THE JEWISH DELI

THE Jewish DELI

AN
ILLUSTRATED GUIDE
TO THE
CHOSEN FOOD

BEN NADLER

CHRONICLE BOOKS
SAN FRANCISCO

Library of Congress Cataloging-in-Publication Data
Names: Nadler, Ben, author.
Title: The Jewish deli : an illustrated guide to the chosen food / Ben Nadler.
Description: San Francisco, California : Chronicle Books, [2023]
Identifiers: LCCN 2021020505 | ISBN 9781797205243
Subjects: LCSH: Jewish cooking. | LCGFT: Cookbooks.
Classification: LCC TX724 .N33 2023 | DDC 641.5/676--dc23
LC record available at https://lccn.loc.gov/2021020505

ISBN 978-1-7972-0524-3

Manufactured in China.

Written and illustrated by Ben Nadler.
Designed by Neil Egan with Evelyn Furuta.

10 9 8 7 6 5 4 3 2 1

Chronicle books and gifts are available at special quantity discounts to corporations, professional associations, literacy programs, and other organizations. For details and discount information, please contact our premiums department at corporatesales@chroniclebooks.com or at 1-800-759-0190.

Chronicle Books LLC
680 Second Street
San Francisco, California 94107
www.chroniclebooks.com

Contents

FEATURES

Introduction

Why do people love Jewish deli food so much? It's hard to explain my passion for the food of the Jewish delicatessen. Is it nature or nurture? A legitimate culinary inheritance or a developed nostalgia for a previous generation's world and culture?

I grew up in Wisconsin, where the Jewish population (0.6%) is significantly lower than what it is nationally (2%), so there were no Jewish delis in sight. My parents are both East Coast Jews, and my family's roots go back to Eastern Europe by way of Montreal and the New York metropolitan area, but we weren't eating smoked meats and knishes. Our family friends were mostly members of the local Jewish community, attending one another's bar and bat mitzvahs at the same synagogue. We would gather for potluck holiday feasts, eating gefilte fish and matzo with horseradish at the Passover seder, hamantaschen from our synagogue's bake sale on Purim, and challah braided and baked at my neighbor's house while we stayed home from school for Rosh Hashanah, the Jewish New Year. Traditional Jewish food has been passed down to me—even pressed upon me—but not specifically deli, not that distinct fusion cuisine of the Jewish immigrant experience. So why is it that when I go into Manhattan, I feel an irresistible impulse to go to Katz's Delicatessen for a pastrami sandwich? Why do I feel the gravitational pull of the bagel and lox at Russ & Daughters? And it's not just me: People around the continent love a good Jewish deli too. Jews may make up only a tiny minority of the population, but Americans and Canadians of all religious (and nonreligious) backgrounds flock to the deli as if it were a national birthright.

What accounts for this passion for a cuisine with roots in the shtetls (small villages) of Eastern Europe? What even *is* this cuisine?

I'm not a chef or a food expert by any means—I'm an illustrator and a wannabe writer. I can say with some confidence that, as a visual person, it was the pure aesthetics of the classic Jewish deli that first drew me in: the faded pastels of the old storefronts; the lined-up jars of colorful dried fruits; the intricate old labels on stacked cans of fish; the gradients of meaty pinks and reds behind the counter glass; the crisp, white uniforms. It's a carefully curated clutter, layers of visual history. The portraits of celebrity customers—Broadway stars, borscht belt comedians—and previous owners plastering the walls among bright neon signs and shelves of preserved goods envelop me in a unique atmosphere that makes me feel like I'm home even before I've eaten anything. A Jewish deli is begging to be illustrated, no detail too small to be appreciated, nowhere to look without some sort of secret delicacy waiting to be discovered.

It is notoriously difficult to convert to Judaism. The Jews have spent a good deal of human history running away from people who want them eradicated, so there are some trust issues here. But the Jewish deli in North America was founded on the mingling of Jews with gentiles from all corners of the world, sharing meat and dairy dishes, supporting one another's businesses, and building a new world together in this mixed-up country. In many ways, the deli is a perfect metaphor for the melting pot. Even today it serves not just to preserve the Jewish culinary past but as an incubator of culinary change. When you are inside a Jewish deli, you're welcomed and treated as a Jew, no matter who you are—no conversion necessary. It is a place to be unapologetically Jewish; you're free to kvech, kvell, and, most importantly, eat as Jews of Eastern European descent have been eating since they arrived in this country. This is inherently comforting to me. The Jewish deli is a place so familiar to me that, even when I enter one for the very first time, I feel perfectly at home.

Still, this is not a book about Jews, and it is definitely not a book about me. It is a book about food. And the food is good. Really, really good. It is fatty, salty, briny, buttery, bright, sweet, smoky, sour, and just about every adjective you could use to describe something delicious. It's homey and comforting, exciting and weird, luxurious and sloppy. When I bite into a good pastrami sandwich, I feel in my Ashkenazi blood that I am satisfying my most basic human instincts. Do I think pickled herring in cream sauce has a universal appeal? Of course not. Yet somehow I cannot get enough of it.

As a Jewish lover of deli food, and as a maker of books, I feel a certain responsibility to do what I can to usher a new generation of hungry customers through the doors of the Jewish delicatessen. I made this book as a visual guide, taking you through the histories of the food; the varieties of meats, fishes, and condiments; the different kinds of preparations; and what to order and how to order it. For the novice who is overwhelmed when entering a deli, I want to guide you up to the counter and help you figure out what to order. For the experienced deli "maven," I hope at least to entertain you and perhaps to fill in some gaps in your knowledge.

A Brief History

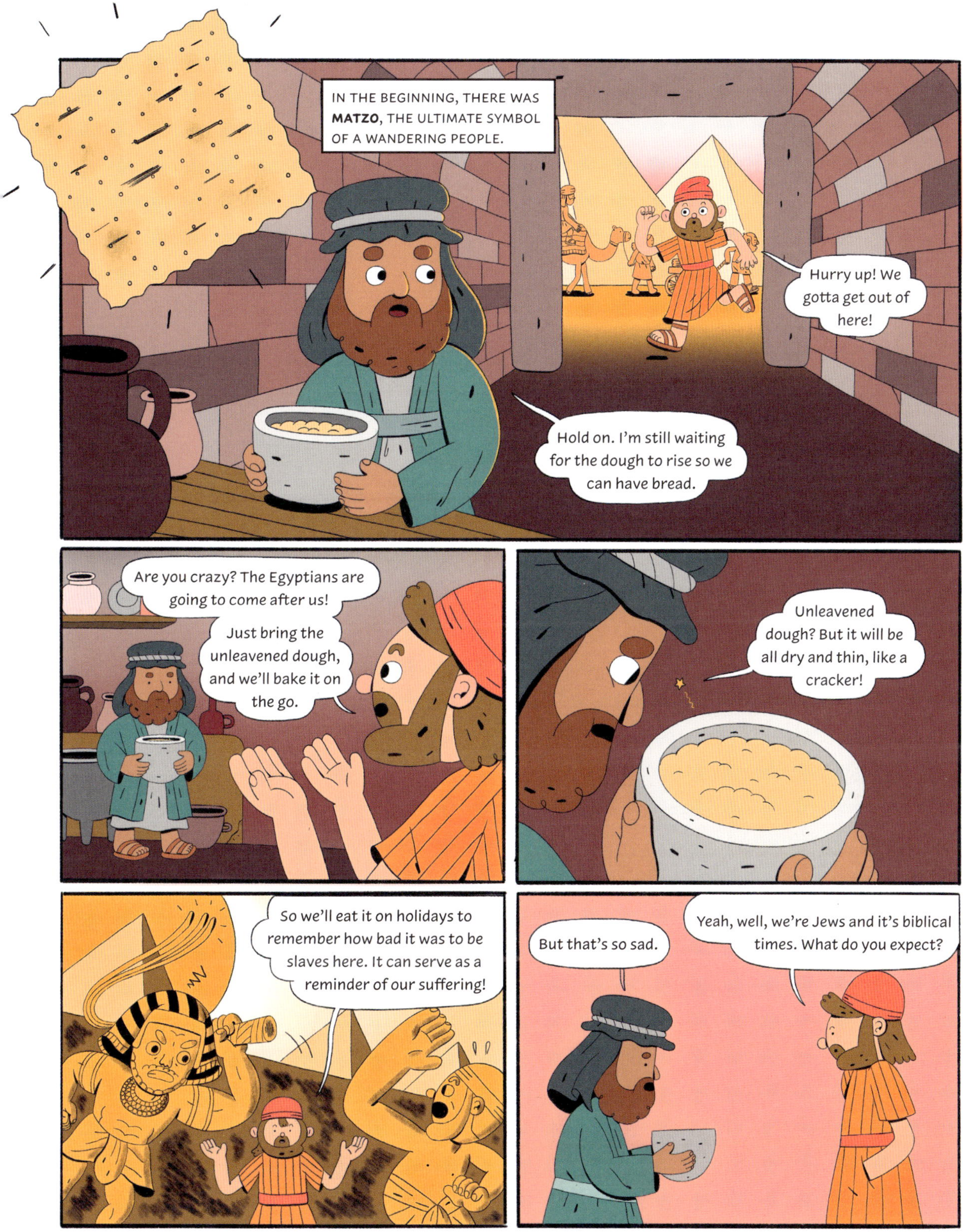
IN THE BEGINNING, THERE WAS **MATZO**, THE ULTIMATE SYMBOL OF A WANDERING PEOPLE.
Hurry up! We gotta get out of here!
Hold on. I'm still waiting for the dough to rise so we can have bread.
Are you crazy? The Egyptians are going to come after us!
Just bring the unleavened dough, and we'll bake it on the go.
Unleavened dough? But it will be all dry and thin, like a cracker!
So we'll eat it on holidays to remember how bad it was to be slaves here. It can serve as a reminder of our suffering!
But that's so sad.
Yeah, well, we're Jews and it's biblical times. What do you expect?

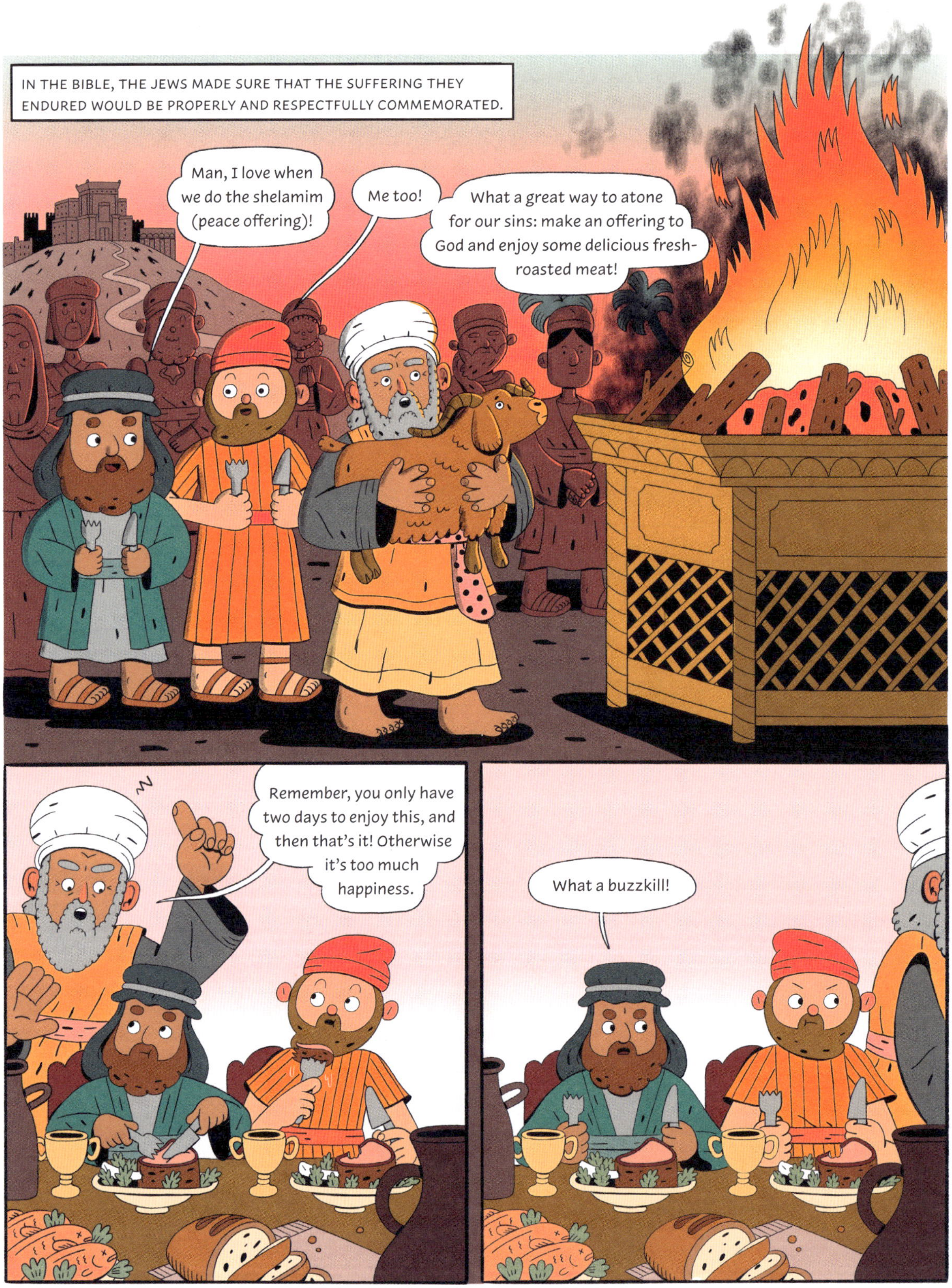
IN THE BIBLE, THE JEWS MADE SURE THAT THE SUFFERING THEY ENDURED WOULD BE PROPERLY AND RESPECTFULLY COMMEMORATED.
Man, I love when we do the shelamim (peace offering)!
Me too!
What a great way to atone for our sins: make an offering to God and enjoy some delicious fresh-roasted meat!
Remember, you only have two days to enjoy this, and then that's it! Otherwise it's too much happiness.
What a buzzkill!

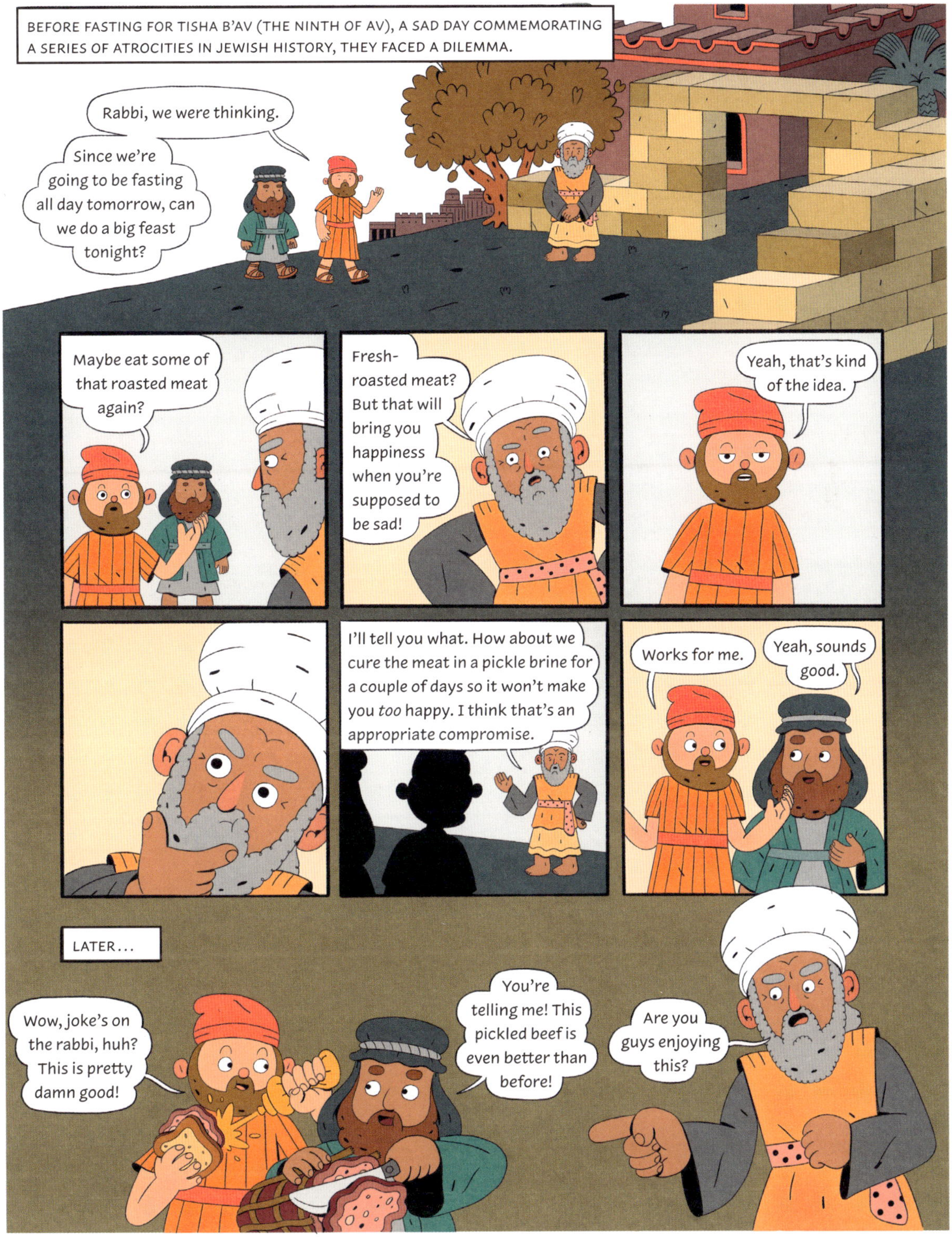
BEFORE FASTING FOR TISHA B'AV (THE NINTH OF AV), A SAD DAY COMMEMORATING A SERIES OF ATROCITIES IN JEWISH HISTORY, THEY FACED A DILEMMA.
Rabbi, we were thinking.
Since we're going to be fasting all day tomorrow, can we do a big feast tonight?
Maybe eat some of that roasted meat again?
Fresh-roasted meat? But that will bring you happiness when you're supposed to be sad!
Yeah, that's kind of the idea.
I'll tell you what. How about we cure the meat in a pickle brine for a couple of days so it won't make you *too* happy. I think that's an appropriate compromise.
Works for me.
Yeah, sounds good.
LATER...
Wow, joke's on the rabbi, huh? This is pretty damn good!
You're telling me! This pickled beef is even better than before!
Are you guys enjoying this?

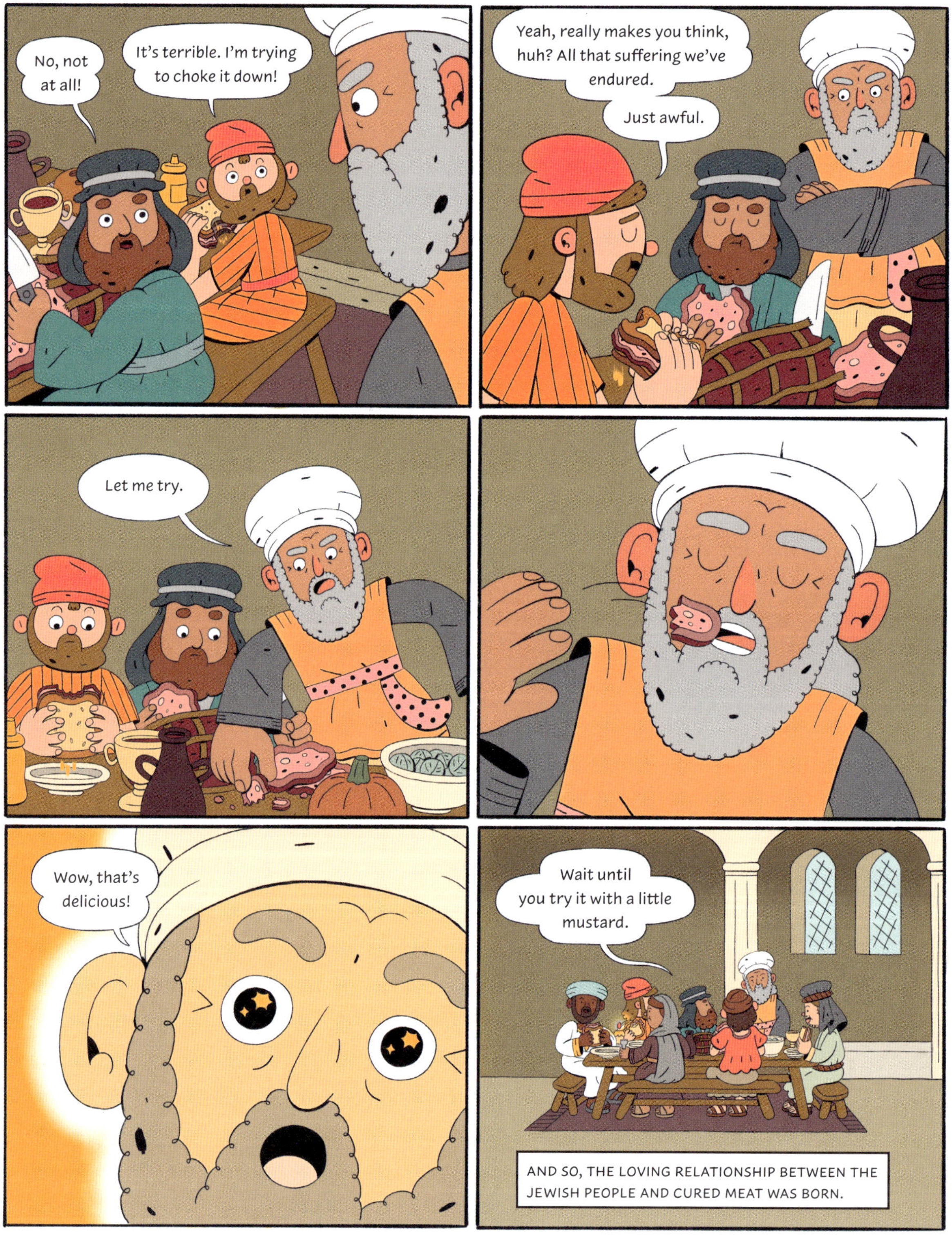
No, not at all!
It's terrible. I'm trying to choke it down!
Yeah, really makes you think, huh? All that suffering we've endured.
Just awful.
Let me try.
Wow, that's delicious!
Wait until you try it with a little mustard.
AND SO, THE LOVING RELATIONSHIP BETWEEN THE JEWISH PEOPLE AND CURED MEAT WAS BORN.

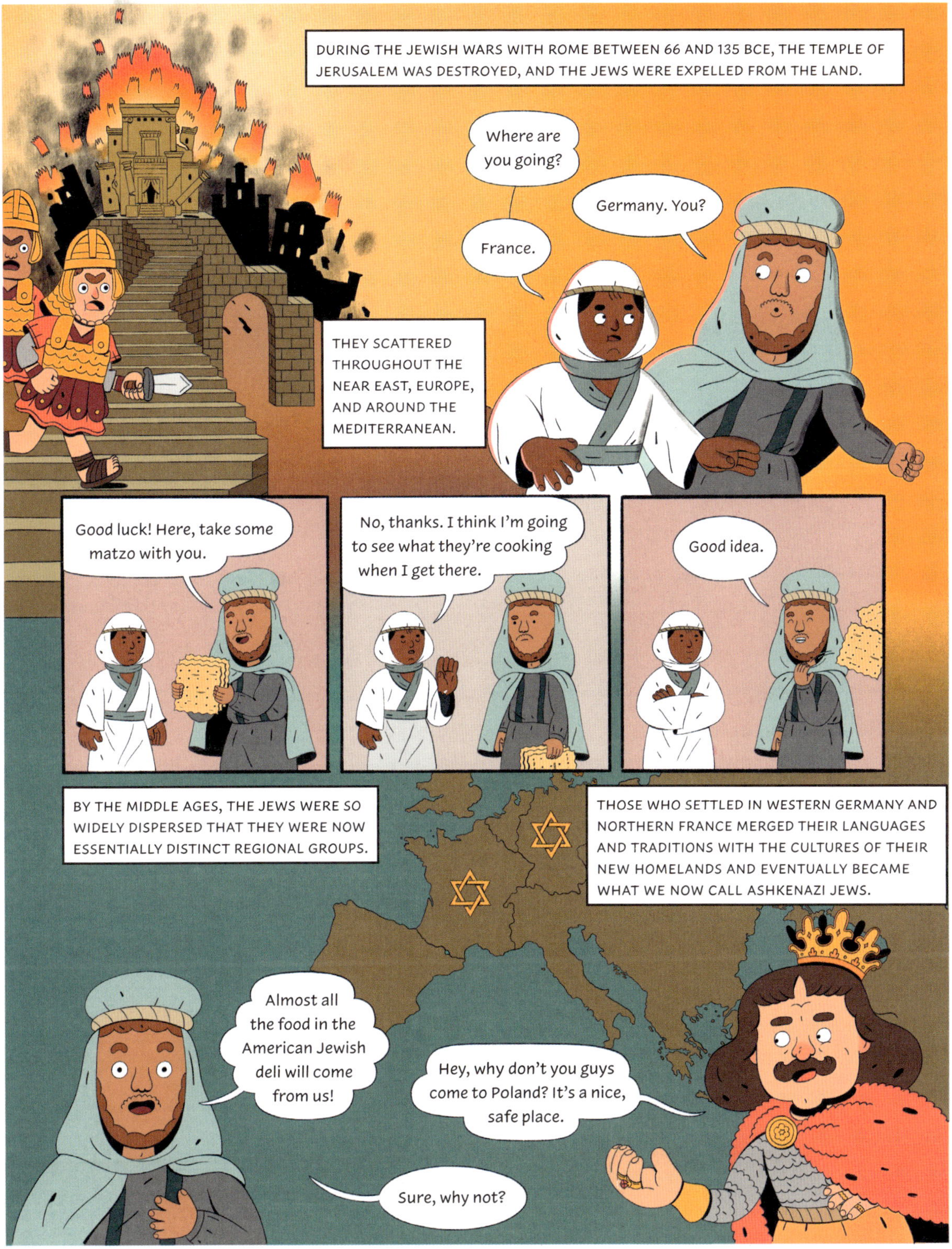

DURING THE JEWISH WARS WITH ROME BETWEEN 66 AND 135 BCE, THE TEMPLE OF JERUSALEM WAS DESTROYED, AND THE JEWS WERE EXPELLED FROM THE LAND.
Where are you going?
Germany. You?
France.
THEY SCATTERED THROUGHOUT THE NEAR EAST, EUROPE, AND AROUND THE MEDITERRANEAN.
Good luck! Here, take some matzo with you.
No, thanks. I think I'm going to see what they're cooking when I get there.
Good idea.
BY THE MIDDLE AGES, THE JEWS WERE SO WIDELY DISPERSED THAT THEY WERE NOW ESSENTIALLY DISTINCT REGIONAL GROUPS.
THOSE WHO SETTLED IN WESTERN GERMANY AND NORTHERN FRANCE MERGED THEIR LANGUAGES AND TRADITIONS WITH THE CULTURES OF THEIR NEW HOMELANDS AND EVENTUALLY BECAME WHAT WE NOW CALL ASHKENAZI JEWS.
Almost all the food in the American Jewish deli will come from us!
Hey, why don't you guys come to Poland? It's a nice, safe place.
Sure, why not?

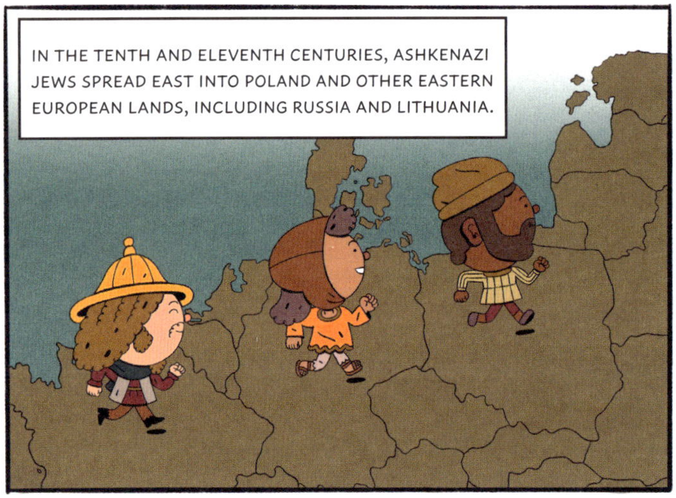
IN THE TENTH AND ELEVENTH CENTURIES, ASHKENAZI JEWS SPREAD EAST INTO POLAND AND OTHER EASTERN EUROPEAN LANDS, INCLUDING RUSSIA AND LITHUANIA.

THE FOODS THAT THEY ATE CAME FROM ADAPTING THE COUNTRY'S LOCAL CUISINE FOR KOSHER LAW AND SUBSTITUTING CHEAPER INGREDIENTS SUCH AS CHICKEN, LAMB, AND BEEF.

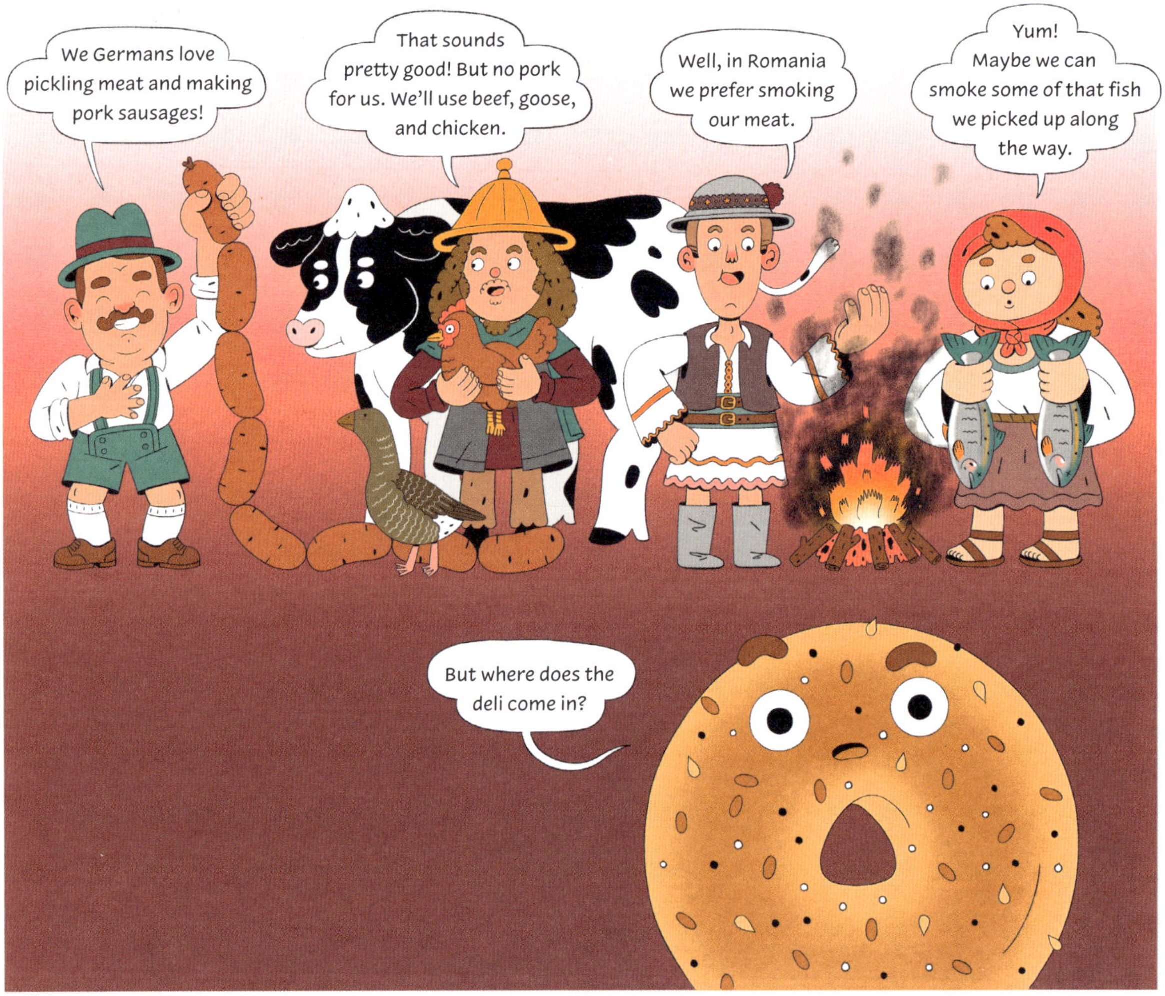
We Germans love pickling meat and making pork sausages!
That sounds pretty good! But no pork for us. We'll use beef, goose, and chicken.
Well, in Romania we prefer smoking our meat.
Yum! Maybe we can smoke some of that fish we picked up along the way.
But where does the deli come in?

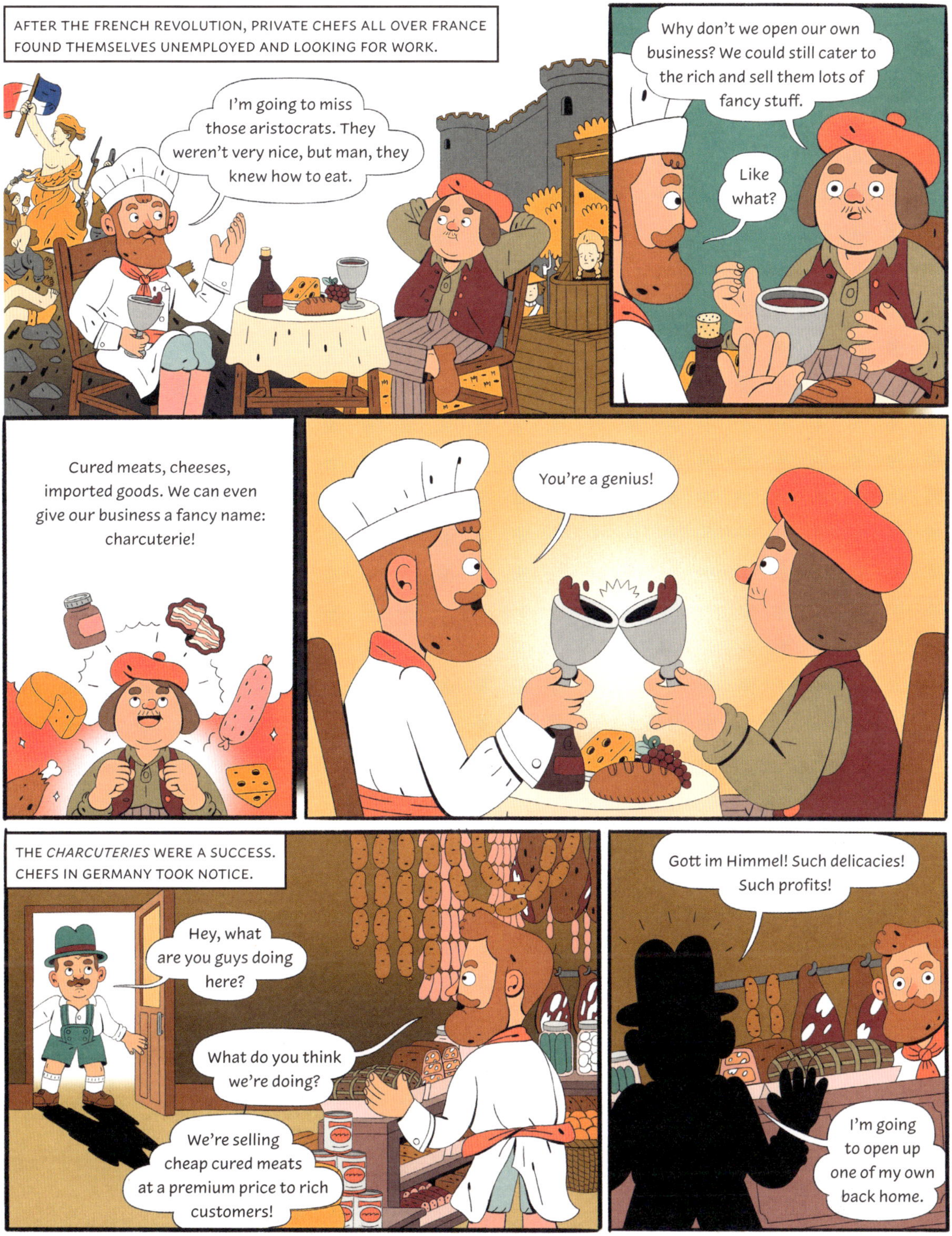
AFTER THE FRENCH REVOLUTION, PRIVATE CHEFS ALL OVER FRANCE FOUND THEMSELVES UNEMPLOYED AND LOOKING FOR WORK.
I'm going to miss those aristocrats. They weren't very nice, but man, they knew how to eat.
Why don't we open our own business? We could still cater to the rich and sell them lots of fancy stuff.
Like what?
Cured meats, cheeses, imported goods. We can even give our business a fancy name: charcuterie!
You're a genius!
THE *CHARCUTERIES* WERE A SUCCESS. CHEFS IN GERMANY TOOK NOTICE.
Hey, what are you guys doing here?
What do you think we're doing?
We're selling cheap cured meats at a premium price to rich customers!
Gott im Himmel! Such delicacies! Such profits!
I'm going to open up one of my own back home.

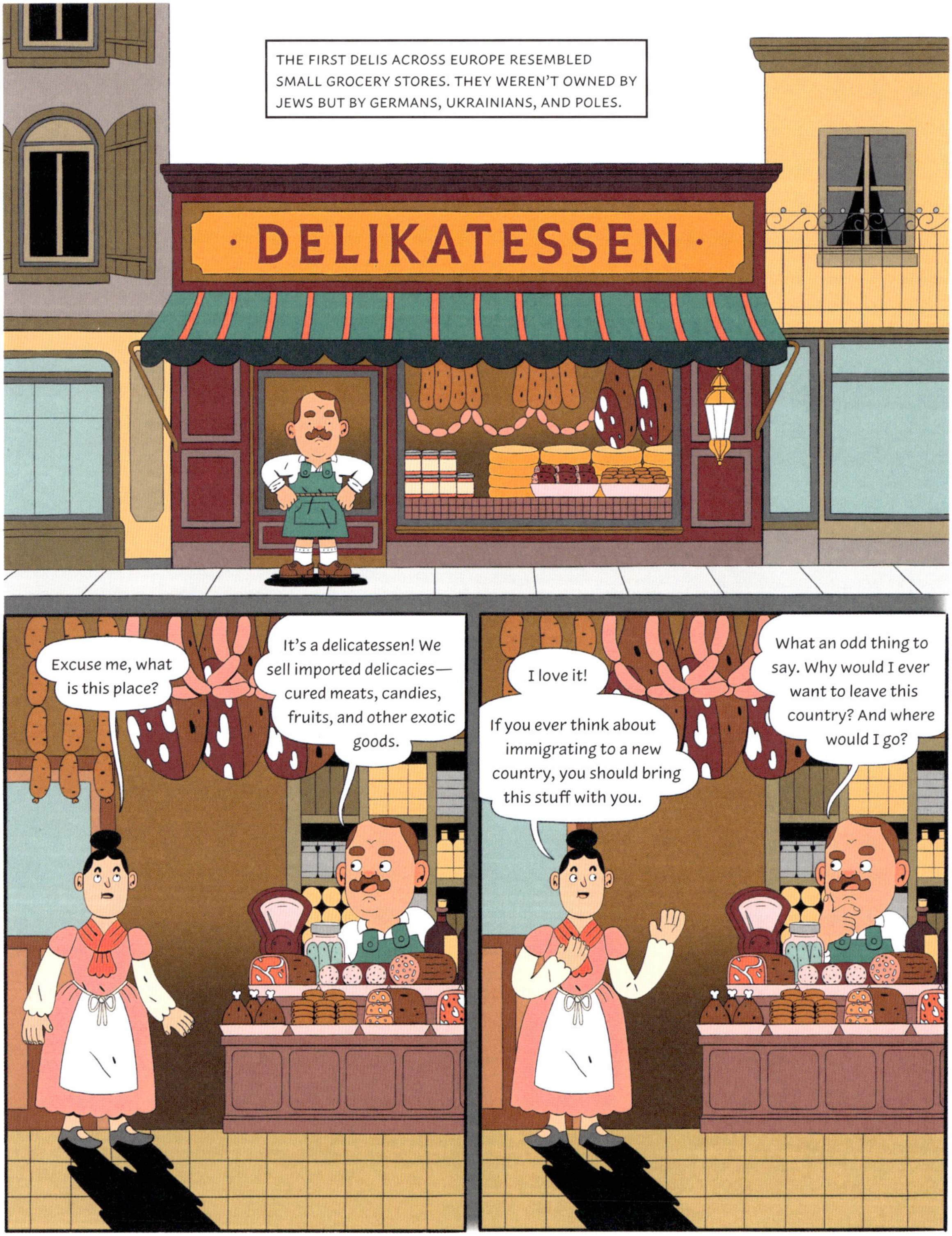
THE FIRST DELIS ACROSS EUROPE RESEMBLED SMALL GROCERY STORES. THEY WEREN'T OWNED BY JEWS BUT BY GERMANS, UKRAINIANS, AND POLES.
DELIKATESSEN
Excuse me, what is this place?
It's a delicatessen! We sell imported delicacies—cured meats, candies, fruits, and other exotic goods.
I love it!
If you ever think about immigrating to a new country, you should bring this stuff with you.
What an odd thing to say. Why would I ever want to leave this country? And where would I go?

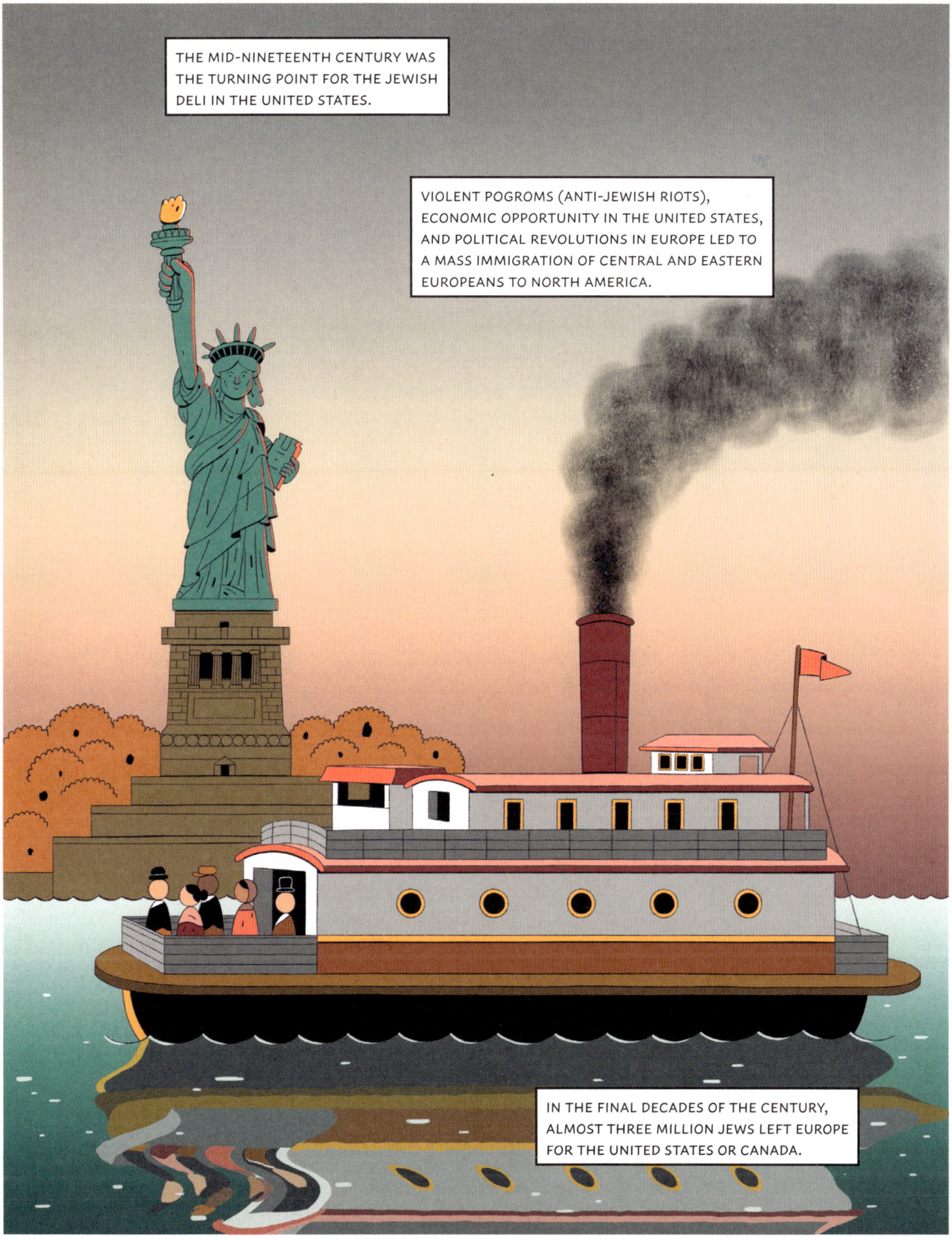
THE MID-NINETEENTH CENTURY WAS THE TURNING POINT FOR THE JEWISH DELI IN THE UNITED STATES.
VIOLENT POGROMS (ANTI-JEWISH RIOTS), ECONOMIC OPPORTUNITY IN THE UNITED STATES, AND POLITICAL REVOLUTIONS IN EUROPE LED TO A MASS IMMIGRATION OF CENTRAL AND EASTERN EUROPEANS TO NORTH AMERICA.
IN THE FINAL DECADES OF THE CENTURY, ALMOST THREE MILLION JEWS LEFT EUROPE FOR THE UNITED STATES OR CANADA.

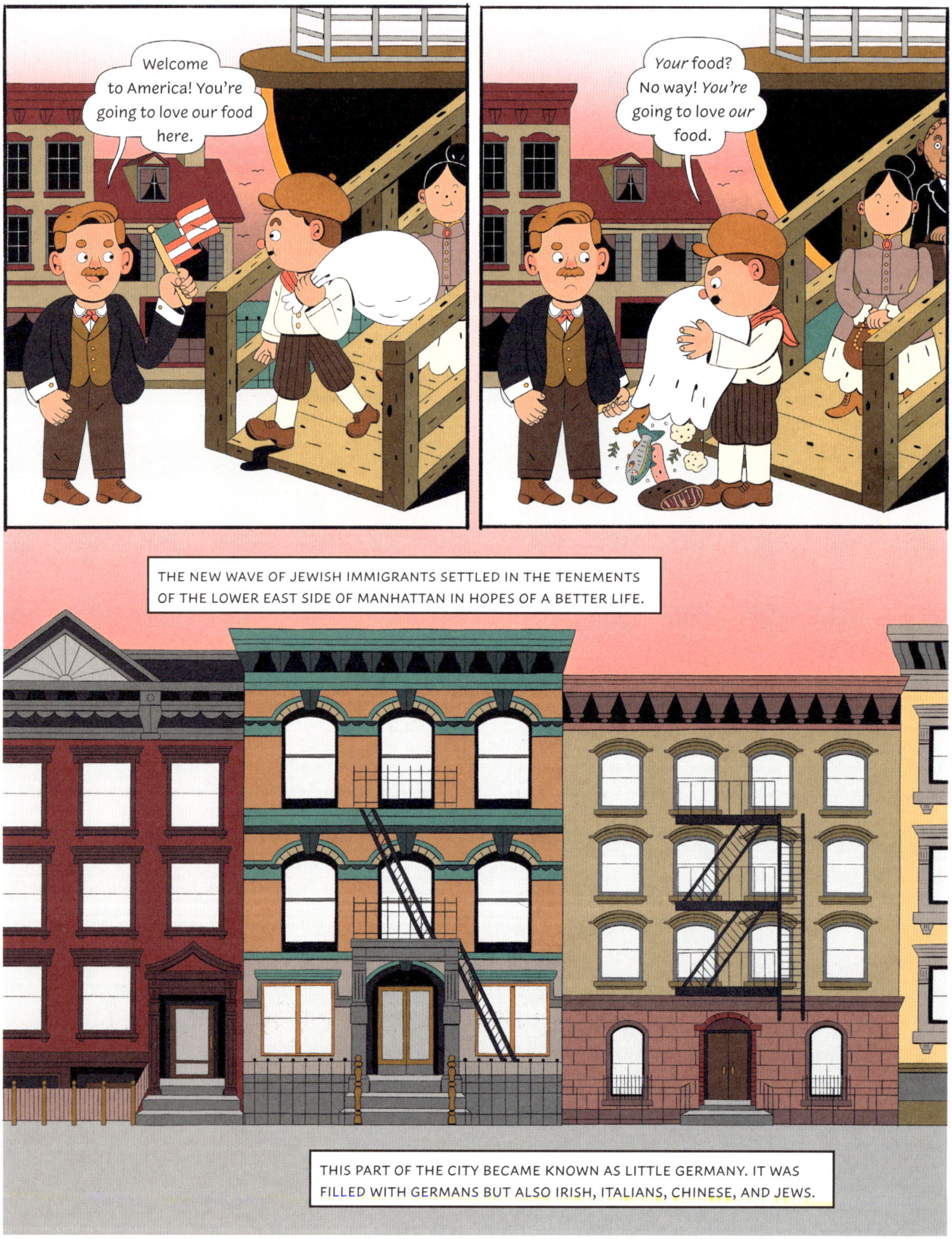
Welcome to America! You're going to love our food here.
Your food? No way! *You're* going to love *our* food.
THE NEW WAVE OF JEWISH IMMIGRANTS SETTLED IN THE TENEMENTS OF THE LOWER EAST SIDE OF MANHATTAN IN HOPES OF A BETTER LIFE.
THIS PART OF THE CITY BECAME KNOWN AS LITTLE GERMANY. IT WAS FILLED WITH GERMANS BUT ALSO IRISH, ITALIANS, CHINESE, AND JEWS.

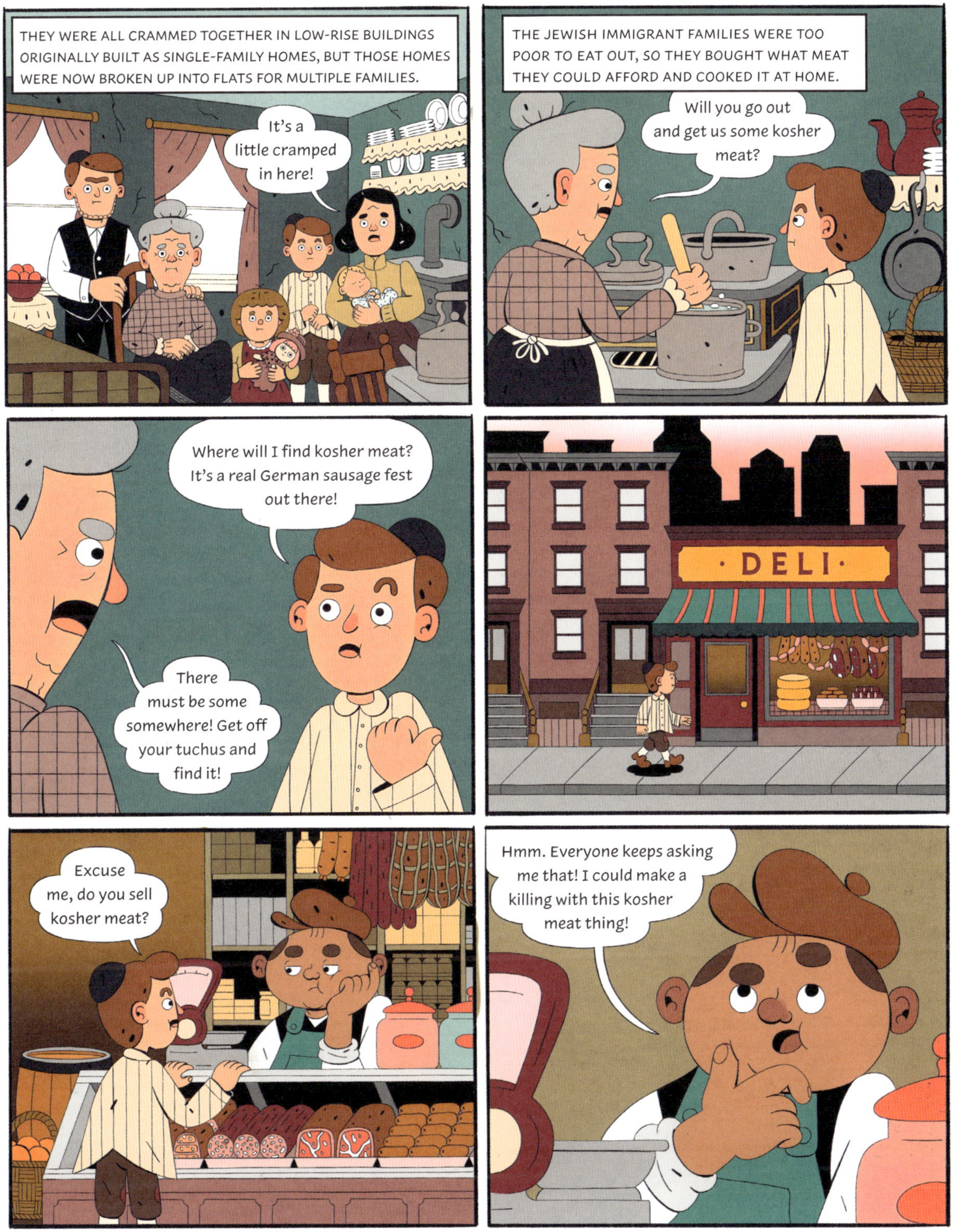
THEY WERE ALL CRAMMED TOGETHER IN LOW-RISE BUILDINGS ORIGINALLY BUILT AS SINGLE-FAMILY HOMES, BUT THOSE HOMES WERE NOW BROKEN UP INTO FLATS FOR MULTIPLE FAMILIES.
It's a little cramped in here!
THE JEWISH IMMIGRANT FAMILIES WERE TOO POOR TO EAT OUT, SO THEY BOUGHT WHAT MEAT THEY COULD AFFORD AND COOKED IT AT HOME.
Will you go out and get us some kosher meat?
Where will I find kosher meat? It's a real German sausage fest out there!
There must be some somewhere! Get off your tuchus and find it!
DELI
Excuse me, do you sell kosher meat?
Hmm. Everyone keeps asking me that! I could make a killing with this kosher meat thing!

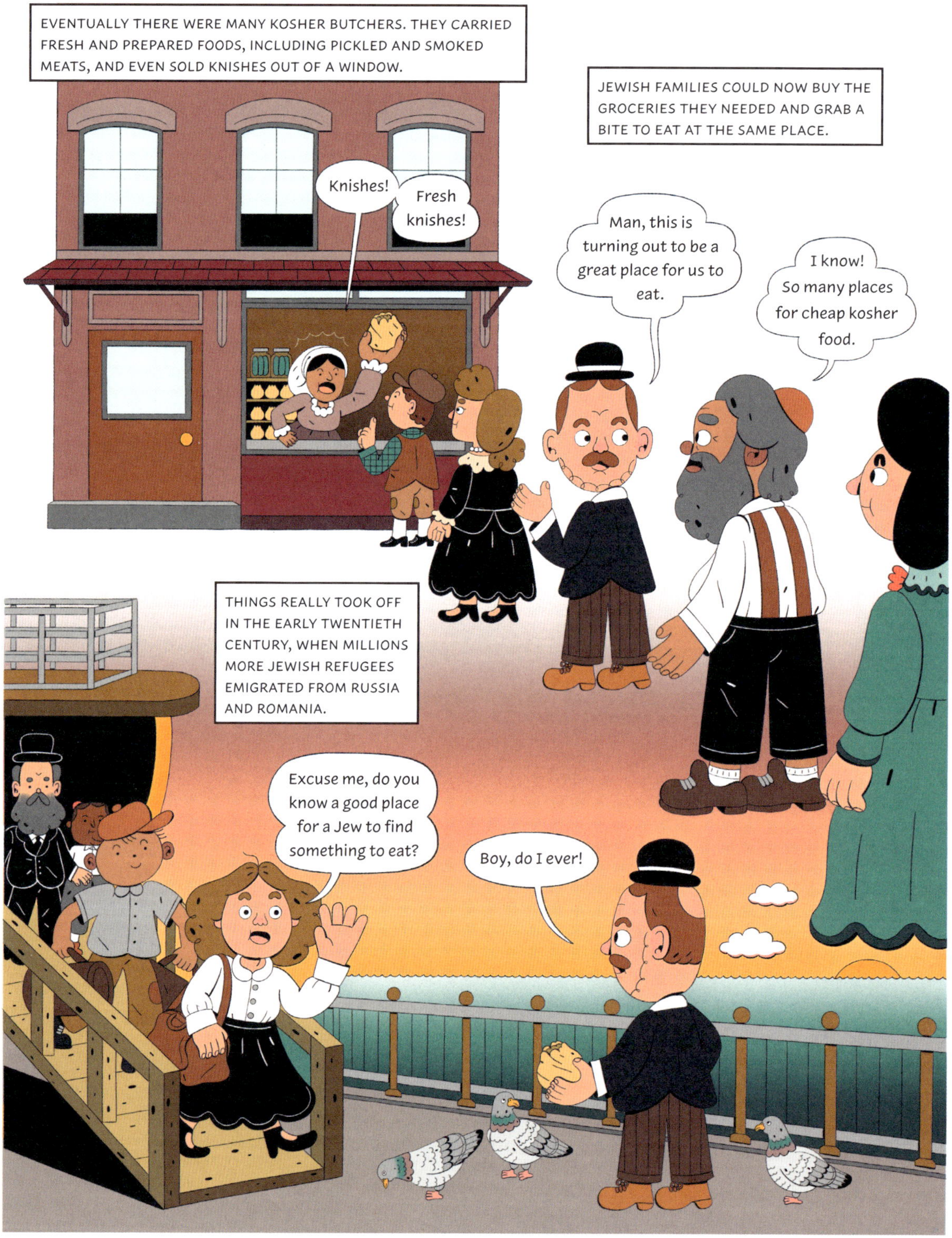
EVENTUALLY THERE WERE MANY KOSHER BUTCHERS. THEY CARRIED FRESH AND PREPARED FOODS, INCLUDING PICKLED AND SMOKED MEATS, AND EVEN SOLD KNISHES OUT OF A WINDOW.
JEWISH FAMILIES COULD NOW BUY THE GROCERIES THEY NEEDED AND GRAB A BITE TO EAT AT THE SAME PLACE.
Knishes!
Fresh knishes!
Man, this is turning out to be a great place for us to eat.
I know! So many places for cheap kosher food.
THINGS REALLY TOOK OFF IN THE EARLY TWENTIETH CENTURY, WHEN MILLIONS MORE JEWISH REFUGEES EMIGRATED FROM RUSSIA AND ROMANIA.
Excuse me, do you know a good place for a Jew to find something to eat?
Boy, do I ever!

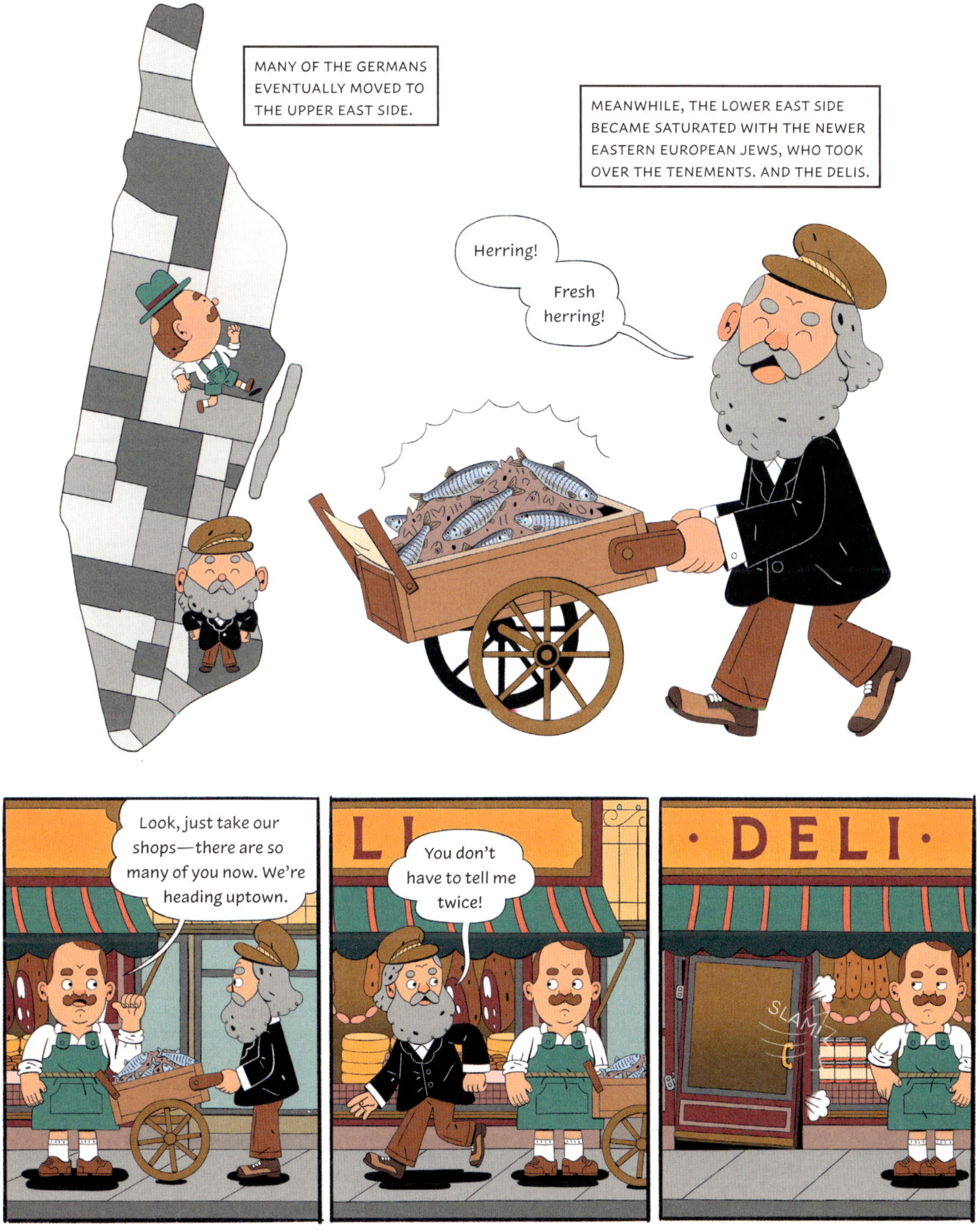
MANY OF THE GERMANS EVENTUALLY MOVED TO THE UPPER EAST SIDE.
MEANWHILE, THE LOWER EAST SIDE BECAME SATURATED WITH THE NEWER EASTERN EUROPEAN JEWS, WHO TOOK OVER THE TENEMENTS. AND THE DELIS.
Herring!
Fresh herring!
Look, just take our shops—there are so many of you now. We're heading uptown.
You don't have to tell me twice!
DELI
SLAM!

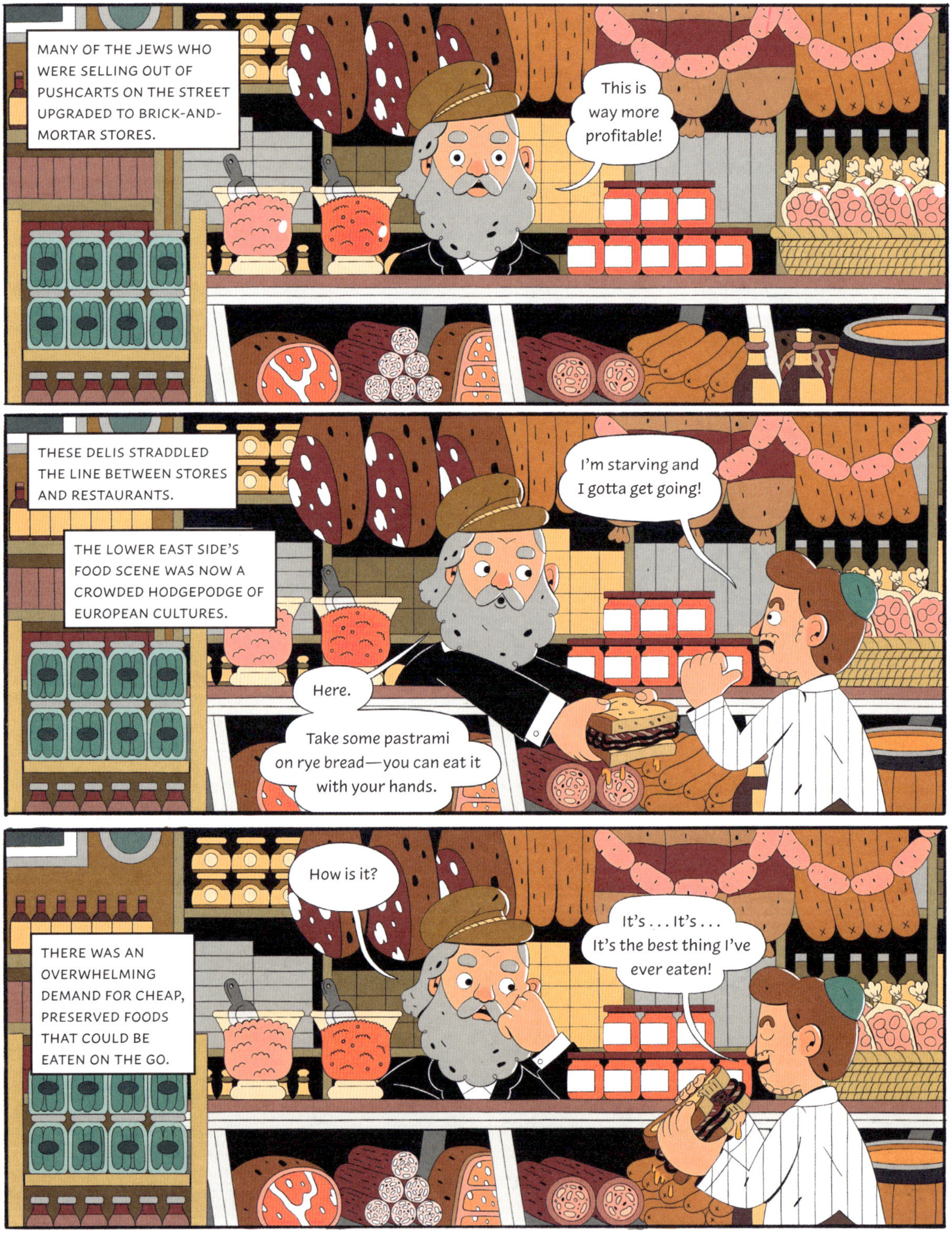
MANY OF THE JEWS WHO WERE SELLING OUT OF PUSHCARTS ON THE STREET UPGRADED TO BRICK-AND-MORTAR STORES.
This is way more profitable!
THESE DELIS STRADDLED THE LINE BETWEEN STORES AND RESTAURANTS.
THE LOWER EAST SIDE'S FOOD SCENE WAS NOW A CROWDED HODGEPODGE OF EUROPEAN CULTURES.
I'm starving and I gotta get going!
Here.
Take some pastrami on rye bread—you can eat it with your hands.
THERE WAS AN OVERWHELMING DEMAND FOR CHEAP, PRESERVED FOODS THAT COULD BE EATEN ON THE GO.
How is it?
It's . . . It's . . . It's the best thing I've ever eaten!

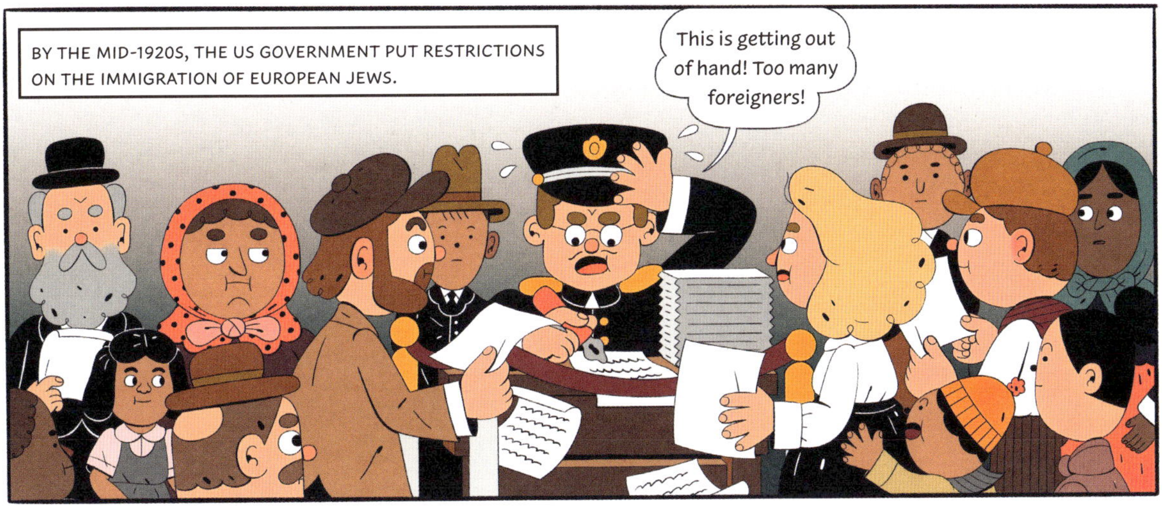
BY THE MID-1920S, THE US GOVERNMENT PUT RESTRICTIONS ON THE IMMIGRATION OF EUROPEAN JEWS.
This is getting out of hand! Too many foreigners!

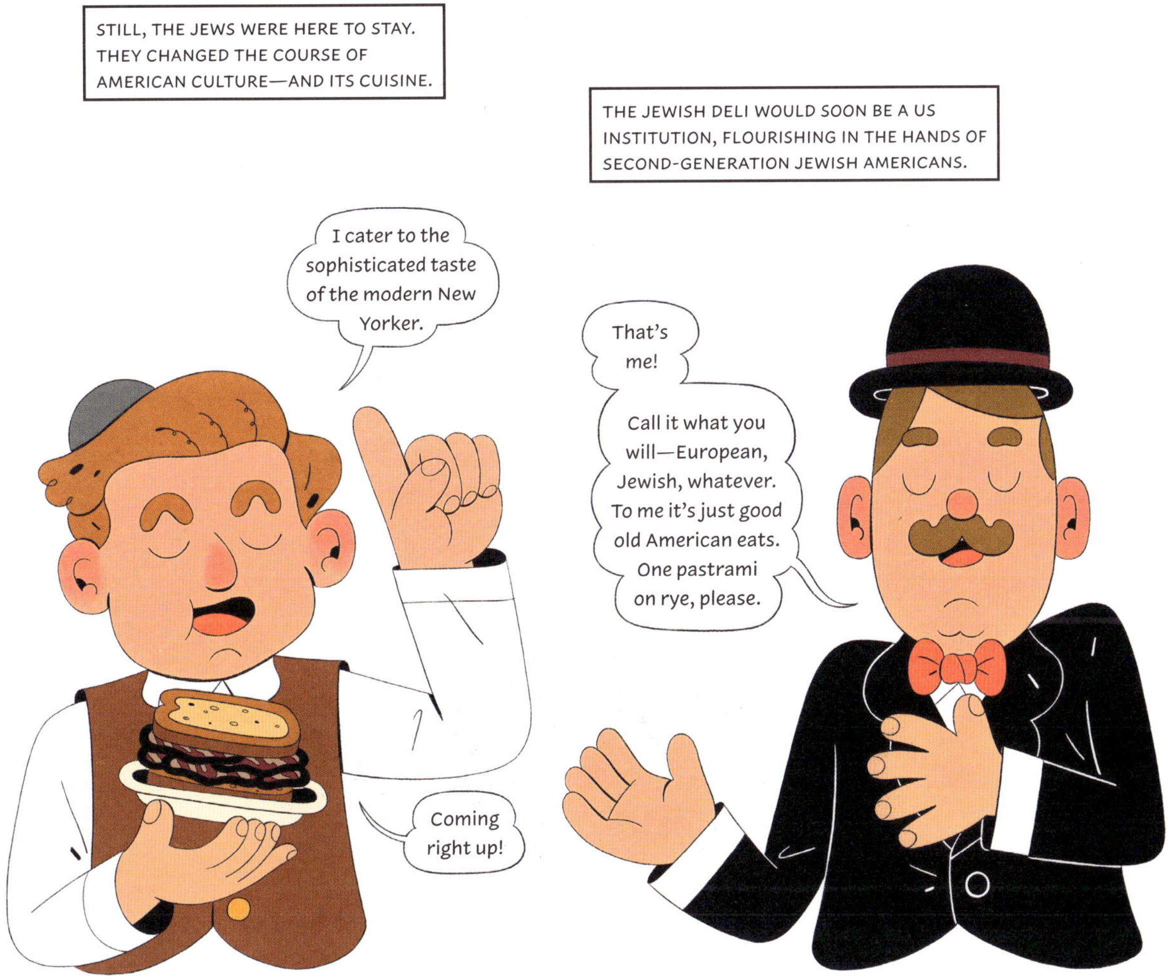
STILL, THE JEWS WERE HERE TO STAY. THEY CHANGED THE COURSE OF AMERICAN CULTURE—AND ITS CUISINE.
THE JEWISH DELI WOULD SOON BE A US INSTITUTION, FLOURISHING IN THE HANDS OF SECOND-GENERATION JEWISH AMERICANS.
I cater to the sophisticated taste of the modern New Yorker.
That's me!
Call it what you will—European, Jewish, whatever. To me it's just good old American eats. One pastrami on rye, please.
Coming right up!

KOSHER

SO, WHAT DOES *KOSHER* MEAN?

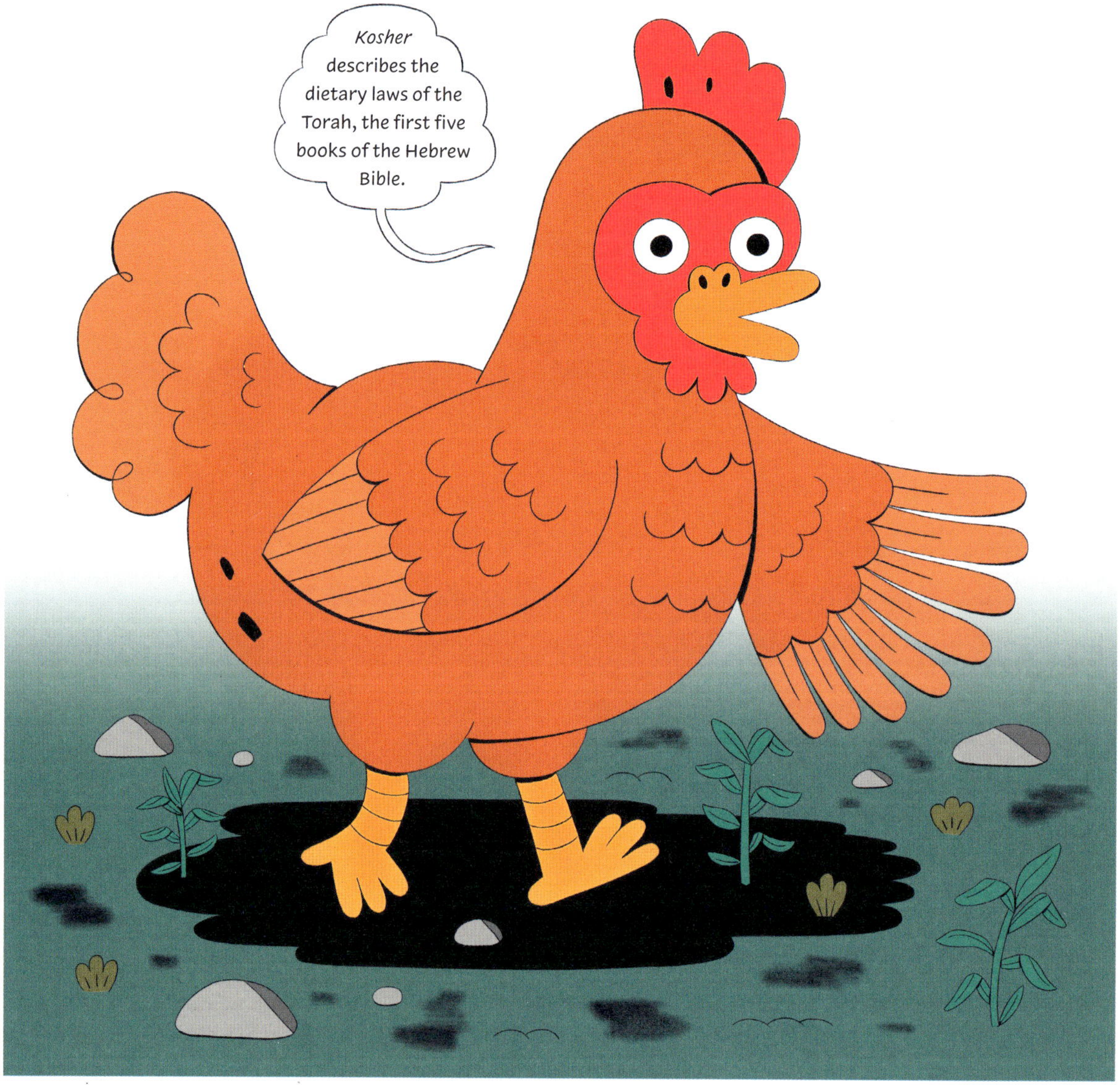
Kosher describes the dietary laws of the Torah, the first five books of the Hebrew Bible.

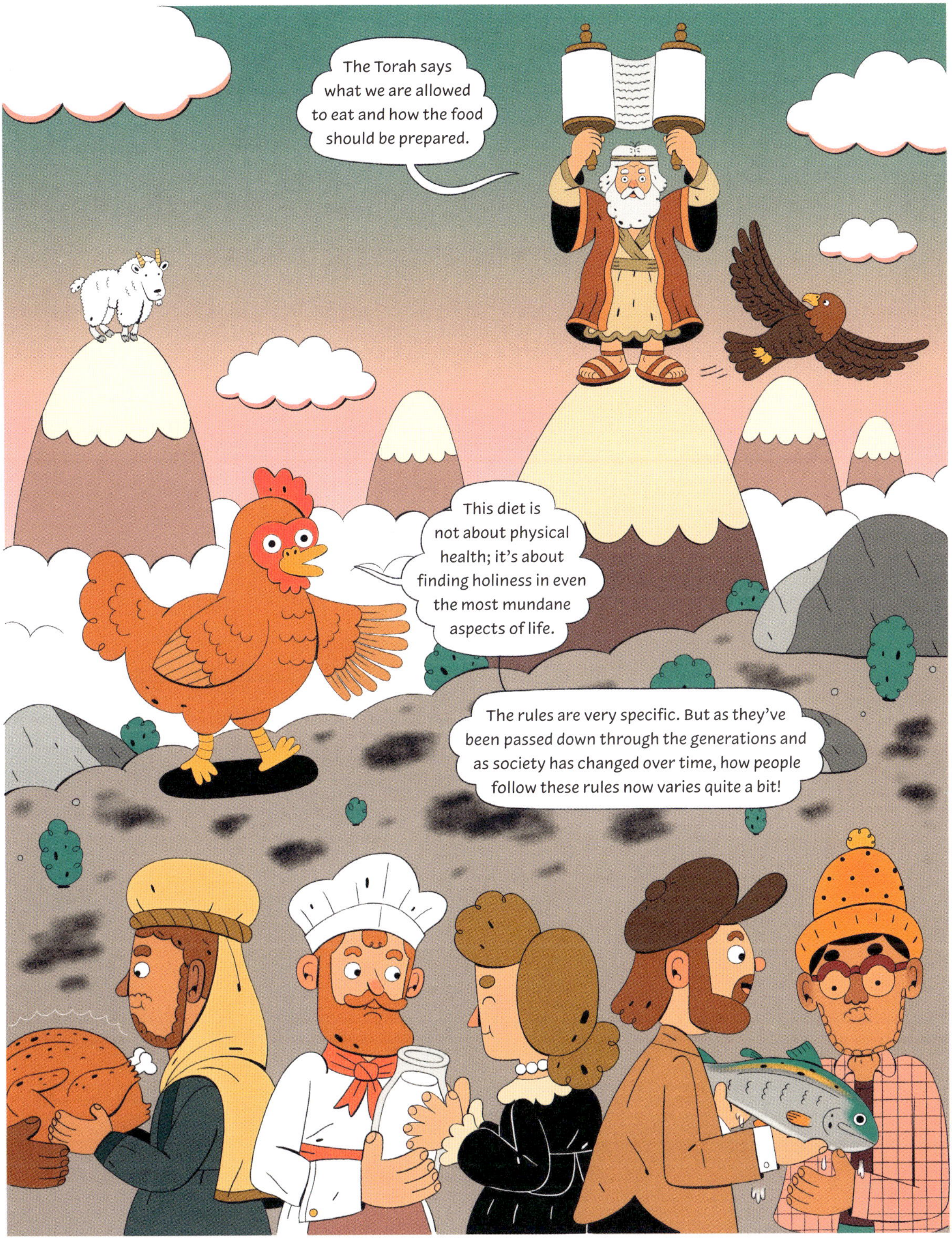
The Torah says what we are allowed to eat and how the food should be prepared.
This diet is not about physical health; it's about finding holiness in even the most mundane aspects of life.
The rules are very specific. But as they've been passed down through the generations and as society has changed over time, how people follow these rules now varies quite a bit!

KOSHER EATING CAN BE BROKEN DOWN INTO THREE MAIN CATEGORIES: MEAT, DAIRY, AND PAREVE (FOOD THAT IS NEITHER MEAT NOR DAIRY).

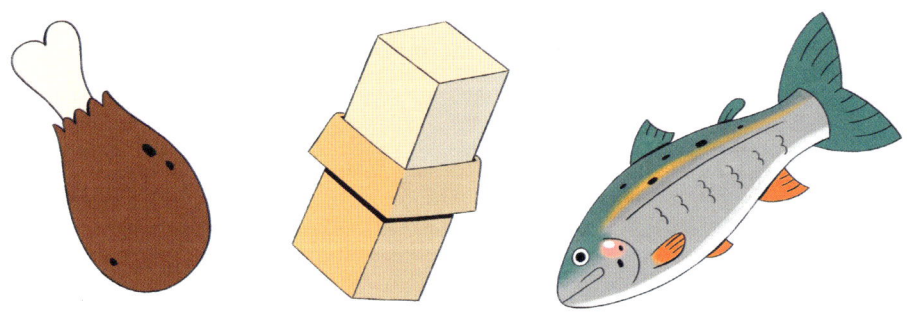

FOR MEATS, ONLY ANIMALS THAT HAVE CLOVEN HOOVES AND CHEW THEIR CUD CAN BE EATEN.

SO COWS, SHEEP, GOATS, AND DEER ARE ALLOWED.

Excuse me for only needing to chew my food *once!*

PIGS HAVE CLOVEN HOOVES, BUT THEY DON'T CHEW CUD, SO NO DICE!

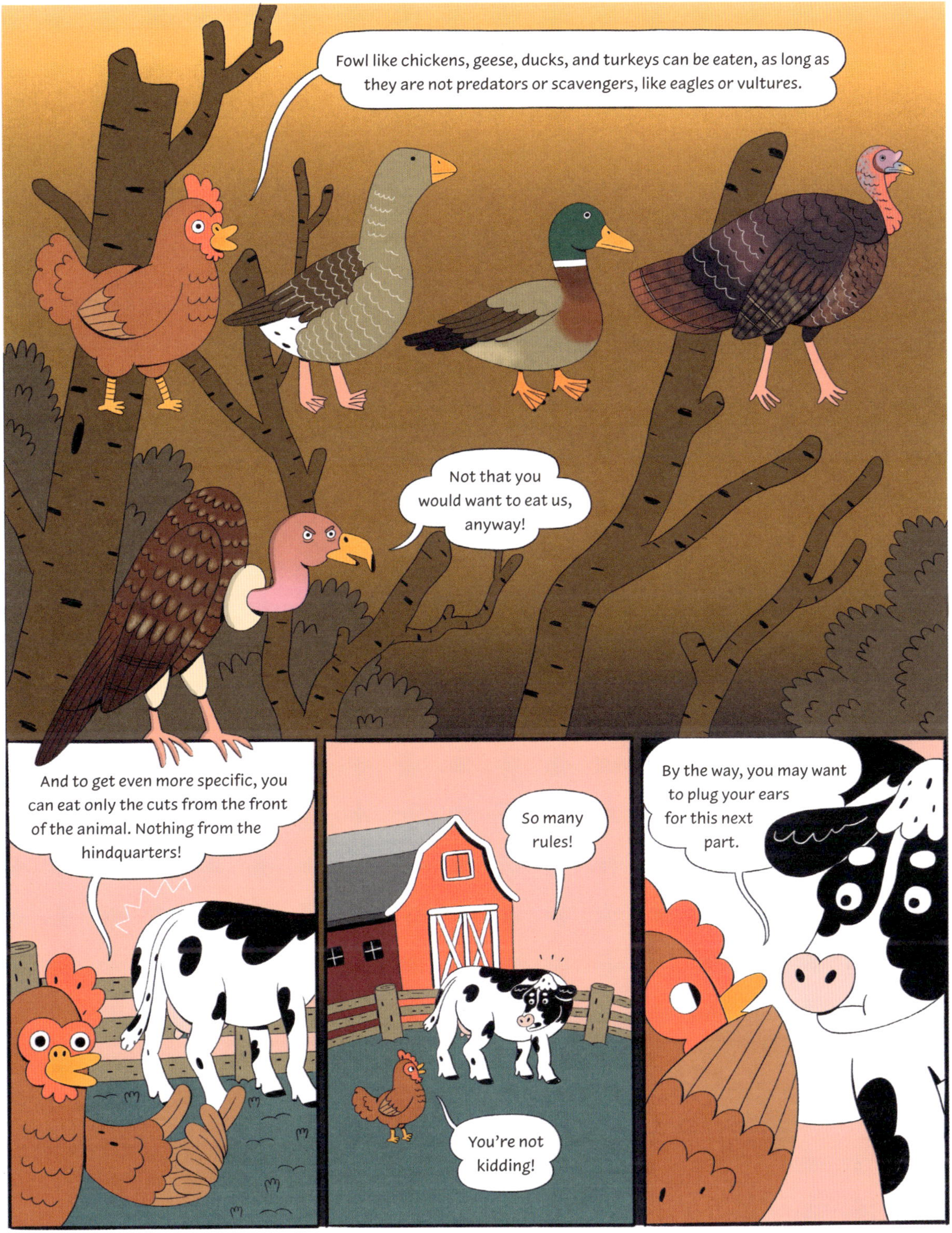

Fowl like chickens, geese, ducks, and turkeys can be eaten, as long as they are not predators or scavengers, like eagles or vultures.
Not that you would want to eat us, anyway!
And to get even more specific, you can eat only the cuts from the front of the animal. Nothing from the hindquarters!
So many rules!
You're not kidding!
By the way, you may want to plug your ears for this next part.

TO BE CONSIDERED KOSHER, THESE ANIMALS MUST BE SLAUGHTERED IN A CERTAIN WAY BY A CERTIFIED BUTCHER CALLED A SHOCHET.

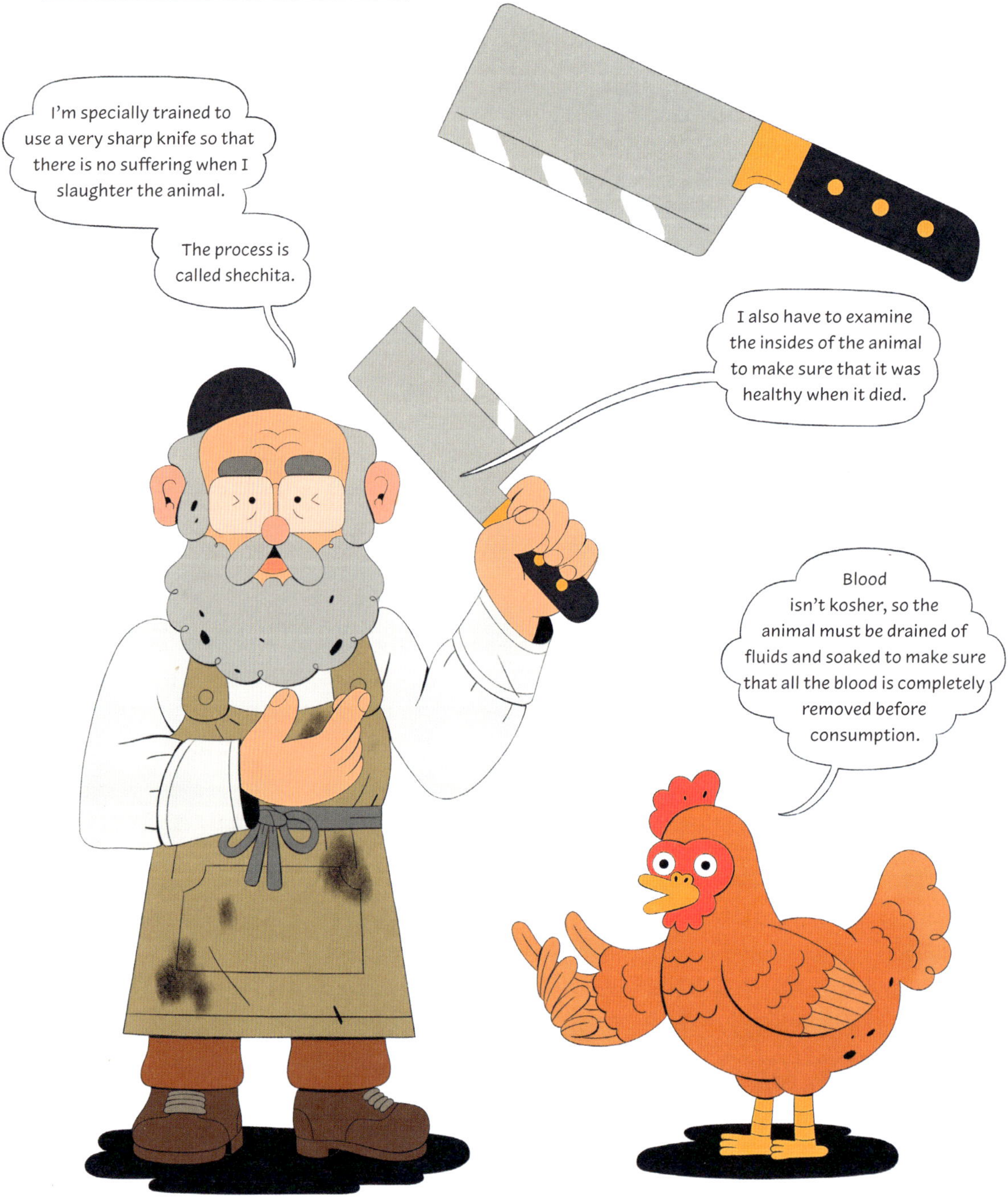

I'm specially trained to use a very sharp knife so that there is no suffering when I slaughter the animal.
The process is called shechita.
I also have to examine the insides of the animal to make sure that it was healthy when it died.
Blood isn't kosher, so the animal must be drained of fluids and soaked to make sure that all the blood is completely removed before consumption.

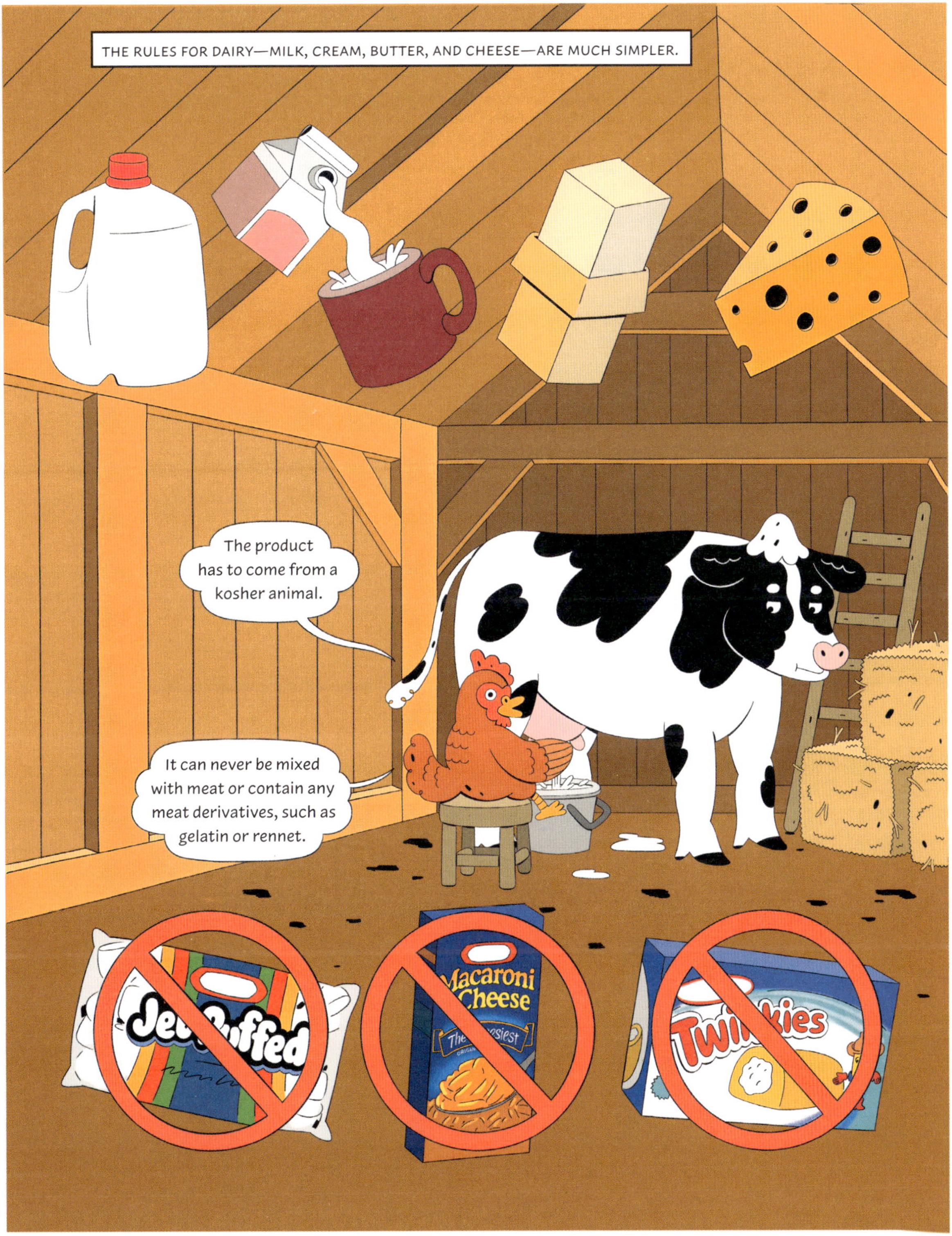
THE RULES FOR DAIRY—MILK, CREAM, BUTTER, AND CHEESE—ARE MUCH SIMPLER.
The product has to come from a kosher animal.
It can never be mixed with meat or contain any meat derivatives, such as gelatin or rennet.
Macaroni Cheese

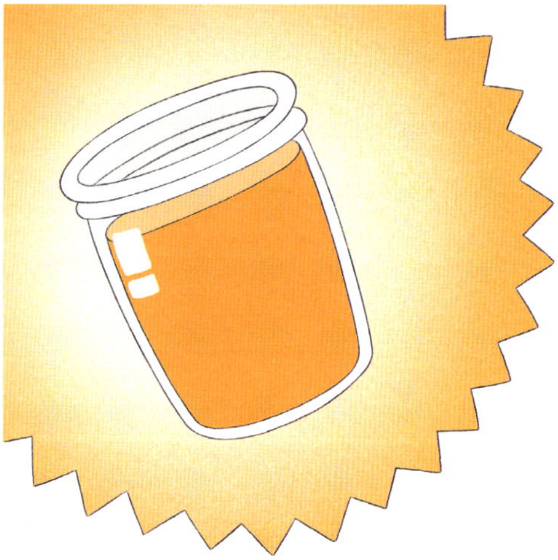

THIS IS WHY CHICKEN FAT, CALLED SCHMALTZ, IS SUCH AN IMPORTANT INGREDIENT IN JEWISH COOKING. IT CAN BE USED IN PLACE OF BUTTER WHEN PREPARING MEAT-BASED MEALS.

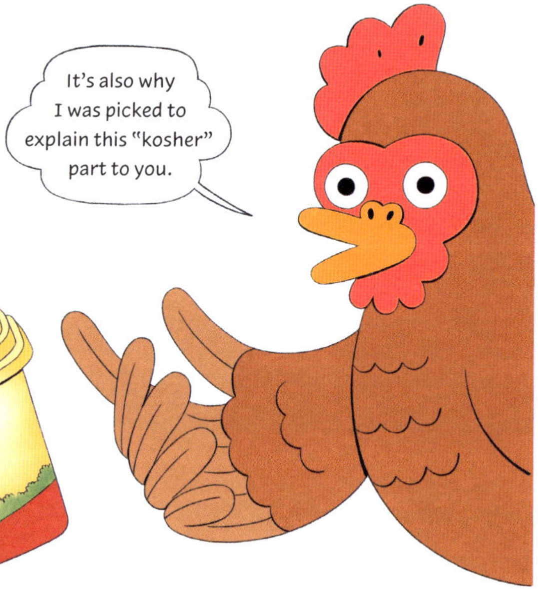
It's also why I was picked to explain this "kosher" part to you.

BECAUSE IT IS A VEGETABLE FAT, NON-DAIRY MARGARINE CAN ALSO BE USED INSTEAD OF BUTTER WHEN EATING A MEAT MEAL.

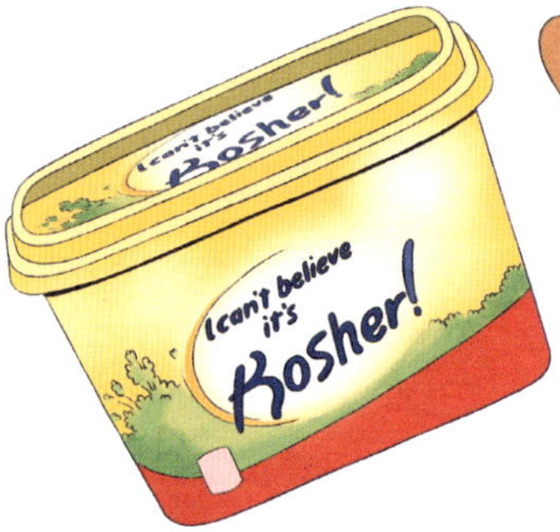
I can't believe it's Kosher!

LASTLY, FISH IS KOSHER AS LONG AS IT HAS FINS AND SCALES AND IS NOT A BOTTOM-FEEDER.

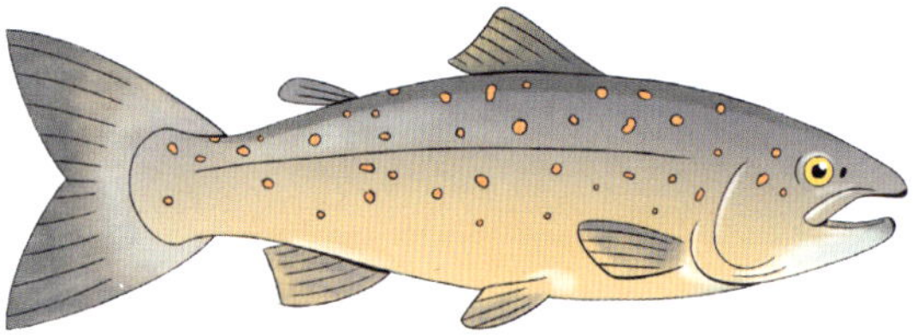

SO **SALMON**,

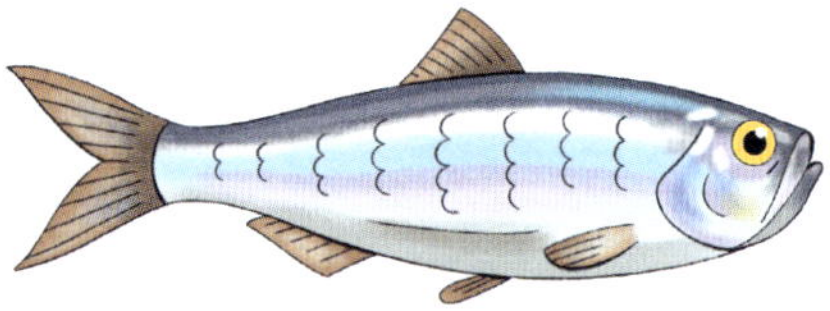

HERRING,

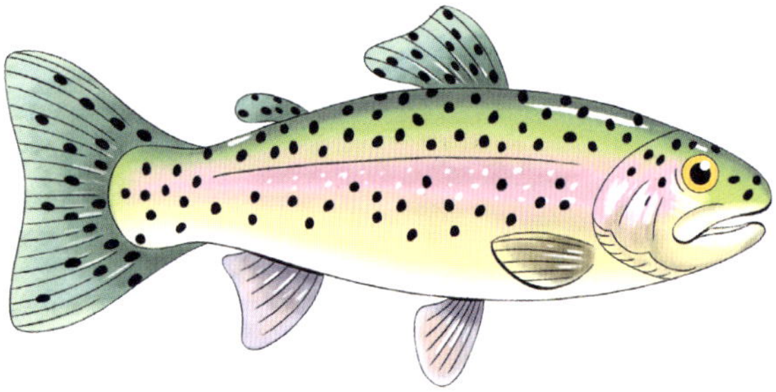

TROUT,

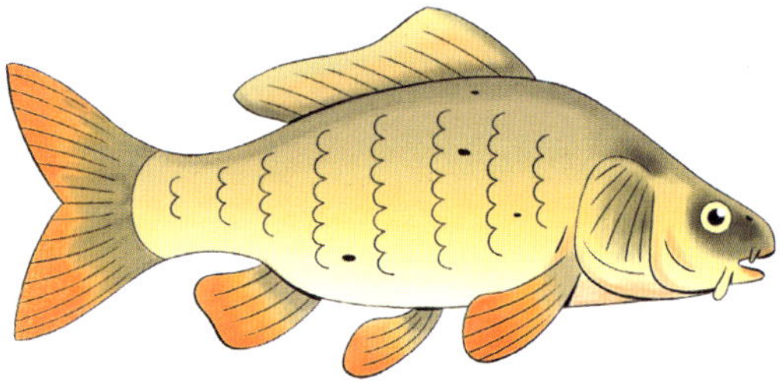

AND **CARP** ARE ON THE MENU.

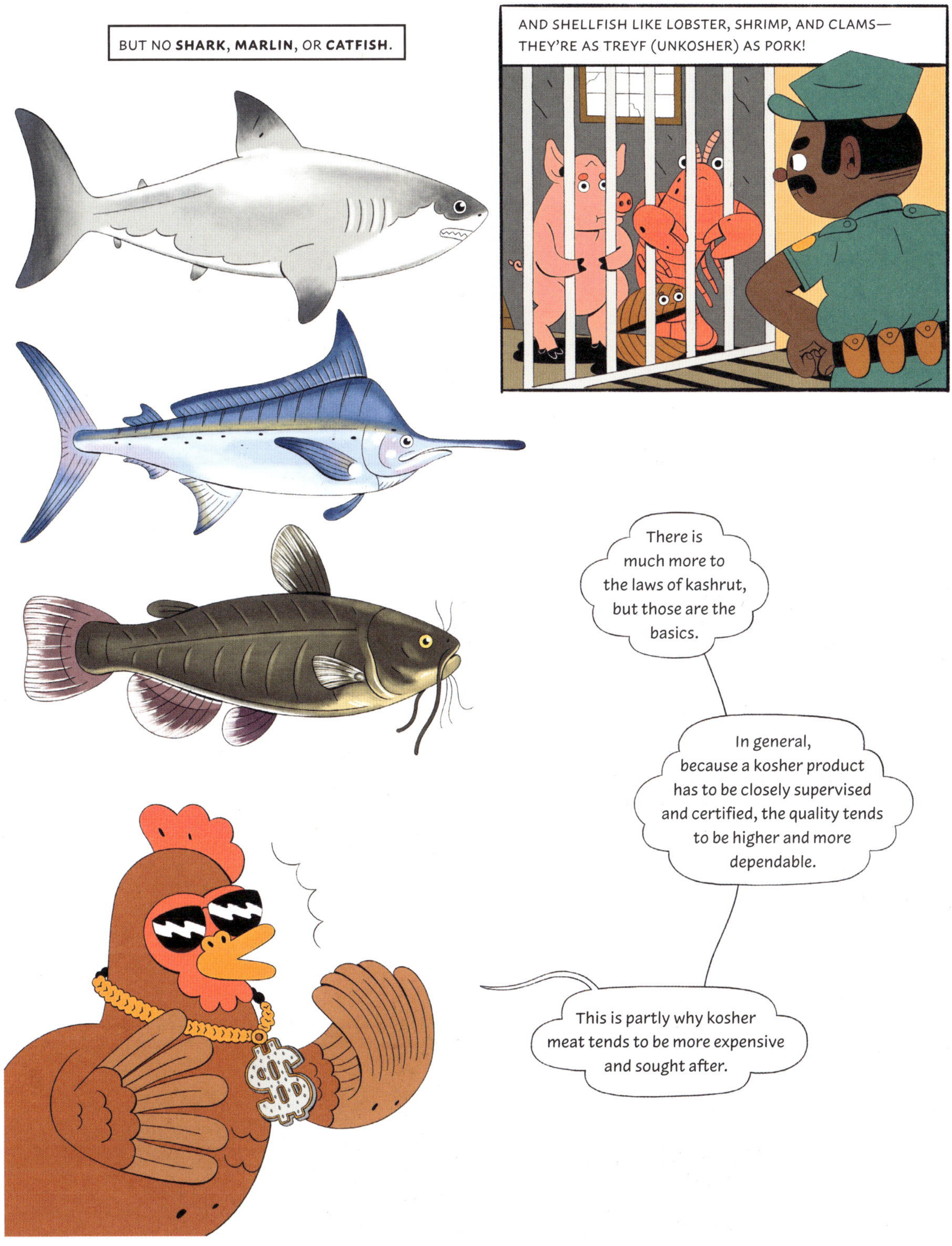
BUT NO **SHARK**, **MARLIN**, OR **CATFISH**.
AND SHELLFISH LIKE LOBSTER, SHRIMP, AND CLAMS—THEY'RE AS TREYF (UNKOSHER) AS PORK!
There is much more to the laws of kashrut, but those are the basics.
In general, because a kosher product has to be closely supervised and certified, the quality tends to be higher and more dependable.
This is partly why kosher meat tends to be more expensive and sought after.

Kosher versus Kosher Style

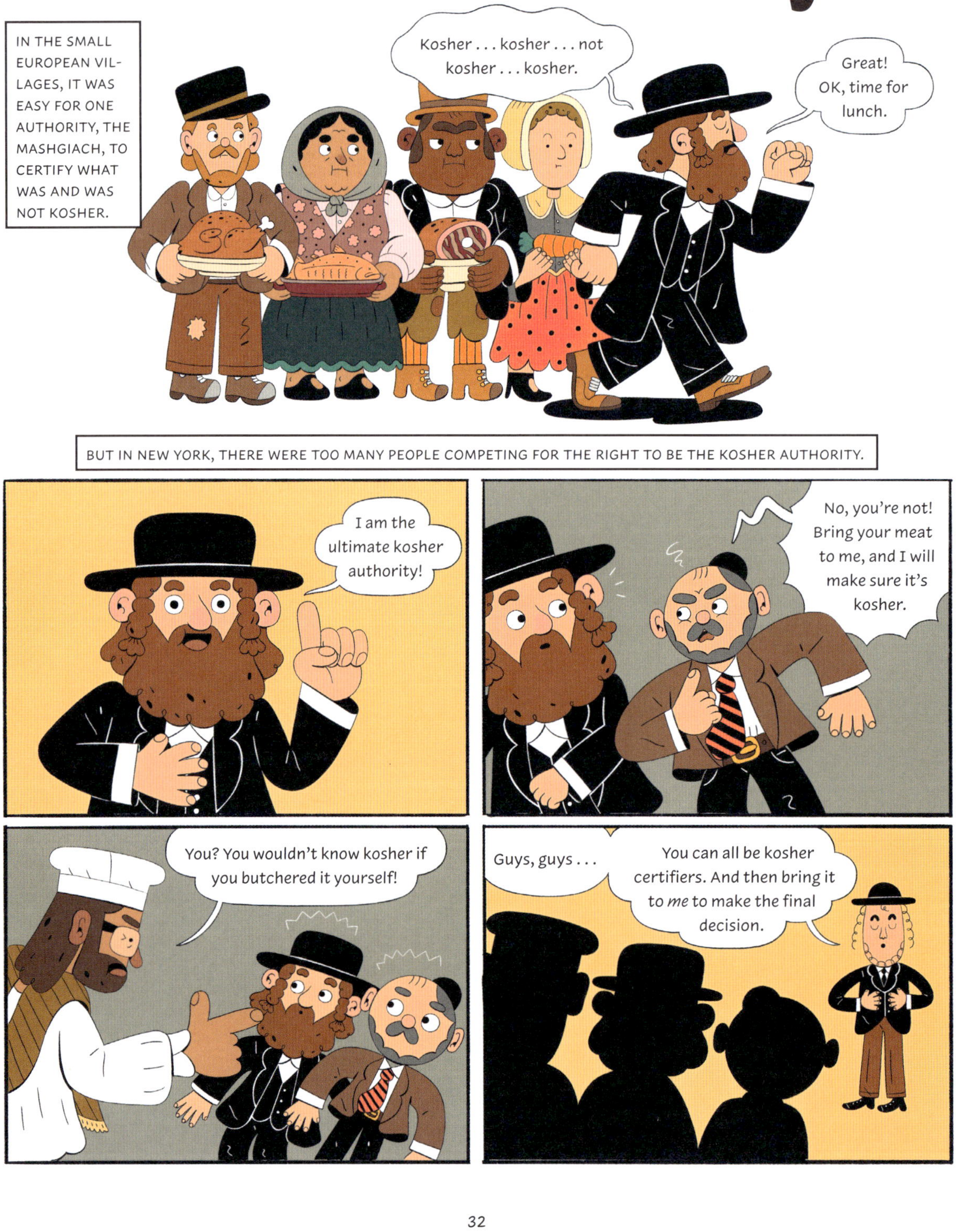
IN THE SMALL EUROPEAN VILLAGES, IT WAS EASY FOR ONE AUTHORITY, THE MASHGIACH, TO CERTIFY WHAT WAS AND WAS NOT KOSHER.
Kosher . . . kosher . . . not kosher . . . kosher.
Great! OK, time for lunch.
BUT IN NEW YORK, THERE WERE TOO MANY PEOPLE COMPETING FOR THE RIGHT TO BE THE KOSHER AUTHORITY.
I am the ultimate kosher authority!
No, you're not! Bring your meat to me, and I will make sure it's kosher.
You? You wouldn't know kosher if you butchered it yourself!
Guys, guys . . .
You can all be kosher certifiers. And then bring it to *me* to make the final decision.

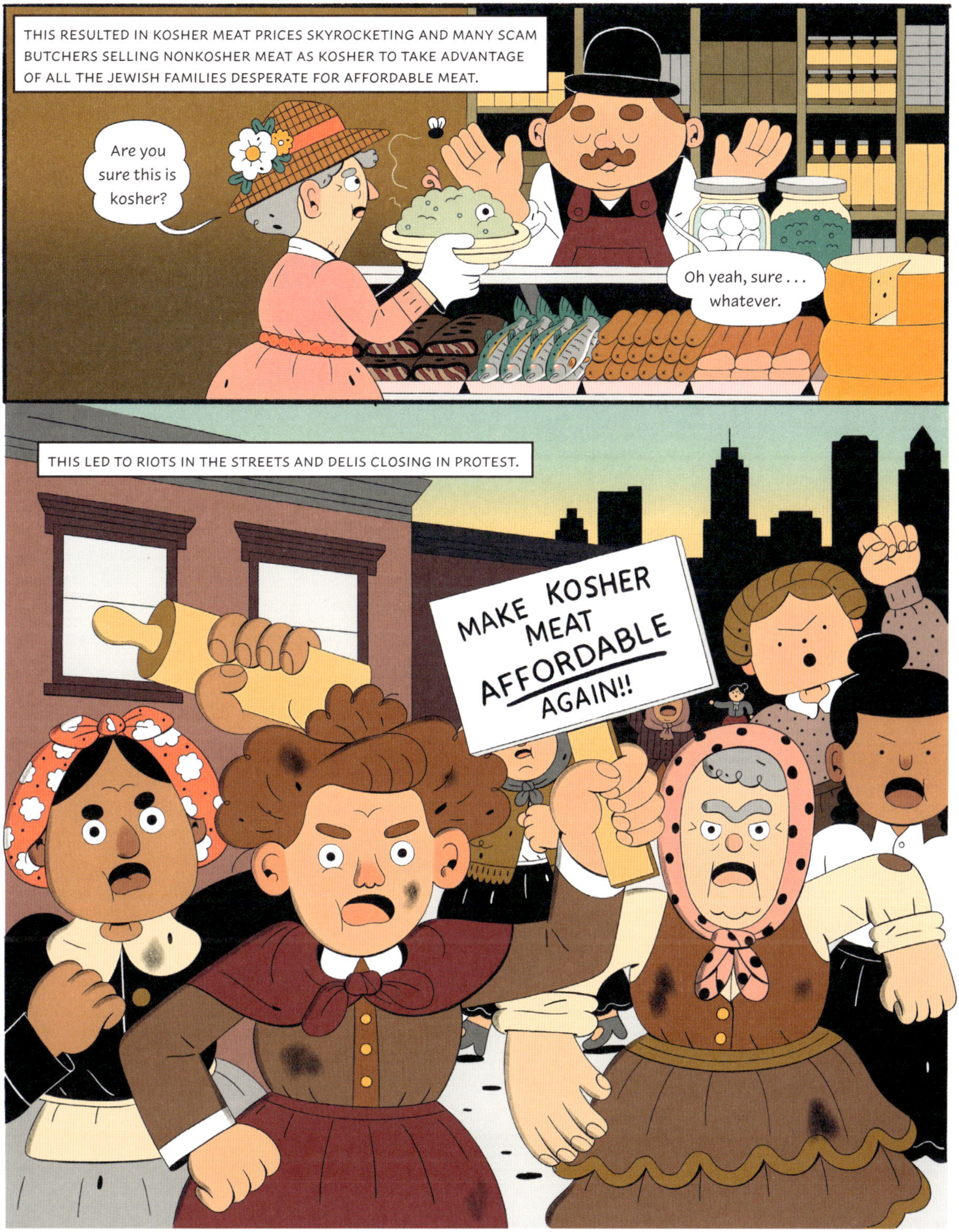
THIS RESULTED IN KOSHER MEAT PRICES SKYROCKETING AND MANY SCAM BUTCHERS SELLING NONKOSHER MEAT AS KOSHER TO TAKE ADVANTAGE OF ALL THE JEWISH FAMILIES DESPERATE FOR AFFORDABLE MEAT.
Are you sure this is kosher?
Oh yeah, sure . . . whatever.
THIS LED TO RIOTS IN THE STREETS AND DELIS CLOSING IN PROTEST.
MAKE KOSHER MEAT AFFORDABLE AGAIN!!

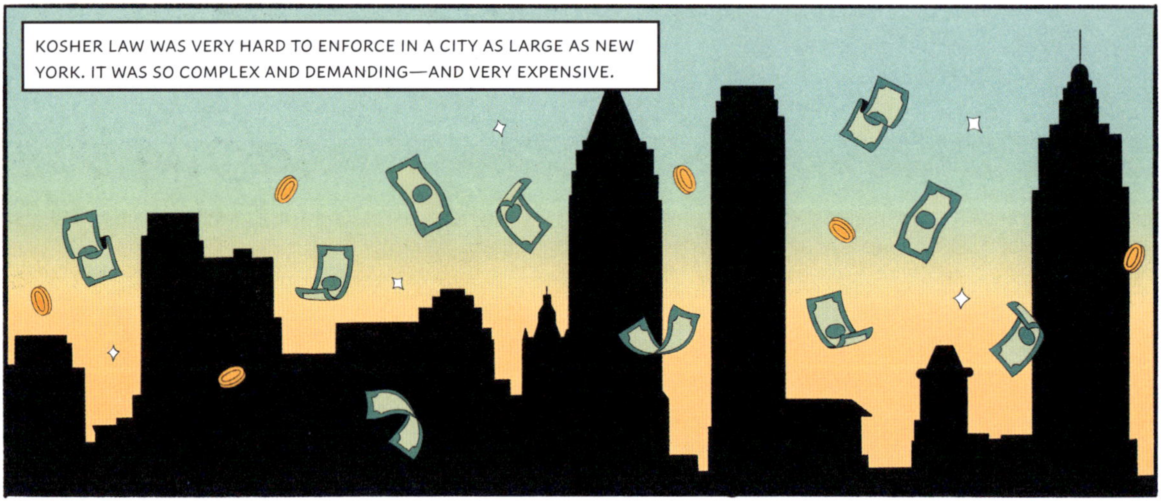
KOSHER LAW WAS VERY HARD TO ENFORCE IN A CITY AS LARGE AS NEW YORK. IT WAS SO COMPLEX AND DEMANDING—AND VERY EXPENSIVE.

THIS LED EVENTUALLY TO A SPLIT BETWEEN KOSHER AND KOSHER-STYLE DELIS.

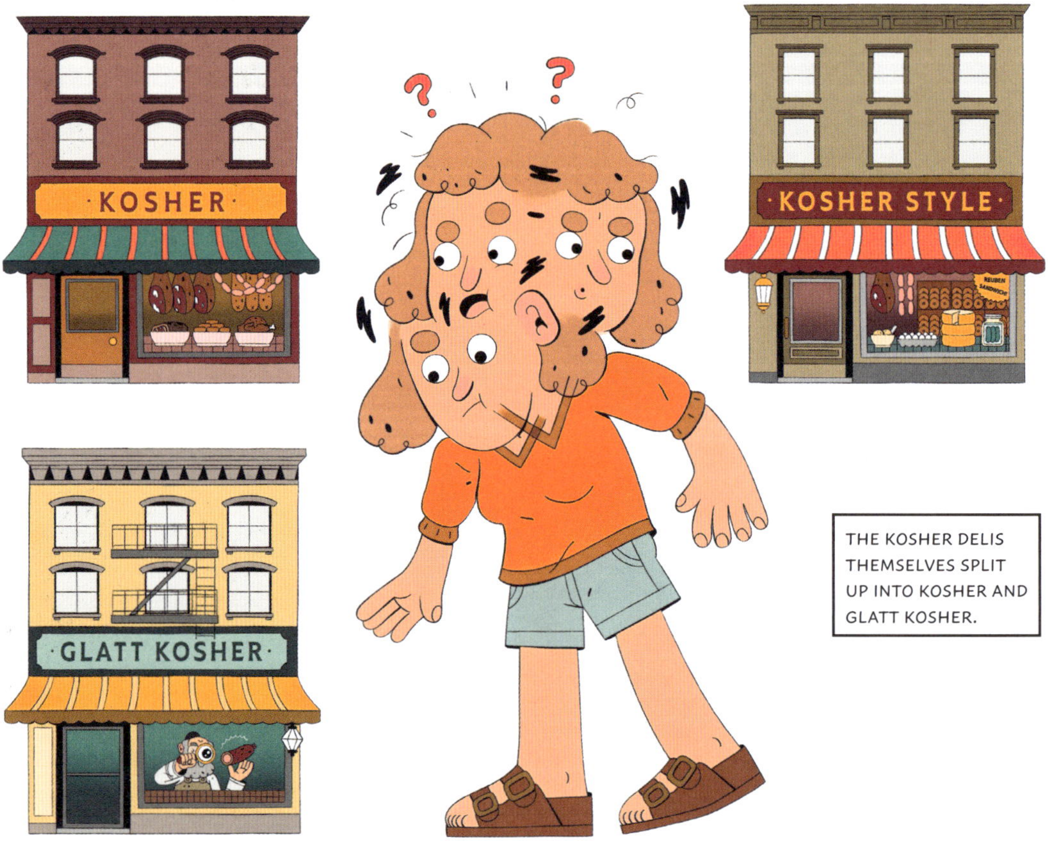
·KOSHER·
·KOSHER STYLE·
·GLATT KOSHER·
THE KOSHER DELIS THEMSELVES SPLIT UP INTO KOSHER AND GLATT KOSHER.

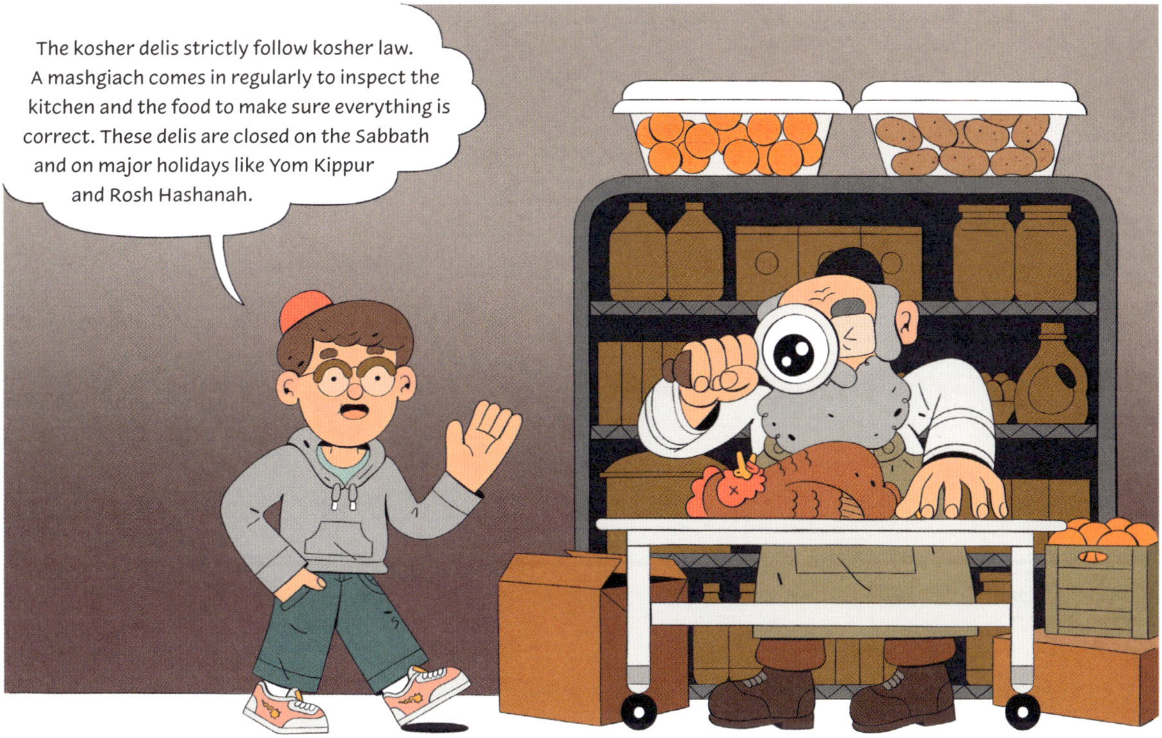
The kosher delis strictly follow kosher law. A mashgiach comes in regularly to inspect the kitchen and the food to make sure everything is correct. These delis are closed on the Sabbath and on major holidays like Yom Kippur and Rosh Hashanah.

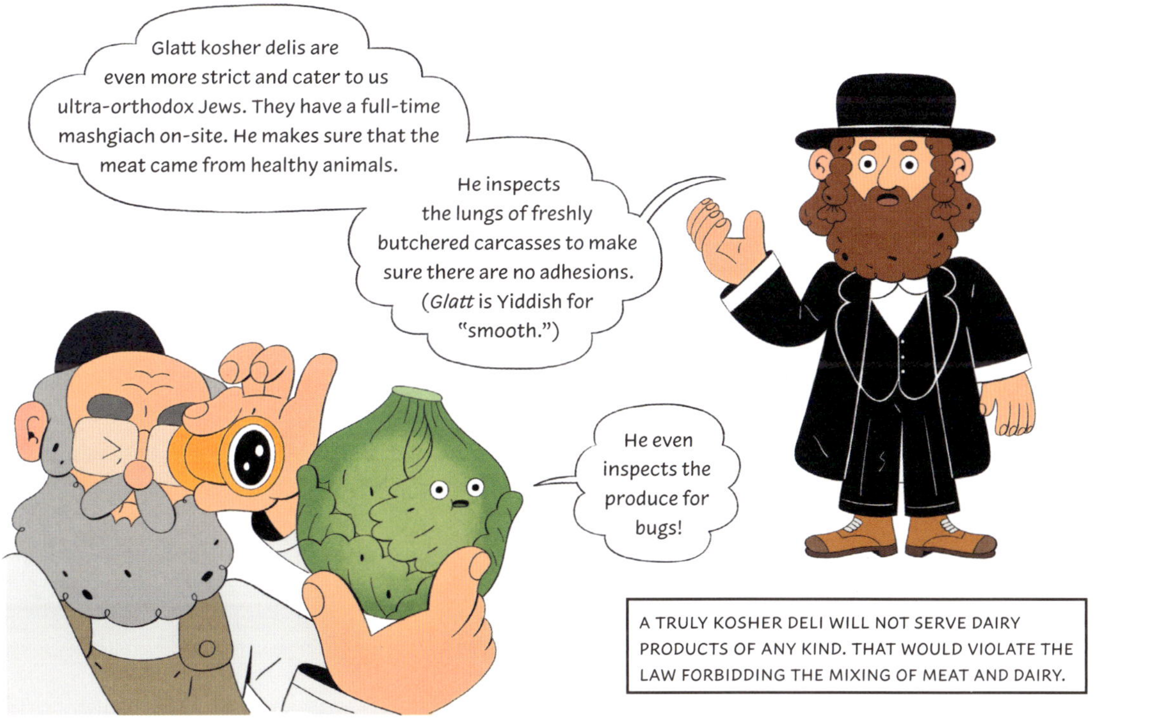
Glatt kosher delis are even more strict and cater to us ultra-orthodox Jews. They have a full-time mashgiach on-site. He makes sure that the meat came from healthy animals.
He inspects the lungs of freshly butchered carcasses to make sure there are no adhesions. (*Glatt* is Yiddish for "smooth.")
He even inspects the produce for bugs!
A TRULY KOSHER DELI WILL NOT SERVE DAIRY PRODUCTS OF ANY KIND. THAT WOULD VIOLATE THE LAW FORBIDDING THE MIXING OF MEAT AND DAIRY.

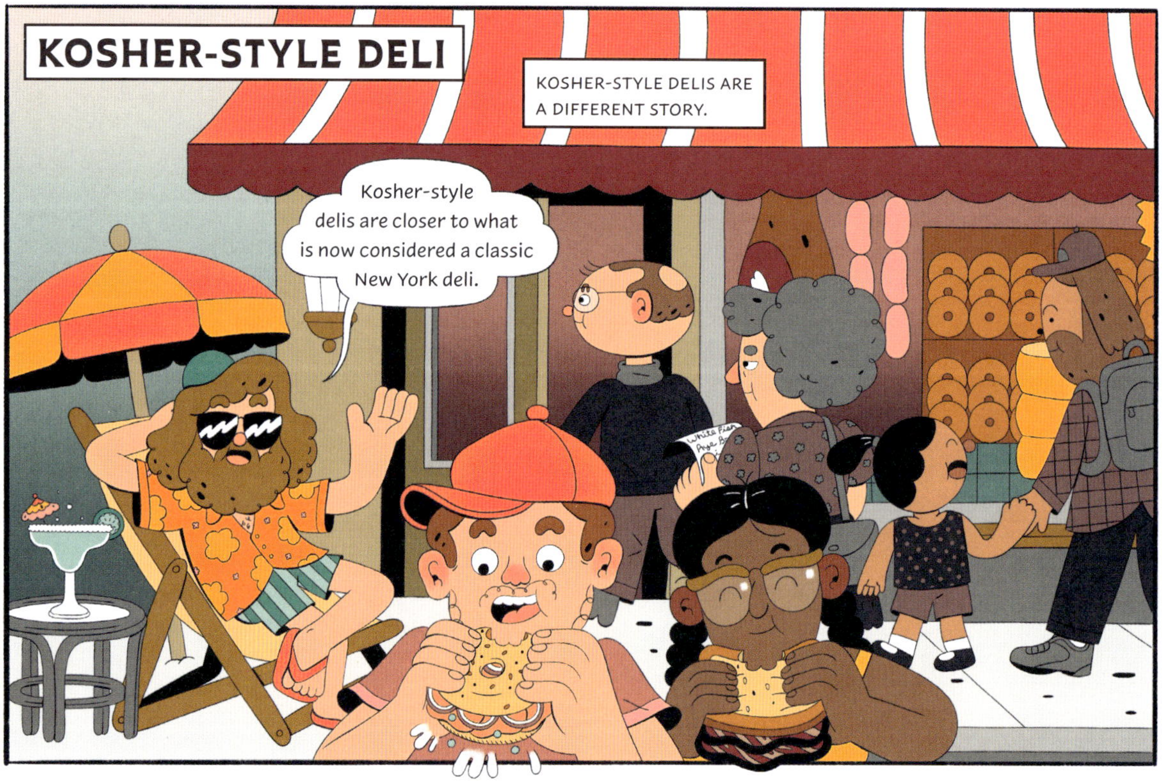
KOSHER-STYLE DELI
KOSHER-STYLE DELIS ARE A DIFFERENT STORY.
Kosher-style delis are closer to what is now considered a classic New York deli.

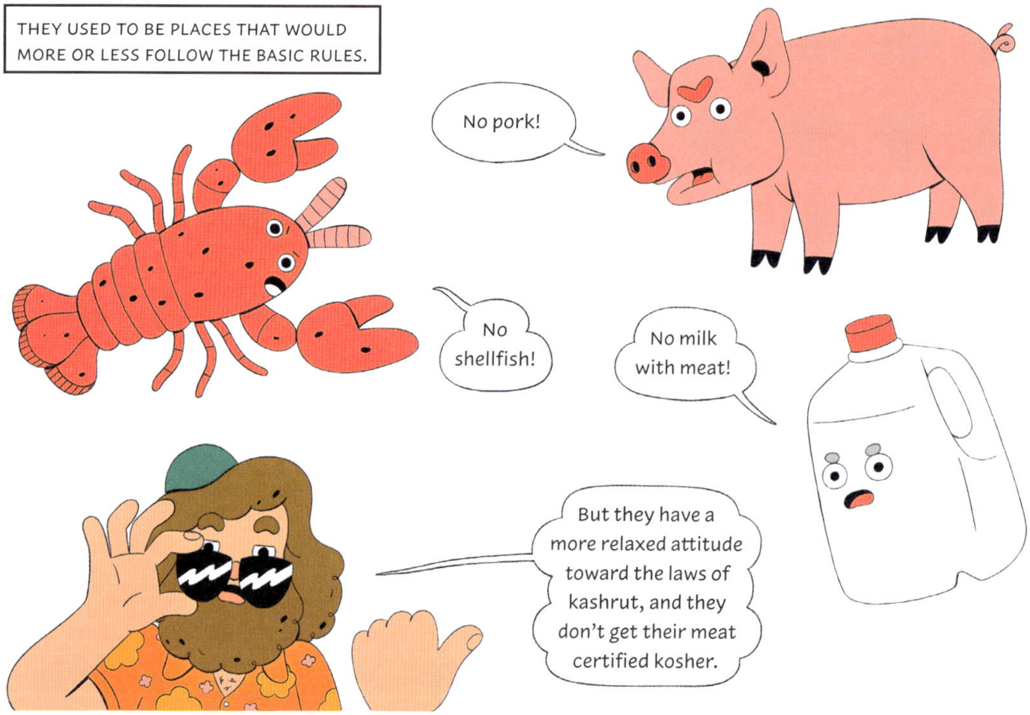
THEY USED TO BE PLACES THAT WOULD MORE OR LESS FOLLOW THE BASIC RULES.
No pork!
No shellfish!
No milk with meat!
But they have a more relaxed attitude toward the laws of kashrut, and they don't get their meat certified kosher.

AS JEWISH FOOD BECAME MORE POPULAR IN THE UNITED STATES, MANY DELIS BEGAN TO RELAX THEIR OBSERVANCE OF THE DIETARY LAWS.

THEY WANTED TO APPEAL TO GENTILES AS WELL AS JEWS.

Can I get that corned beef sandwich with some cheese?
Sorry, we don't do that here.
Why not?
It's against the rules!
Rules be damned! It would be so delicious!

THIS MEANT BREAKING THE RULES TO INVENT THINGS LIKE THE REUBEN.

More on that later!

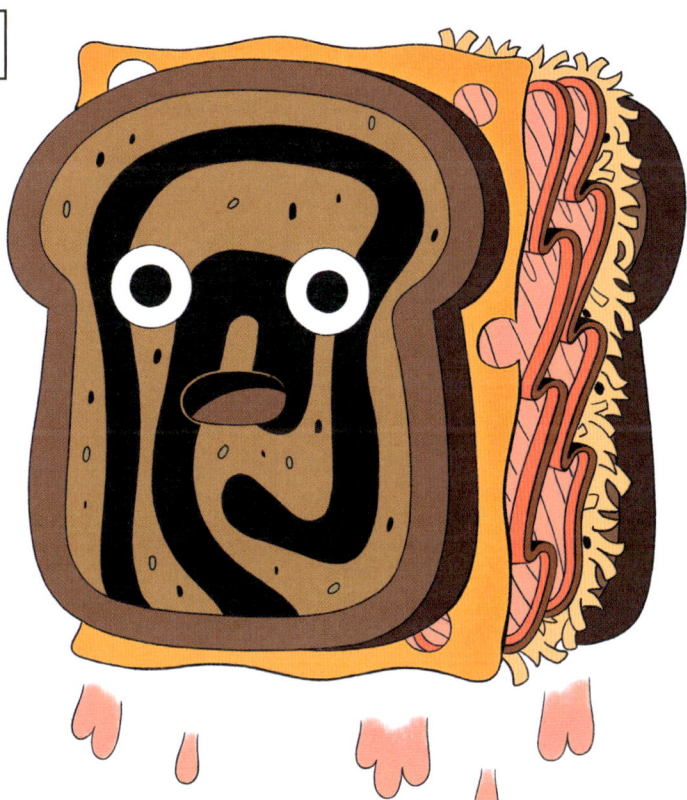

THESE DELIS ARE DEFINITELY NOT KOSHER, BUT THEY WOULD EVENTUALLY DOMINATE THE BUSINESS.

DELICATESSEN VERSUS APPETIZING STORE

DELIS AND APPETIZING STORES ARE OFTEN LUMPED TOGETHER, BUT THEY ARE NOT THE SAME THING!

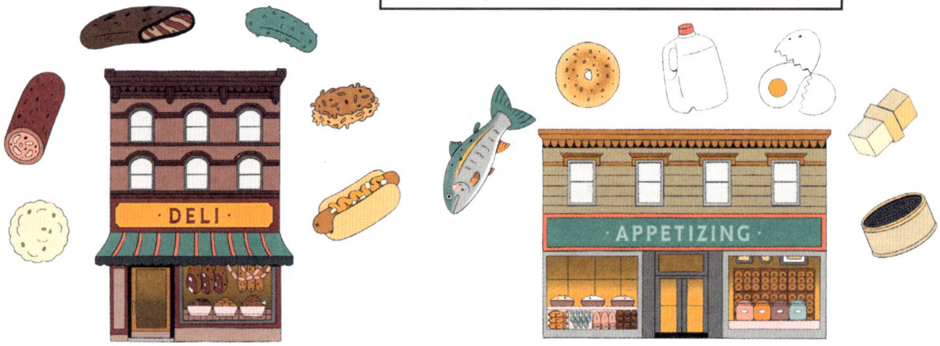

DELI
APPETIZING

BECAUSE KOSHER LAW PROHIBITS THE MIXING OF DAIRY AND MEAT, AND DELIS SELL MEATS SUCH AS PASTRAMI, SALAMI, AND CORNED BEEF, THEY CANNOT ALSO SELL DAIRY.

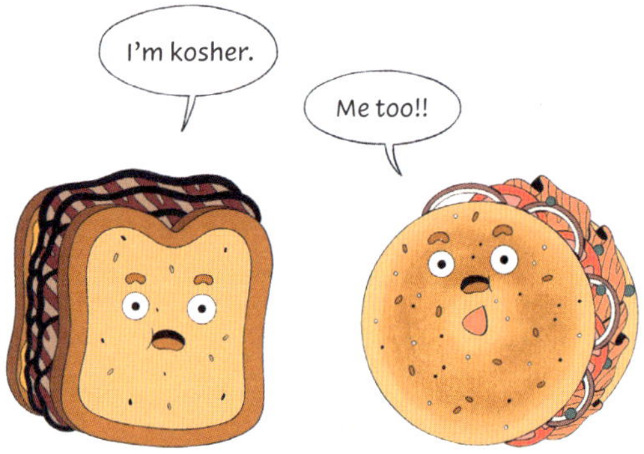

I'm kosher.
Me too!!

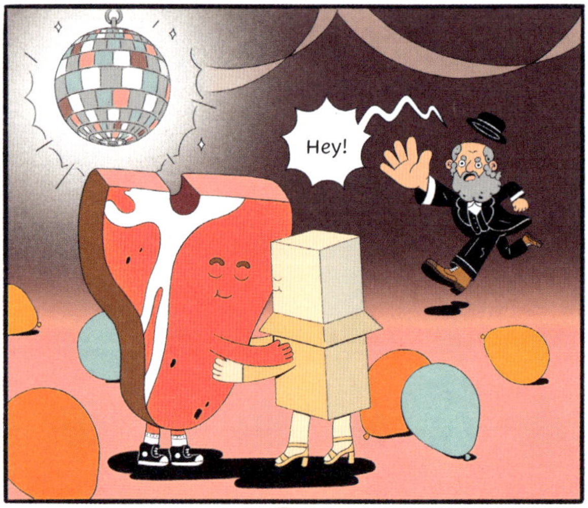

Hey!

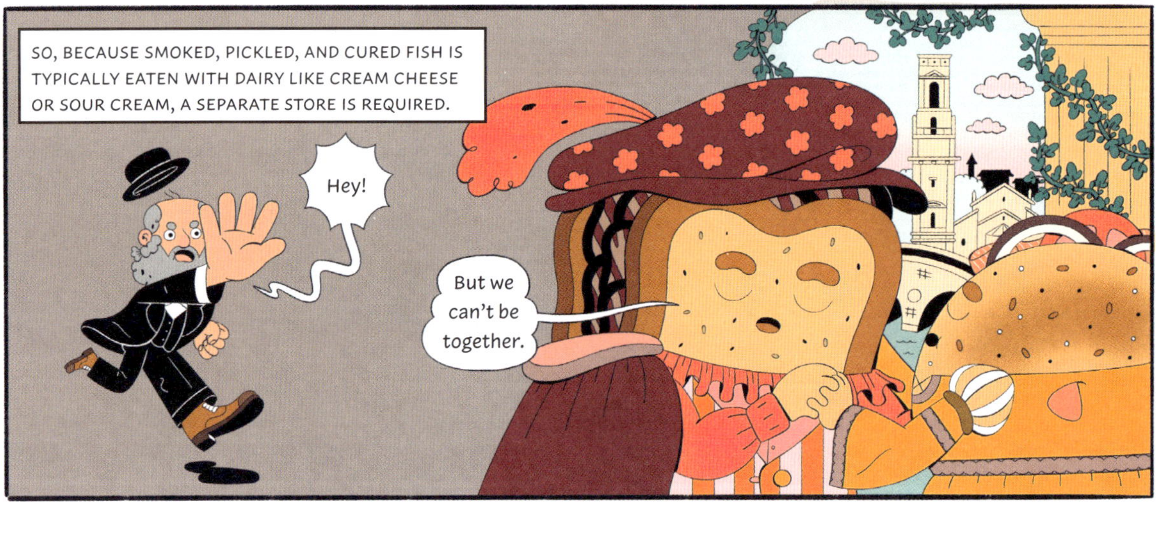

SO, BECAUSE SMOKED, PICKLED, AND CURED FISH IS TYPICALLY EATEN WITH DAIRY LIKE CREAM CHEESE OR SOUR CREAM, A SEPARATE STORE IS REQUIRED.
Hey!
But we can't be together.

YOU WILL SEE KOSHER-STYLE DELIS THAT SERVE BOTH DAIRY PRODUCTS AND MEAT DISHES, BUT THEY ARE NOT *REALLY* KOSHER.

MEANWHILE, THERE ARE APPETIZING STORES THAT SELL NONKOSHER FISH—STURGEON, FOR EXAMPLE.

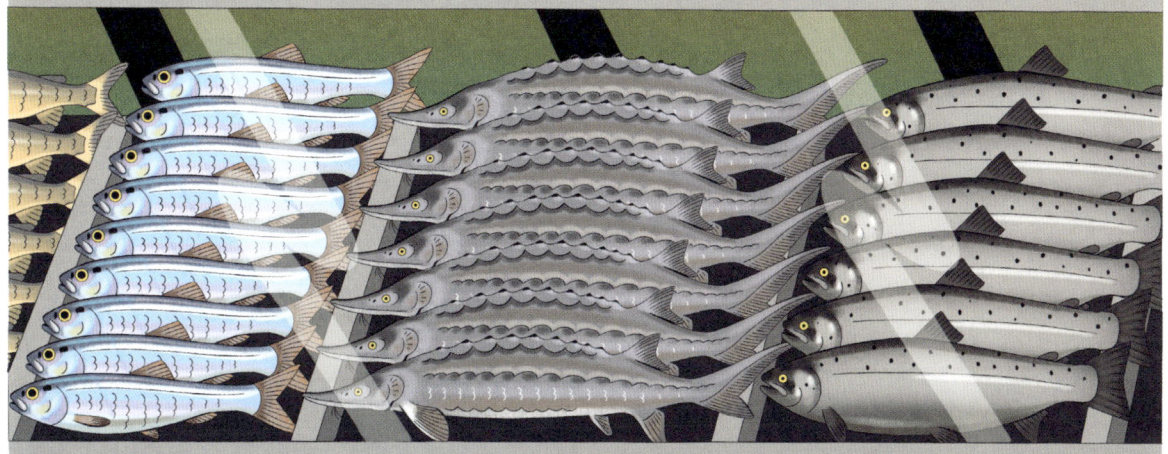

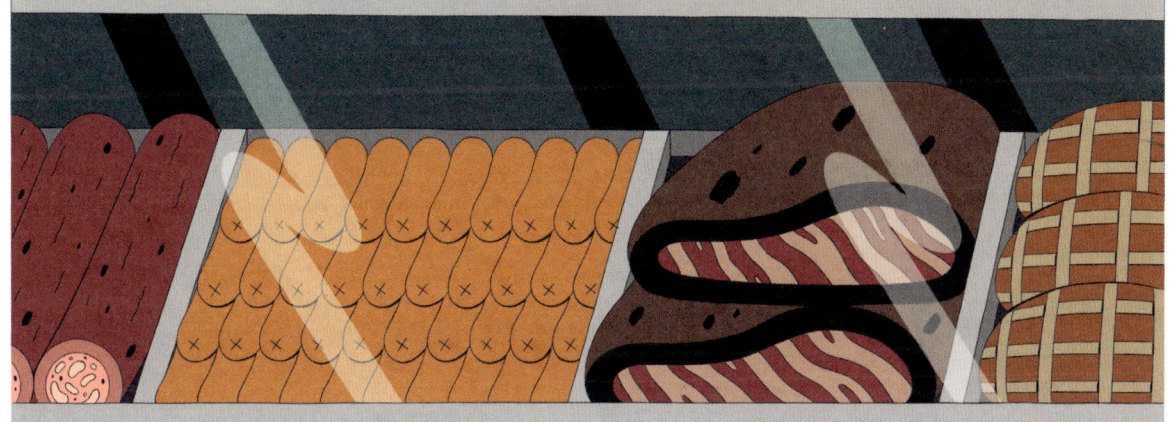

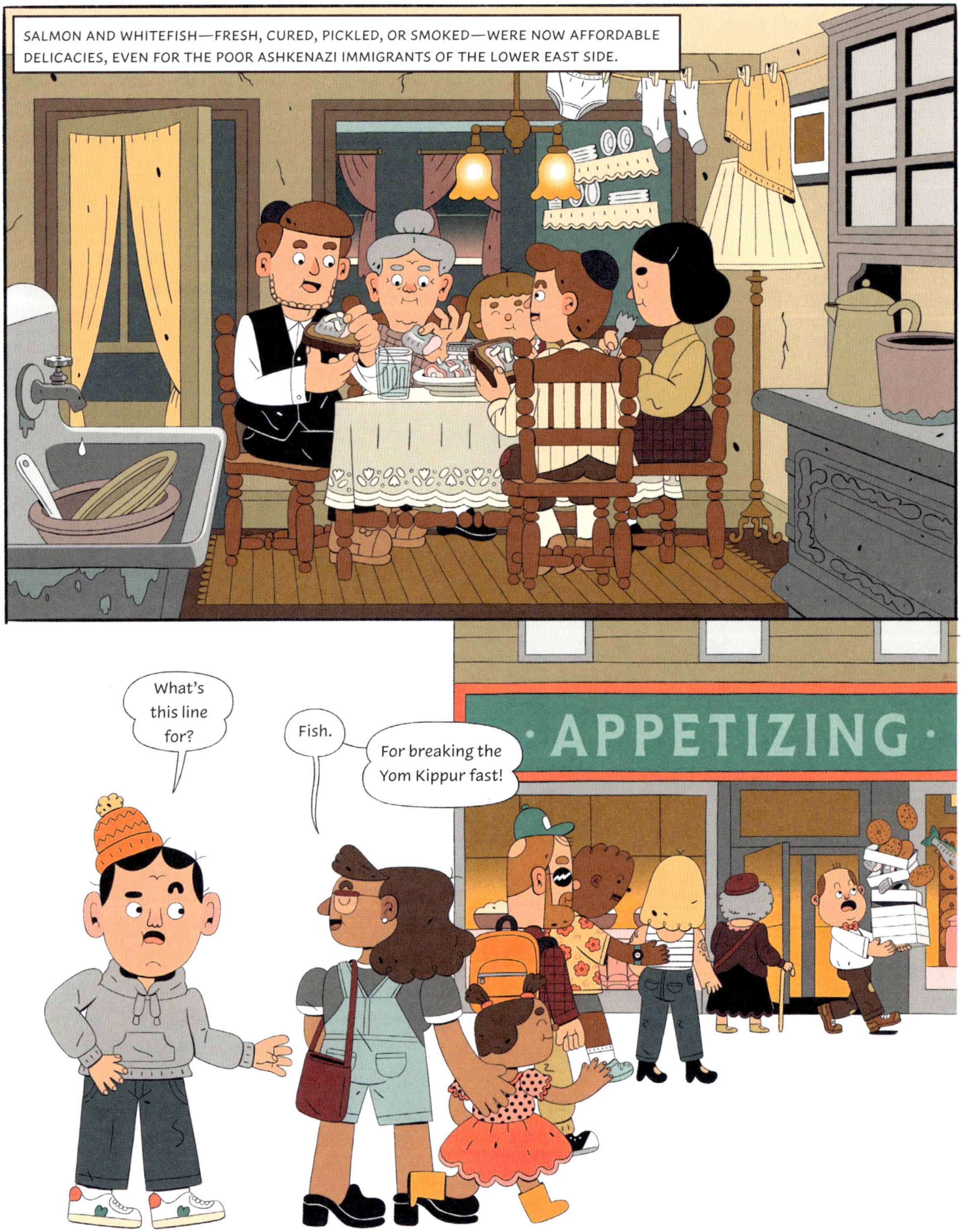
SALMON AND WHITEFISH—FRESH, CURED, PICKLED, OR SMOKED—WERE NOW AFFORDABLE DELICACIES, EVEN FOR THE POOR ASHKENAZI IMMIGRANTS OF THE LOWER EAST SIDE.
What's this line for?
Fish.
For breaking the Yom Kippur fast!
·APPETIZING·

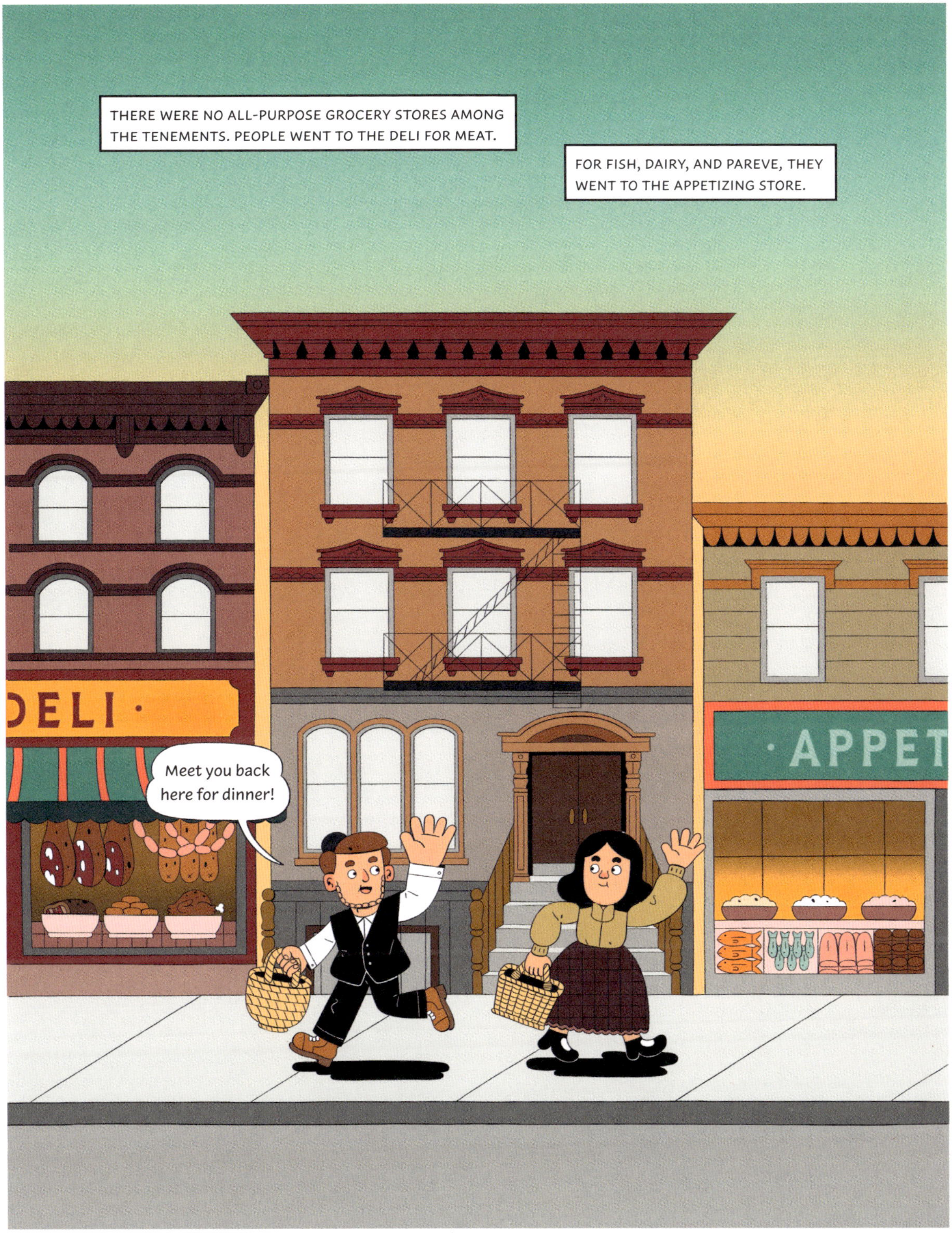
THERE WERE NO ALL-PURPOSE GROCERY STORES AMONG THE TENEMENTS. PEOPLE WENT TO THE DELI FOR MEAT.
FOR FISH, DAIRY, AND PAREVE, THEY WENT TO THE APPETIZING STORE.
DELI
Meet you back here for dinner!
APPET

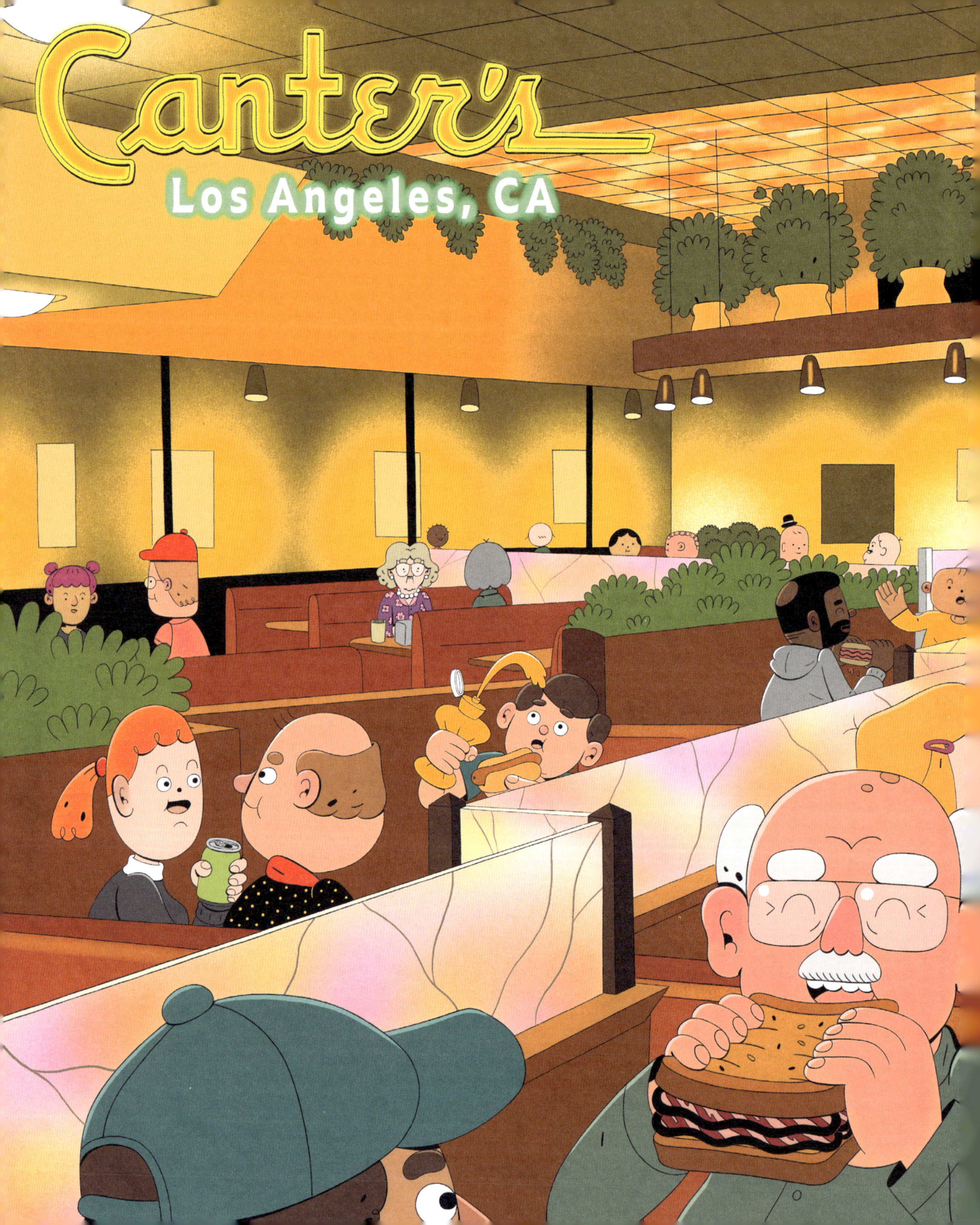
Canter's
Los Angeles, CA

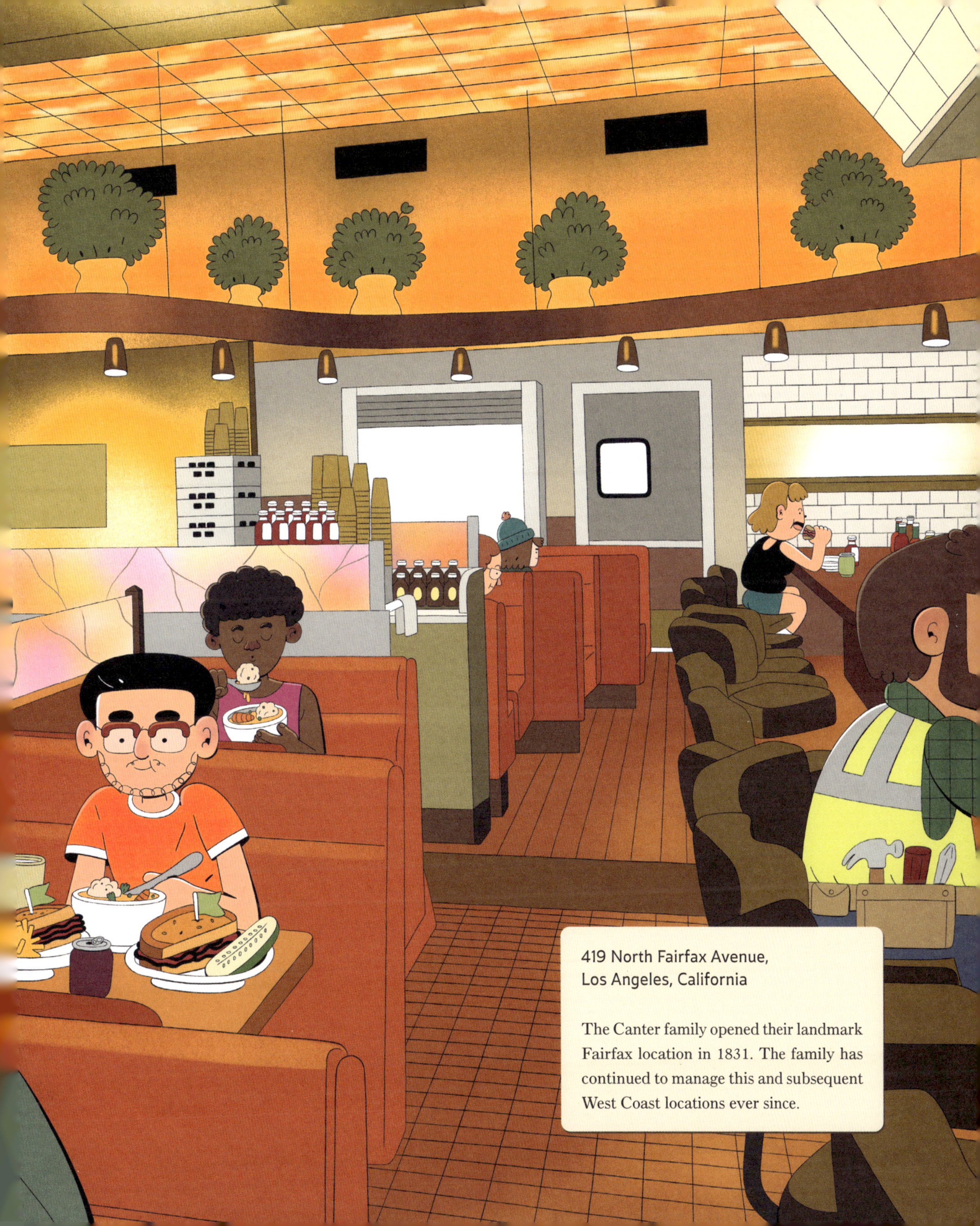

419 North Fairfax Avenue,
Los Angeles, California

The Canter family opened their landmark Fairfax location in 1831. The family has continued to manage this and subsequent West Coast locations ever since.

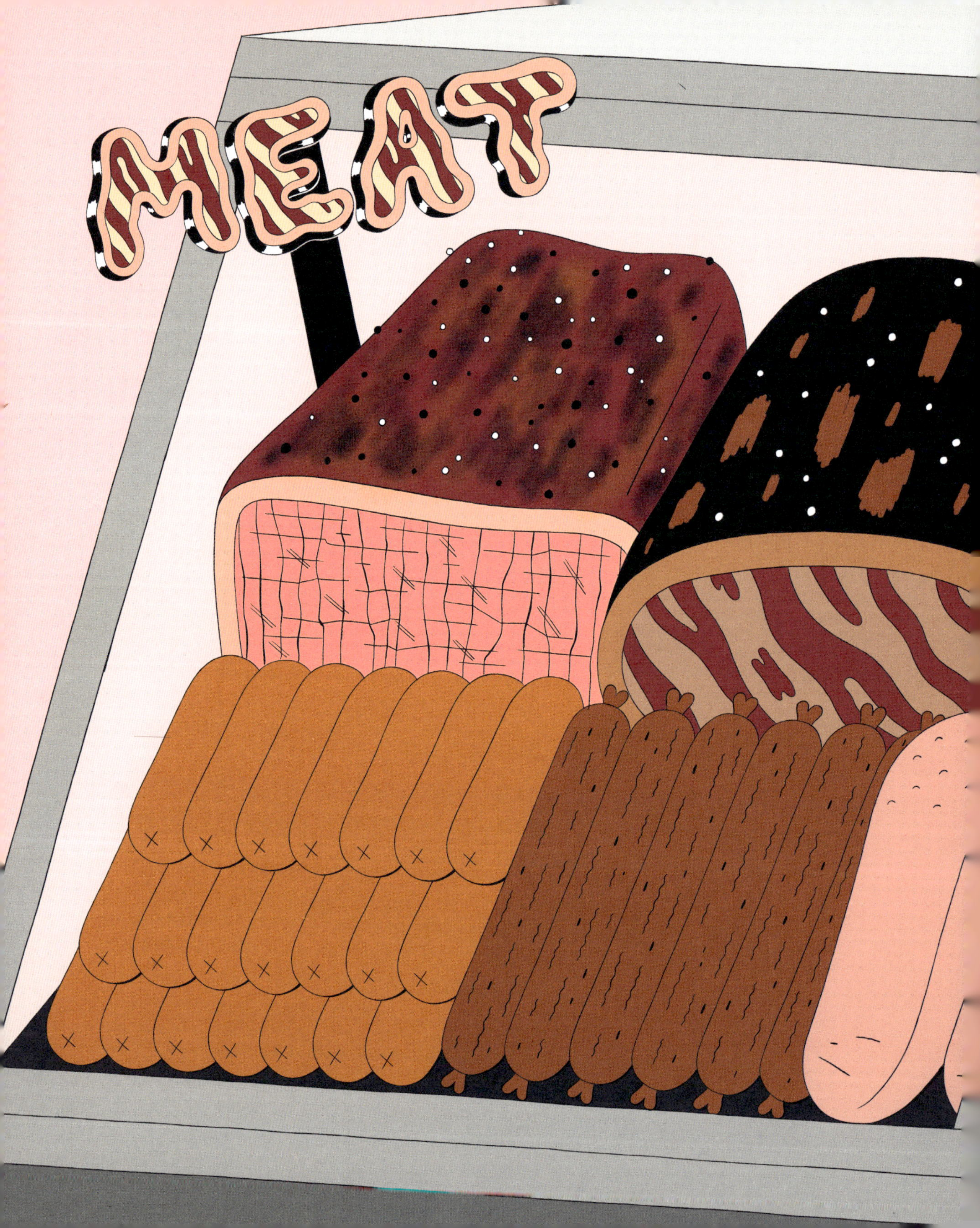
MEAT

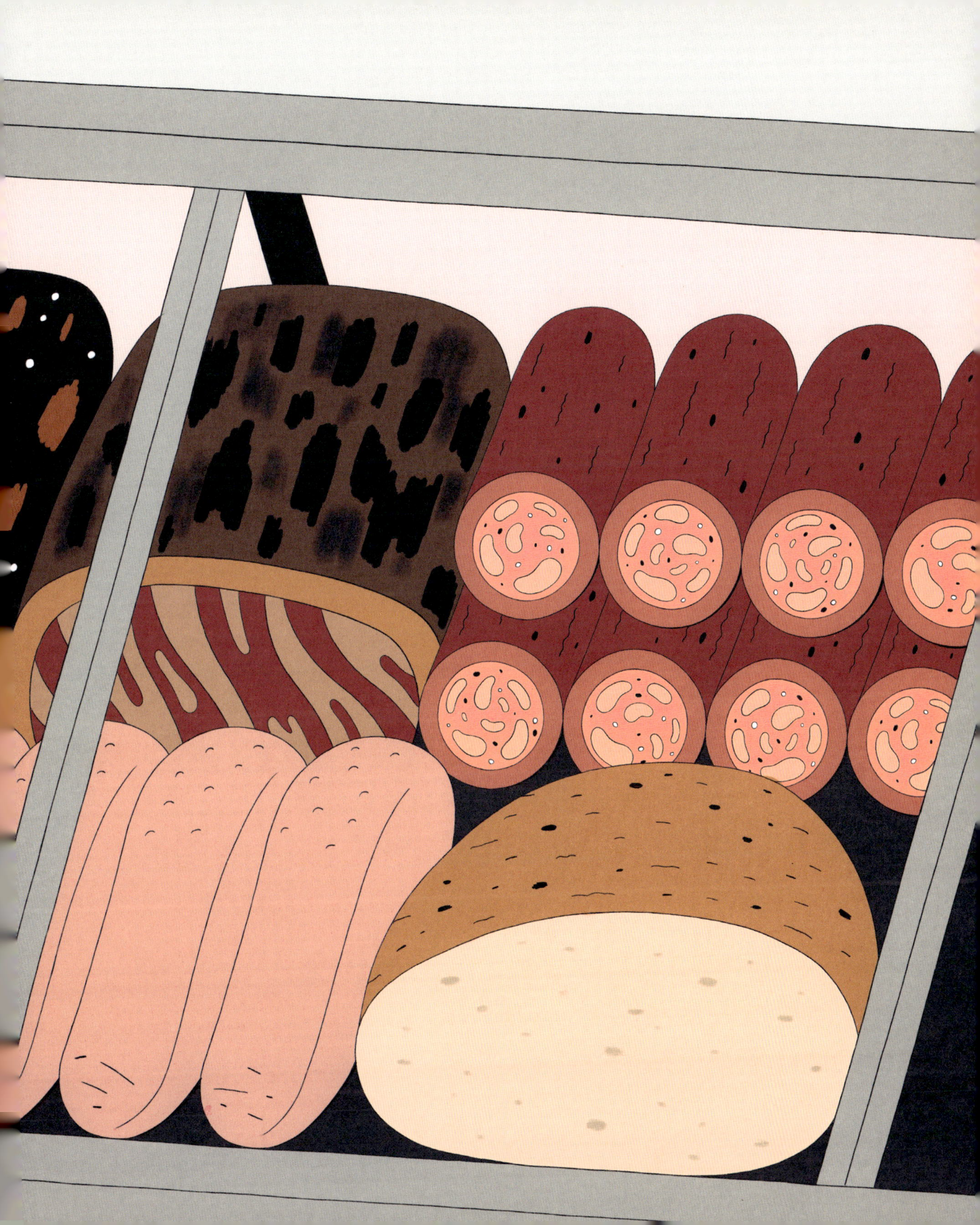

IN THE BOOK OF GENESIS, JACOB WRESTLES WITH AN ANGEL. WHILE THEY ARE FIGHTING, THE ANGEL TOUCHES JACOB'S HIP SOCKET, CAUSING IT TO BECOME DISLOCATED.

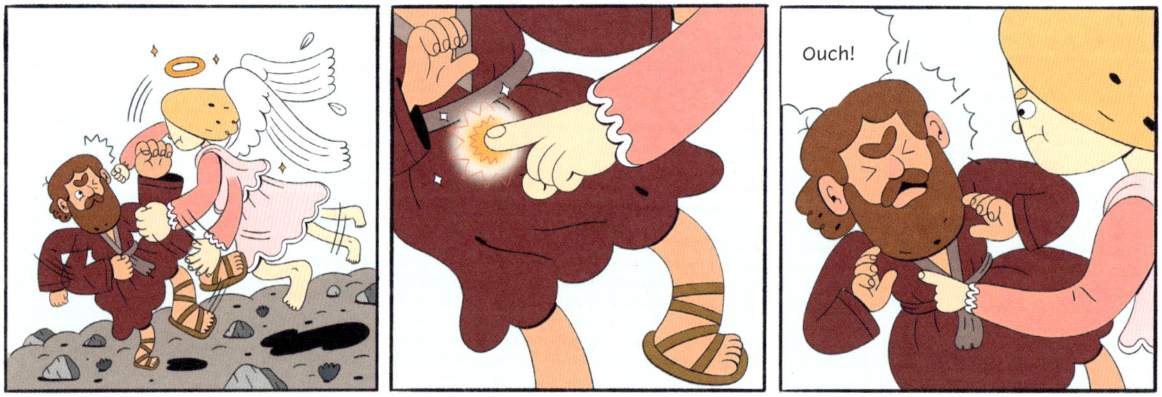
Ouch!

THIS IS THE ORIGIN FOR THE KOSHER LAW THAT ONE MUST NOT EAT AN ANIMAL'S SCIATIC NERVE.

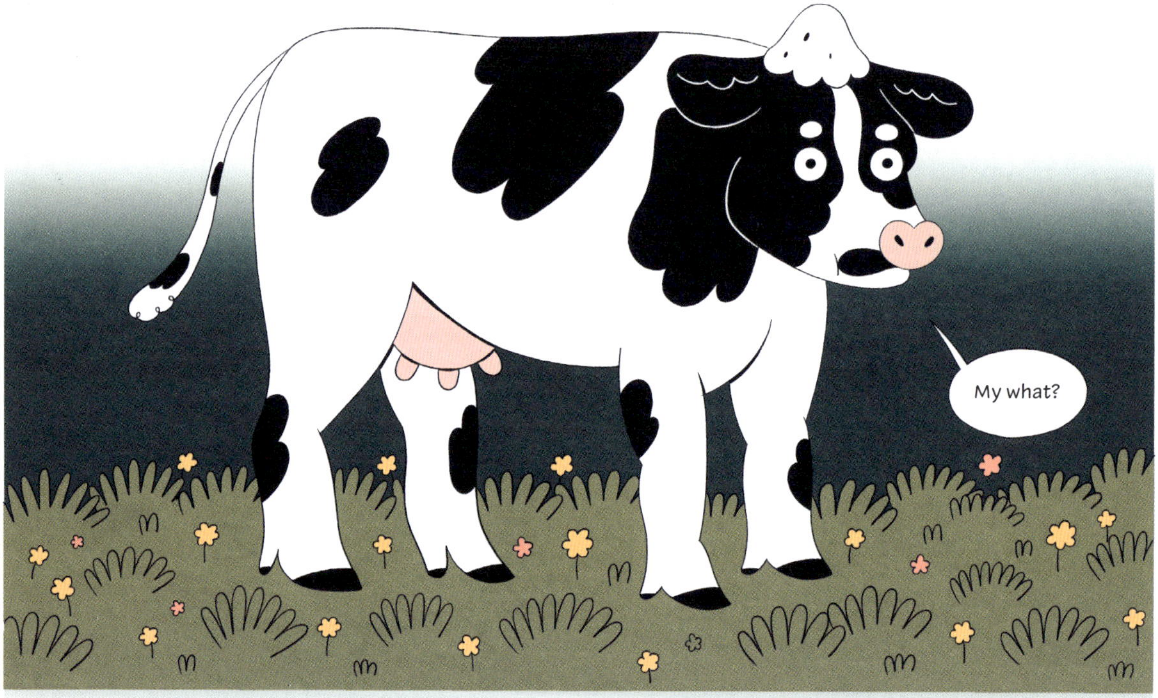
My what?

THE SCIATIC NERVE IS A LARGE NERVE THAT RUNS ALONG A COW'S BACK AND OVER THE HIPS.

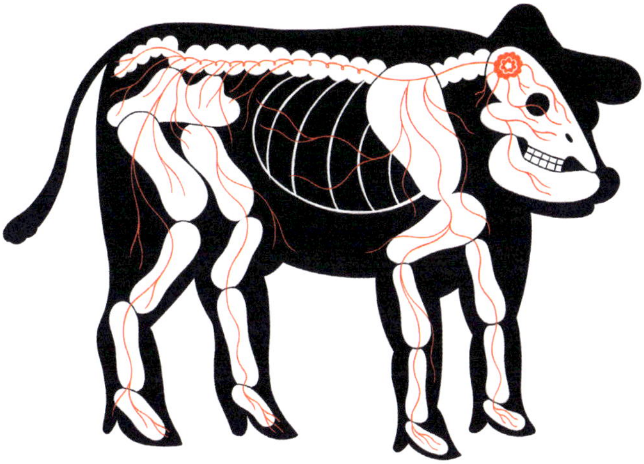

IT IS EXPENSIVE AND DIFFICULT FOR BUTCHERS TO REMOVE THIS NERVE FROM HINDQUARTER CUTS OF BEEF.

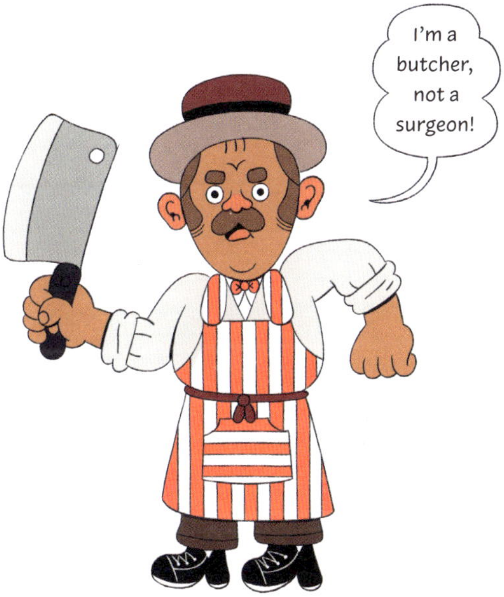
I'm a butcher, not a surgeon!

THUS, ONLY CUTS FROM THE FRONT OF THE ANIMAL ARE KOSHER.

HOWEVER, THE MOST DESIRABLE FOREQUARTER CUTS, INCLUDING RIB AND CHUCK, WERE TOO EXPENSIVE FOR POOR JEWISH IMMIGRANTS.

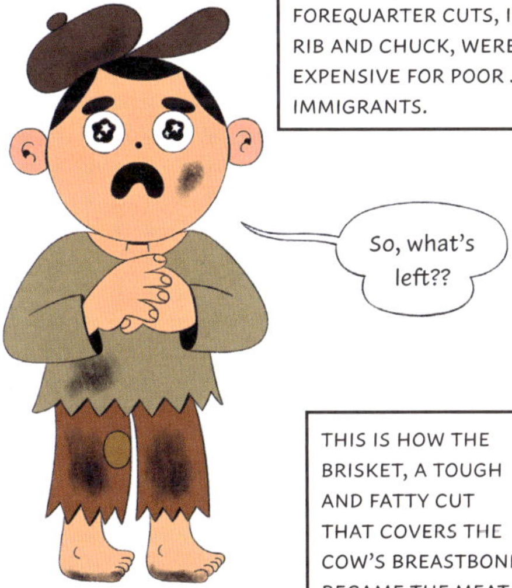
So, what's left??

THIS IS HOW THE BRISKET, A TOUGH AND FATTY CUT THAT COVERS THE COW'S BREASTBONE, BECAME THE MEAT OF CHOICE FOR DISHES IN THE JEWISH DELI.

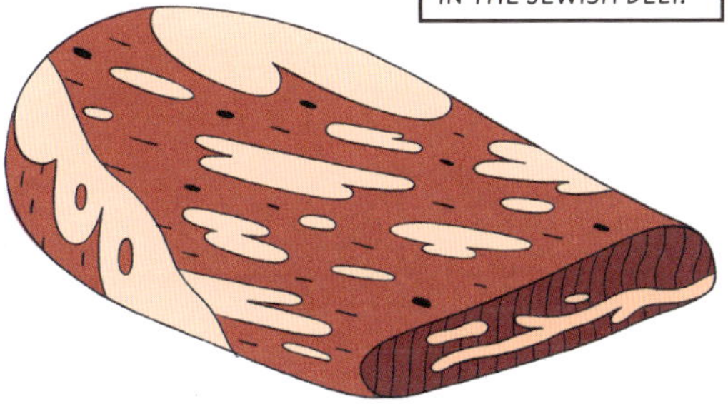

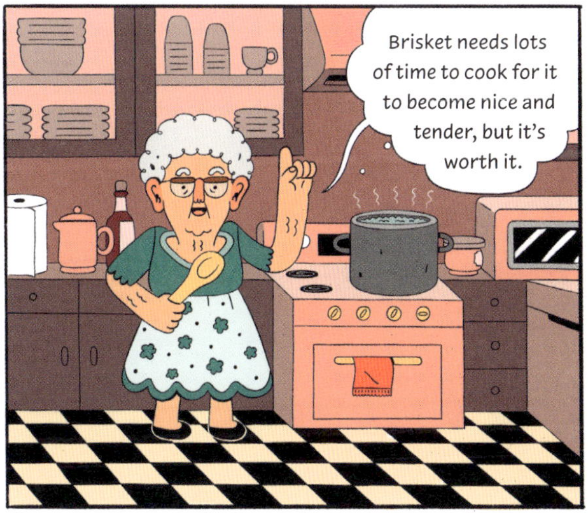
Brisket needs lots of time to cook for it to become nice and tender, but it's worth it.

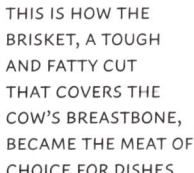

Corned Beef

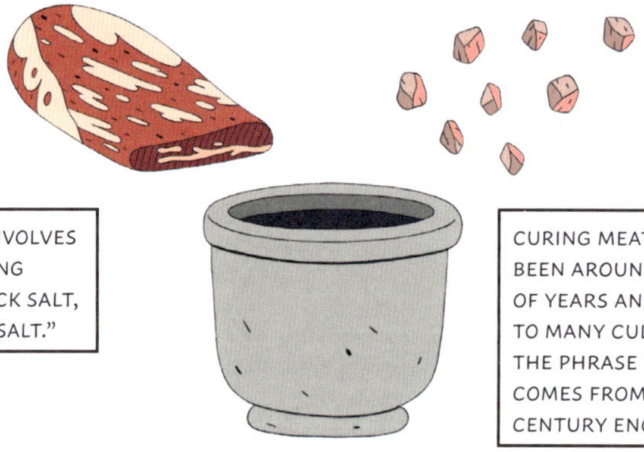

THE PROCESS OF CORNING INVOLVES PUTTING MEAT IN A POT ALONG WITH LARGE KERNELS OF ROCK SALT, REFERRED TO AS "CORNS OF SALT."

CURING MEAT WITH SALT HAS BEEN AROUND FOR THOUSANDS OF YEARS AND IS COMMON TO MANY CULTURES, BUT THE PHRASE "CORNED MEAT" COMES FROM SEVENTEENTH-CENTURY ENGLAND.

WHEN THE ENGLISH CONQUERED IRELAND, THEY BROUGHT THEIR CATTLE TO THE IRISH COUNTRYSIDE. SUDDENLY, BEEF WAS PLENTIFUL AND AFFORDABLE IN IRELAND.

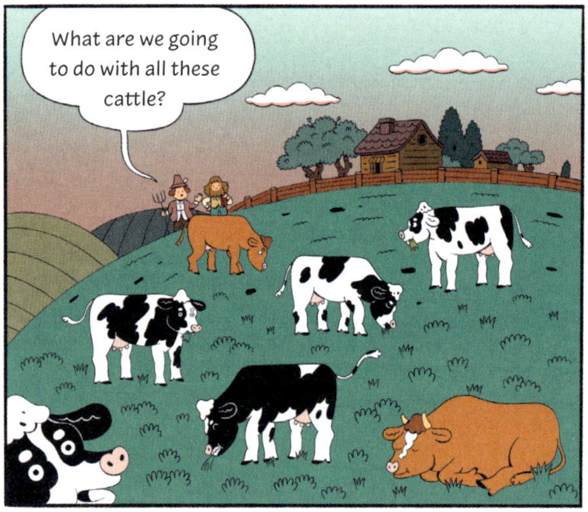
What are we going to do with all these cattle?

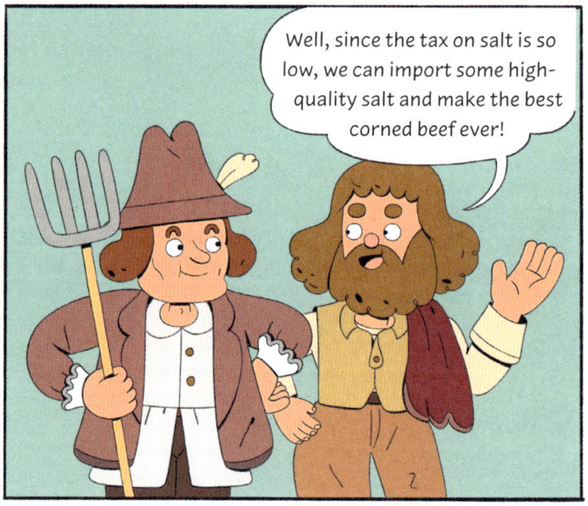
Well, since the tax on salt is so low, we can import some high-quality salt and make the best corned beef ever!

THE JEWS IN EASTERN EUROPE COULDN'T AFFORD MUCH MEAT AT ALL, AND BEEF WAS ESPECIALLY EXPENSIVE.

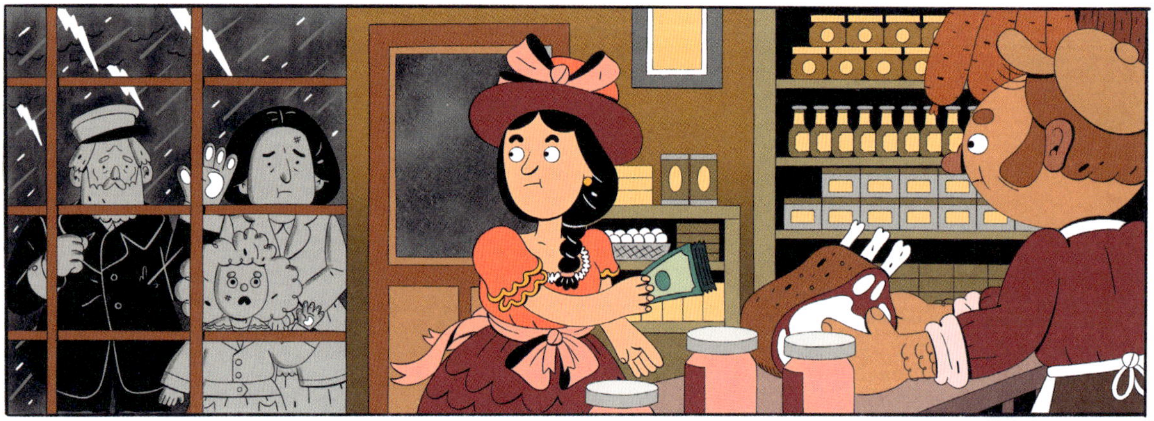

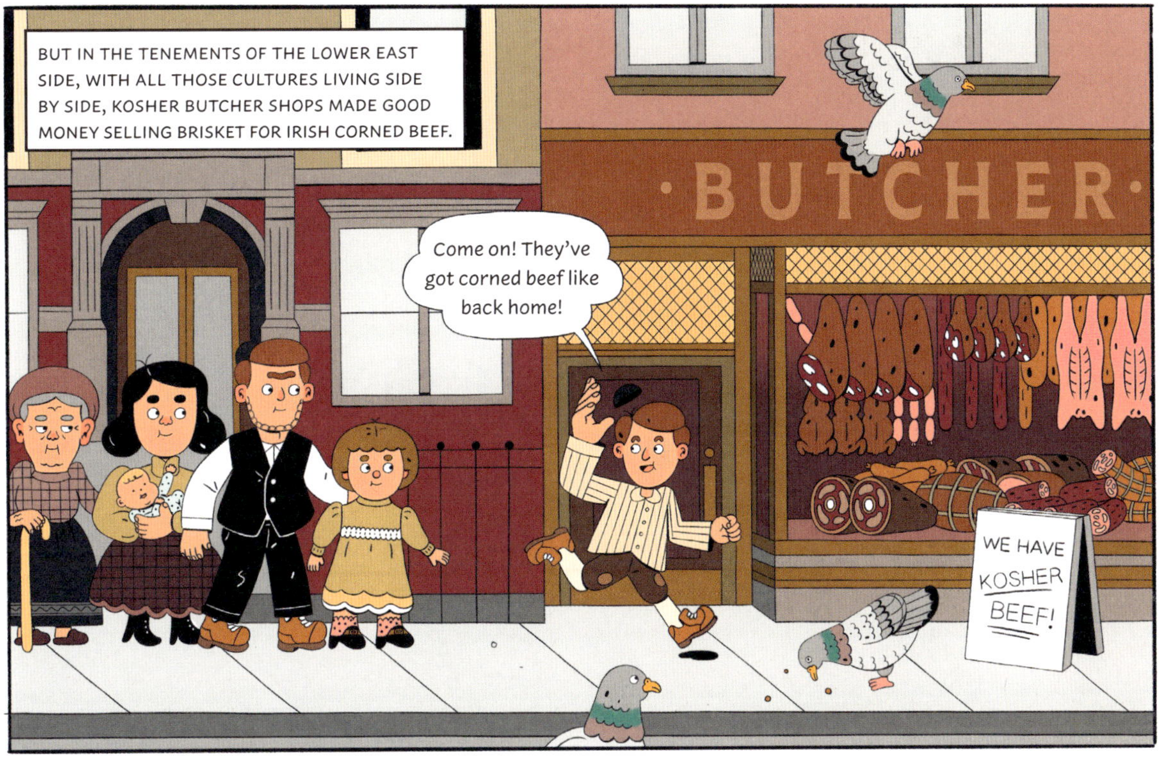
BUT IN THE TENEMENTS OF THE LOWER EAST SIDE, WITH ALL THOSE CULTURES LIVING SIDE BY SIDE, KOSHER BUTCHER SHOPS MADE GOOD MONEY SELLING BRISKET FOR IRISH CORNED BEEF.
·BUTCHER·
Come on! They've got corned beef like back home!
WE HAVE KOSHER BEEF!

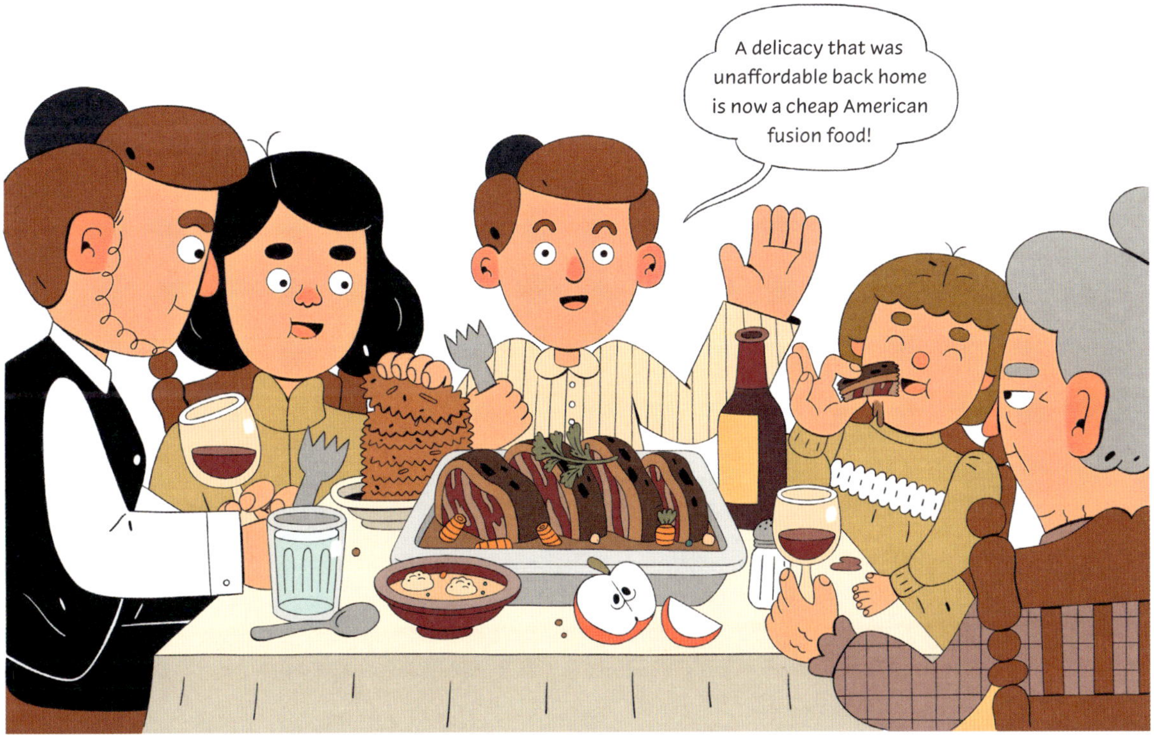
A delicacy that was unaffordable back home is now a cheap American fusion food!

BRISKET HAS A THICK LAYER OF FAT ON TOP CALLED THE DECKLE.

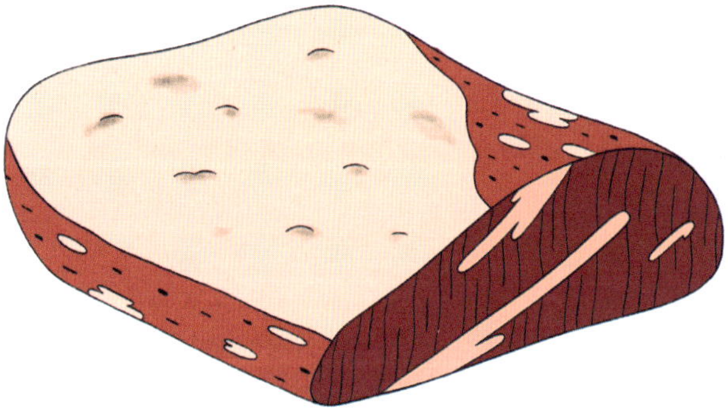

THE DECKLE IS POKED FULL OF HOLES SO THAT THE BRINE CAN PENETRATE TO THE MEAT.

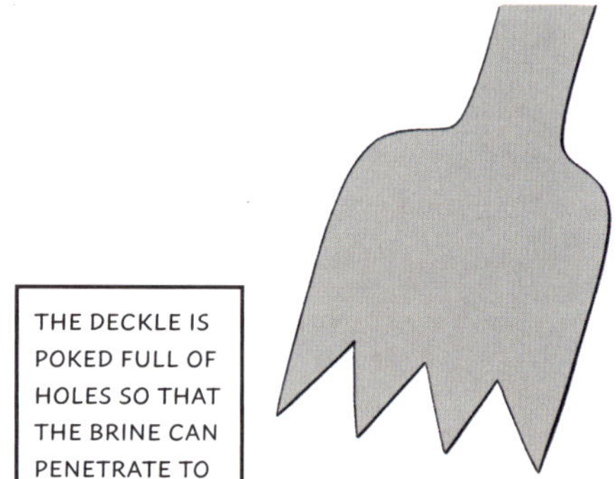

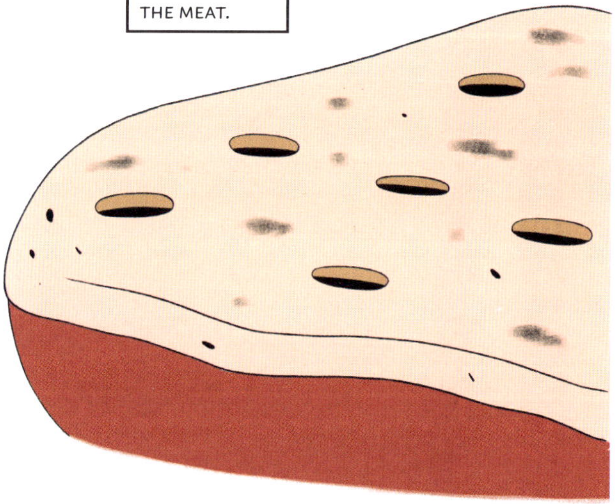

THE BRISKET THEN CURES IN BARRELS OF WET, SALTY BRINE WITH GARLIC, SUGAR, AND A VARIETY OF SPICES.

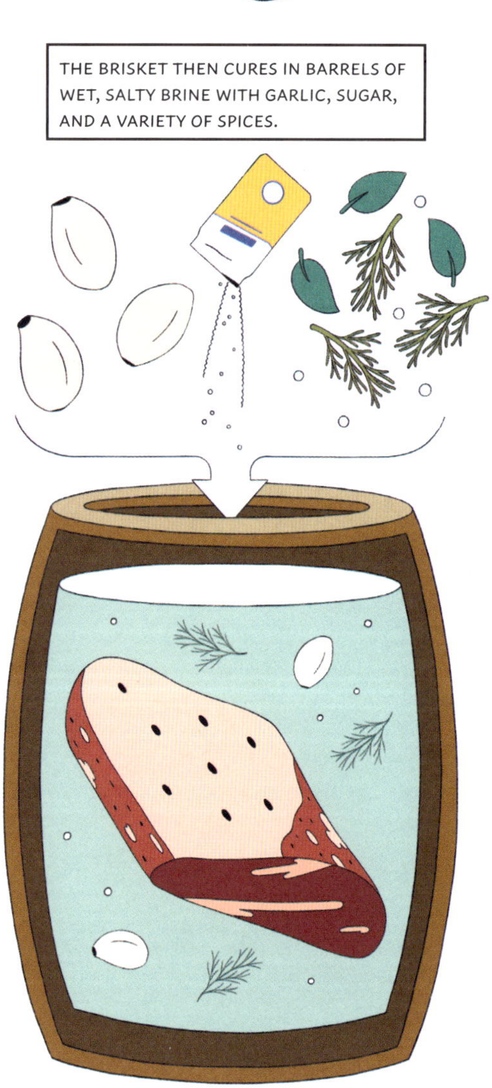

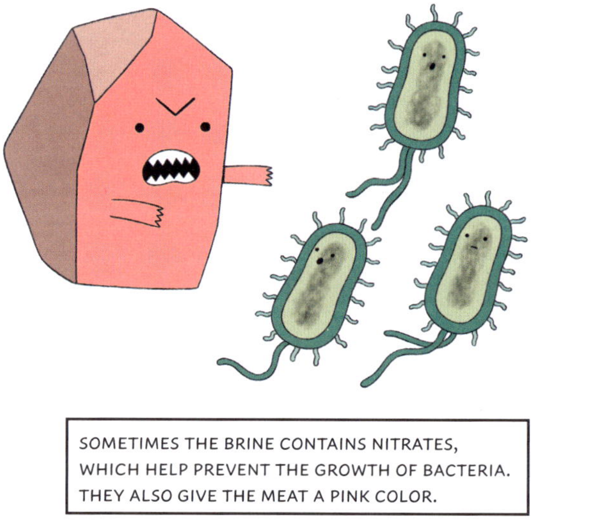

SOMETIMES THE BRINE CONTAINS NITRATES, WHICH HELP PREVENT THE GROWTH OF BACTERIA. THEY ALSO GIVE THE MEAT A PINK COLOR.

THE BRISKET SOAKS UP THE BRINE, AND IN ABOUT FIVE DAYS IT'S PICKLED.

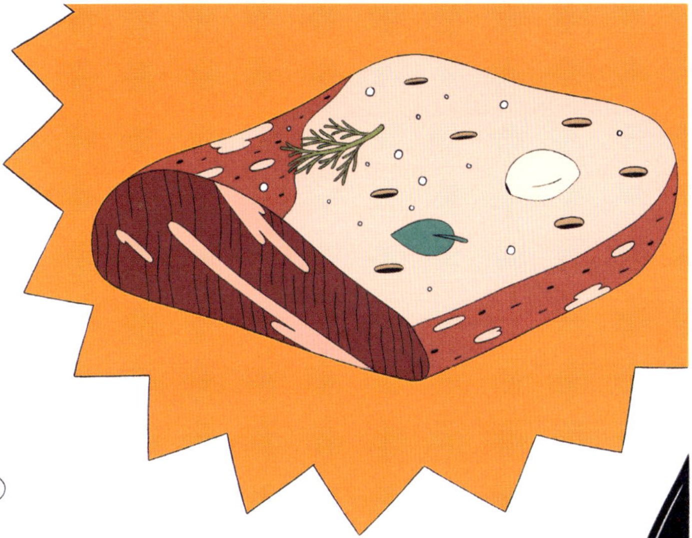

THE CURED BRISKET IS THEN SLOWLY BOILED. THIS IS WHAT GIVES CORNED BEEF ITS SOFT TEXTURE.

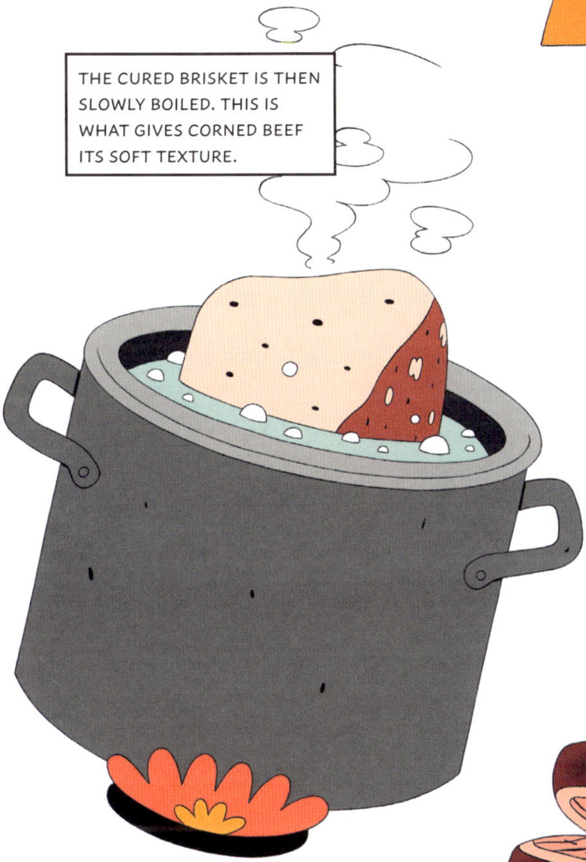

THE MEAT IS CUT THINLY ACROSS THE GRAIN TO PRODUCE TENDER, FATTY SLICES.

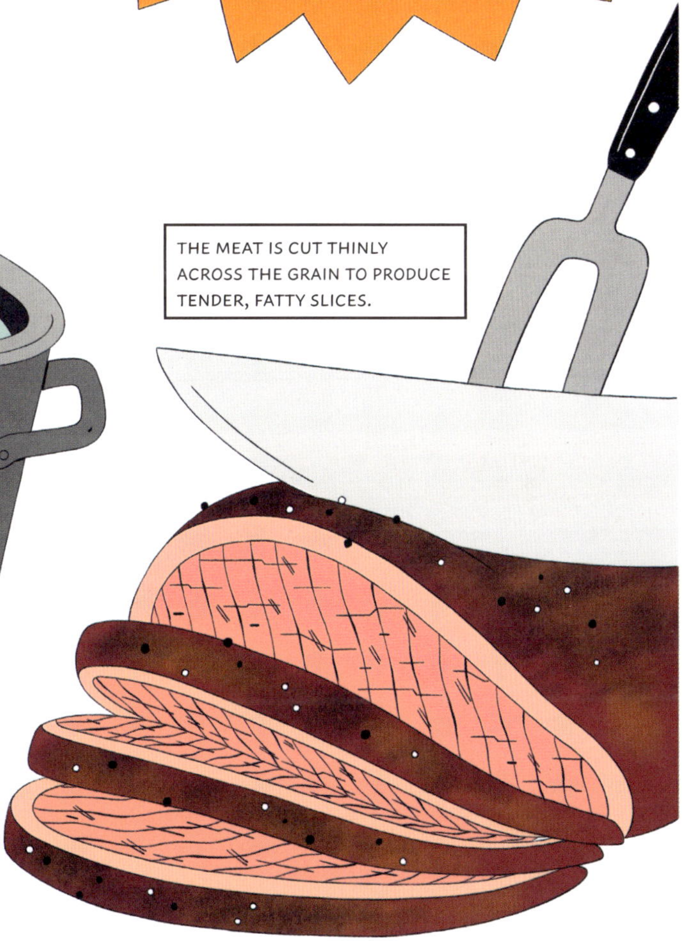

THE TASTE IS SALTY, SOUR, AND PEPPERY.

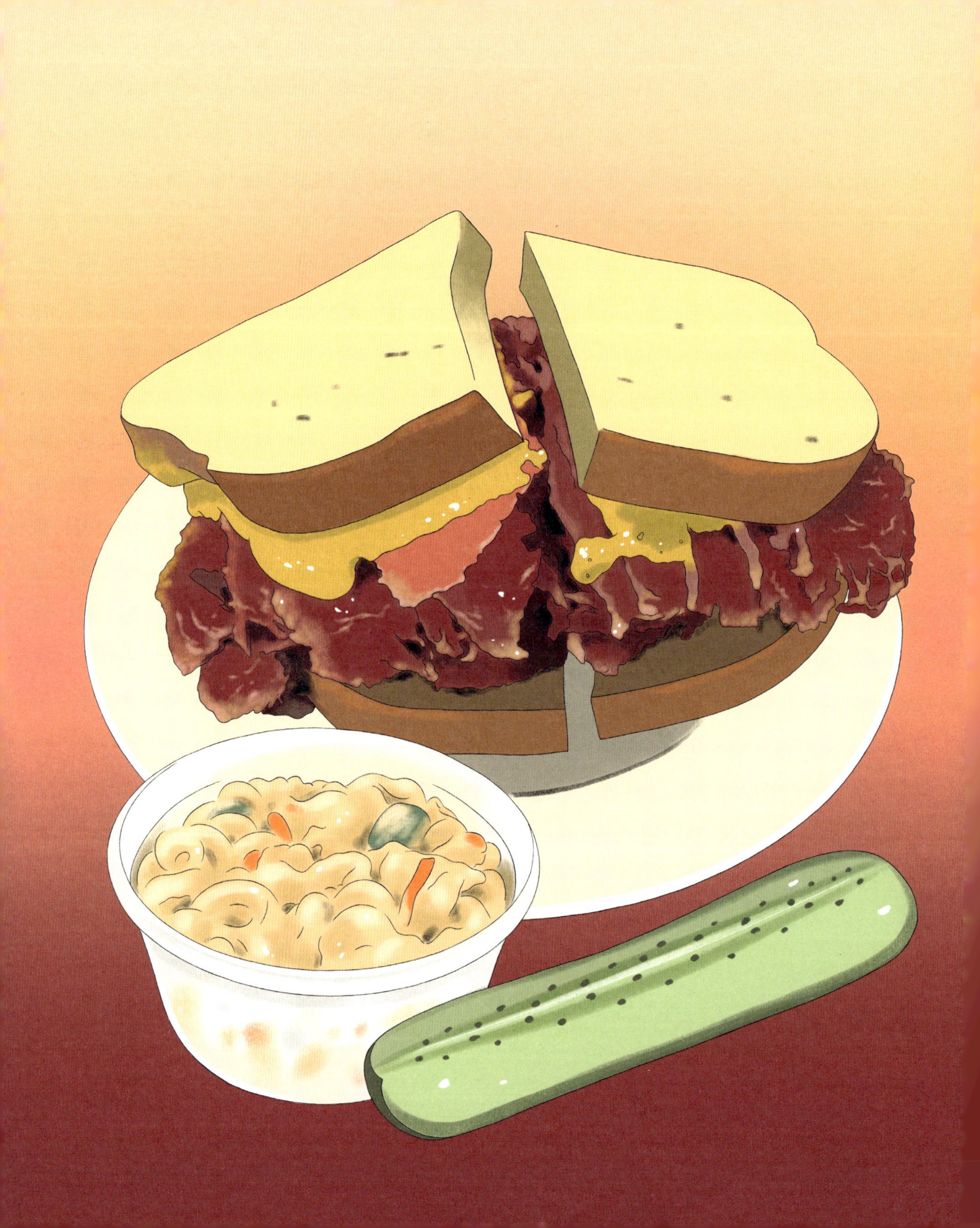

The Corned Beef Sandwich

It doesn't seem fair that corned beef and pastrami are sometimes mistaken for one another. While they are both brined beef, their distinct origins and preparation make for very different eating experiences. A corned beef on rye with brown mustard is leaner and more toothsome than a pastrami sandwich, with more chew and less fatty richness (coming from briskct rather than the fattier navel). It's tender and moist; but without the melty quality of so much rendered fat, it holds its shape better and is more (delicious) work to get through than its pastrami counterpart. Corned beef is salty and sour, and if the meat isn't good quality or if it's been cured for too long, the flavor can seem overly salty or metallic.

When corned beef has been expertly cured and boiled, its meaty fibers come away in bite-size chunks. Its salty and sour tang harmonizes perfectly with the mustard and rye. I recommend a side of creamy macaroni salad and bright, acidic pickles to balance the corned beef flavors.

In a world of Wagyu and Kobe beef, corned beef on rye is appealingly humble in nature. It's about doing the best with what you've got, and there's something noble about giving a tough hunk of brisket so much care that it becomes succulent even without the aid of so much belly fat. It is a sandwich celebrating perseverance, and to my mind it deserves a chance to stand on its own without being draped with a slice of Swiss cheese.

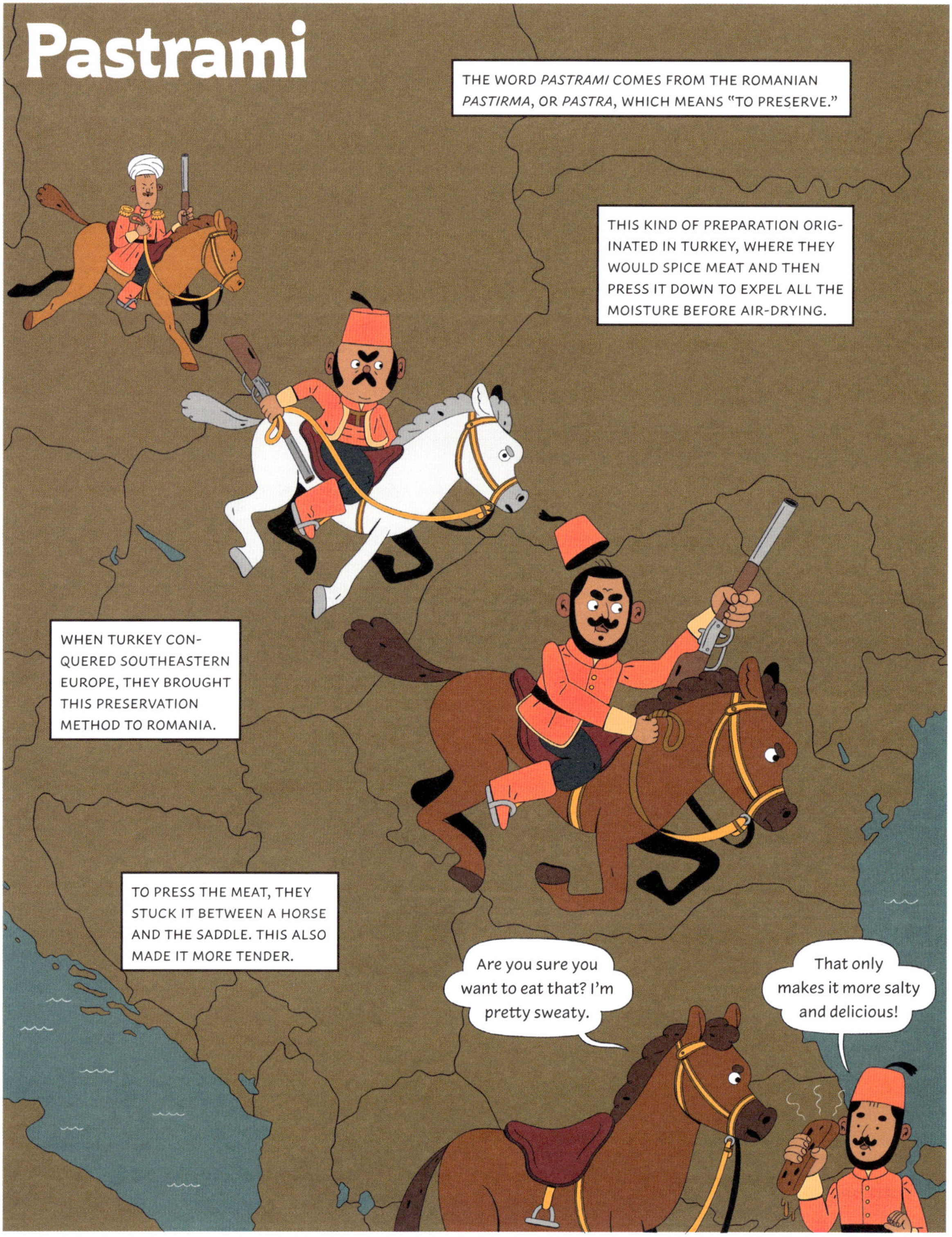
Pastrami
THE WORD *PASTRAMI* COMES FROM THE ROMANIAN *PASTIRMA*, OR *PASTRA*, WHICH MEANS "TO PRESERVE."
THIS KIND OF PREPARATION ORIGINATED IN TURKEY, WHERE THEY WOULD SPICE MEAT AND THEN PRESS IT DOWN TO EXPEL ALL THE MOISTURE BEFORE AIR-DRYING.
WHEN TURKEY CONQUERED SOUTHEASTERN EUROPE, THEY BROUGHT THIS PRESERVATION METHOD TO ROMANIA.
TO PRESS THE MEAT, THEY STUCK IT BETWEEN A HORSE AND THE SADDLE. THIS ALSO MADE IT MORE TENDER.
Are you sure you want to eat that? I'm pretty sweaty.
That only makes it more salty and delicious!

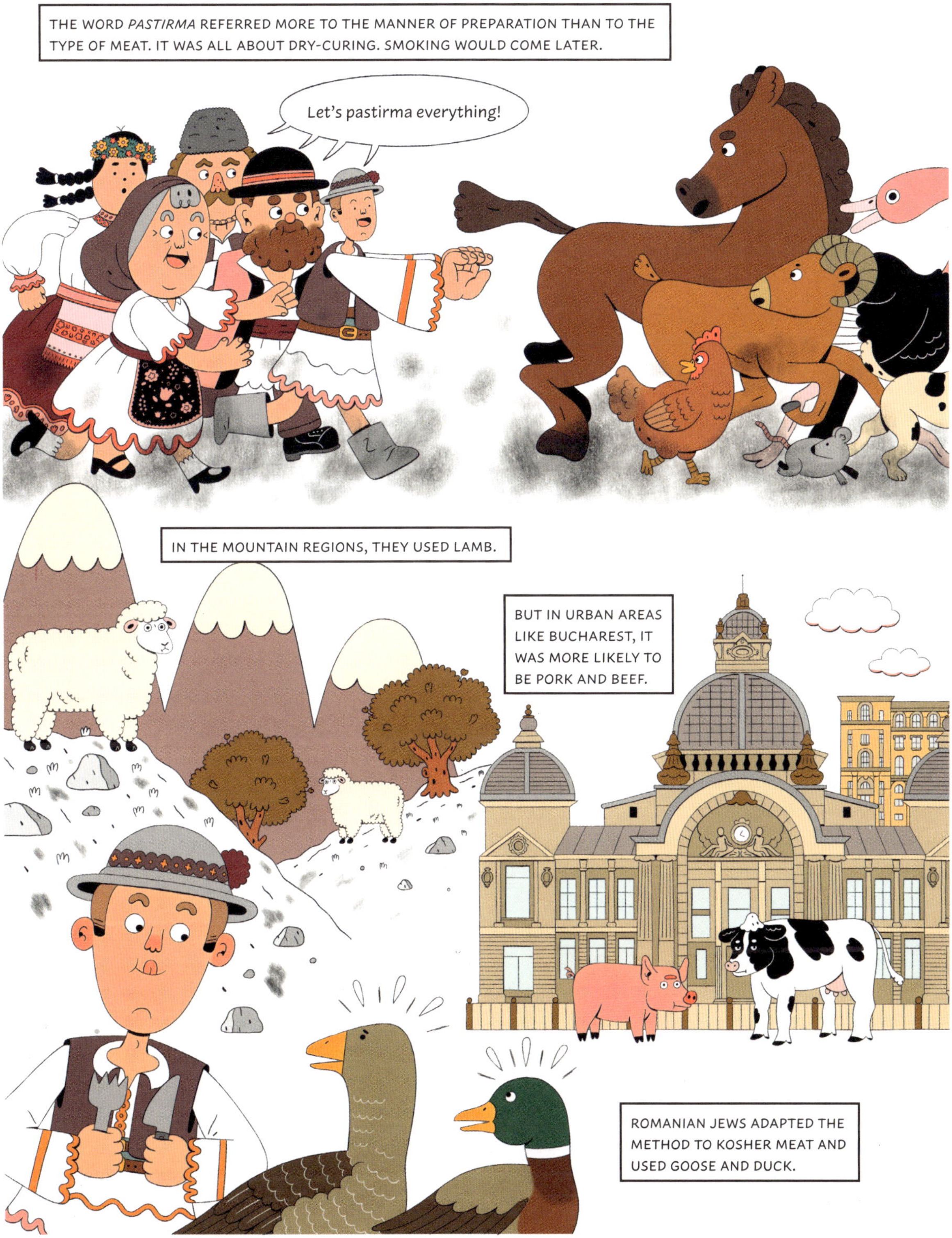
THE WORD *PASTIRMA* REFERRED MORE TO THE MANNER OF PREPARATION THAN TO THE TYPE OF MEAT. IT WAS ALL ABOUT DRY-CURING. SMOKING WOULD COME LATER.
Let's pastirma everything!
IN THE MOUNTAIN REGIONS, THEY USED LAMB.
BUT IN URBAN AREAS LIKE BUCHAREST, IT WAS MORE LIKELY TO BE PORK AND BEEF.
ROMANIAN JEWS ADAPTED THE METHOD TO KOSHER MEAT AND USED GOOSE AND DUCK.

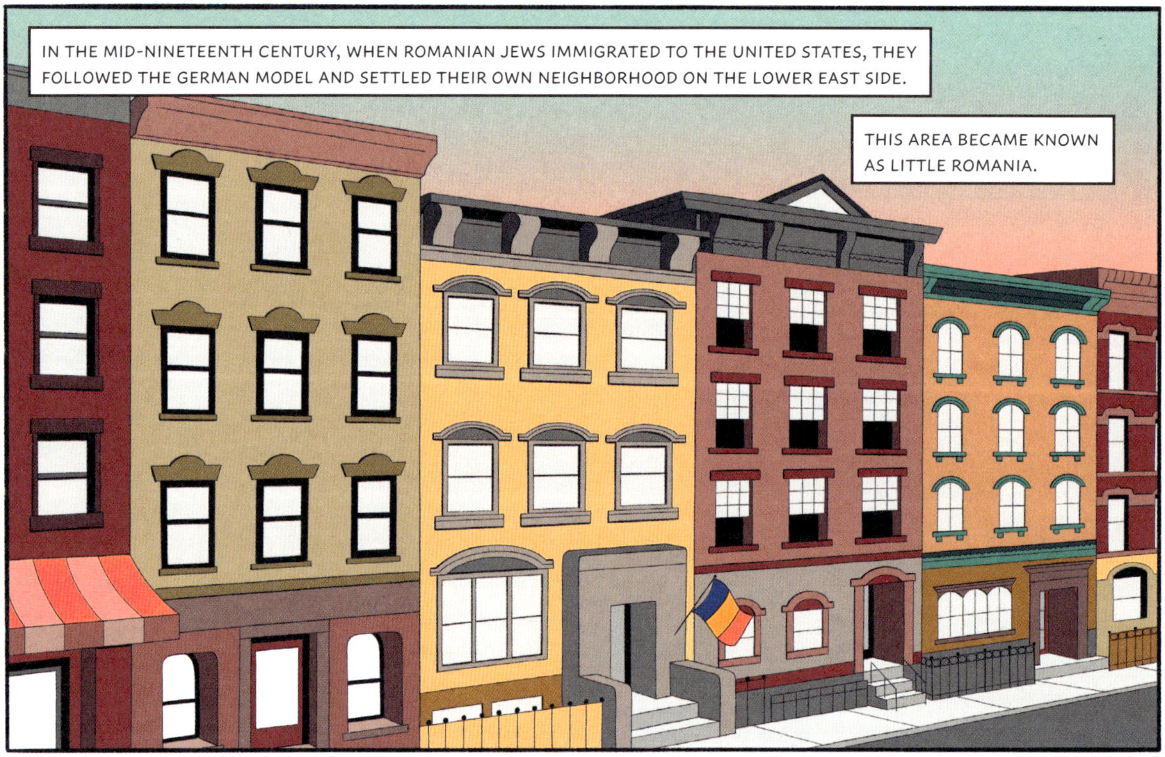
IN THE MID-NINETEENTH CENTURY, WHEN ROMANIAN JEWS IMMIGRATED TO THE UNITED STATES, THEY FOLLOWED THE GERMAN MODEL AND SETTLED THEIR OWN NEIGHBORHOOD ON THE LOWER EAST SIDE.
THIS AREA BECAME KNOWN AS LITTLE ROMANIA.

BEEF WAS THE MOST AVAILABLE MEAT, SO BRISKET BECAME THE CUT OF CHOICE FOR MAKING PASTIRMA.

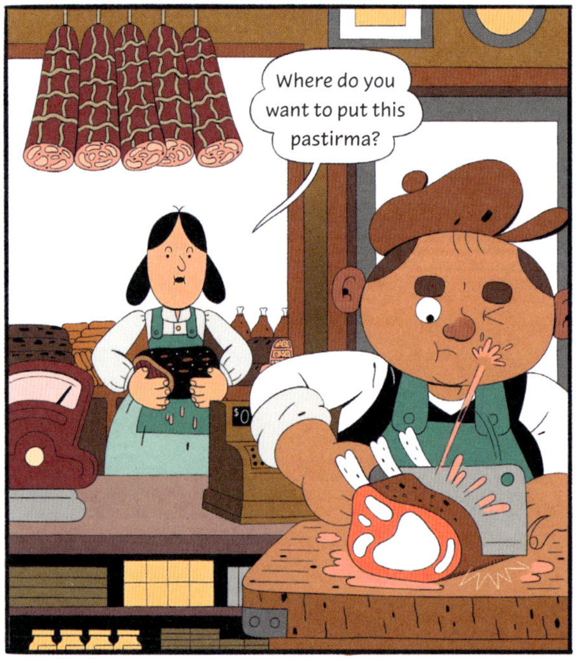
Where do you want to put this pastirma?

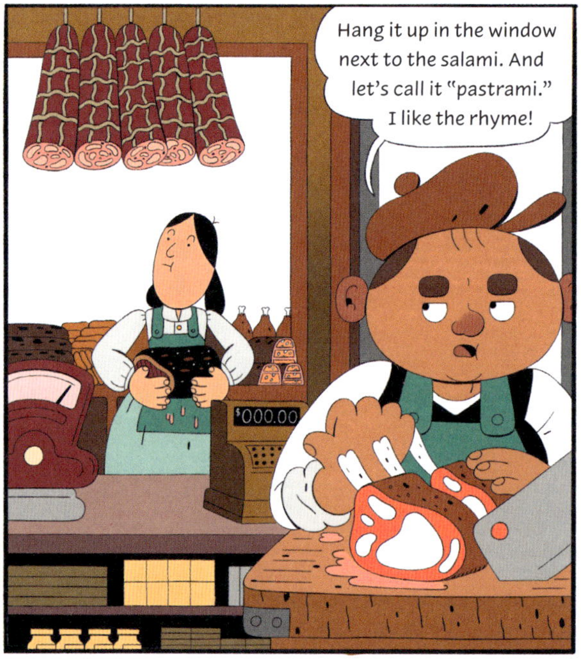
Hang it up in the window next to the salami. And let's call it "pastrami." I like the rhyme!
$000.00

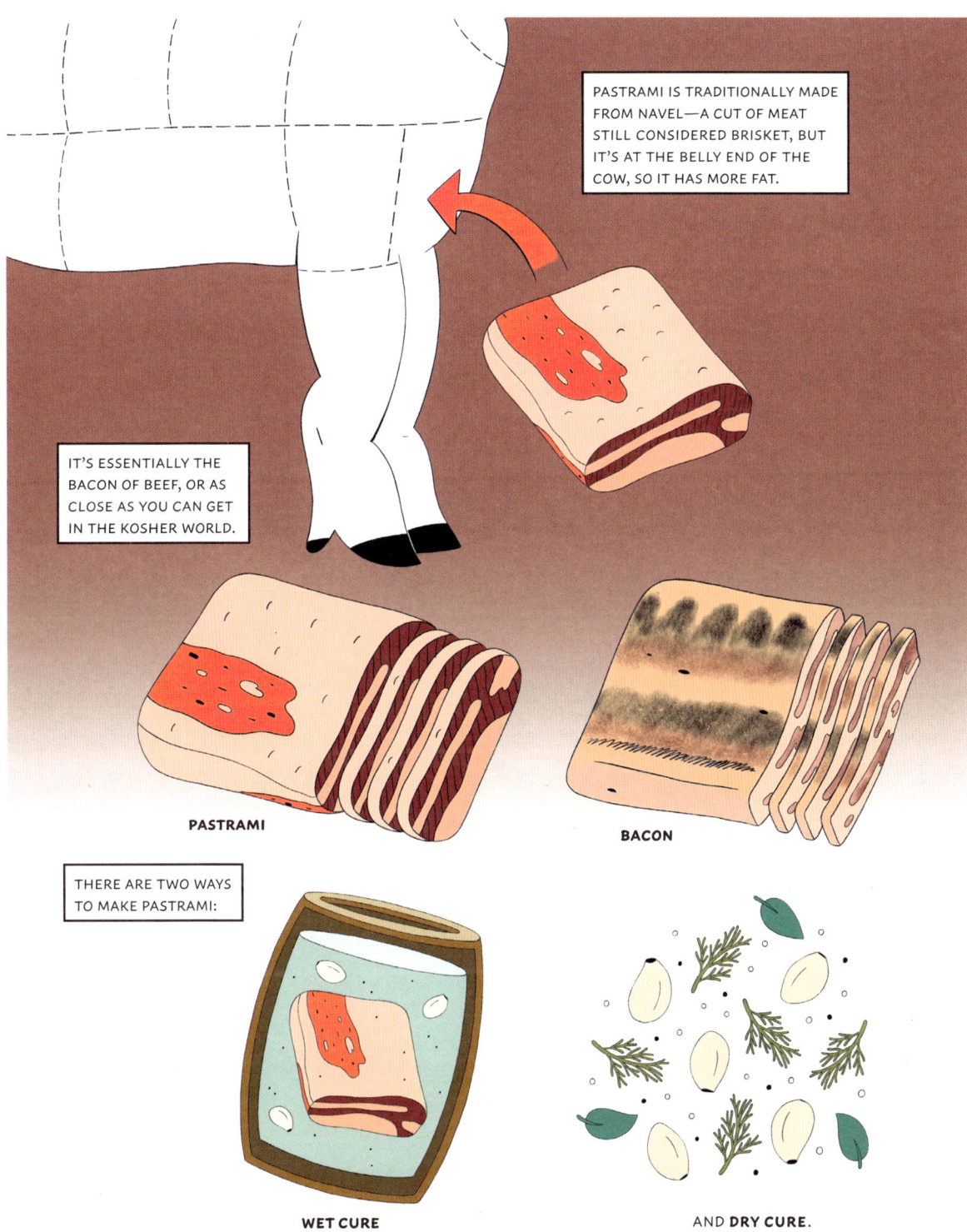

PASTRAMI IS TRADITIONALLY MADE FROM NAVEL—A CUT OF MEAT STILL CONSIDERED BRISKET, BUT IT'S AT THE BELLY END OF THE COW, SO IT HAS MORE FAT.

IT'S ESSENTIALLY THE BACON OF BEEF, OR AS CLOSE AS YOU CAN GET IN THE KOSHER WORLD.

PASTRAMI

BACON

THERE ARE TWO WAYS TO MAKE PASTRAMI:

WET CURE

AND **DRY CURE.**

THE WET BRINE IS LIKE CORNED BEEF. FIRST, THE NAVEL IS PERFORATED WITH HOLES.

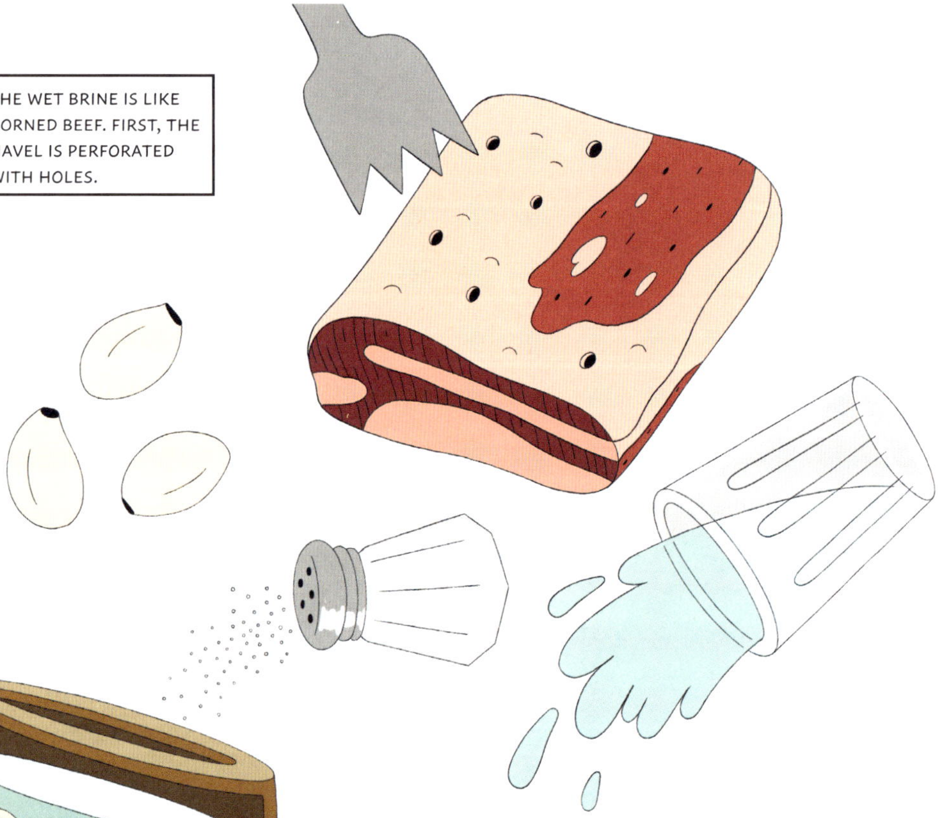

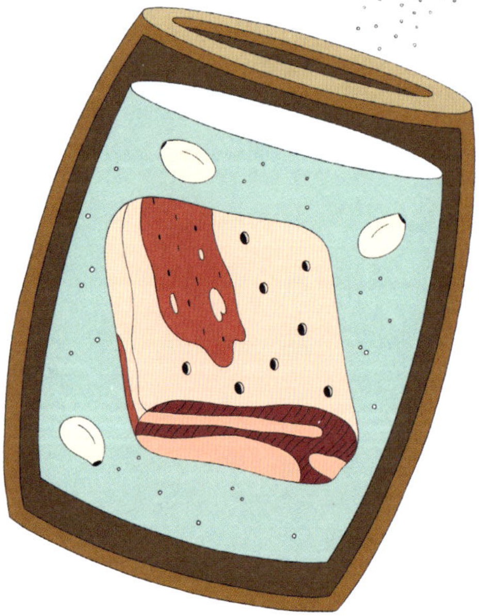

THEN IT'S LEFT TO SOAK FOR SEVERAL DAYS IN A BARREL FILLED WITH A MARINADE OF SALT, GARLIC, AND WATER.

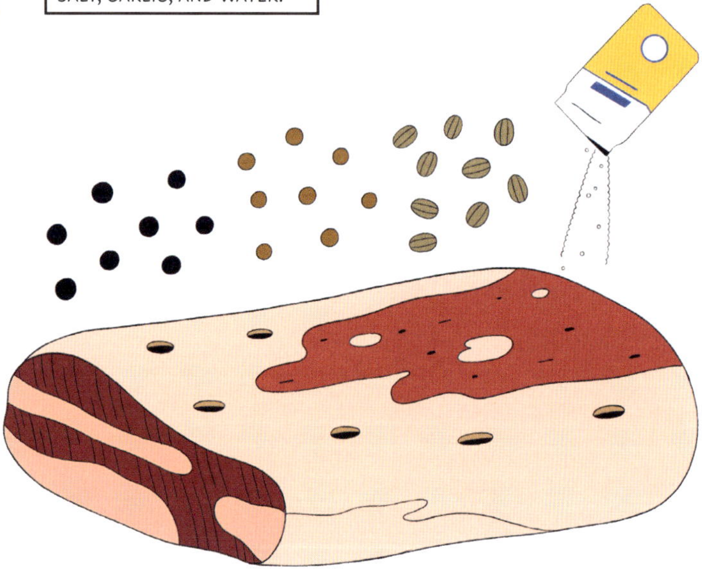

AFTER BEING PICKLED, THE NAVEL IS RUBBED WITH A DRY MIXTURE OF SPICES SUCH AS BLACK PEPPER, MUSTARD SEED, CORIANDER, AND SUGAR.

THE MORE COMMON WAY TO MAKE PASTRAMI IS THE DRY CURE.

THIS INVOLVES RUBBING THE SPICE MIXTURE ON RAW, NONPICKLED NAVEL AND LEAVING IT TO CURE FOR A COUPLE OF WEEKS.

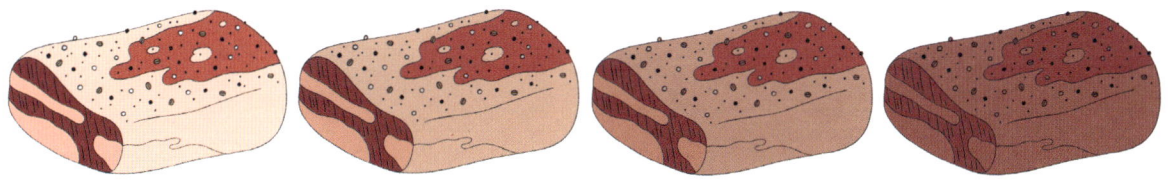

THIS METHOD OF CURING PRODUCES A DRIER MEAT THAN THE WET BRINE.

EITHER WAY, ONCE THE BEEF IS FULLY CURED, IT'S HUNG UP OR PLACED ON A RACK AND HOT-SMOKED.

THE END RESULT IS A DEEP, DARK CRUST OF SMOKED SPICE WITH A ROBUST RED COLOR WITHIN.

IT IS IMPORTANT FOR PASTRAMI TO BE CUT BY HAND. THIS KEEPS THE MOISTURE IN THE MEAT.

A MACHINE SLICER TENDS TO FORCE THE MOISTURE— AND THE FLAVOR—OUT OF THE MEAT.

THE CUTTERS WILL ASK YOU IF YOU WANT IT LEAN OR JUICY,

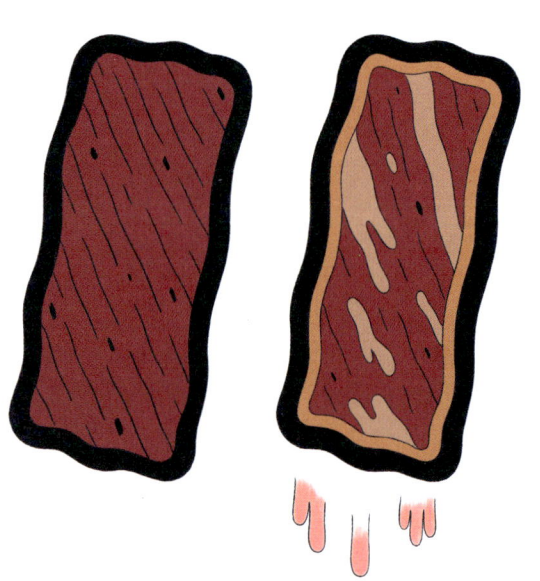

AND THEY'LL GIVE YOU A SAMPLE OF THE CUT TO MAKE SURE IT'S THE RIGHT THICKNESS.

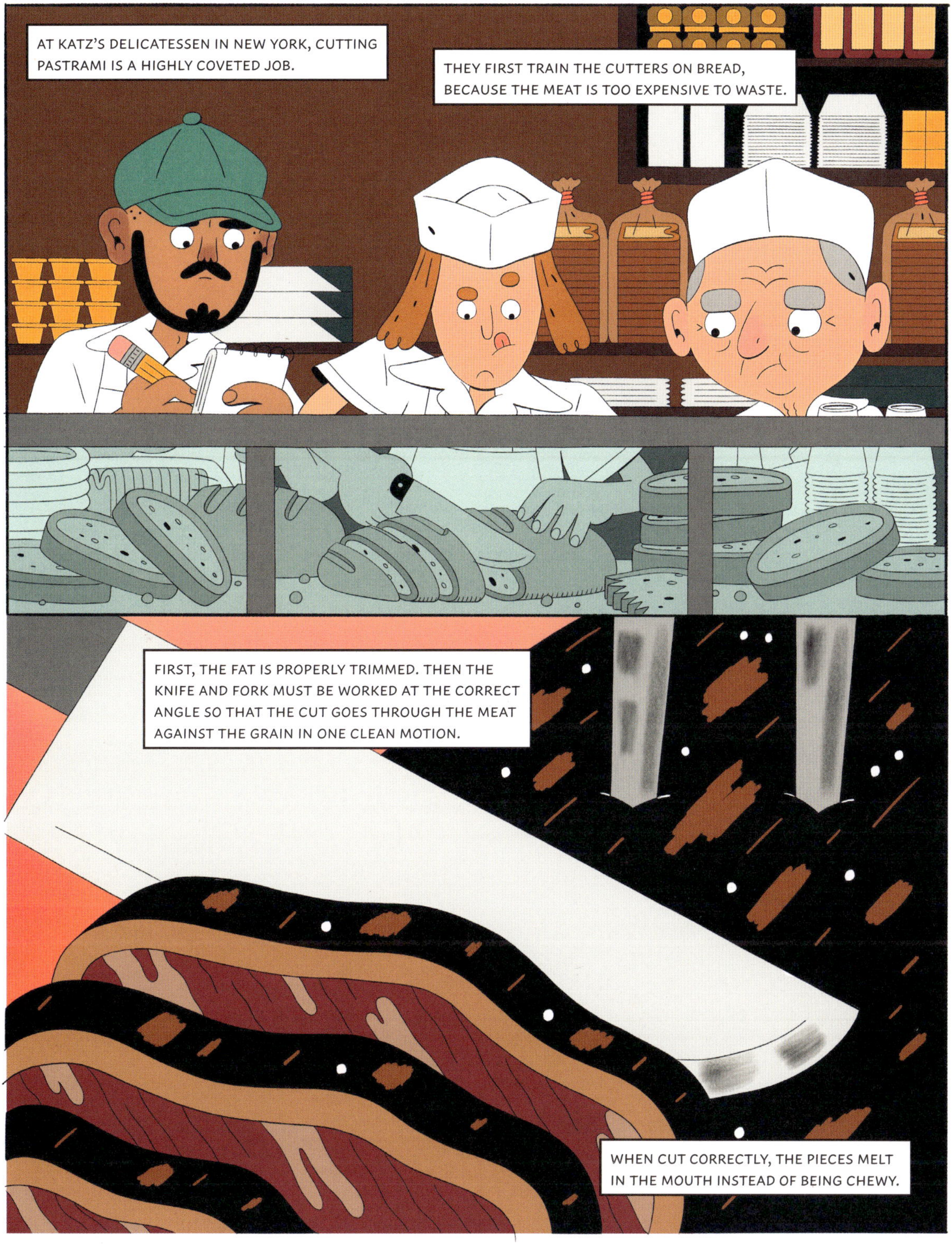
AT KATZ'S DELICATESSEN IN NEW YORK, CUTTING PASTRAMI IS A HIGHLY COVETED JOB.
THEY FIRST TRAIN THE CUTTERS ON BREAD, BECAUSE THE MEAT IS TOO EXPENSIVE TO WASTE.
FIRST, THE FAT IS PROPERLY TRIMMED. THEN THE KNIFE AND FORK MUST BE WORKED AT THE CORRECT ANGLE SO THAT THE CUT GOES THROUGH THE MEAT AGAINST THE GRAIN IN ONE CLEAN MOTION.
WHEN CUT CORRECTLY, THE PIECES MELT IN THE MOUTH INSTEAD OF BEING CHEWY.

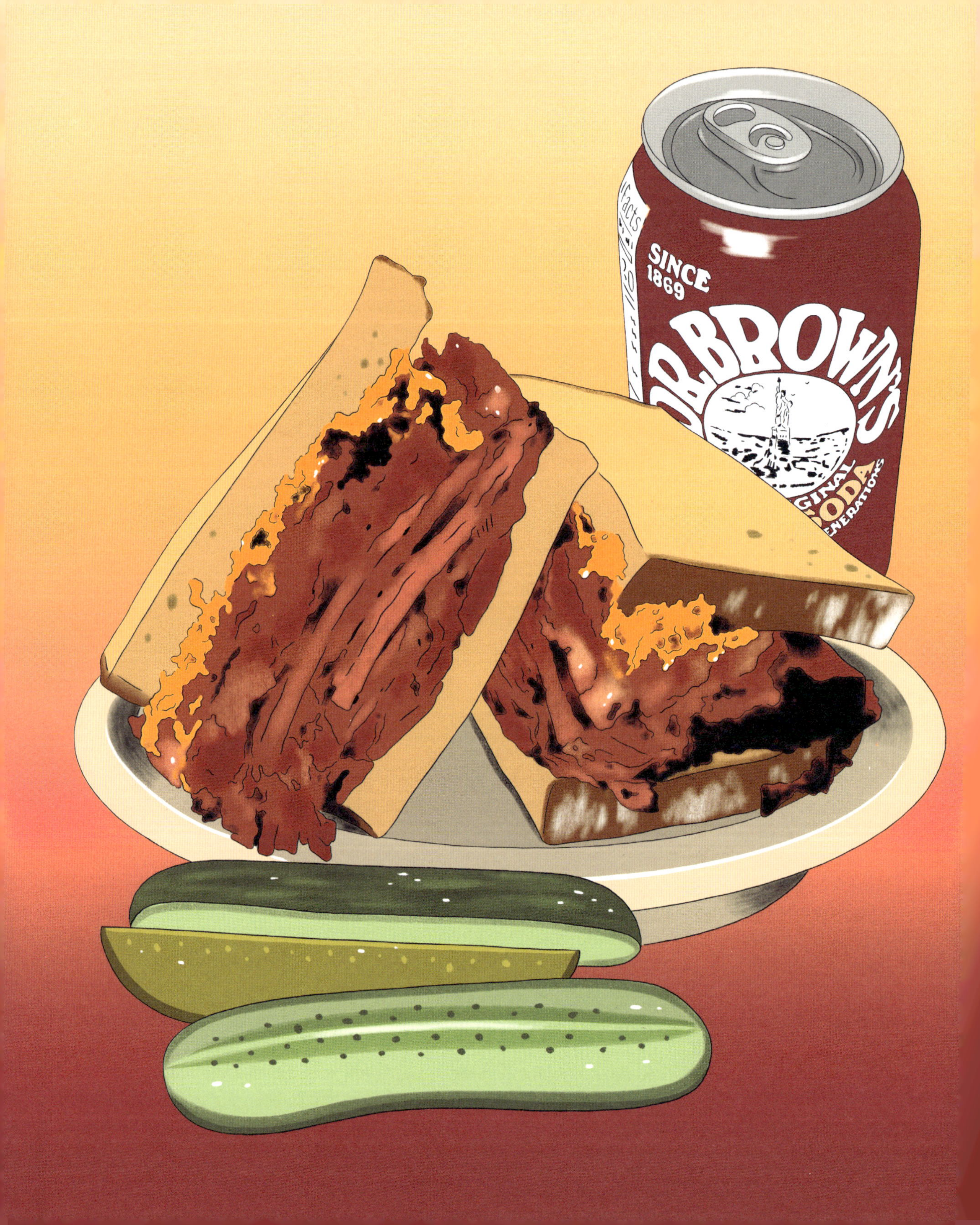
SINCE 1869
BROWN'S
SODA

The Pastrami Sandwich

When I eat a pastrami sandwich from Katz's, it occurs to me that the most important ingredient is time. The way the pastrami melts in your mouth is a result of three time-intensive processes—and no shortcuts. The cure tenderizes the meat and breaks down the fibers, the smoking renders the fat in the center of the navel cut and draws it out to the edges, and the steaming softens everything to the point of nearly falling apart.

If the point of a sandwich is to showcase a variety of ingredients and how well they go together, then the pastrami sandwich isn't really a sandwich. It's a vessel for the meat—and a perfect excuse to eat a lot of it. The kick of the mustard and the tang of the rye bread are perfect complements, but they serve at the throne of the moist and peppery meat, so satisfying and expertly crafted. The pickles (my preference is for half sour, for brightness) are there to cut the fatty richness, but they're still on the side as if to say, "We don't need to be a part of this, but we're here if you need us."

I'm not here to tell you how to eat your sandwich, but I *urgently suggest* that you resist adding anything to this already ideal sandwich (no ketchup, no mayo, no cheese). You would be robbing yourself of the unique experience of eating something the way it's been eaten since the beginning of the Jewish American story.

Montreal Smoked Meat

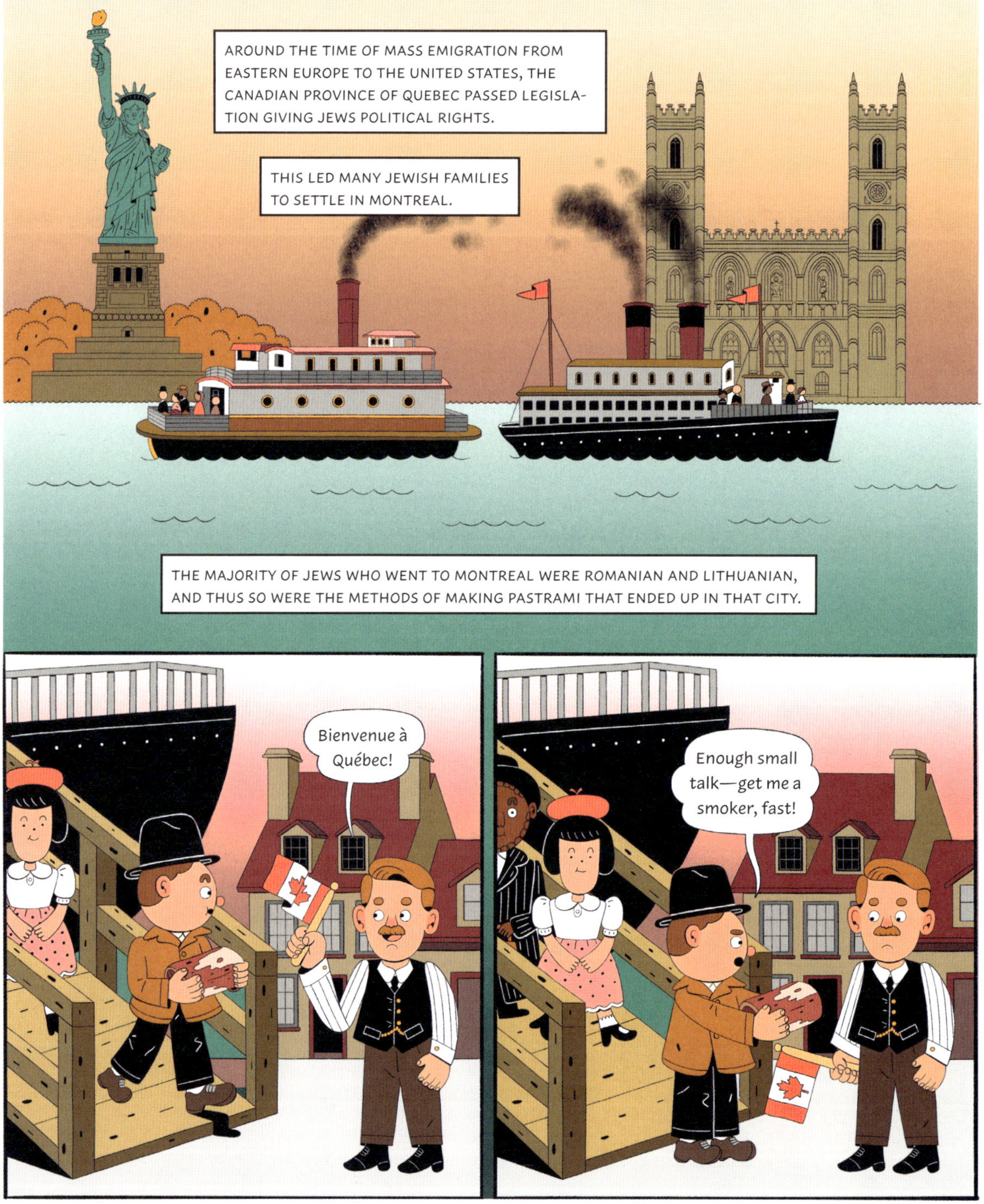
AROUND THE TIME OF MASS EMIGRATION FROM EASTERN EUROPE TO THE UNITED STATES, THE CANADIAN PROVINCE OF QUEBEC PASSED LEGISLATION GIVING JEWS POLITICAL RIGHTS.
THIS LED MANY JEWISH FAMILIES TO SETTLE IN MONTREAL.
THE MAJORITY OF JEWS WHO WENT TO MONTREAL WERE ROMANIAN AND LITHUANIAN, AND THUS SO WERE THE METHODS OF MAKING PASTRAMI THAT ENDED UP IN THAT CITY.
Bienvenue à Québec!
Enough small talk—get me a smoker, fast!

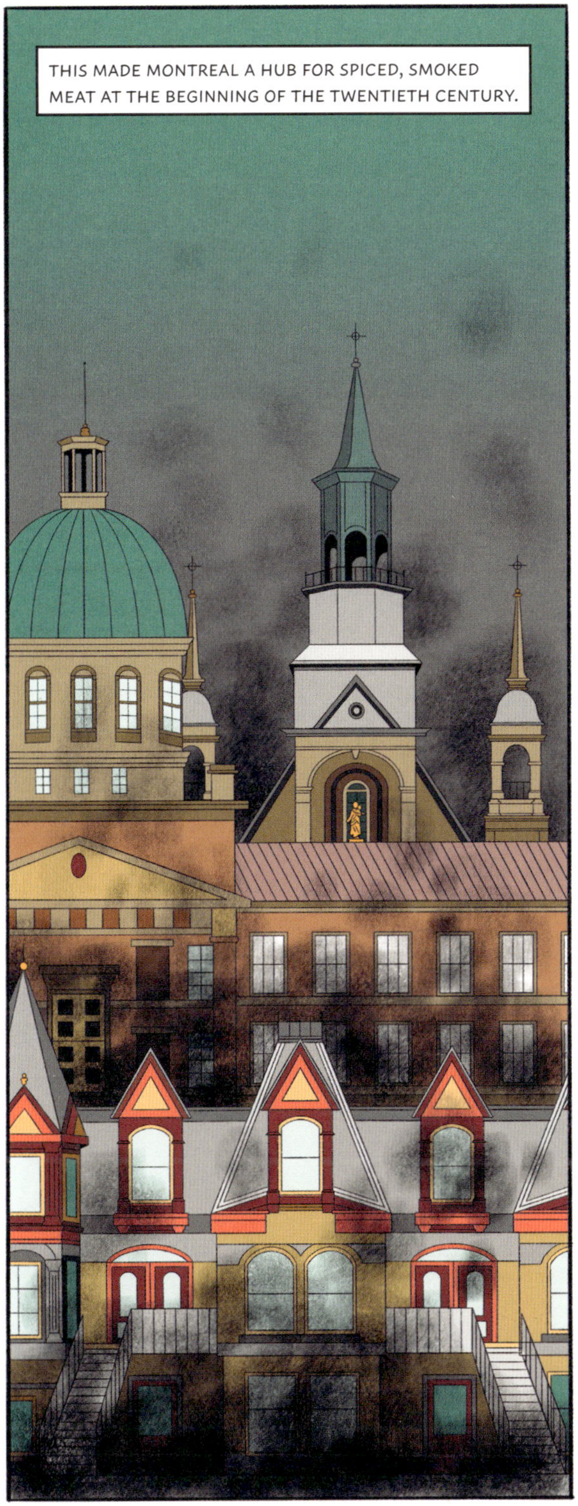
THIS MADE MONTREAL A HUB FOR SPICED, SMOKED MEAT AT THE BEGINNING OF THE TWENTIETH CENTURY.

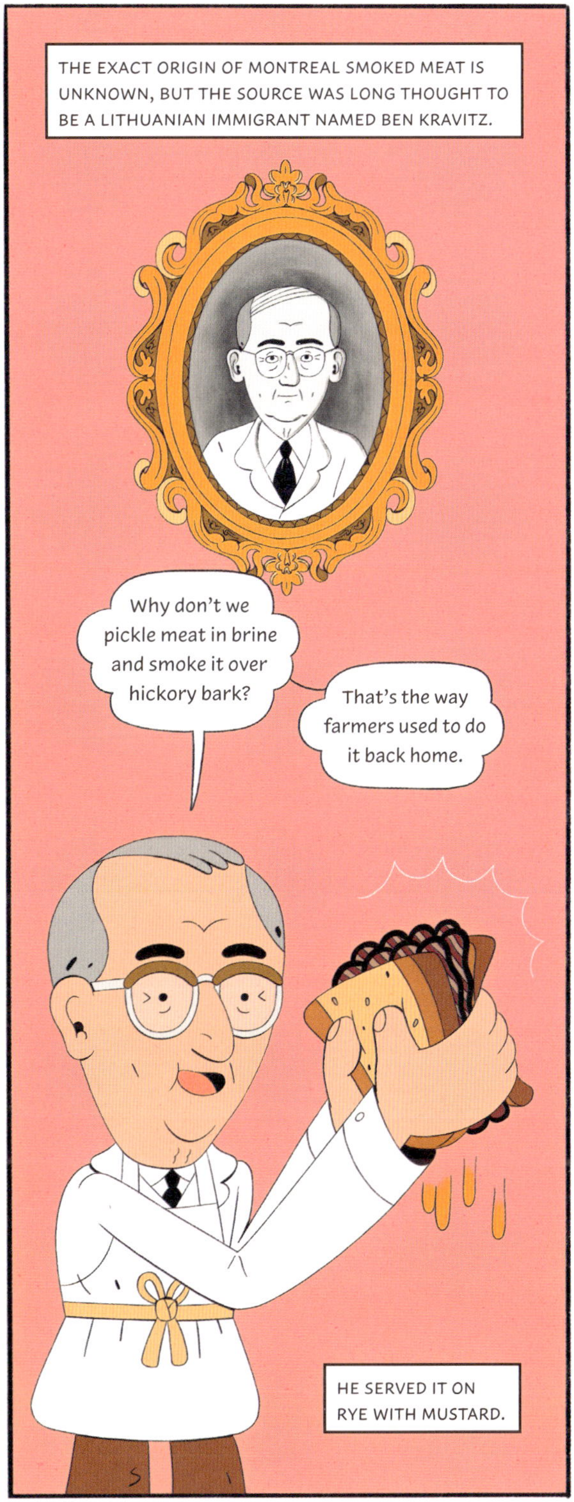
THE EXACT ORIGIN OF MONTREAL SMOKED MEAT IS UNKNOWN, BUT THE SOURCE WAS LONG THOUGHT TO BE A LITHUANIAN IMMIGRANT NAMED BEN KRAVITZ.
Why don't we pickle meat in brine and smoke it over hickory bark?
That's the way farmers used to do it back home.
HE SERVED IT ON RYE WITH MUSTARD.

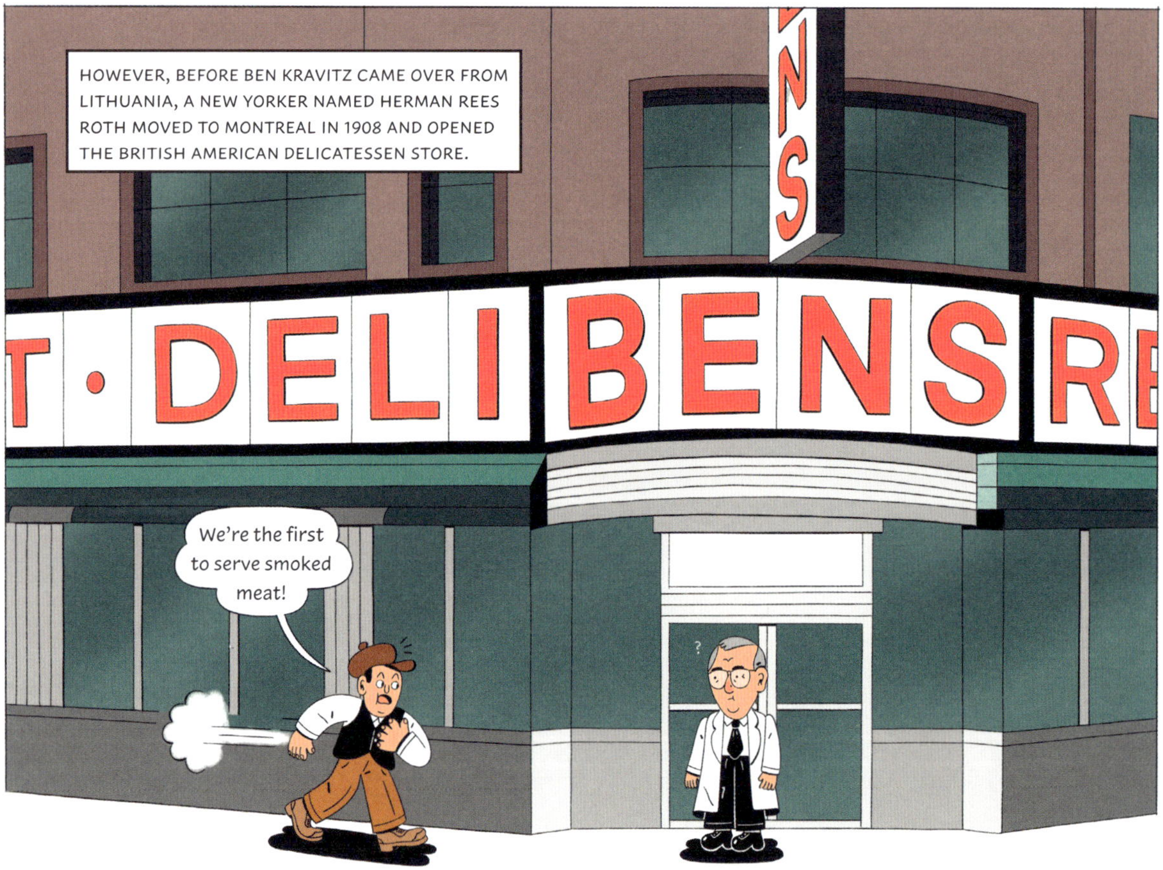
HOWEVER, BEFORE BEN KRAVITZ CAME OVER FROM LITHUANIA, A NEW YORKER NAMED HERMAN REES ROTH MOVED TO MONTREAL IN 1908 AND OPENED THE BRITISH AMERICAN DELICATESSEN STORE.
DELI BENS
We're the first to serve smoked meat!

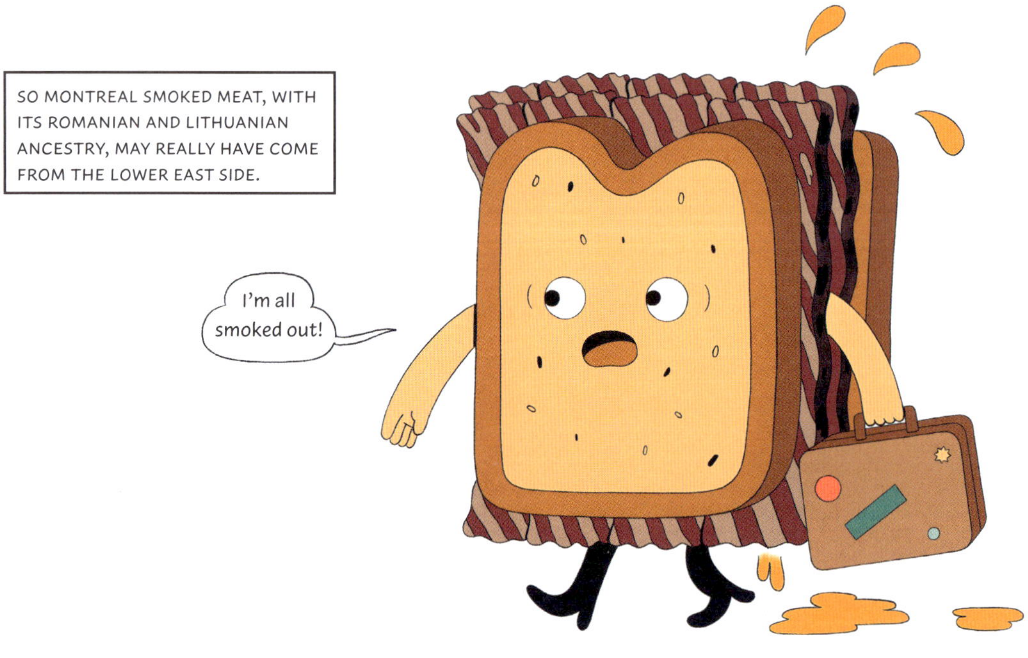
SO MONTREAL SMOKED MEAT, WITH ITS ROMANIAN AND LITHUANIAN ANCESTRY, MAY REALLY HAVE COME FROM THE LOWER EAST SIDE.
I'm all smoked out!

MONTREAL SMOKED MEAT IS A FRANKENSTEIN COMBINATION OF PASTRAMI AND CORNED BEEF.

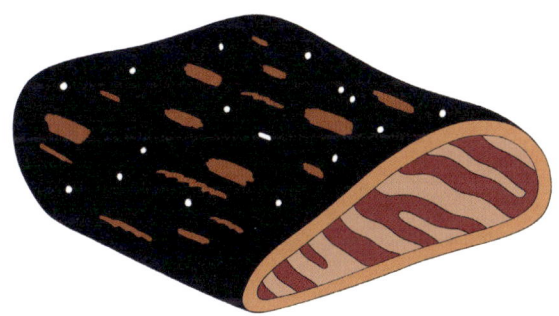

PASTRAMI IS SPICED, SMOKED NAVEL.

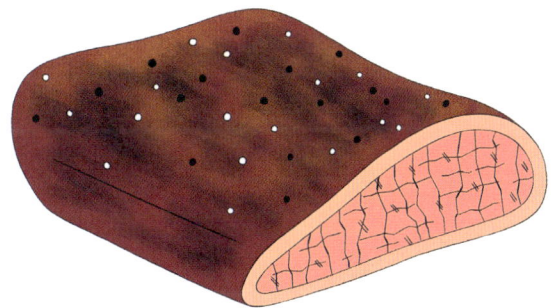

CORNED BEEF IS PICKLED, BOILED BRISKET.

MONTREAL SMOKED MEAT TAKES LESSONS FROM EACH ONE.

LIKE CORNED BEEF, MONTREAL SMOKED MEAT IS MADE FROM BRISKET; LIKE PASTRAMI, IT IS CURED AND SMOKED.

BUT WHEREAS PASTRAMI IS USUALLY DRY-CURED, THEN SPICED AND SMOKED, MONTREAL SMOKED MEAT IS DRY-CURED AND THEN PICKLED IN BRINE (LIKE CORNED BEEF) BEFORE BEING SMOKED FOR A LONGER PERIOD OF TIME.

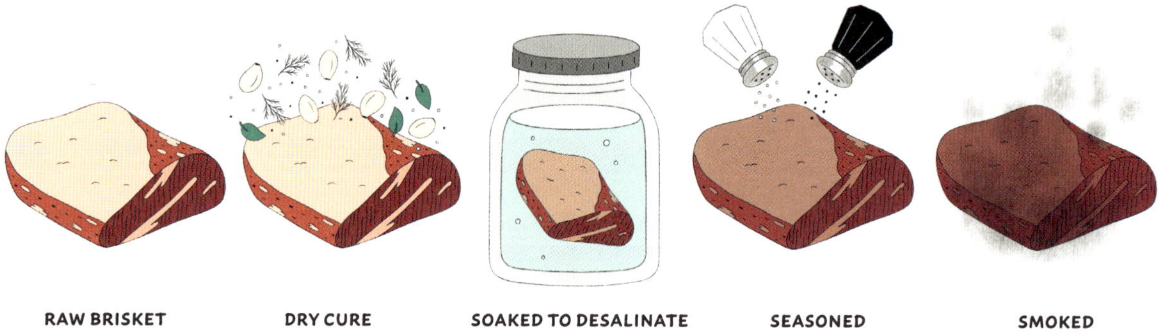
RAW BRISKET
DRY CURE
SOAKED TO DESALINATE
SEASONED
SMOKED

THE RESULT IS LESS SALTY, WITH MORE EMPHASIS ON THE SMOKY FLAVOR.

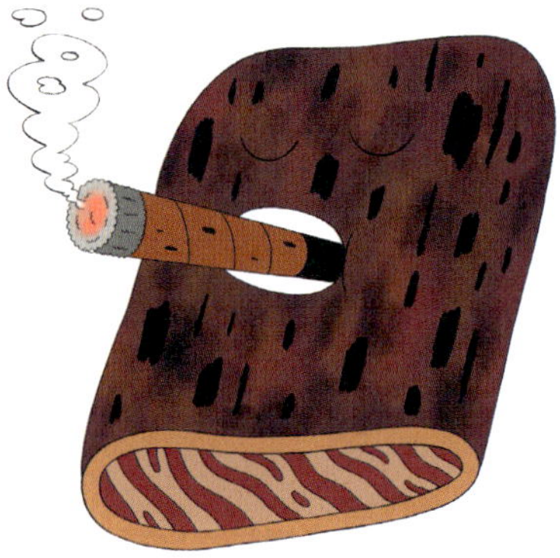

ANOTHER DIFFERENCE IS IN THE PICKLING SPICES. MONTREAL SMOKED MEAT HAS LESS SUGAR AND MORE PEPPER THAN PASTRAMI.

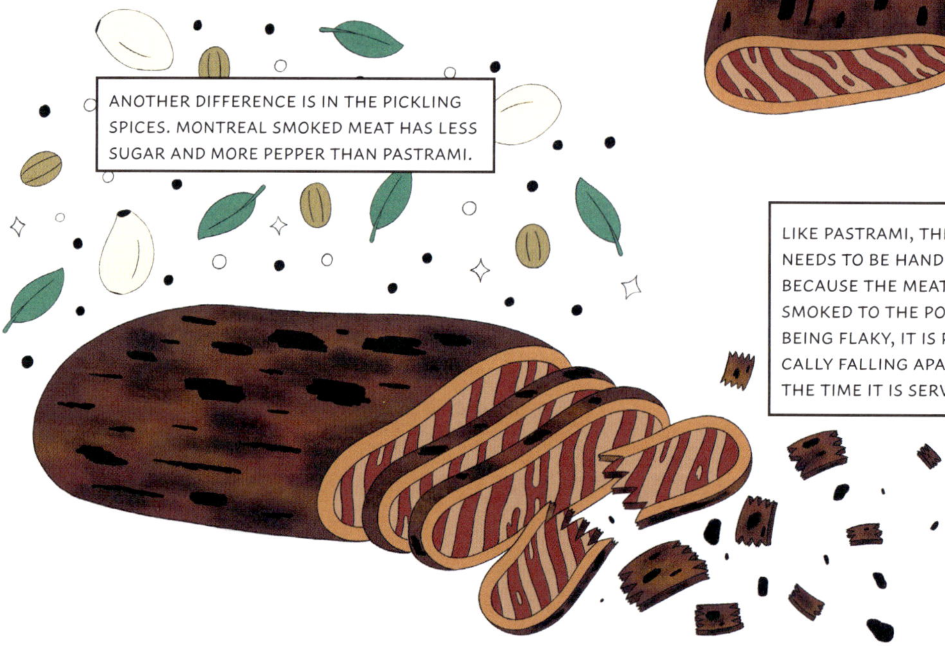

LIKE PASTRAMI, THE MEAT NEEDS TO BE HAND-SLICED. BECAUSE THE MEAT IS SMOKED TO THE POINT OF BEING FLAKY, IT IS PRACTICALLY FALLING APART BY THE TIME IT IS SERVED.

WITH A MACHINE YOU WOULD END UP WITH NOTHING BUT SHAVINGS.

LIKE PASTRAMI, CUSTOMERS CAN ORDER THEIR SMOKED MEAT ACCORDING TO FAT CONTENT.

Choose your fat!

THEY USED TO SERVE CUTS WHERE THE GIANT FAT CAP, THE DECKLE, WAS SPICED AND RESMOKED, BUT THAT WAS DEEMED TOO CRAZY, EVEN BY JEWISH DELI STANDARDS!

LEAN SLICES HAVE A THIN LAYER OF FAT BUT ARE VERY DRY.

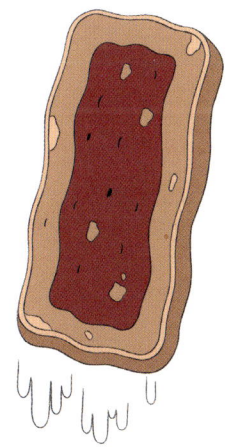

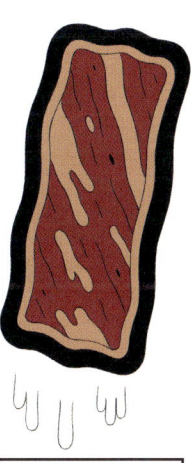

MEDIUM HAS MORE FAT AND MOISTURE THAN LEAN.

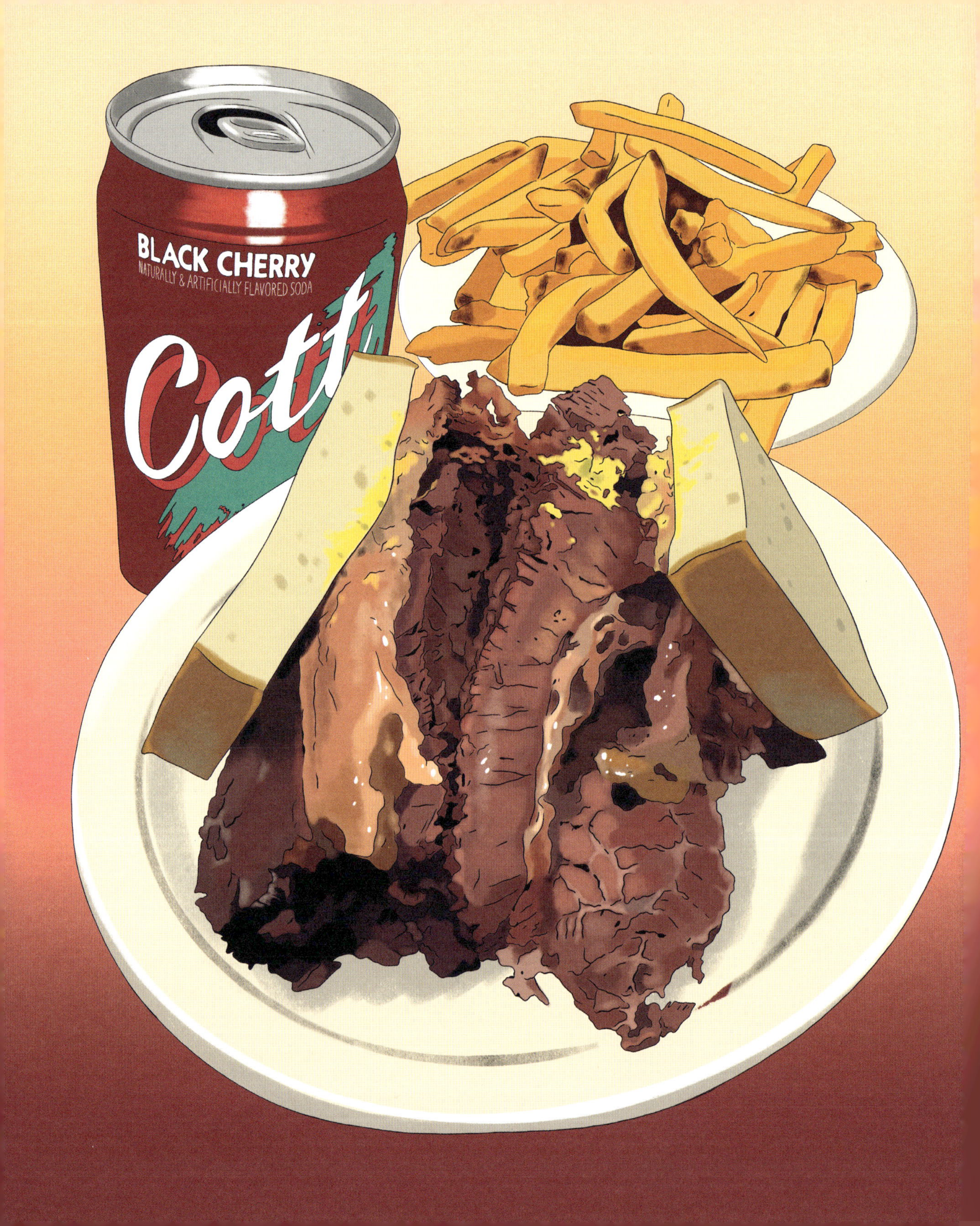
BLACK CHERRY
NATURALLY & ARTIFICIALLY FLAVORED SODA
Cott

The Smoked Meat Sandwich

I think of pastrami and Montreal-style smoked meat as immigrant siblings who arrived on the same boat but disembarked to settle in different environments, briny smoky brothers who are sometimes compared but who each have their own character.

The most notable difference is texture, with smoked meat coming from brisket (as opposed to the navel), making it leaner, more dense, and apt to come apart in stringy bits. Even without the richness of a navel cut, smoked meat still has plenty of fat, and its marinade, spices, and smoke combine to give it intensely rich layers of flavor. This is why it tends to be piled less high than the tsunami of meat that we often see with pastrami on rye.

Much like at Katz's, eating a smoked meat sandwich at Schwartz's is an all-consuming, unique experience. The smells and the sounds of the century-old institution are part of the flavor—they enhance the smoke and spice of the meat and soak into the rye. This is another discovery I've made while eating food that's been perfected by generations of local Jews: The environment itself is an ingredient. Katz's pastrami tastes best in New York, Schwartz's smoked meat is at its most delicious in Montreal, and the sandwiches of local delis across North America are best eaten at their respective counters.

LET'S TALK ABOUT

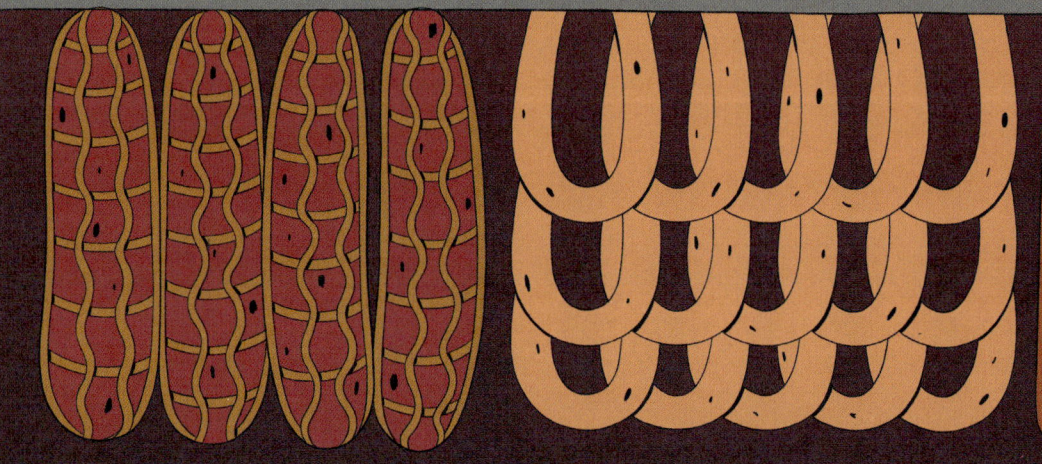

SAUSAGE HAS BEEN A PART OF GERMAN CULTURE AS FAR BACK AS THE FOURTEENTH CENTURY. IT WAS TYPICALLY MADE FROM PORK.

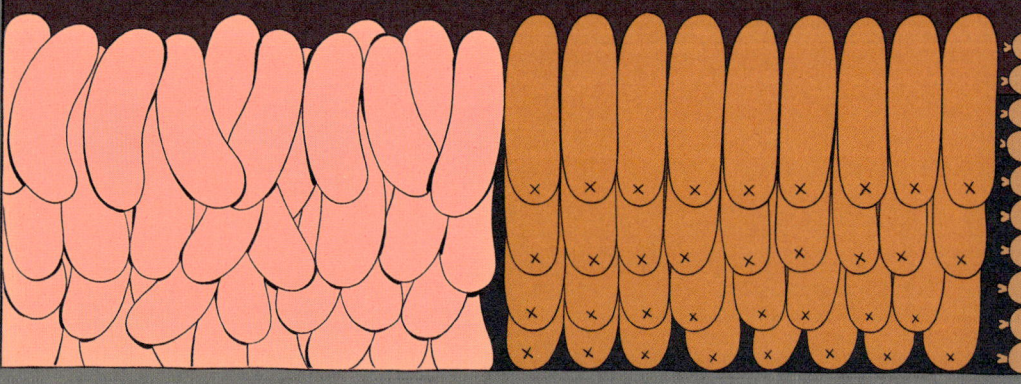

SAUSAGE

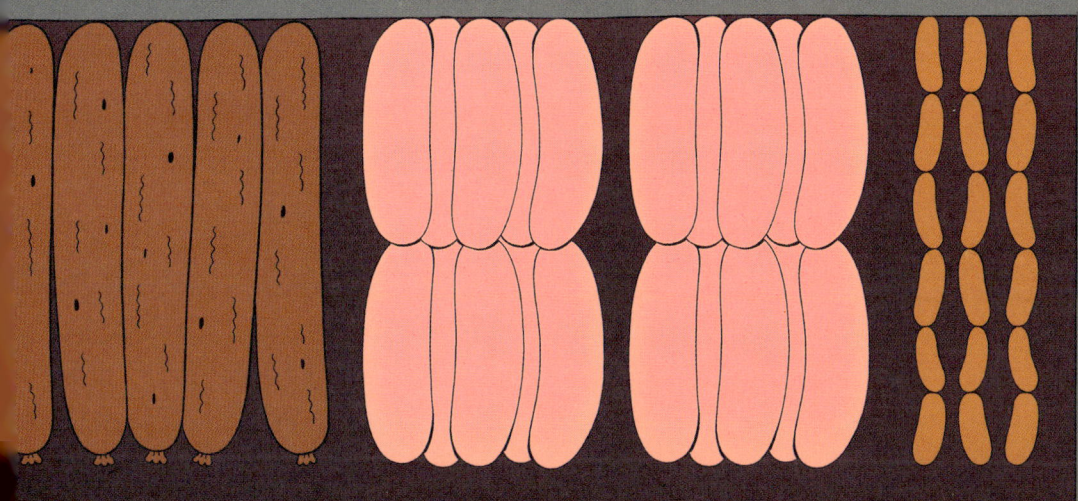

BECAUSE OF ITS RICH HISTORY—NOT JUST IN GERMANY BUT ALSO IN ROMANIA AND LITHUANIA—IT WAS INEVITABLE THAT VARIOUS KINDS OF SAUSAGE WOULD END UP HANGING IN THE WINDOWS OF US DELIS.

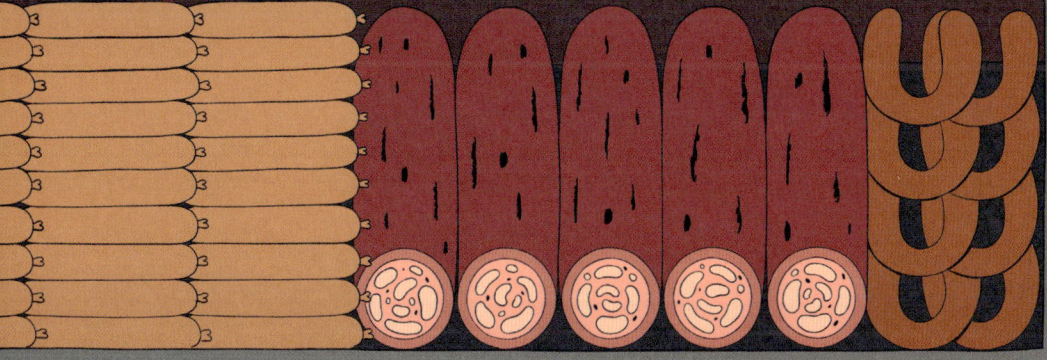

Hot Dogs

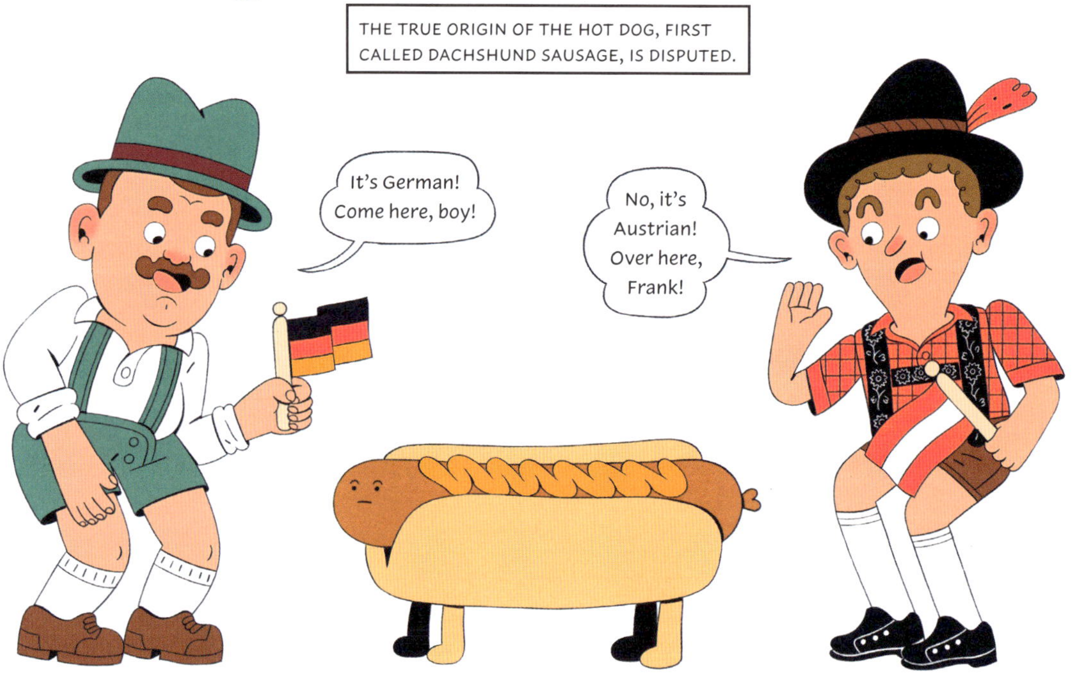
THE TRUE ORIGIN OF THE HOT DOG, FIRST CALLED DACHSHUND SAUSAGE, IS DISPUTED.
It's German! Come here, boy!
No, it's Austrian! Over here, Frank!

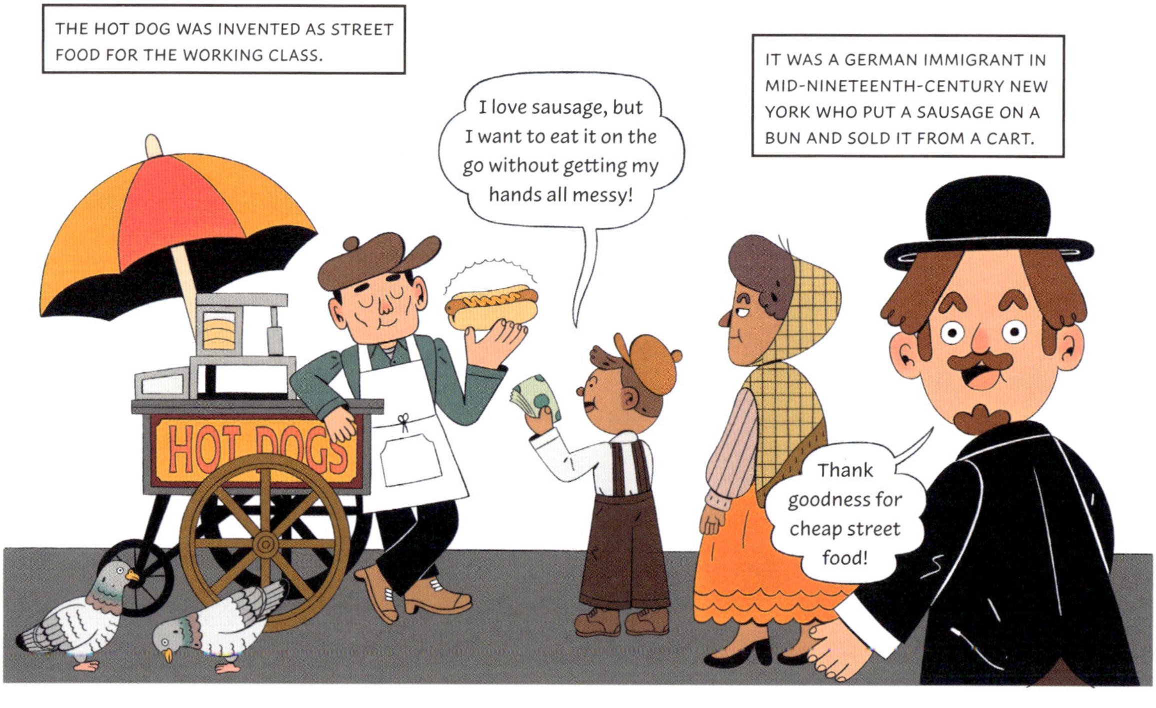
THE HOT DOG WAS INVENTED AS STREET FOOD FOR THE WORKING CLASS.
IT WAS A GERMAN IMMIGRANT IN MID-NINETEENTH-CENTURY NEW YORK WHO PUT A SAUSAGE ON A BUN AND SOLD IT FROM A CART.
HOT DOGS
I love sausage, but I want to eat it on the go without getting my hands all messy!
Thank goodness for cheap street food!

WHEN THE EASTERN EUROPEAN JEWS FIRST CAME TO NEW YORK, THE GERMAN AMERICAN SAUSAGE MAKERS, SEEING A NEW AND OPEN MARKET, STARTED SELLING THEM KOSHER BEEF SAUSAGES.

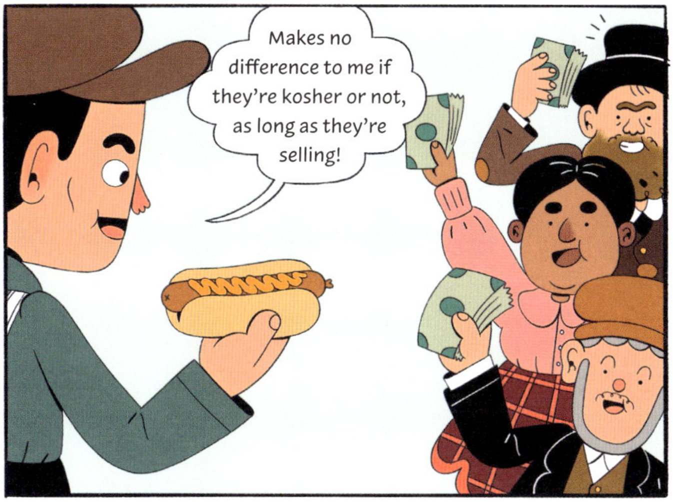
Makes no difference to me if they're kosher or not, as long as they're selling!

THE HEBREW NATIONAL BRAND WAS FOUNDED IN 1905 BY A RUSSIAN JEWISH IMMIGRANT NAMED THEODORE KRAININ.

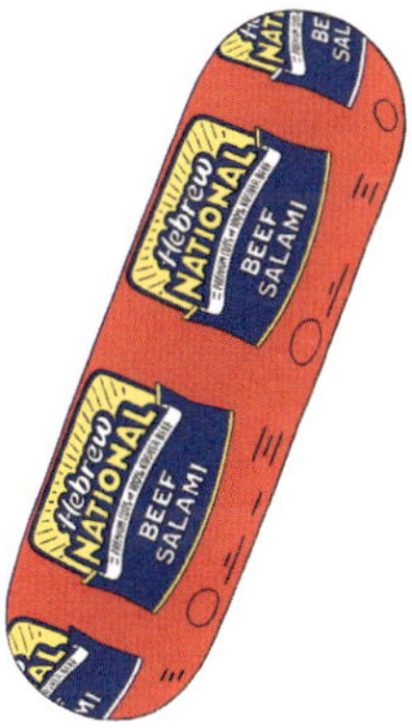
Hebrew NATIONAL
BEEF SALAMI

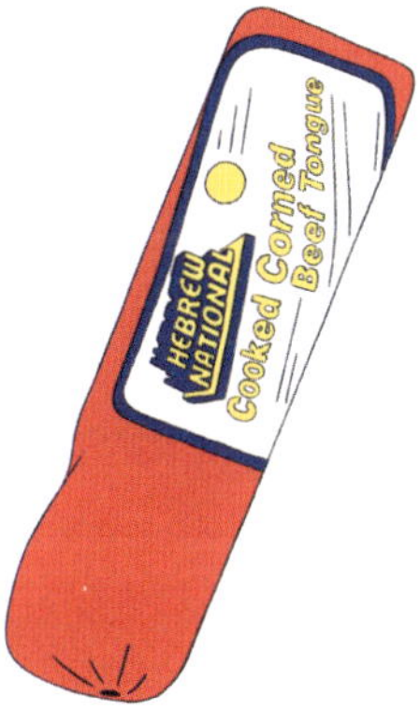
HEBREW NATIONAL
Cooked Corned Beef Tongue

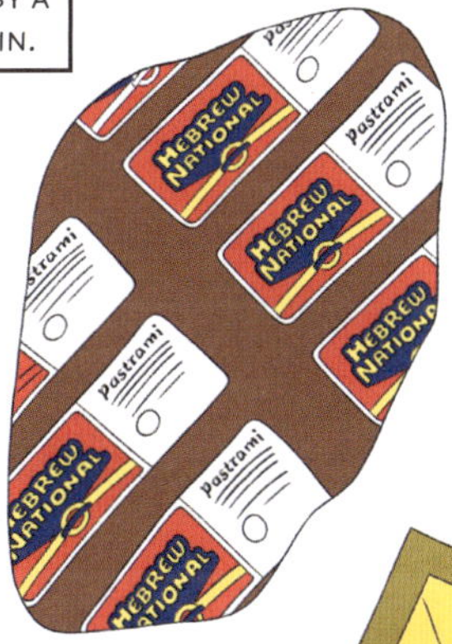
HEBREW NATIONAL
Pastrami

THE COMPANY SOLD KOSHER SALAMI, PICKLED TONGUE, CORNED BEEF,

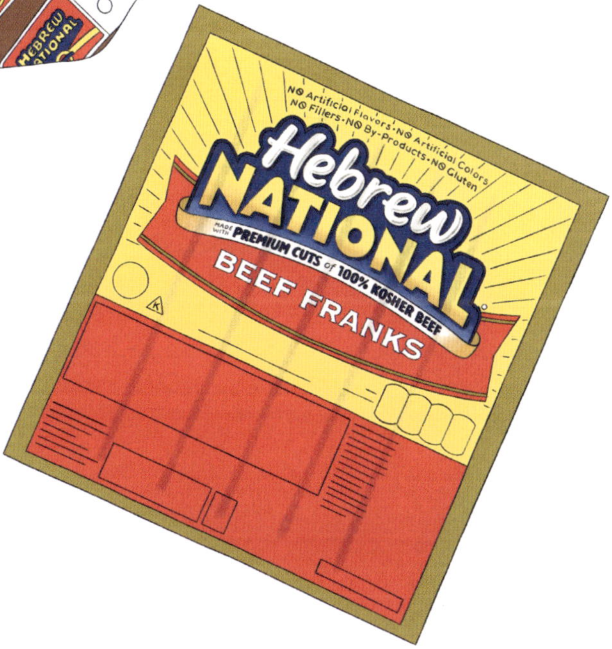
NO Artificial Flavors · NO Artificial Colors
NO Fillers · NO By-Products · NO Gluten
Hebrew NATIONAL
MADE WITH PREMIUM CUTS of 100% KOSHER BEEF
BEEF FRANKS

AND, OF COURSE, **HOT DOGS**.

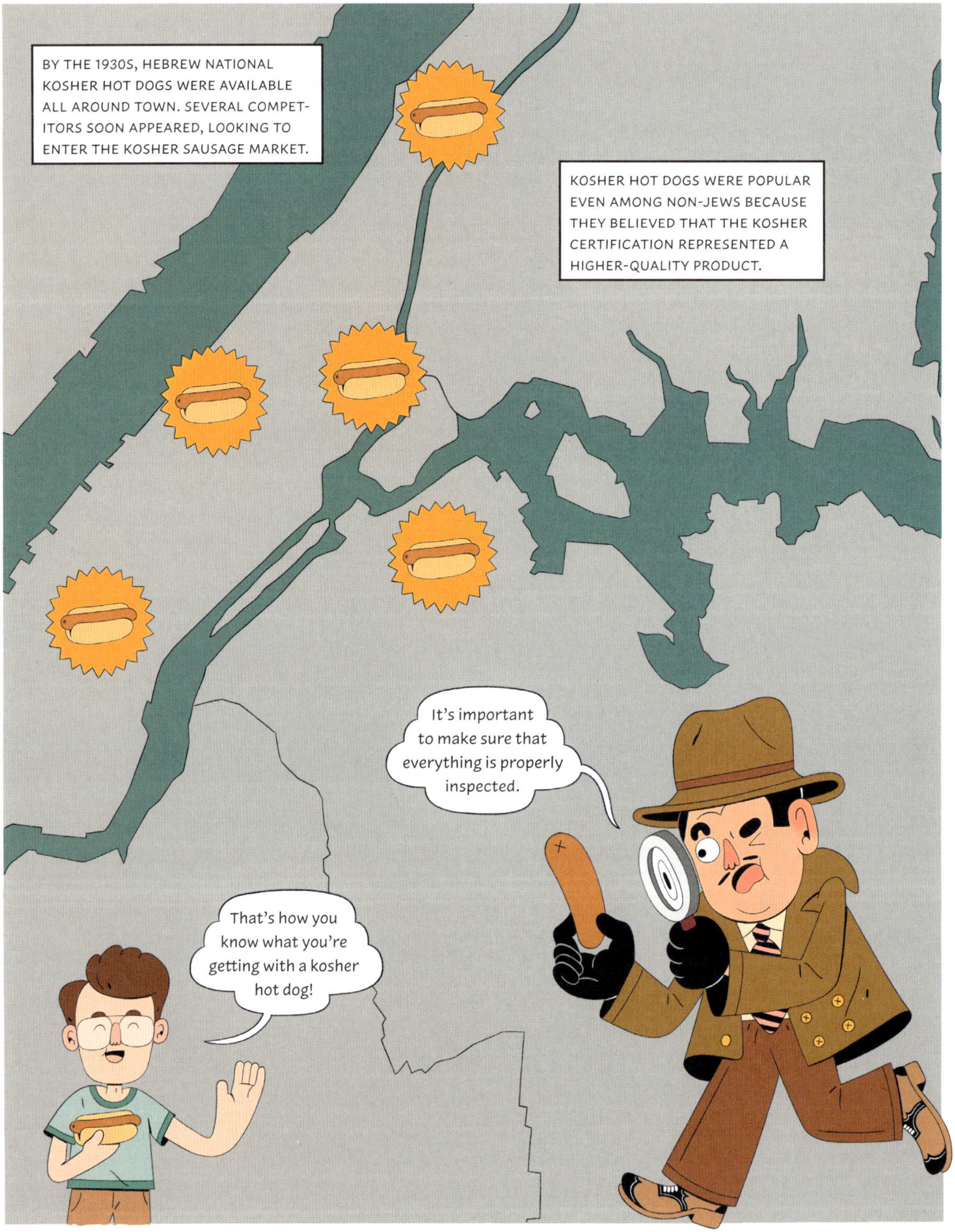
BY THE 1930S, HEBREW NATIONAL KOSHER HOT DOGS WERE AVAILABLE ALL AROUND TOWN. SEVERAL COMPETITORS SOON APPEARED, LOOKING TO ENTER THE KOSHER SAUSAGE MARKET.
KOSHER HOT DOGS WERE POPULAR EVEN AMONG NON-JEWS BECAUSE THEY BELIEVED THAT THE KOSHER CERTIFICATION REPRESENTED A HIGHER-QUALITY PRODUCT.
It's important to make sure that everything is properly inspected.
That's how you know what you're getting with a kosher hot dog!

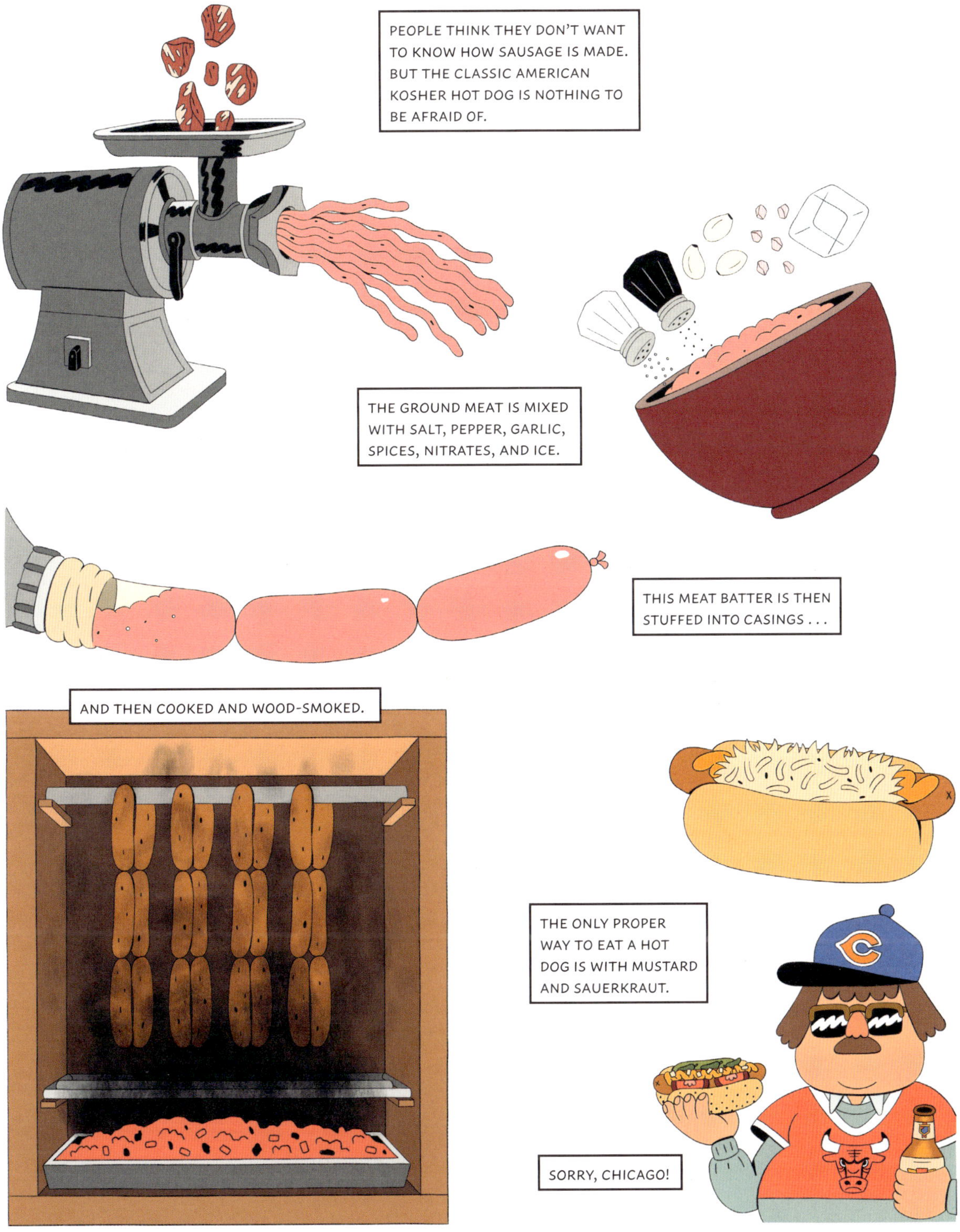
PEOPLE THINK THEY DON'T WANT TO KNOW HOW SAUSAGE IS MADE. BUT THE CLASSIC AMERICAN KOSHER HOT DOG IS NOTHING TO BE AFRAID OF.
THE GROUND MEAT IS MIXED WITH SALT, PEPPER, GARLIC, SPICES, NITRATES, AND ICE.
THIS MEAT BATTER IS THEN STUFFED INTO CASINGS . . .
AND THEN COOKED AND WOOD-SMOKED.
THE ONLY PROPER WAY TO EAT A HOT DOG IS WITH MUSTARD AND SAUERKRAUT.
SORRY, CHICAGO!

Salami

THE HISTORY OF SALAMI—A HARD, DRY, FERMENTED SAUSAGE—GOES BACK THOUSANDS OF YEARS . . .

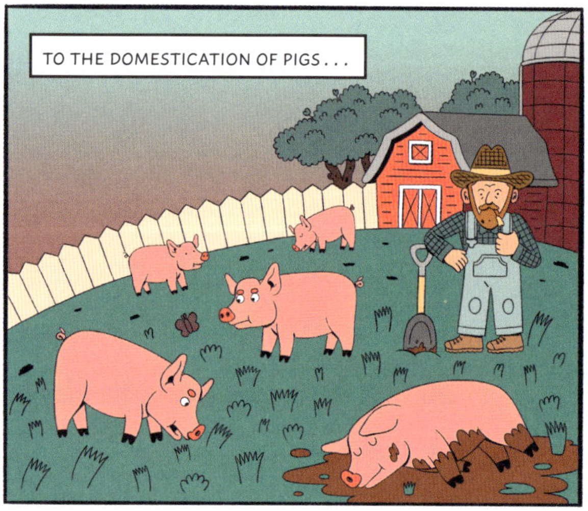
TO THE DOMESTICATION OF PIGS . . .

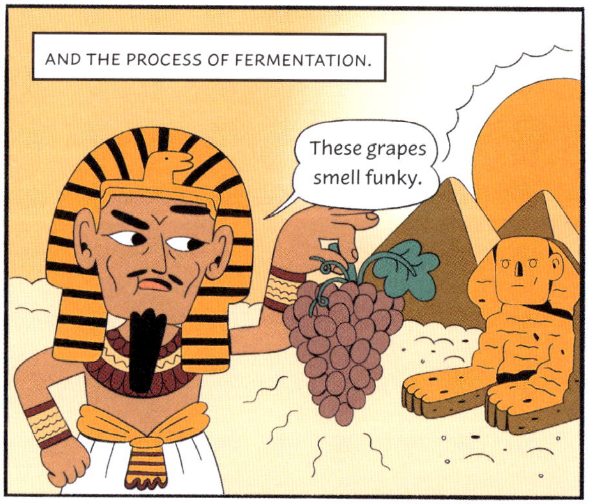
AND THE PROCESS OF FERMENTATION.
These grapes smell funky.

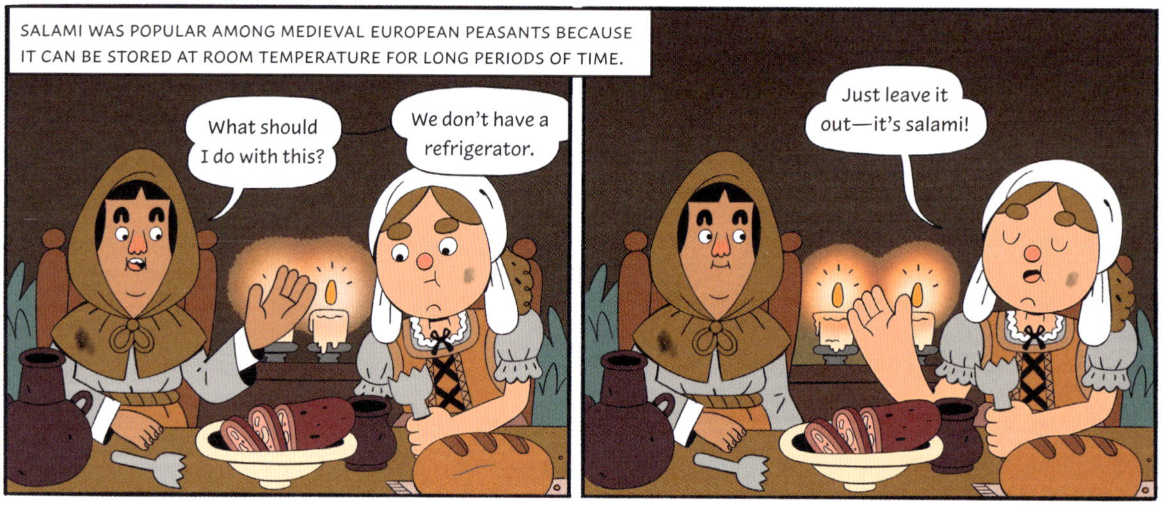
SALAMI WAS POPULAR AMONG MEDIEVAL EUROPEAN PEASANTS BECAUSE IT CAN BE STORED AT ROOM TEMPERATURE FOR LONG PERIODS OF TIME.
What should I do with this?
We don't have a refrigerator.
Just leave it out—it's salami!

LIKE HOT DOGS, KOSHER BEEF SALAMI IN DELIS ORIGINATED WITH GERMAN IMMIGRANTS.

EVENTUALLY, HEBREW NATIONAL TOOK OVER AND WOULD BECOME THE NUMBER ONE PRODUCER OF KOSHER SALAMI.

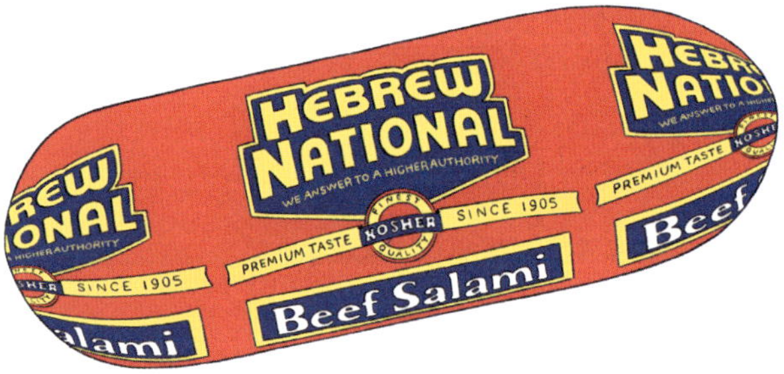
HEBREW NATIONAL
WE ANSWER TO A HIGHER AUTHORITY
PREMIUM TASTE
KOSHER
SINCE 1905
Beef Salami

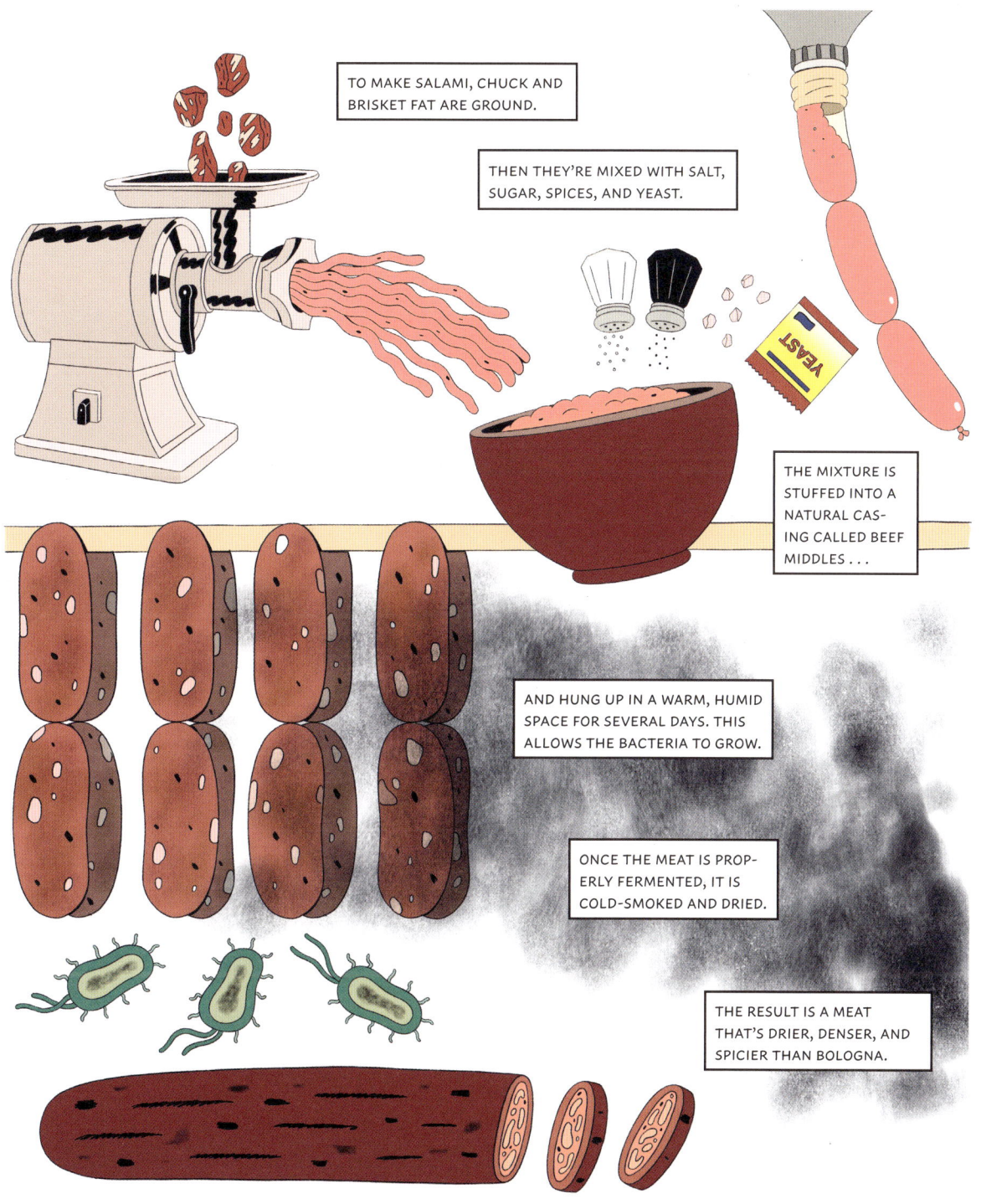

TO MAKE SALAMI, CHUCK AND BRISKET FAT ARE GROUND.

THEN THEY'RE MIXED WITH SALT, SUGAR, SPICES, AND YEAST.

THE MIXTURE IS STUFFED INTO A NATURAL CASING CALLED BEEF MIDDLES . . .

AND HUNG UP IN A WARM, HUMID SPACE FOR SEVERAL DAYS. THIS ALLOWS THE BACTERIA TO GROW.

ONCE THE MEAT IS PROPERLY FERMENTED, IT IS COLD-SMOKED AND DRIED.

THE RESULT IS A MEAT THAT'S DRIER, DENSER, AND SPICIER THAN BOLOGNA.

BEEF SALAMI IS PREPARED LIKE OTHER MEATS IN THE DELI COUNTER, SLICED AND SERVED ON RYE BREAD WITH MUSTARD.

Karnatzel

A KARNATZEL IS A LONG, THIN, DRIED BEEF SAUSAGE THAT ORIGINATED IN ROMANIA AND IS ESPECIALLY POPULAR IN MONTREAL.

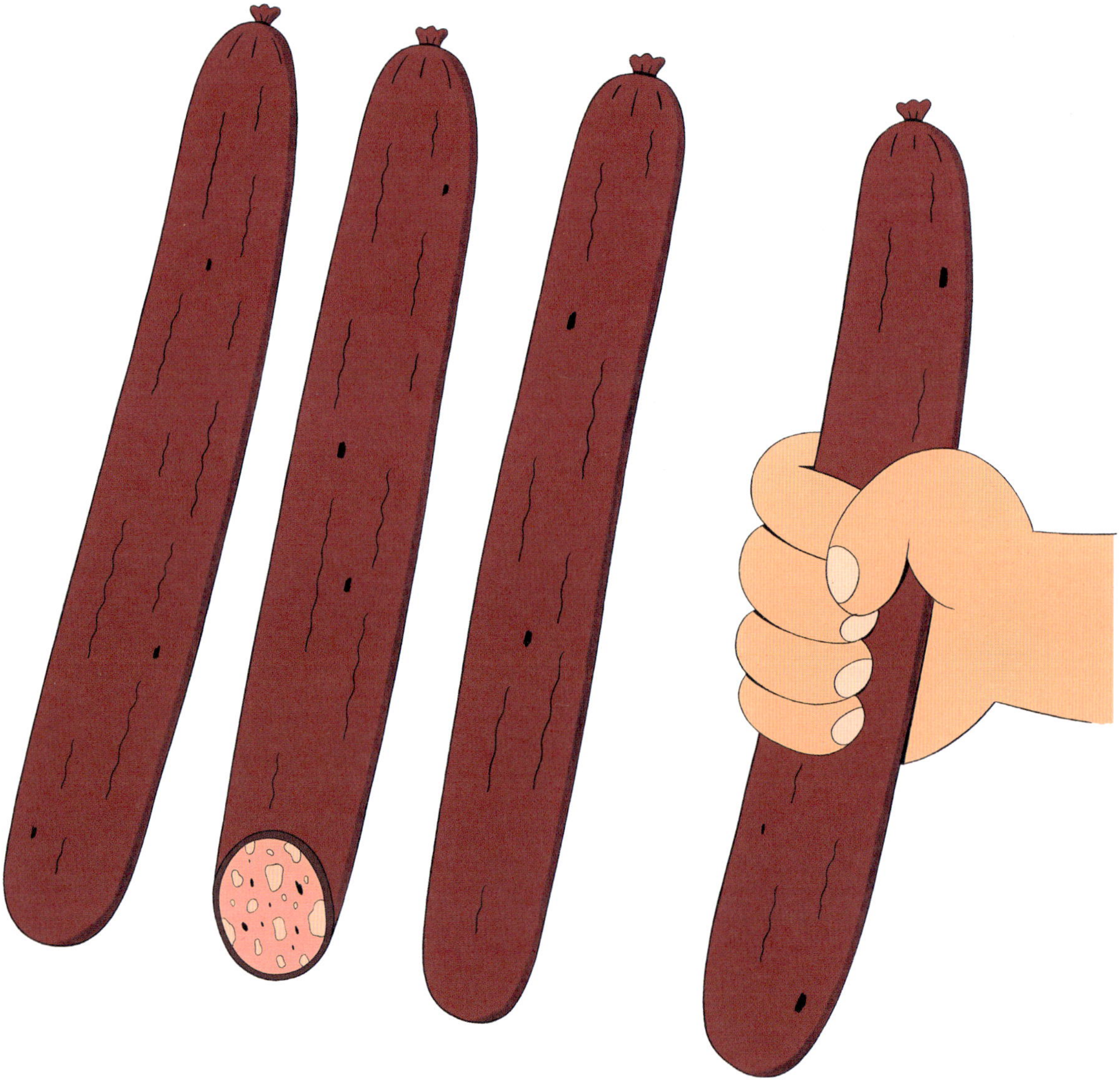

THE MEAT IS SEASONED WITH GARLIC, SALT, AND PEPPER AND THEN SMOKED.

Tongue

PICKLED BEEF TONGUE IS ONE OF SEVERAL KOSHER PRODUCTS MADE FROM OFFAL, THE NONMUSCULAR ORGAN MEATS.

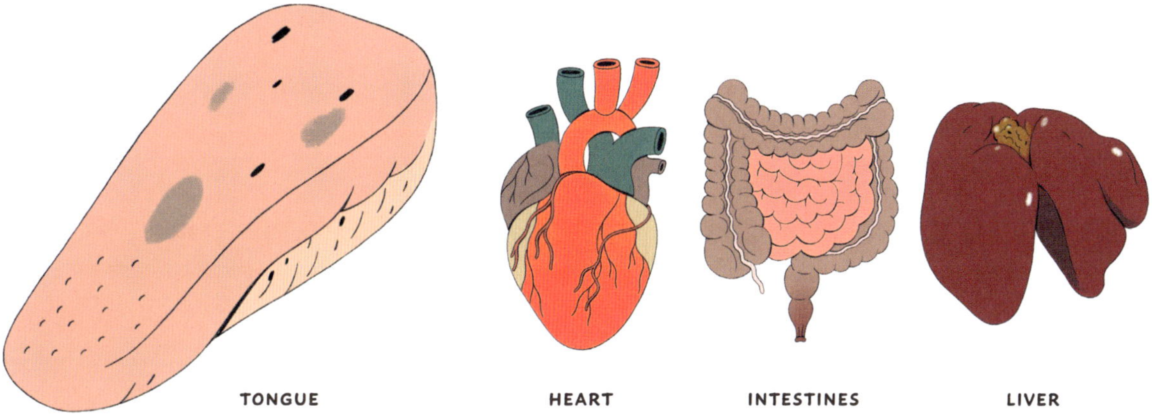
TONGUE
HEART
INTESTINES
LIVER

THE JEWISH PEOPLE HAVE HAD A LONG AND LOVING RELATIONSHIP WITH THESE MEATS, WHICH WERE CHEAP AND REGARDED AS UNDESIRABLE BY THE UPPER CLASSES.

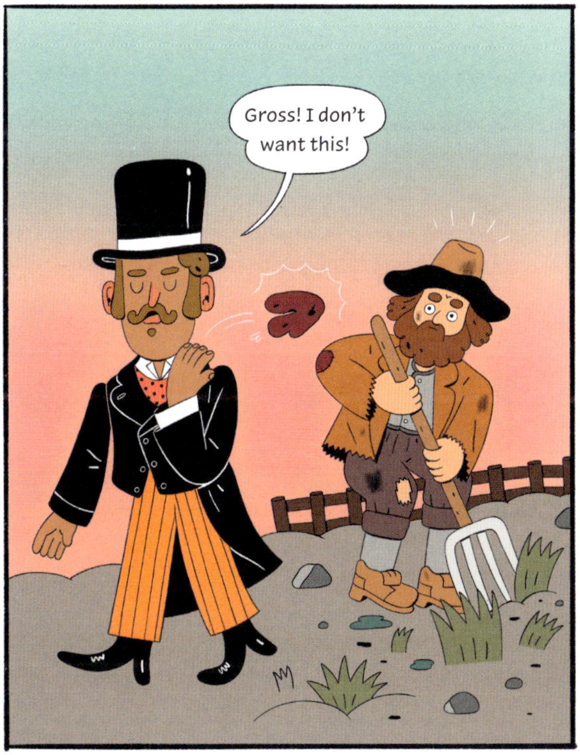
Gross! I don't want this!

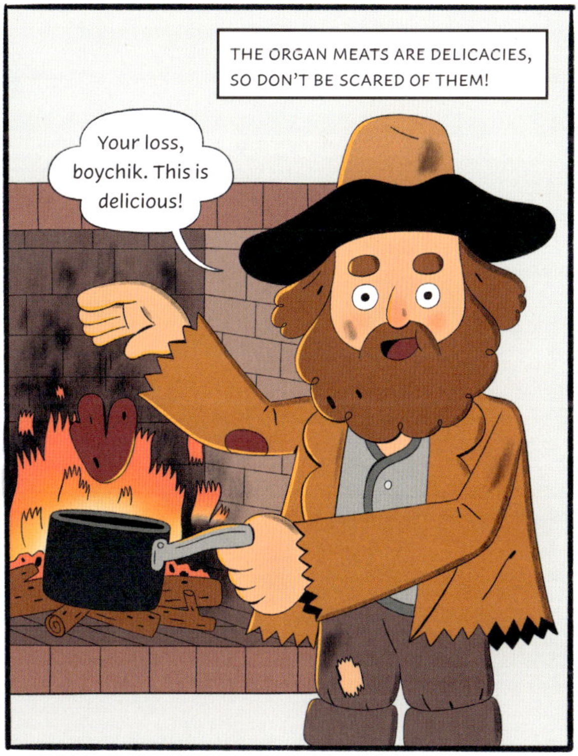
THE ORGAN MEATS ARE DELICACIES, SO DON'T BE SCARED OF THEM!
Your loss, boychik. This is delicious!

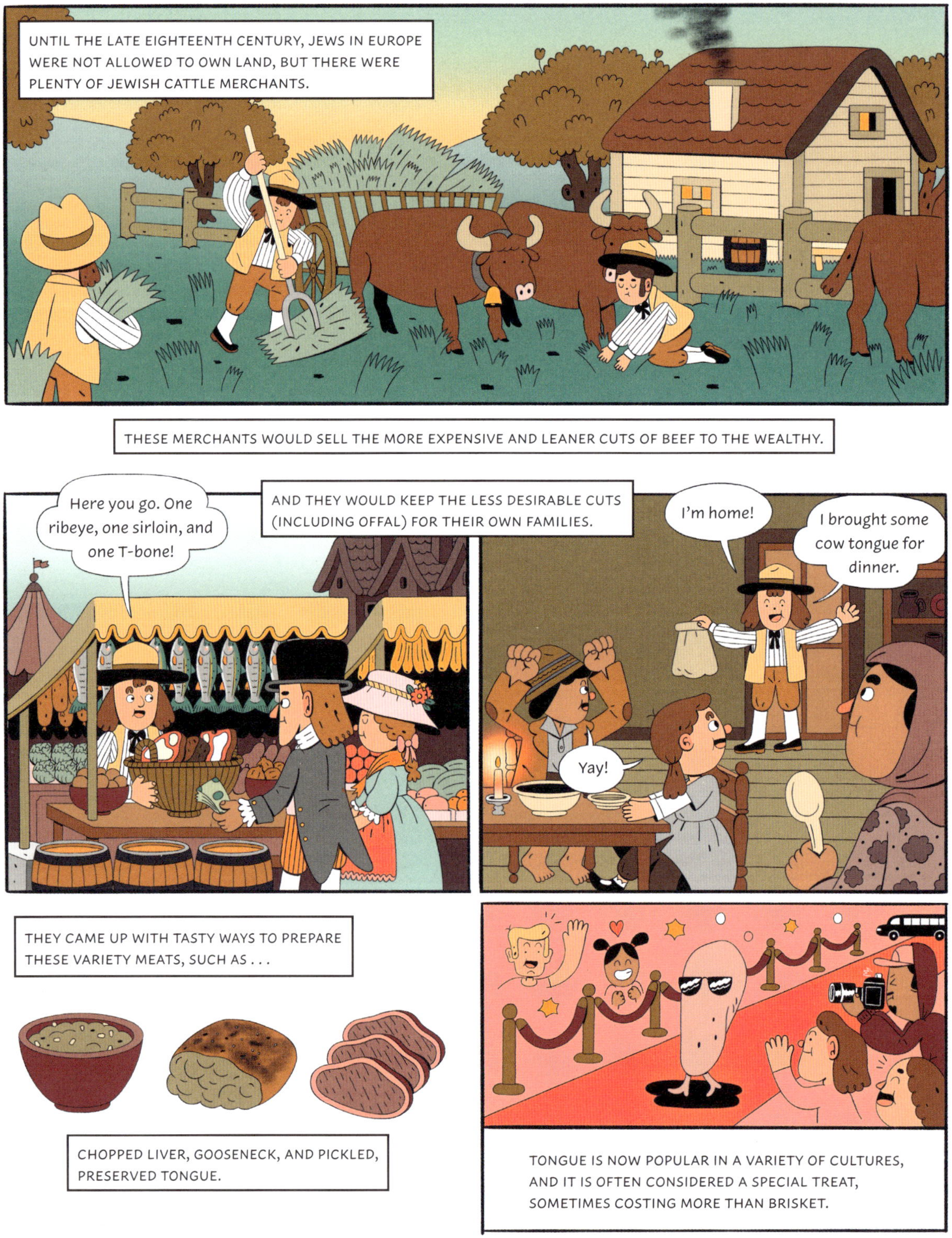
UNTIL THE LATE EIGHTEENTH CENTURY, JEWS IN EUROPE WERE NOT ALLOWED TO OWN LAND, BUT THERE WERE PLENTY OF JEWISH CATTLE MERCHANTS.
THESE MERCHANTS WOULD SELL THE MORE EXPENSIVE AND LEANER CUTS OF BEEF TO THE WEALTHY.
Here you go. One ribeye, one sirloin, and one T-bone!
AND THEY WOULD KEEP THE LESS DESIRABLE CUTS (INCLUDING OFFAL) FOR THEIR OWN FAMILIES.
I'm home!
I brought some cow tongue for dinner.
Yay!
THEY CAME UP WITH TASTY WAYS TO PREPARE THESE VARIETY MEATS, SUCH AS . . .
CHOPPED LIVER, GOOSENECK, AND PICKLED, PRESERVED TONGUE.
TONGUE IS NOW POPULAR IN A VARIETY OF CULTURES, AND IT IS OFTEN CONSIDERED A SPECIAL TREAT, SOMETIMES COSTING MORE THAN BRISKET.

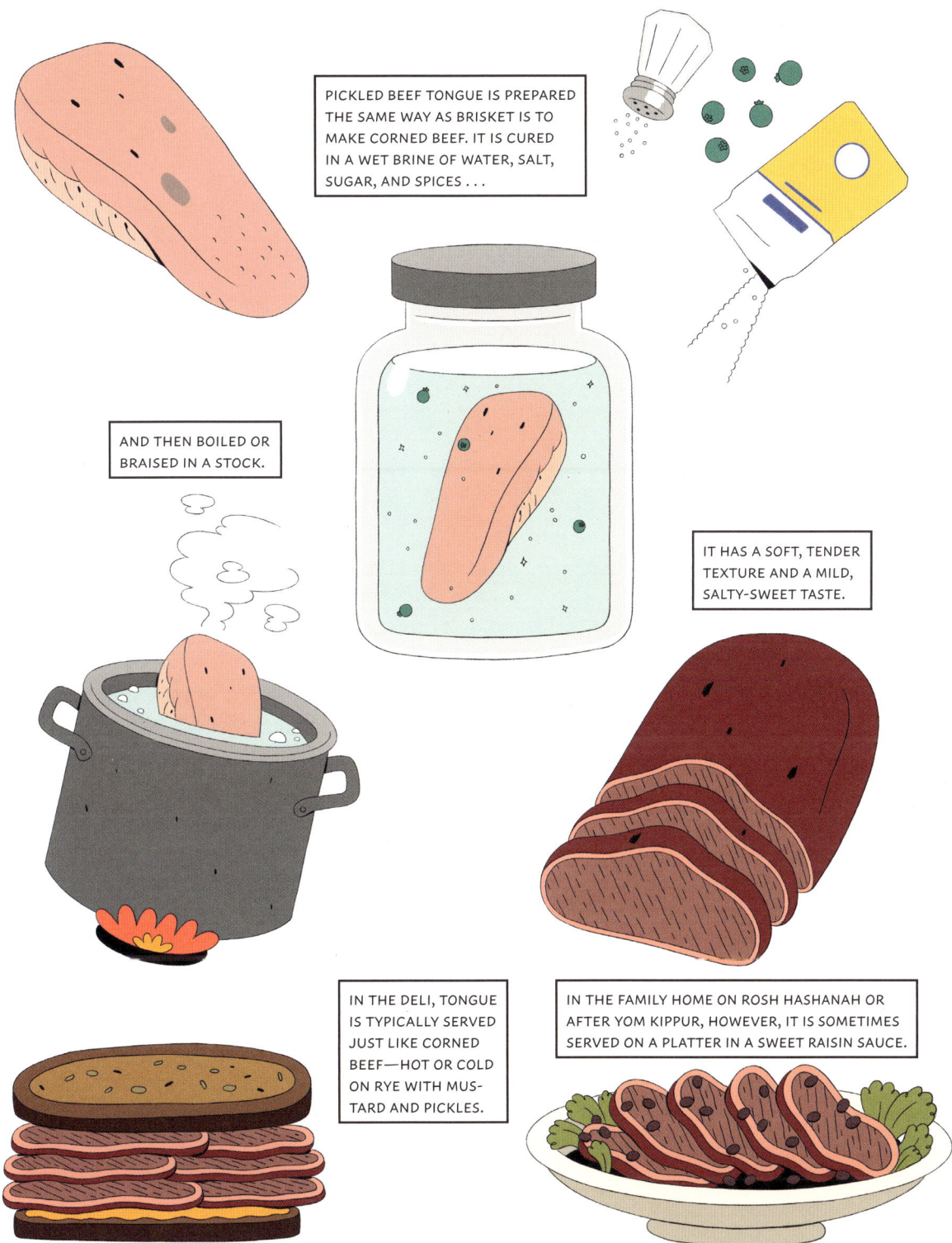

PICKLED BEEF TONGUE IS PREPARED THE SAME WAY AS BRISKET IS TO MAKE CORNED BEEF. IT IS CURED IN A WET BRINE OF WATER, SALT, SUGAR, AND SPICES . . .

AND THEN BOILED OR BRAISED IN A STOCK.

IT HAS A SOFT, TENDER TEXTURE AND A MILD, SALTY-SWEET TASTE.

IN THE DELI, TONGUE IS TYPICALLY SERVED JUST LIKE CORNED BEEF—HOT OR COLD ON RYE WITH MUSTARD AND PICKLES.

IN THE FAMILY HOME ON ROSH HASHANAH OR AFTER YOM KIPPUR, HOWEVER, IT IS SOMETIMES SERVED ON A PLATTER IN A SWEET RAISIN SAUCE.

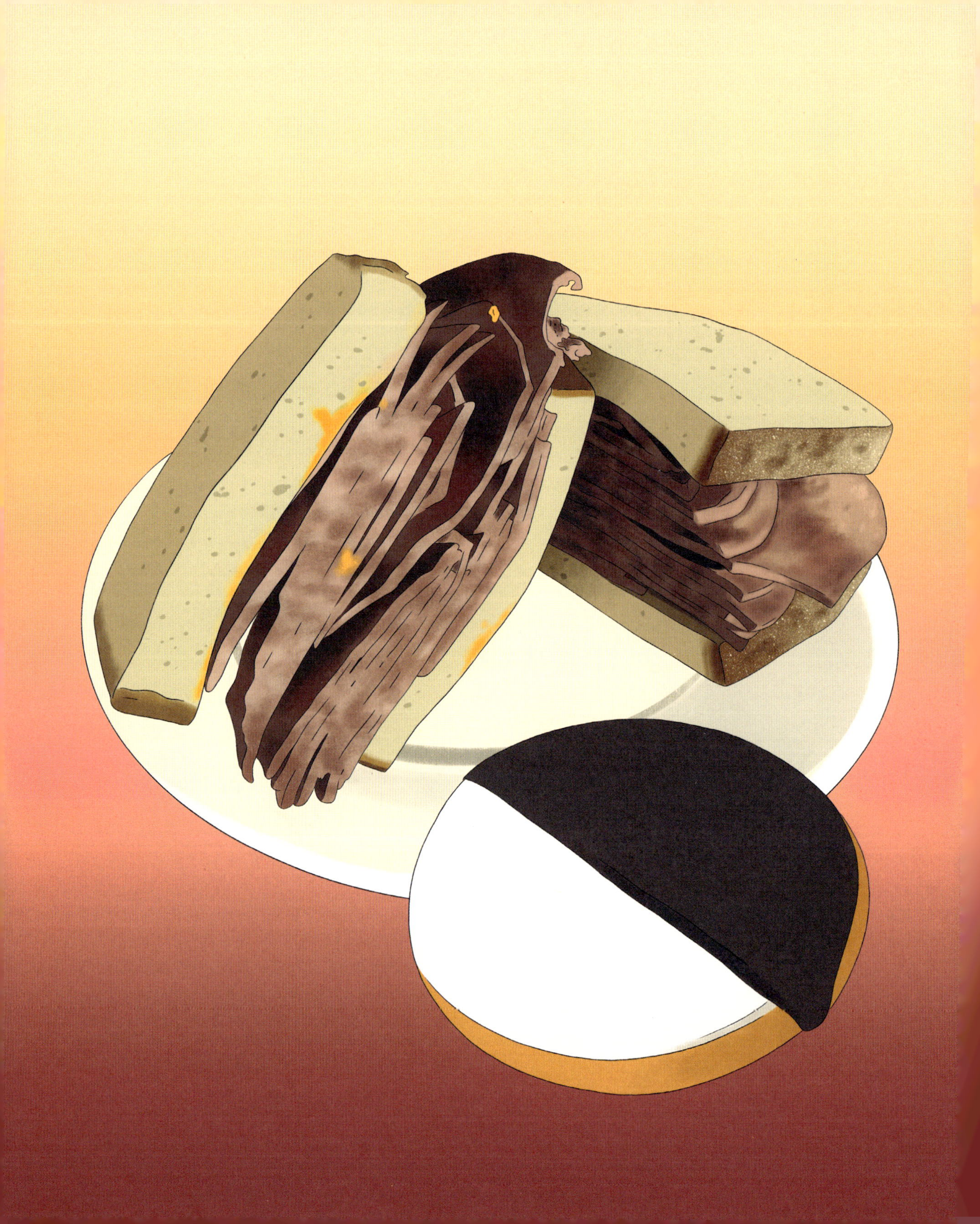

The Tongue Sandwich

Tongue is among the meats that can seem a little unsettling to some, less familiar than cuts from the shoulder or ribs, and yet weirdly intimate and personal. Our tongues are right there, up front, tasting another tongue.

But often the best food can seem a little scary at first, and the dishes that work harder to earn our trust frequently yield the greatest rewards. Beef tongue was discarded by the bourgeoisie and developed skillfully by more resourceful and more adventurous eaters. Like pastrami, it's cooked low and slow for hours on end. Tongue is high in fat, and when treated right, it yields incredibly rich and soft meat, perfect for slicing thin and piling high with mustard.

Tongue can be served steamed, but I believe it's best eaten cold. Sliced, it's comparable to bologna, but without the overprocessed quality. Its flavor profile is not unlike corned beef—both are pickled the same way—but the higher fat content makes for a smoother mouthfeel. When I bite into a tongue sandwich, and the meat's soft and bouncy character combines with mustard and bread and presses against the roof of my mouth, I get a comforting and nostalgic feeling, one that calls out for potato chips and soda after a soccer game. For anyone with a childhood full of bologna sandwiches, tongue might actually be the most familiar way to get started if you're new to the world of deli sandwiches. It's oddly inviting, easy to love, and satisfying as all heck.

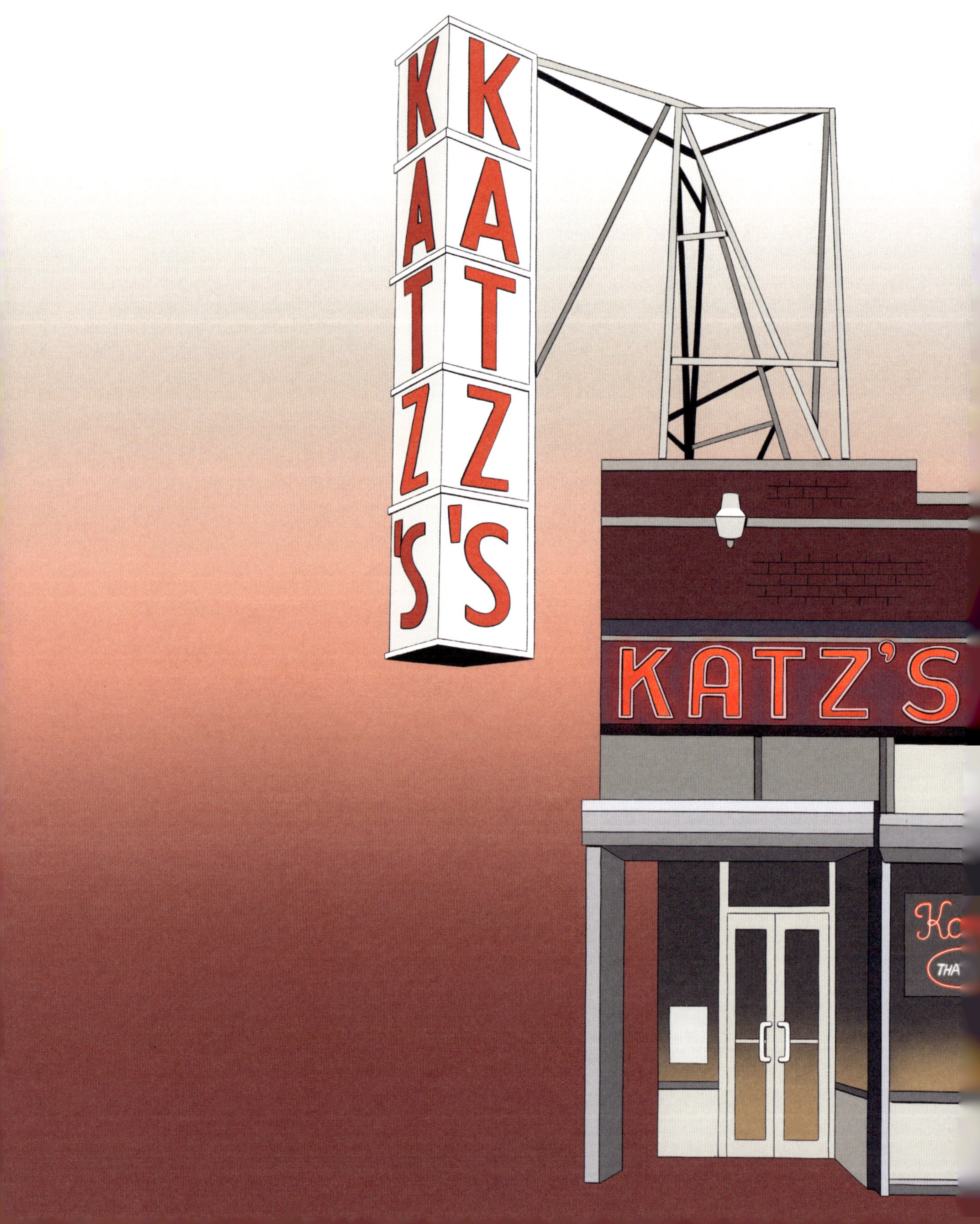
KATZ'S
KATZ'S

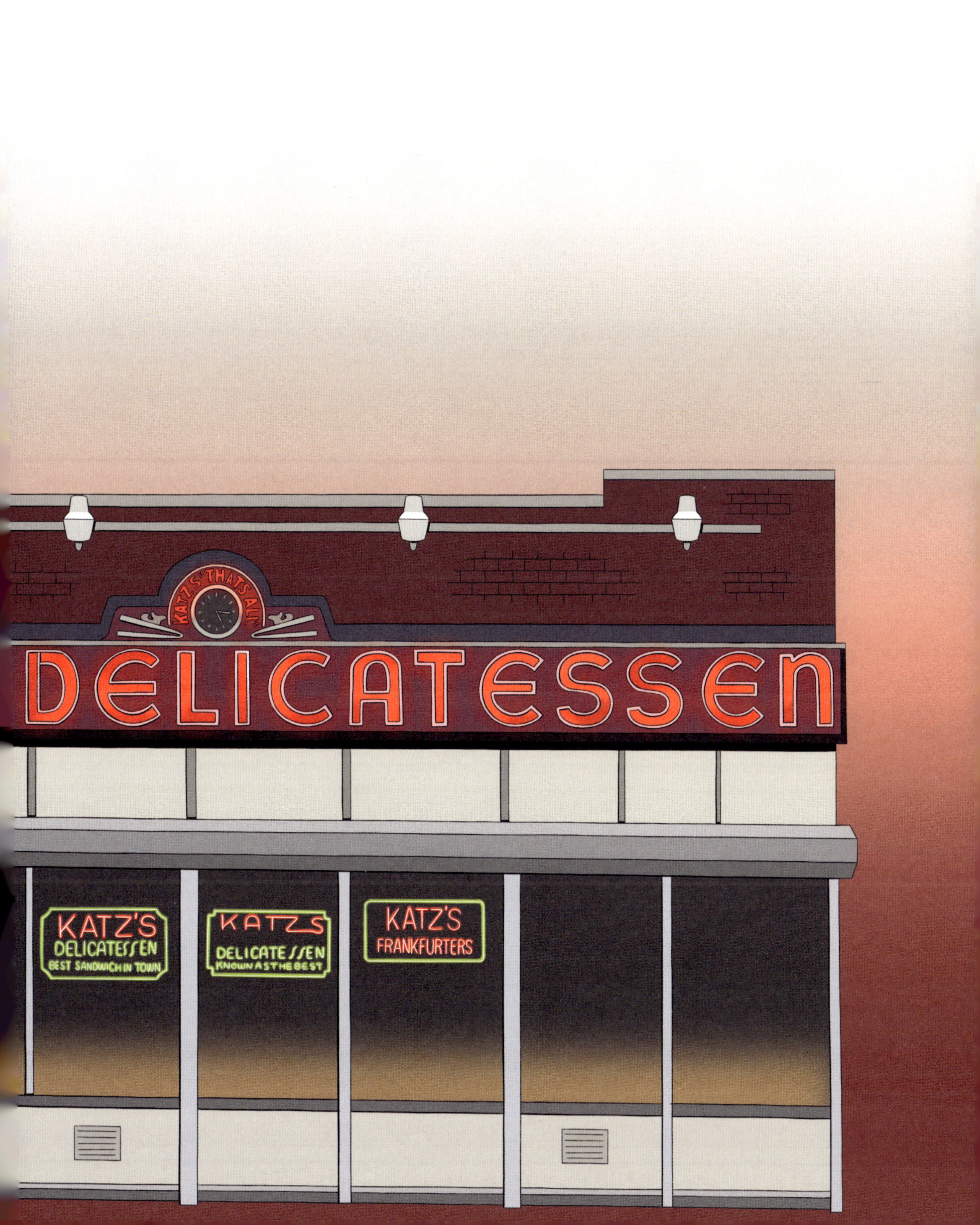
KATZ'S THAT'S ALL
DELICATESSEN
KATZ'S
DELICATESSEN
BEST SANDWICH IN TOWN
KATZ'S
DELICATESSEN
KNOWN AS THE BEST
KATZ'S
FRANKFURTERS

KATZ'S DELICATESSEN

205 East Houston Street,
Manhattan, New York City

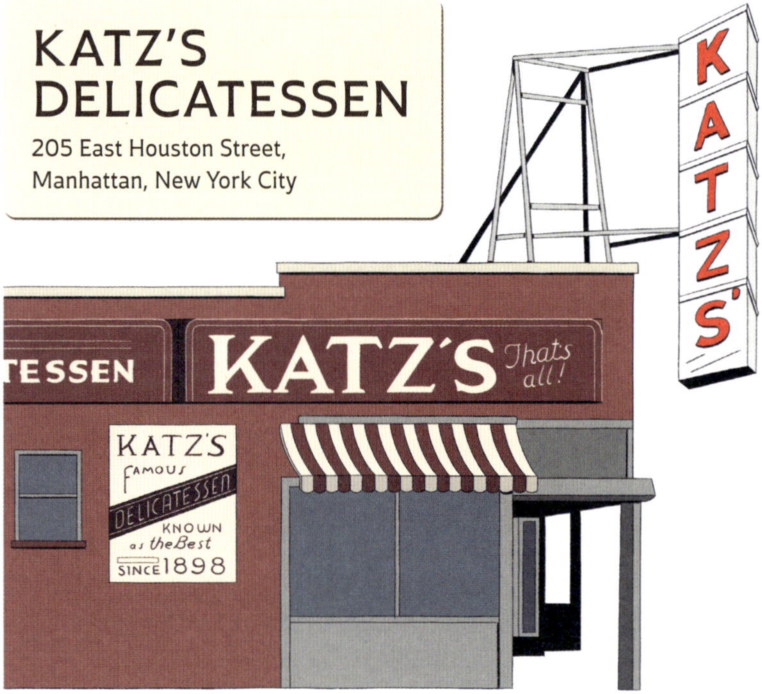
KATZ'S
TESSEN
KATZ'S Thats all!
KATZ'S FAMOUS DELICATESSEN KNOWN as the Best SINCE 1898

ORIGINALLY OPENED UNDER THE NAME ICELAND'S DELICATESSEN BY TWO BROTHERS OF THE YIDDISH POET REUVEN ICELAND, KATZ'S WAS PERHAPS THE FIRST TRUE JEWISH DELI.

WHEN WILLY KATZ JOINED THE BROTHERS IN 1903, THE NAME OF THE ESTABLISHMENT WAS CHANGED TO ICELAND AND KATZ.

IN 1910, WILLY AND HIS COUSIN BENNY BOUGHT OUT THE ICELAND BROTHERS, MOVED THE DELI TO THE WEST SIDE OF LUDLOW STREET, AND RENAMED IT KATZ'S DELICATESSEN.

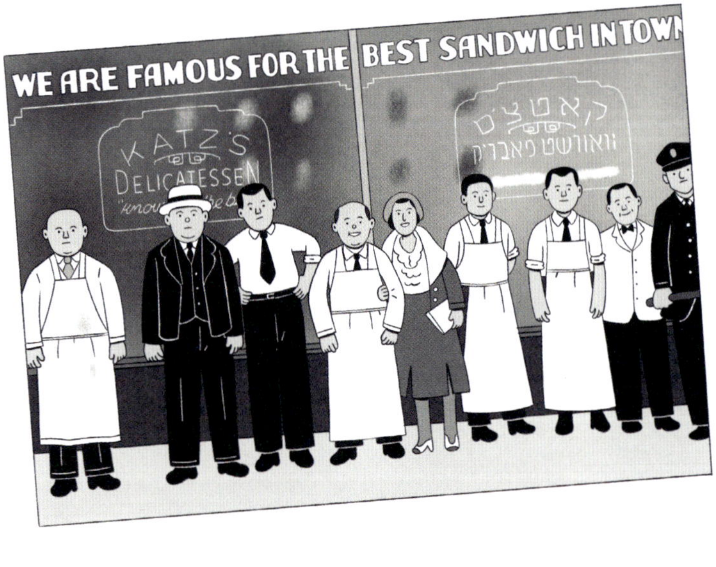
WE ARE FAMOUS FOR THE BEST SANDWICH IN TOWN
KATZ'S DELICATESSEN

DURING THE IMMIGRATION BOOM OF THE MID-NINETEENTH CENTURY, KATZ'S BECAME AN ESSENTIAL OUTPOST OF JEWISH AMERICAN CULTURE.

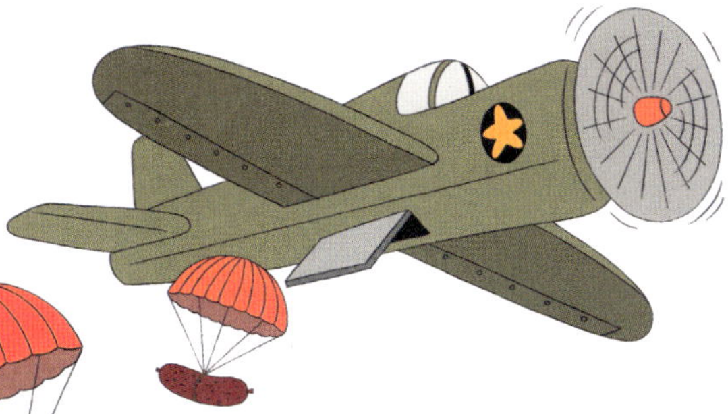

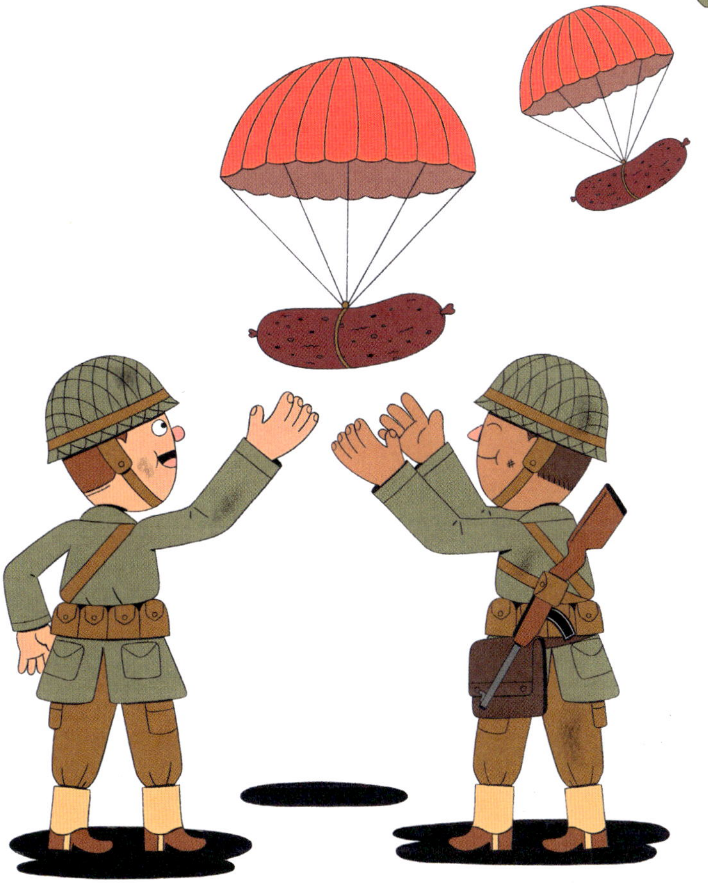

IT SOLD PASTRAMI TO THE ENTIRE NEW YORK JEWISH COMMUNITY AND, LATER, DURING WORLD WAR II, SENT SALAMI CARE PACKAGES OVER TO SOLDIERS IN EUROPE. (THEIR MOTTO WAS "SEND A SALAMI TO YOUR BOY IN THE ARMY.")

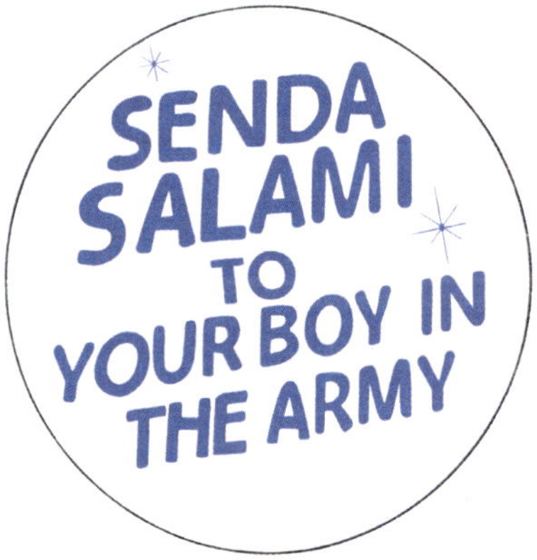
SEND A
SALAMI
TO
YOUR BOY IN
THE ARMY

OWNERSHIP OF KATZ'S HAS SINCE BEEN PASSED DOWN THROUGH GENERATIONS, AND THE DELI REMAINS AN INTEGRAL PART OF NEW YORK CITY CULTURE, SERVING QUALITY MEATS TO LOCALS AND TOURISTS ALIKE, JEWISH OR OTHERWISE.

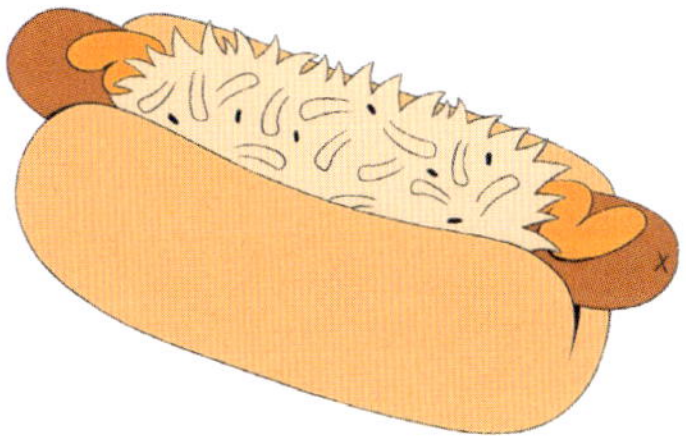

ACCORDING TO CURRENT OWNER JAKE DELL, TWO LESSER KNOWN ITEMS WORTH TRYING AT KATZ'S ARE THE HOT DOG (WITH MUSTARD AND KRAUT) AND THE TURKEY SANDWICH.

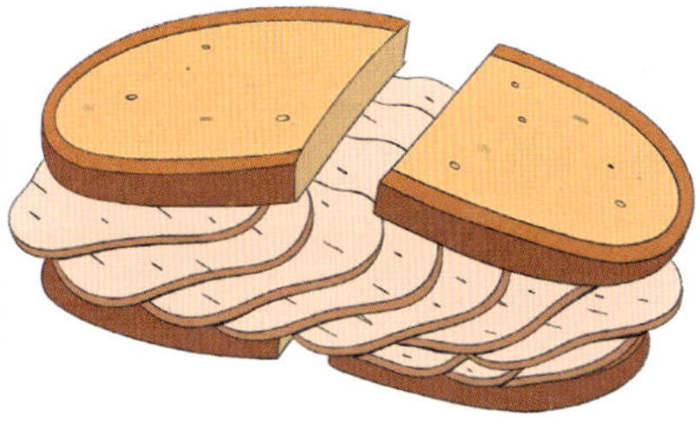

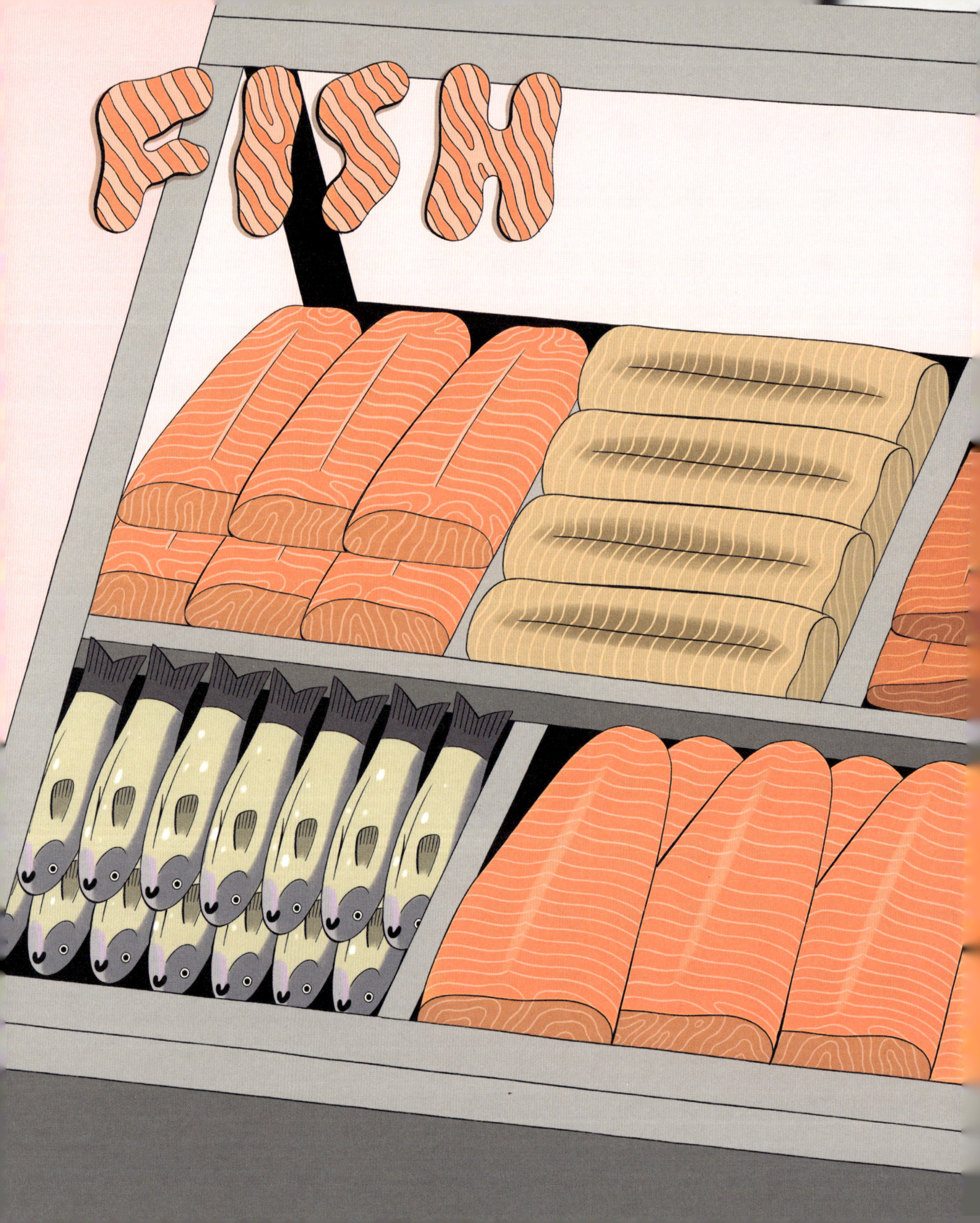
FISH

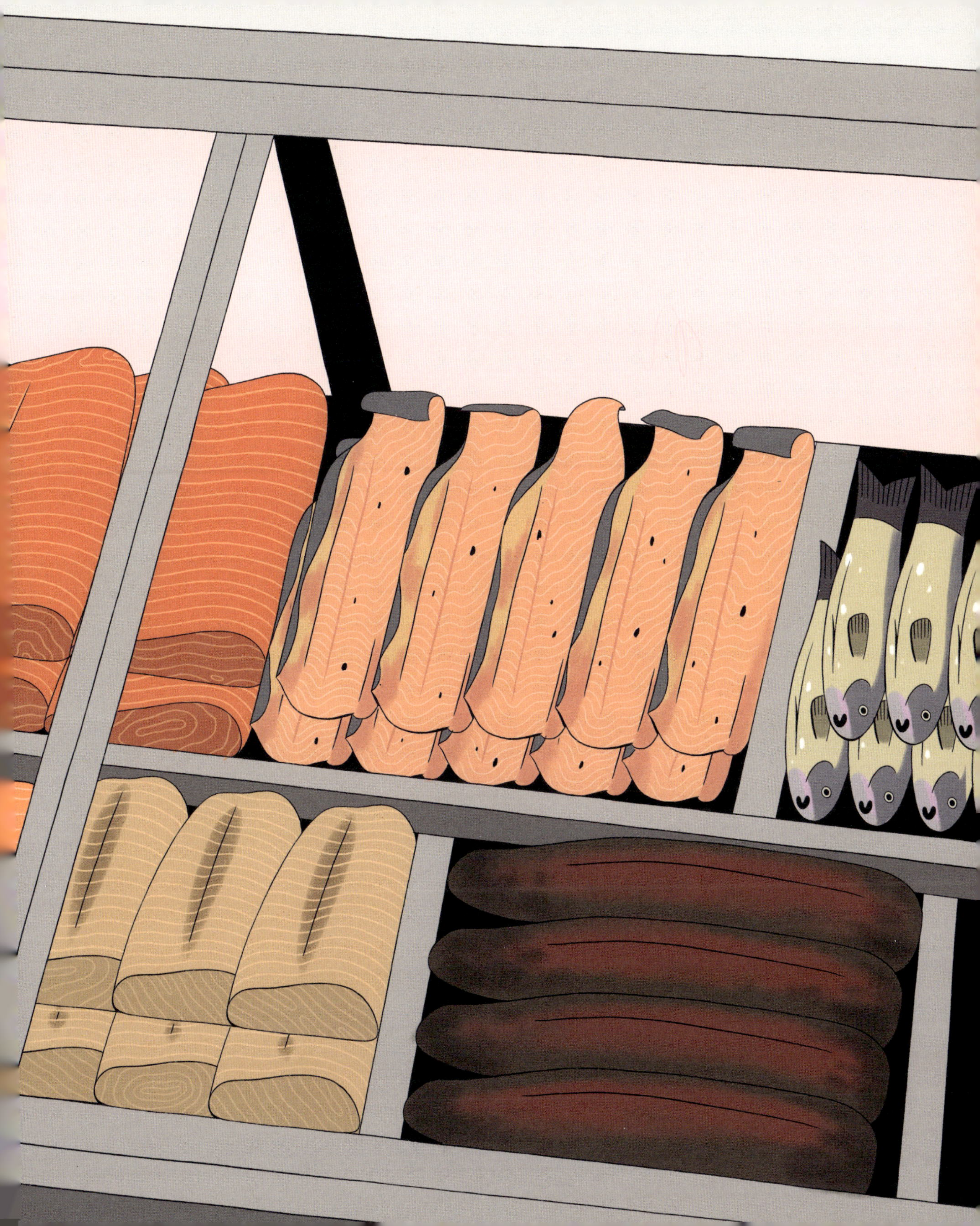

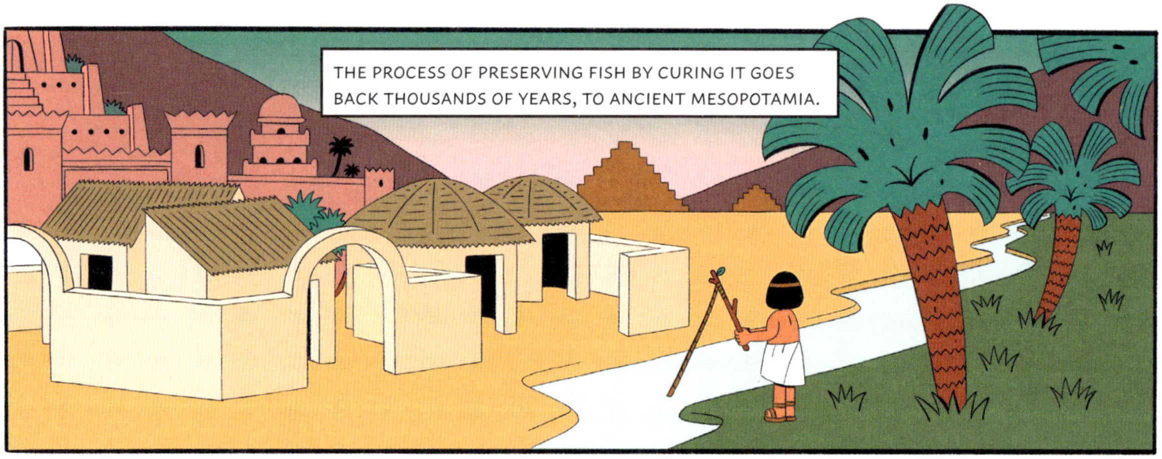
THE PROCESS OF PRESERVING FISH BY CURING IT GOES BACK THOUSANDS OF YEARS, TO ANCIENT MESOPOTAMIA.

THE ANCIENT ISRAELITES WERE CURING FISH WITH SALT FROM THE DEAD SEA AS EARLY AS 1600 BCE.

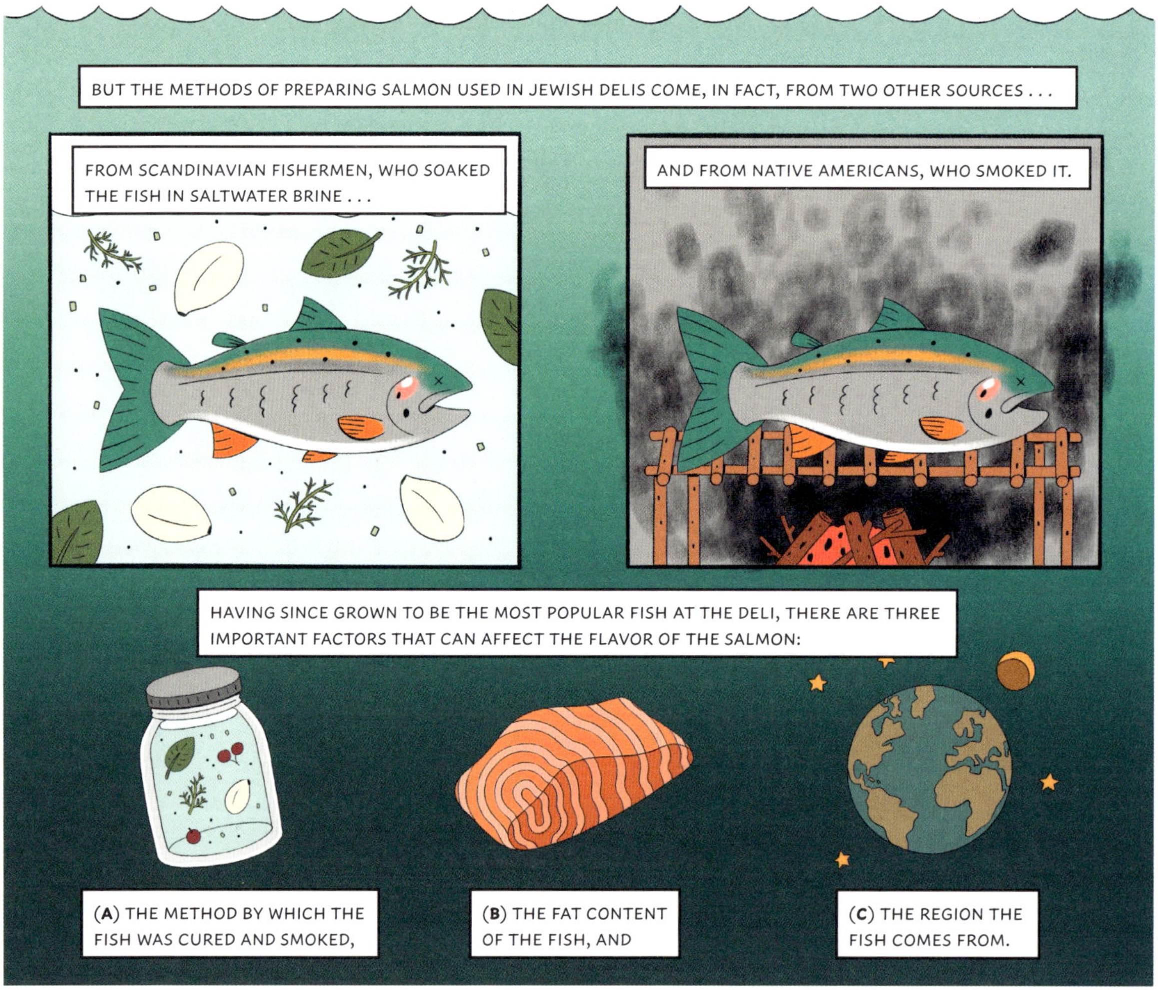
BUT THE METHODS OF PREPARING SALMON USED IN JEWISH DELIS COME, IN FACT, FROM TWO OTHER SOURCES . . .
FROM SCANDINAVIAN FISHERMEN, WHO SOAKED THE FISH IN SALTWATER BRINE . . .
AND FROM NATIVE AMERICANS, WHO SMOKED IT.
HAVING SINCE GROWN TO BE THE MOST POPULAR FISH AT THE DELI, THERE ARE THREE IMPORTANT FACTORS THAT CAN AFFECT THE FLAVOR OF THE SALMON:
(A) THE METHOD BY WHICH THE FISH WAS CURED AND SMOKED,
(B) THE FAT CONTENT OF THE FISH, AND
(C) THE REGION THE FISH COMES FROM.

Lox

THE WORD *LOX* COMES FROM THE YIDDISH WORD *LAKS*, WHICH IN TURN IS RELATED TO THE GERMAN WORD FOR SALMON, *LACHS*. PERHAPS THE MOST COMMON MISCONCEPTION IN DELI FOOD IS THAT THE TERM *LOX* REFERS TO ALL KINDS OF SMOKED SALMON.

IN FACT, THERE ARE GREAT DIFFERENCES IN KINDS OF CURED AND SMOKED SALMON, FROM THE TYPE OF FISH USED TO THE WAY IT IS PREPARED.

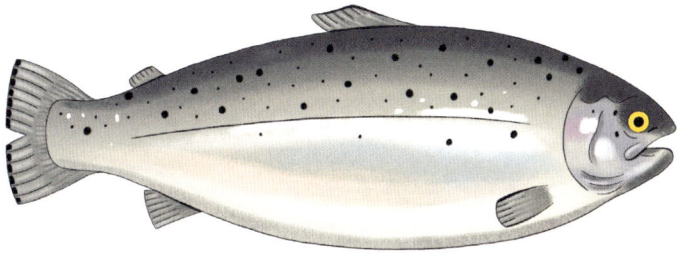

Actually, traditional lox may surprise you!

HOWEVER, SALMON WAS GENERALLY TOO EXPENSIVE FOR JEWISH PEASANTS, SO THEY USED HERRING OR CARP INSTEAD.

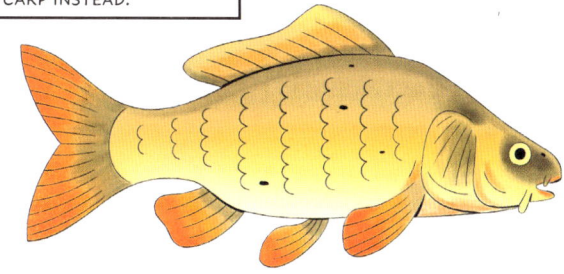

JEWS STARTED MAKING LOX IN MEDIEVAL GERMANY, WITH ITS RICH PICKLING HISTORY.

IN THE MID-NINETEENTH CENTURY, GERMAN AMERICANS WERE PEDDLING PICKLED FISH.

Herring! Fresh herring!

BUT IT WAS THE JEWISH IMMIGRANTS WHO TOOK ADVANTAGE OF THE NEW ABUNDANCE OF SALMON FROM THE PACIFIC NORTHWEST.

Herring? Get over it!

This is America! There's salmon here, and it's affordable.

THEY MADE LOX OUT OF SALMON BELLY, WHICH IS A LUXURIOUSLY FATTY PIECE OF FISH.

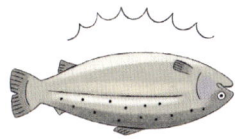

LOX IS NOT SMOKED!

TRADITIONAL LOX, REFERRED TO AS BELLY LOX, IS CURED IN A WET BRINE OF SALT, SUGAR, AND DILL.

THE BRINE DRAWS OUT SOME OF THE MOISTURE OF THE SALMON AND DEEPLY FLAVORS THE MEAT. THE RESULT IS CURED FISH THAT'S SOFT AND BUTTERY BUT ALSO VERY SALTY.

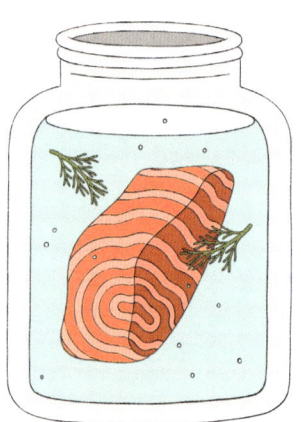

IN FACT, LOX IS SO SALTY ON ITS OWN THAT YOU WILL USUALLY WANT SOMETHING LIKE CREAM CHEESE TO BALANCE IT OUT.

More on that later!

THE TEXTURE AND COLOR OF LOX CAN VARY BASED ON THE KIND OF SALMON USED—

WHETHER IT IS THE LEANER WESTERN PACIFIC KING SALMON . . .

OR THE FATTIER AND MORE FLAVORFUL ATLANTIC SALMON.

PICKLED LOX

PICKLED LOX IS BELLY LOX THAT HAS BEEN SOAKED IN WATER TO LOWER ITS SALT CONTENT AND THEN PICKLED IN A VINEGAR BRINE.

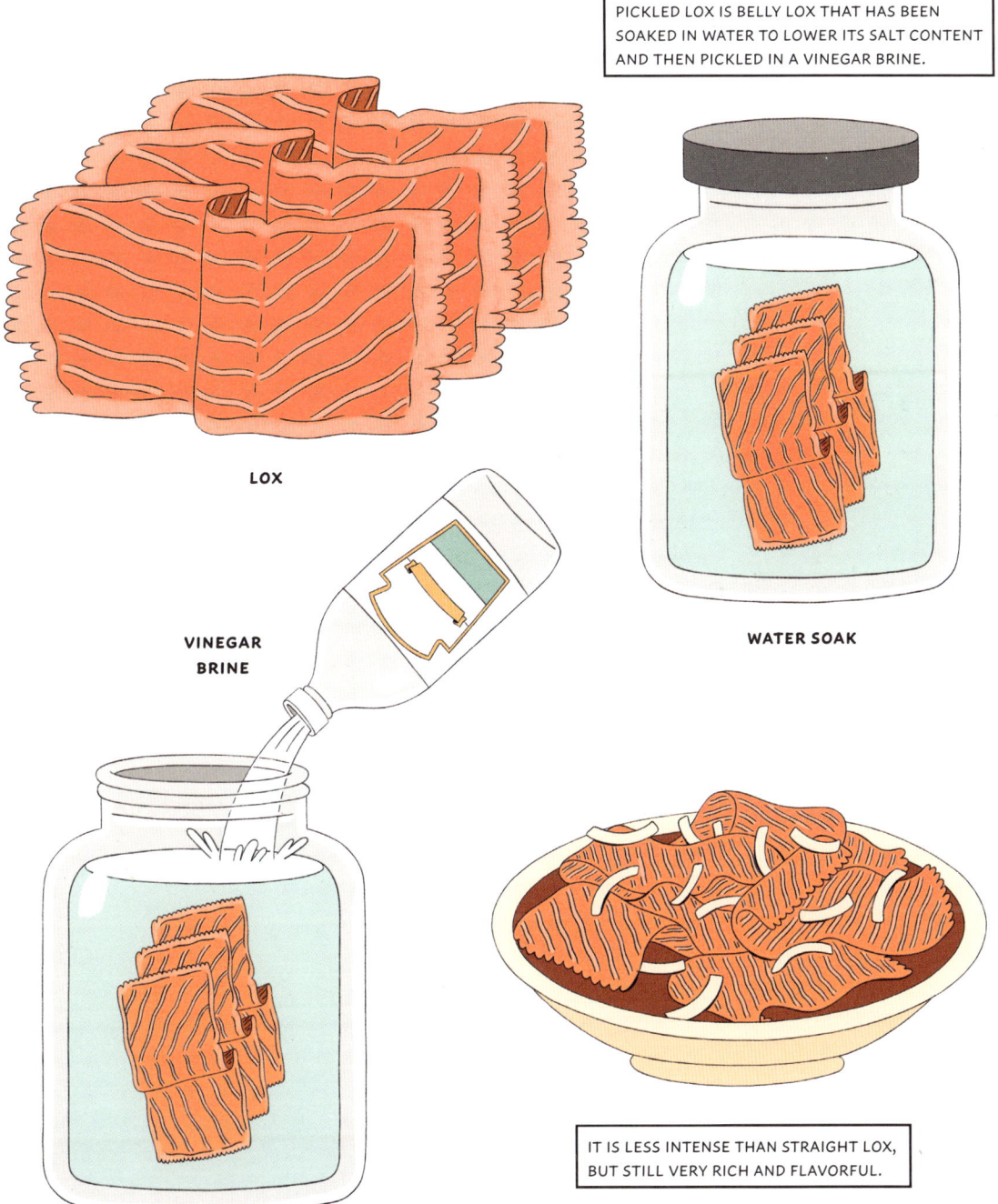

LOX

WATER SOAK

VINEGAR BRINE

IT IS LESS INTENSE THAN STRAIGHT LOX, BUT STILL VERY RICH AND FLAVORFUL.

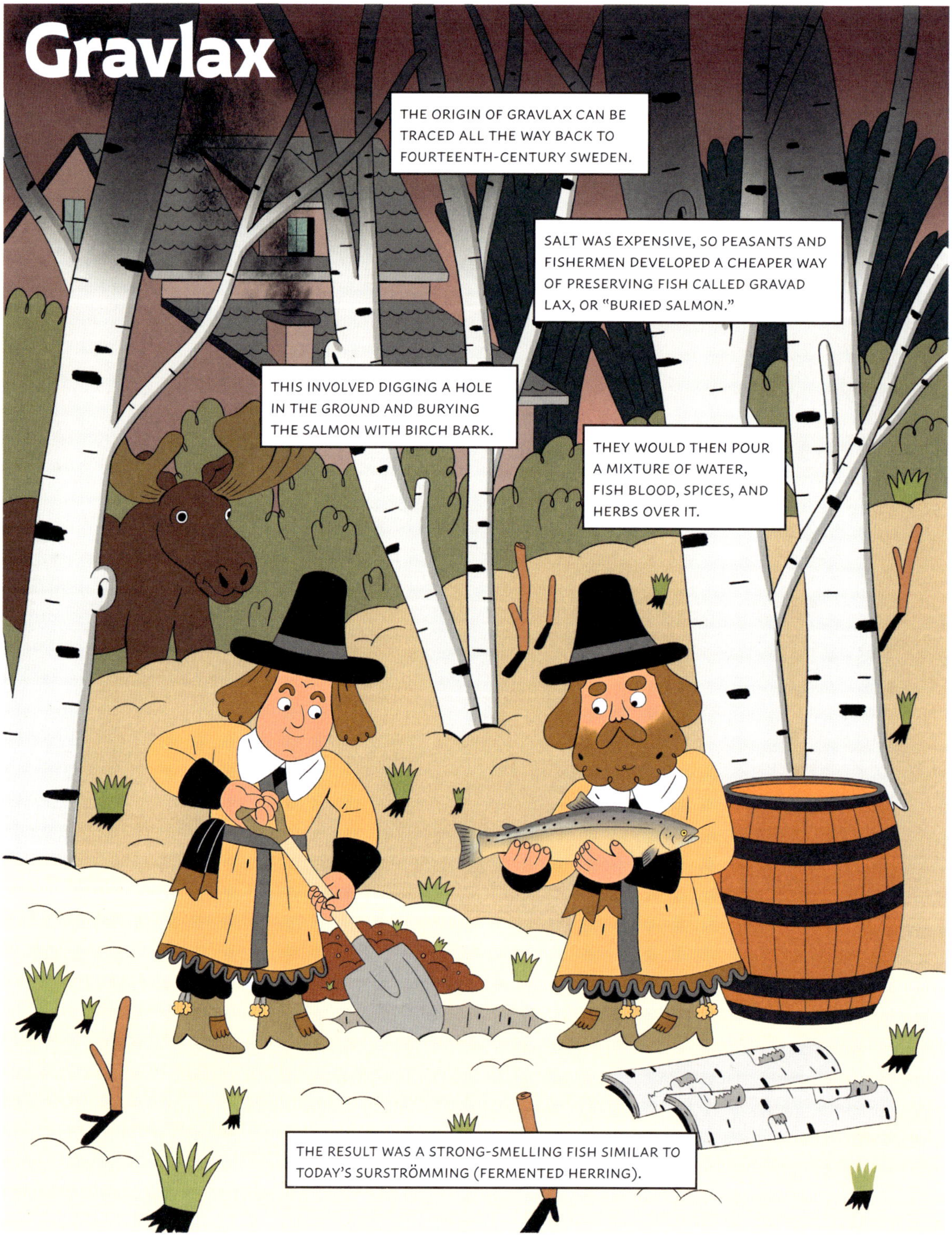
Gravlax
THE ORIGIN OF GRAVLAX CAN BE TRACED ALL THE WAY BACK TO FOURTEENTH-CENTURY SWEDEN.
SALT WAS EXPENSIVE, SO PEASANTS AND FISHERMEN DEVELOPED A CHEAPER WAY OF PRESERVING FISH CALLED GRAVAD LAX, OR "BURIED SALMON."
THIS INVOLVED DIGGING A HOLE IN THE GROUND AND BURYING THE SALMON WITH BIRCH BARK.
THEY WOULD THEN POUR A MIXTURE OF WATER, FISH BLOOD, SPICES, AND HERBS OVER IT.
THE RESULT WAS A STRONG-SMELLING FISH SIMILAR TO TODAY'S SURSTRÖMMING (FERMENTED HERRING).

A QUICK DIGRESSION: SURSTRÖMMING

YES, THE TIN OF SALTY FISH HAS A PUNGENT ODOR, AND, YES, THERE ARE MANY COMPILATIONS ON YOUTUBE OF PEOPLE ATTEMPTING AND FAILING TO CHOKE IT DOWN. BUT IT'S NOT MEANT TO BE CONSUMED STRAIGHT FROM THE CAN.

THOUGH NOT A JEWISH DELICACY, SURSTRÖMMING IS SWEDISH FERMENTED HERRING THAT COULD BE A COUSIN OF SOMETHING YOU'D FIND IN THE DELI.

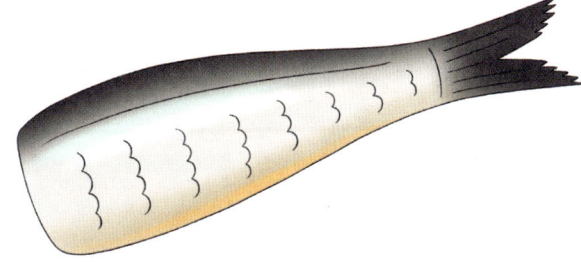

TRADITIONALLY PREPARED, SURSTRÖMMING IS MADE BY FIRST REMOVING THE MEAT OF THE FISH FROM THE SPINE.

IT IS THEN MIXED INTO BOILED POTATOES AND CHOPPED ONIONS BEFORE BEING SPREAD ONTO BUTTERED FLATBREAD.

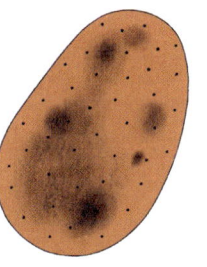

THE TASTE IS COMPARABLE TO SARDINES BUT A BIT STRONGER AND WITH MORE OF A SOUR, FERMENTED FLAVOR.
OK, BACK TO GRAVLAX!

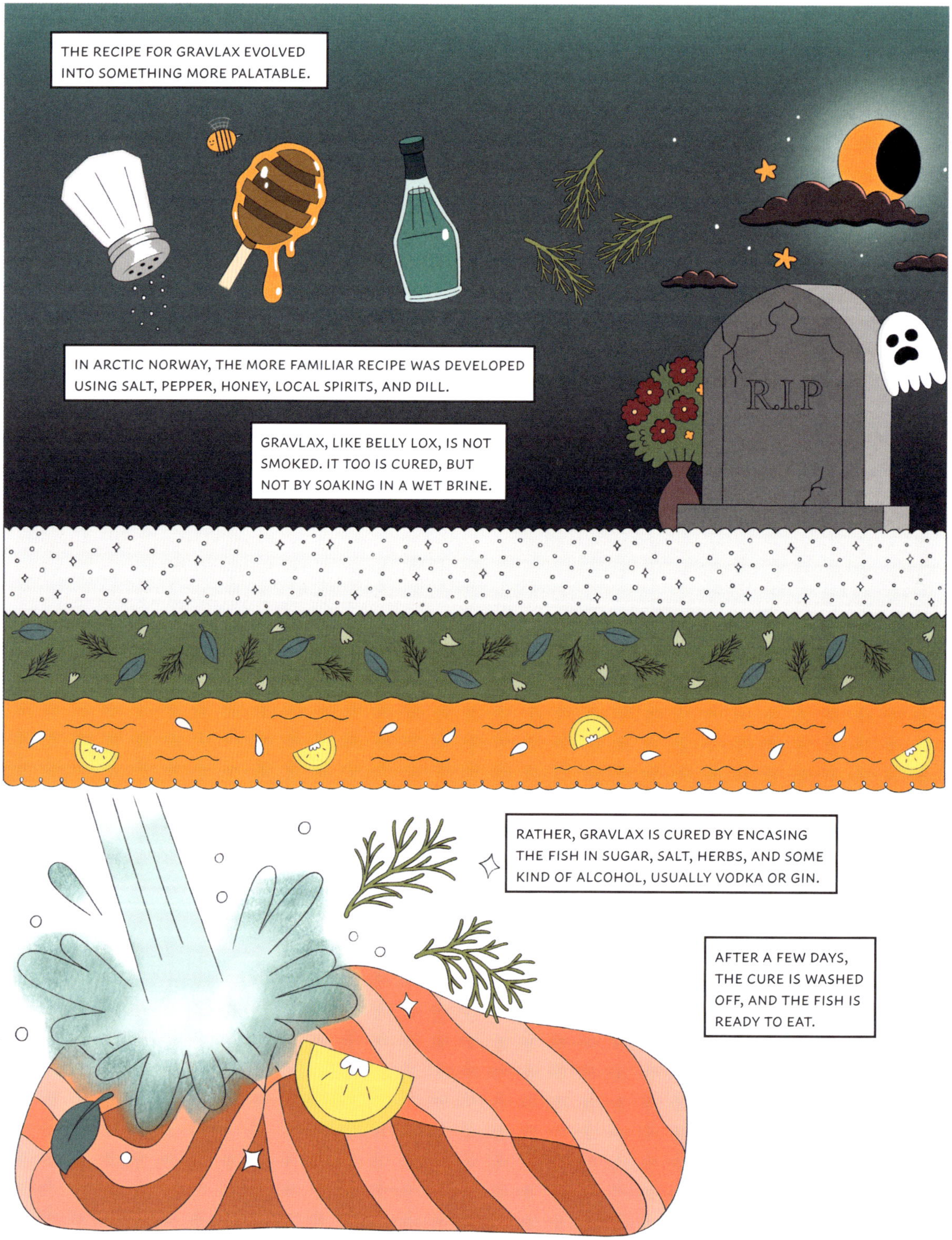
THE RECIPE FOR GRAVLAX EVOLVED INTO SOMETHING MORE PALATABLE.
IN ARCTIC NORWAY, THE MORE FAMILIAR RECIPE WAS DEVELOPED USING SALT, PEPPER, HONEY, LOCAL SPIRITS, AND DILL.
GRAVLAX, LIKE BELLY LOX, IS NOT SMOKED. IT TOO IS CURED, BUT NOT BY SOAKING IN A WET BRINE.
R.I.P
RATHER, GRAVLAX IS CURED BY ENCASING THE FISH IN SUGAR, SALT, HERBS, AND SOME KIND OF ALCOHOL, USUALLY VODKA OR GIN.
AFTER A FEW DAYS, THE CURE IS WASHED OFF, AND THE FISH IS READY TO EAT.

IN APPEARANCE, GRAVLAX LOOKS LIKE REGULAR LOX, BUT IT IS A BIT FIRMER AND DARKER IN COLOR.

BECAUSE OF THE ADDITIONAL INGRE-DIENTS IN THE CURE, GRAVLAX HAS A MORE COMPLEX FLAVOR THAN LOX. IT IS SWEETER AND MORE HERBAL.

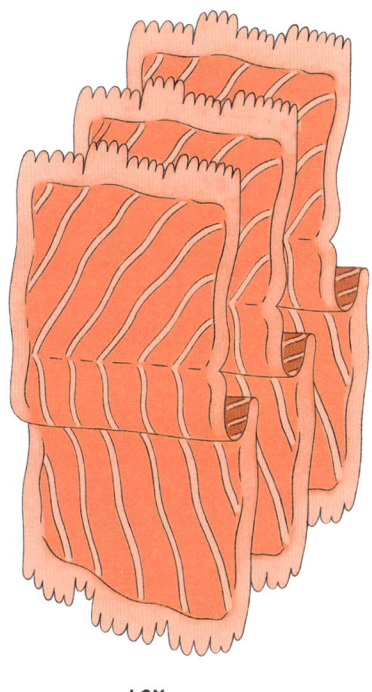

LOX

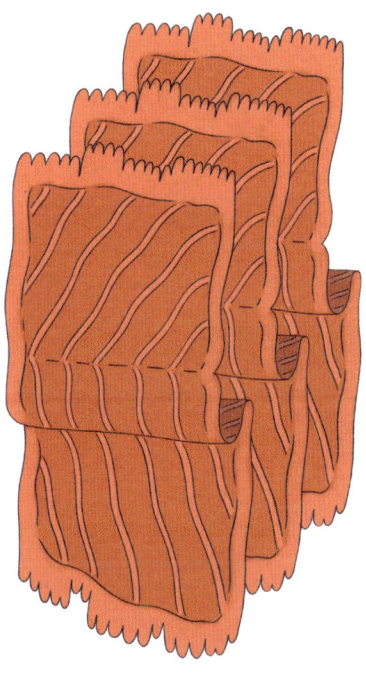

GRAVLOX

TRADITIONAL FLAVORINGS INCLUDE DILL, PEPPER, FENNEL, LEMON, AND JUNIPER BERRIES.

Cold-Smoked Salmon

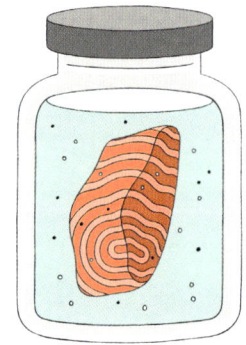

WITH COLD SMOKING, THE SALMON IS FIRST CURED LIKE LOX IN EITHER A DRY OR WET BRINE.

IT IS THEN SMOKED BY BURNING CHERRY, HICKORY, OR OAK WOOD.

BECAUSE A LOW TEMPERATURE IS REQUIRED TO KEEP THE SALMON FROM COOKING, THE FISH DOES NOT SIT DIRECTLY OVER THE WOOD BUT IN A SEPARATE COMPARTMENT, WITH FANS BLOWING SMOKE OVER IT.

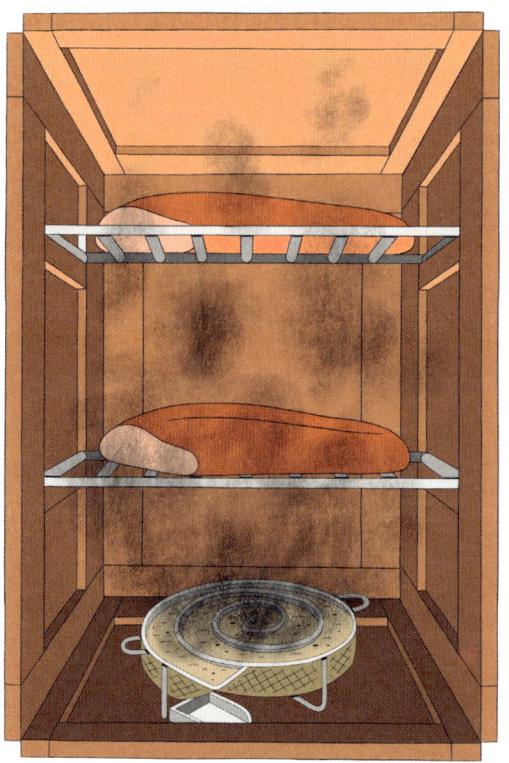

THE RESULT IS A VERY DELICATE TEXTURE AND SMOKY FLAVOR.

NOVA

COLD-SMOKED SALMON CAN COME FROM VARIOUS GEOGRAPHICAL REGIONS BUT MOST COMMONLY FROM THE ATLANTIC COAST.

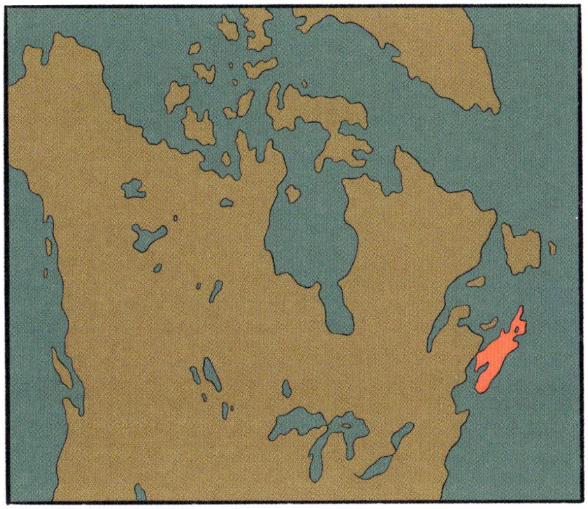

NOVA GETS ITS NAME FROM NOVA SCOTIA, CANADA, WHICH IS WHERE MOST NEW YORK FOOD ESTABLISHMENTS USED TO GET THEIR SALMON.

THE NAME HAS SINCE EVOLVED TO DESCRIBE ANY SALMON THAT HAS BEEN SLIGHTLY CURED LIKE LOX IN EITHER A DRY OR WET BRINE AND THEN COLD-SMOKED.

THE FLAVOR AND TEXTURE OF NOVA DIFFER DEPENDING ON WHERE THE FISH IS FROM.

THE GASPÉ PENINSULA EXTENDS OUT
INTO THE GULF OF SAINT LAWRENCE,
NORTH OF NOVA SCOTIA. THIS IS
THE BIRTHPLACE OF COLD-SMOKED
ATLANTIC SALMON.

NEW BRUNSWICK

GASPÉ NOVA

ATLANTIC SALMON HAS A FATTY AND
MILD SMOKE FLAVOR.

WESTERN NOVA

COLD-SMOKED WILD PACIFIC SALMON
NOVA IS RICHER AND SOFTER THAN GASPÉ
AND MUCH LESS SMOKY.

NORWEGIAN NOVA

NORWEGIAN SALMON IS MILDLY SMOKY AND
LEANER THAN OTHER SALMON.

SCOTTISH NOVA

THE FANCIER SCOTTISH NOVA
IS SMOKED FOR A LONGER
PERIOD OF TIME THAN OTHER
TYPES OF NOVA.

THIS GIVES IT A SOMEWHAT
DRIER TEXTURE. WOOD
CHIPS FROM OLD WHISKEY
BARRELS SMOKE THE FISH.

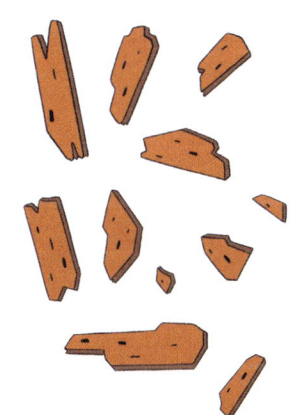

SCOTTISH NOVA TENDS TO BE SILKIER AND MORE OILY THAN
THE OTHER VARIETIES. THE SMOKINESS IS MORE SUBTLE
THAN NORWEGIAN, BUT THE FLESH IS MORE BUTTERY.

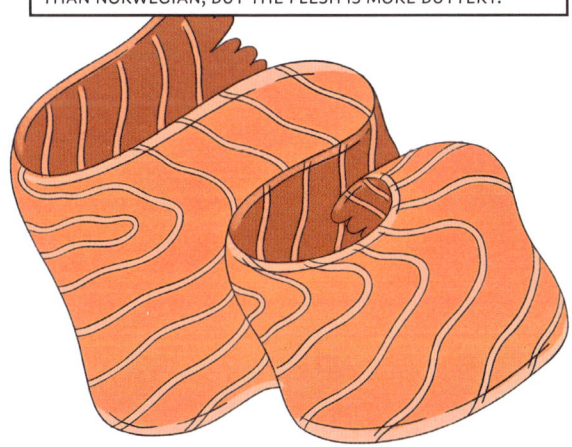

It pays to be a
Scottish fish!

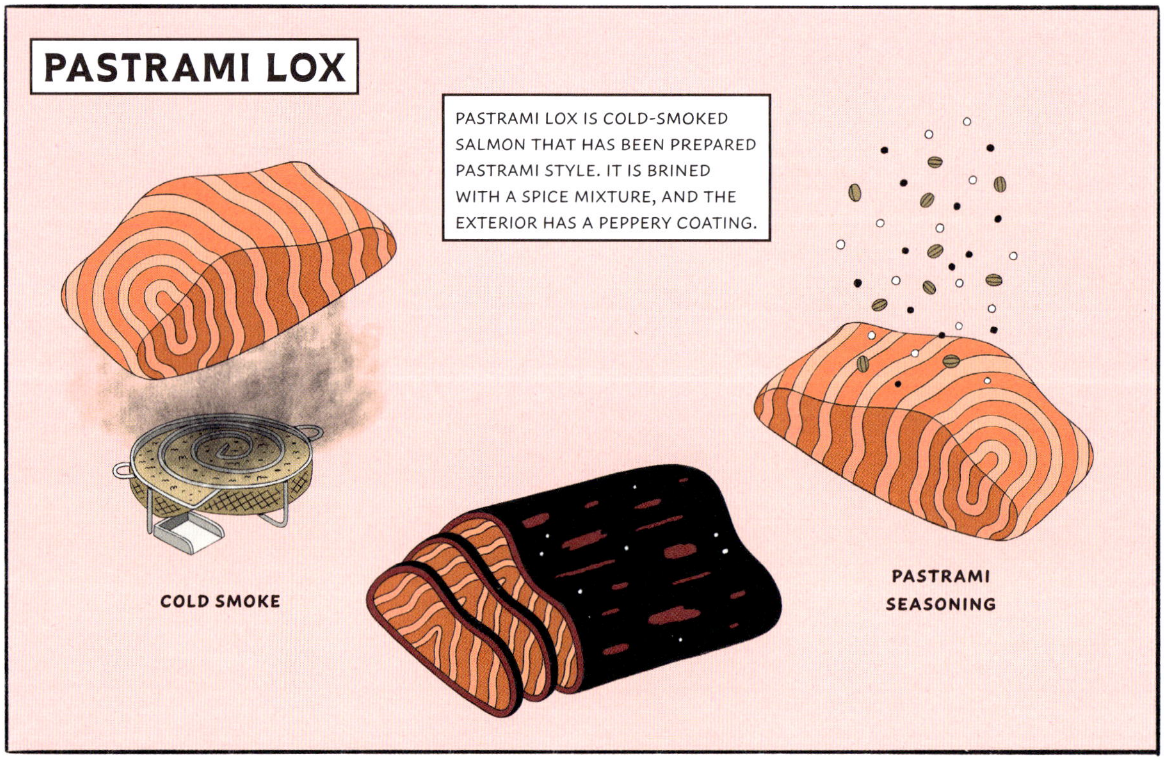
PASTRAMI LOX
PASTRAMI LOX IS COLD-SMOKED SALMON THAT HAS BEEN PREPARED PASTRAMI STYLE. IT IS BRINED WITH A SPICE MIXTURE, AND THE EXTERIOR HAS A PEPPERY COATING.
COLD SMOKE
PASTRAMI SEASONING

Hot-Smoked Fish

SALMON

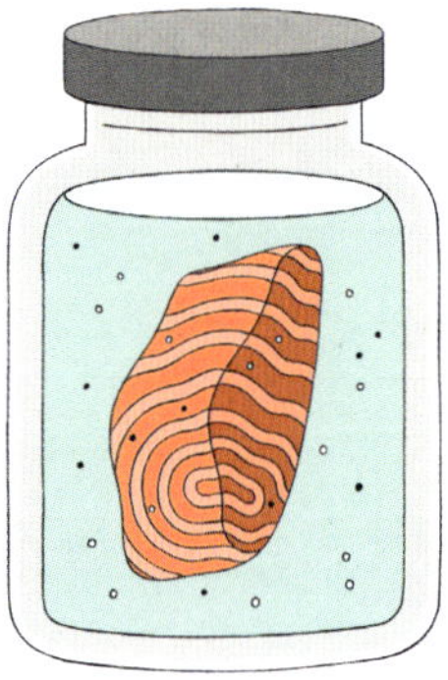

IT IS TRADITIONALLY WET-BRINED AND HOT-SMOKED, DIRECTLY OVER THE WOOD.

WET-BRINED SALMON HAS A FLAKY, COOKED TEXTURE AND A STRONG SMOKY FLAVOR.

BUT NOT ALL SMOKED FISH IS LOX OR NOVA!

HOT-SMOKED SALMON

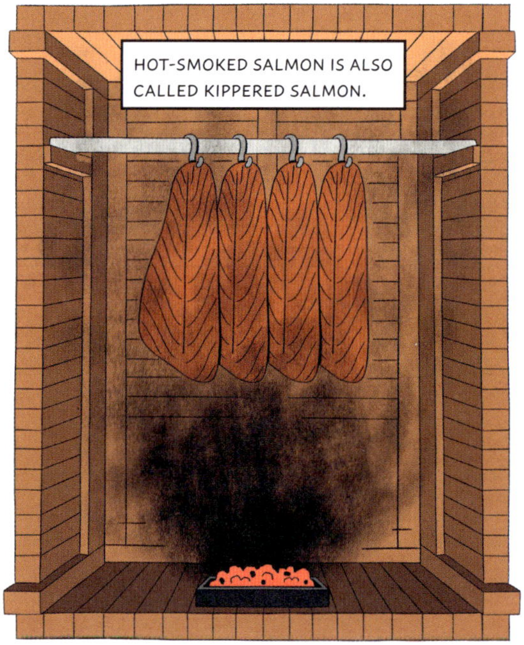
HOT-SMOKED SALMON IS ALSO CALLED KIPPERED SALMON.

SMOKED WHITEFISH

WHITEFISH REFERS TO SEVERAL DIFFERENT SPECIES OF INEXPENSIVE, FRESHWATER FISH.

SMOKED WHITEFISH CAN HAVE A MILD OR STRONG FLAVOR, DEPENDING ON HOW LONG IT HAS SMOKED.

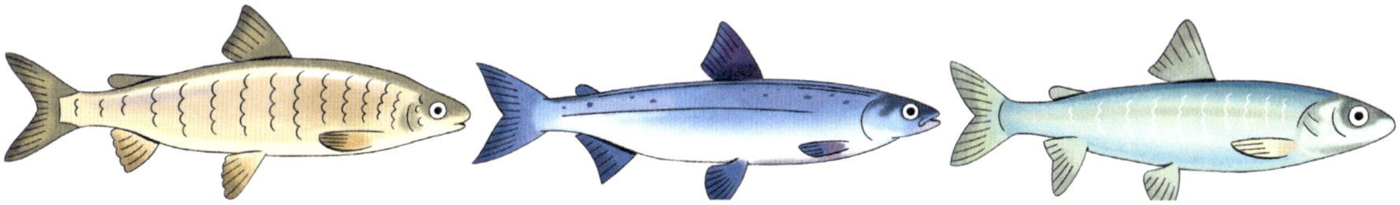
LAKE
ALASKAN
MOUNTAIN

IT IS SOLD EITHER WHOLE OR IN A SPREAD (SCHMEAR) AND IS USUALLY LAKE WHITE-FISH, NATIVE TO THE GREAT LAKES.

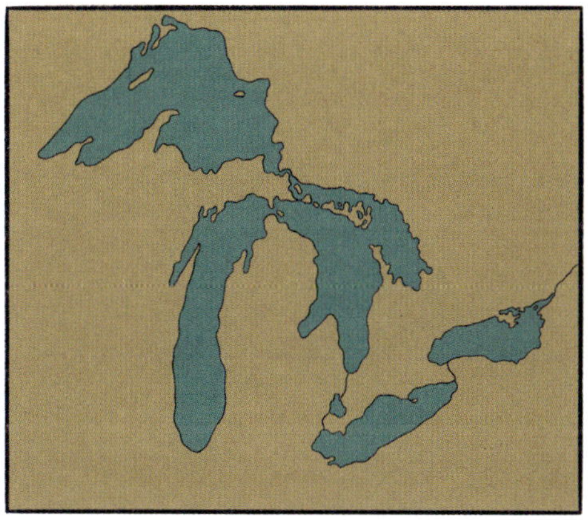

TO MAKE THE SPREAD, THE WHITEFISH FLESH IS SHREDDED INTO SMALL PIECES . . .

AND THEN MIXED WITH MAYONNAISE, SOUR CREAM, DILL, LEMON, AND MUSTARD.

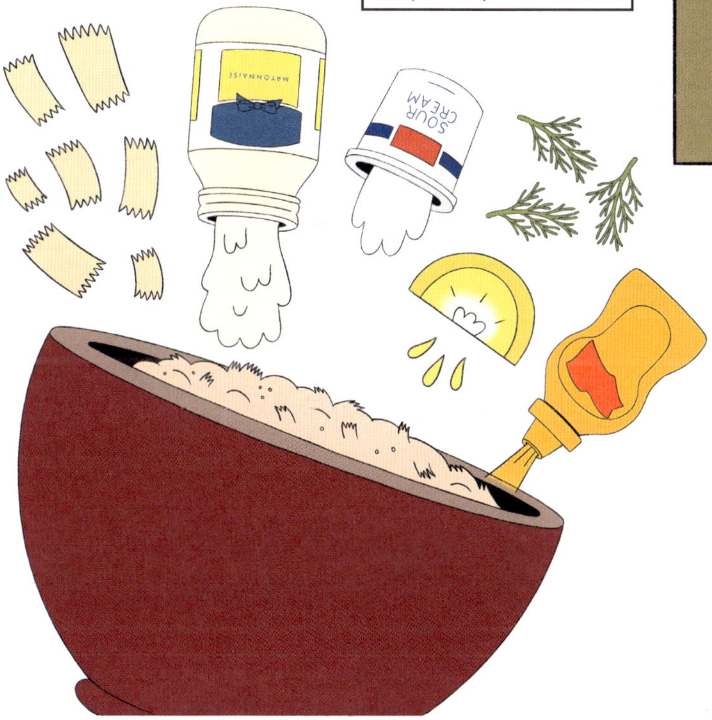

IT CAN BE SERVED ON BAGELS, BIALYS, OR CHALLAH.

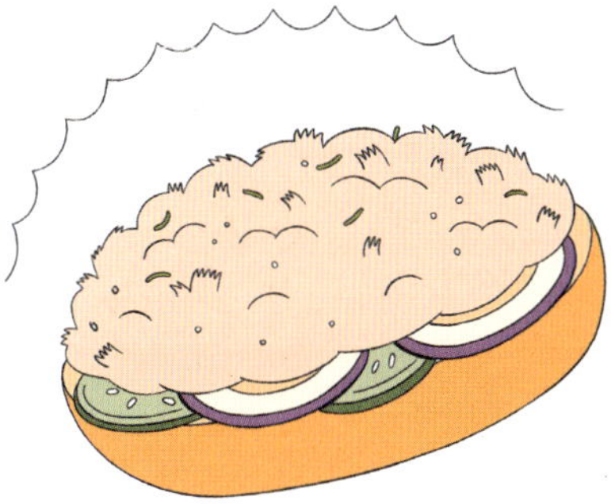

SMOKED STURGEON

STURGEON IS A NORTH AMERICAN FRESHWATER FISH.

IT IS PERHAPS MOST FAMOUS FOR ITS CAVIAR (SALTED ROE OR EGGS).

THE FISH ITSELF IS RICH AND FATTY.

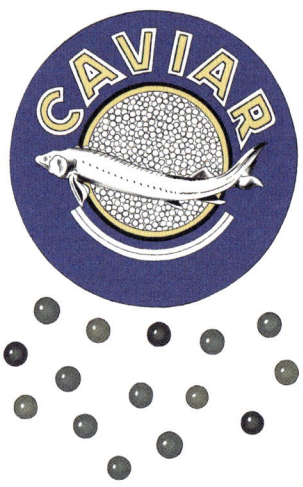

IN THE EIGHTEENTH AND NINETEENTH CENTURIES, STURGEON WAS SO PLENTIFUL IN THE UNITED STATES THAT IT WAS EXPORTED TO EUROPE, ALONG WITH THE CAVIAR.

Why don't we just send the whole fish?

BUT BY THE TWENTIETH CENTURY, OVERFISHING HAD TURNED STURGEON INTO A RARE AND EXPENSIVE DELICACY.

SMOKED STURGEON IS DRY-CURED BEFORE BEING HOT-SMOKED.

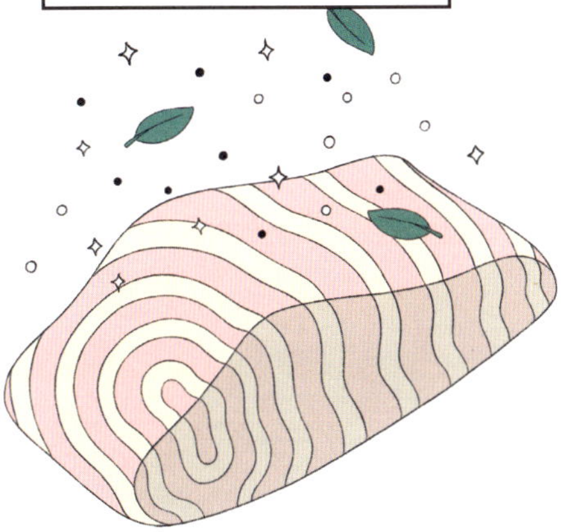

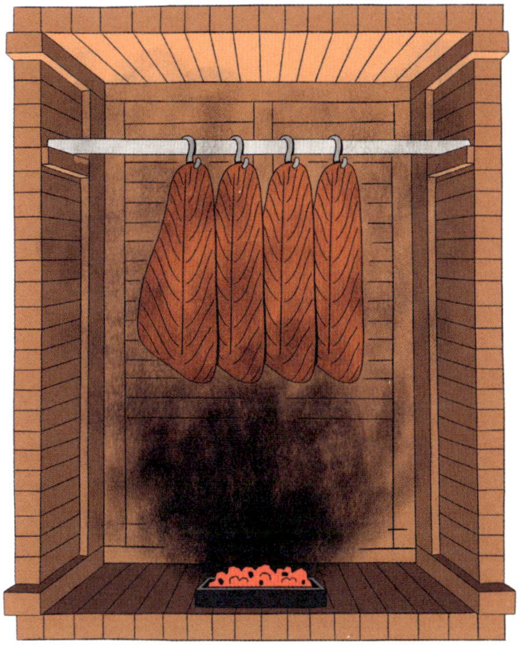

YOU CAN ALSO BUY STURGEON ENDS. BECAUSE THE FISH IS SO FLAKY AFTER BEING SMOKED, IT IS HARD TO SLICE, AND SO LARGE STURGEON PIECES ARE ALSO SOLD SEPARATELY IN CHUNKS.

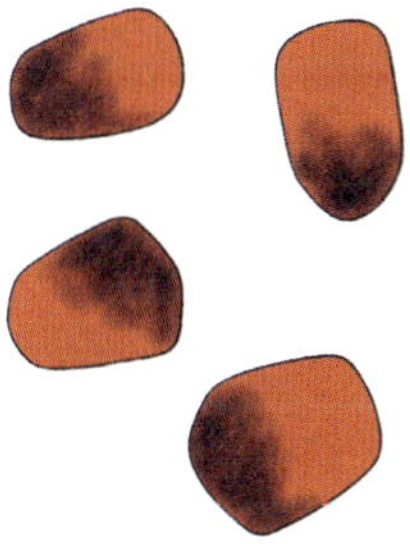

IS STURGEON KOSHER? THE RABBIS HAVE DEBATED THIS FOR A LONG TIME.

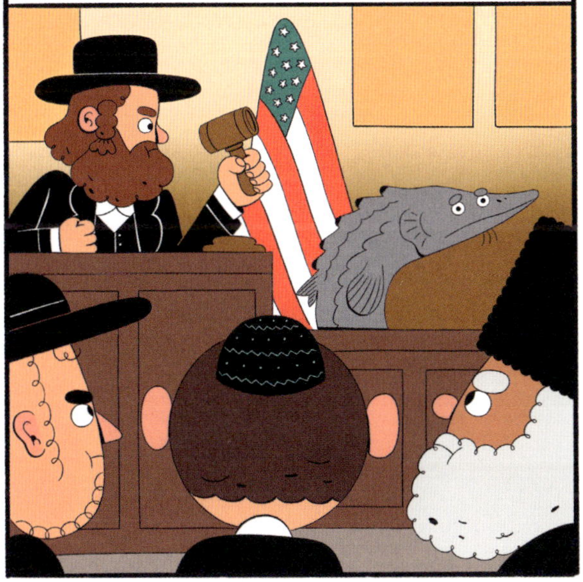

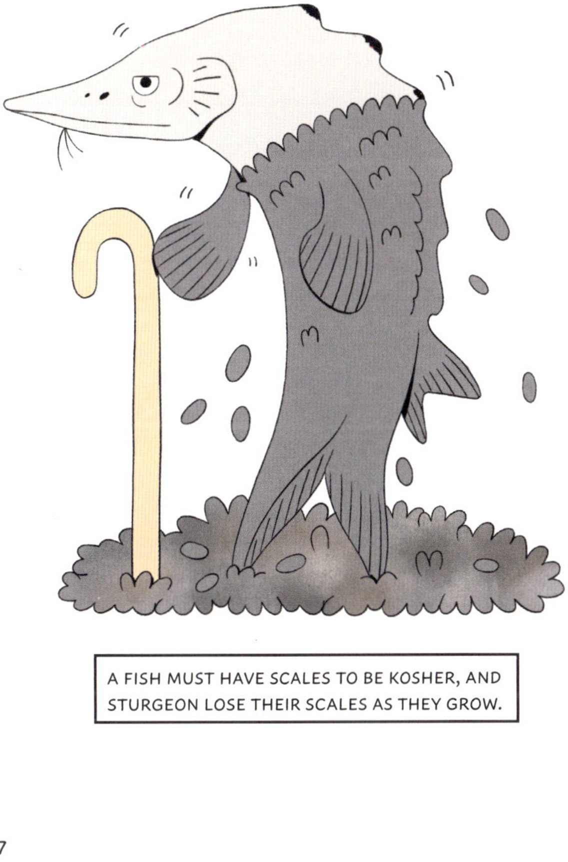

A FISH MUST HAVE SCALES TO BE KOSHER, AND STURGEON LOSE THEIR SCALES AS THEY GROW.

Herring

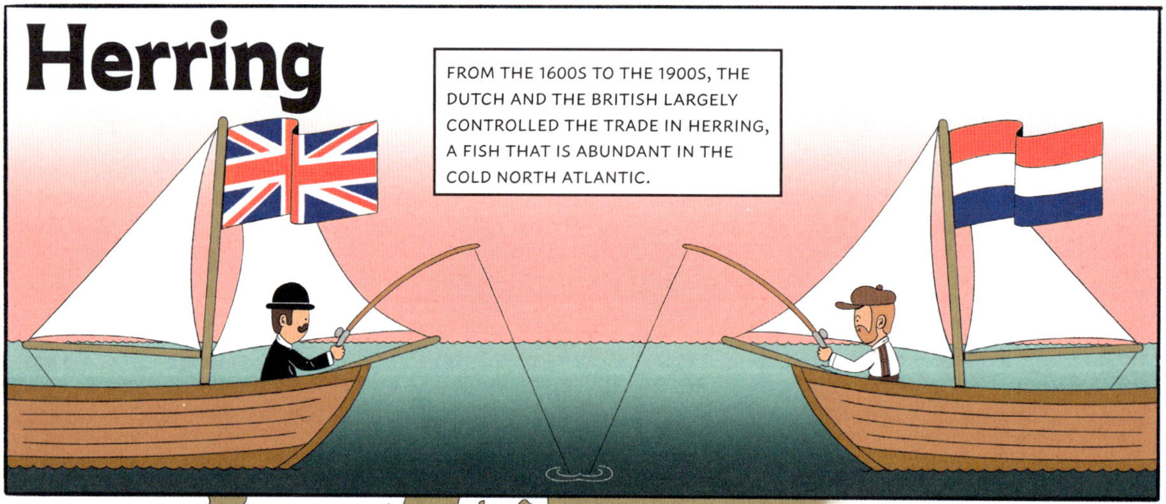
FROM THE 1600S TO THE 1900S, THE DUTCH AND THE BRITISH LARGELY CONTROLLED THE TRADE IN HERRING, A FISH THAT IS ABUNDANT IN THE COLD NORTH ATLANTIC.

HERRING ENTERED THE JEWISH DIET AS FAMILIES MIGRATED EAST FROM FRANCE TO UKRAINE.

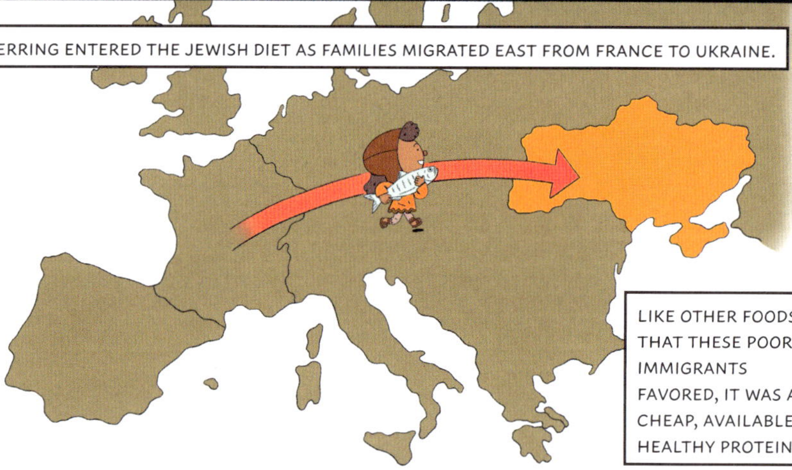

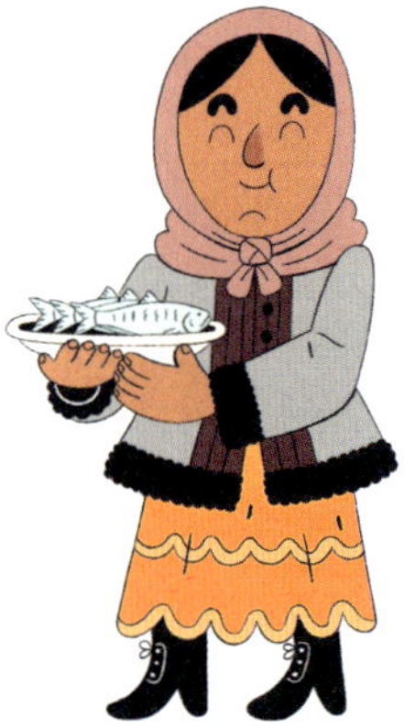

LIKE OTHER FOODS THAT THESE POOR IMMIGRANTS FAVORED, IT WAS A CHEAP, AVAILABLE, HEALTHY PROTEIN.

PICKLED AND PREPARED EITHER IN A SWEET WINE DRESSING OR SOUR CREAM, HERRING HAS BECOME A POPULAR DISH ON JEWISH HOLIDAYS: FROM KIDDUSH ON SHABBAT (JEWISH SABBATH) TO THE BRIS (CIRCUMCISION CEREMONY) TO WEDDINGS AND FUNERALS.

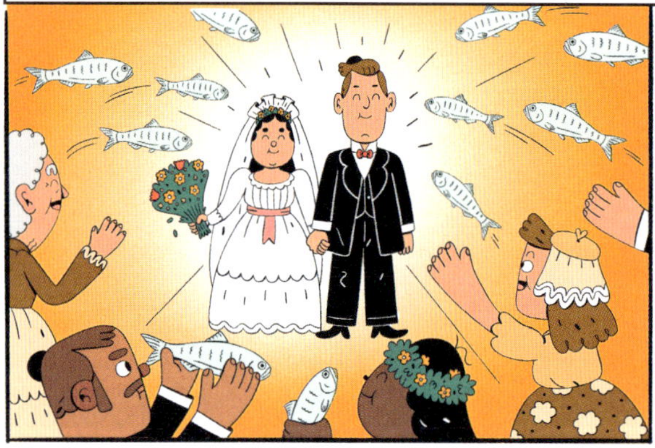

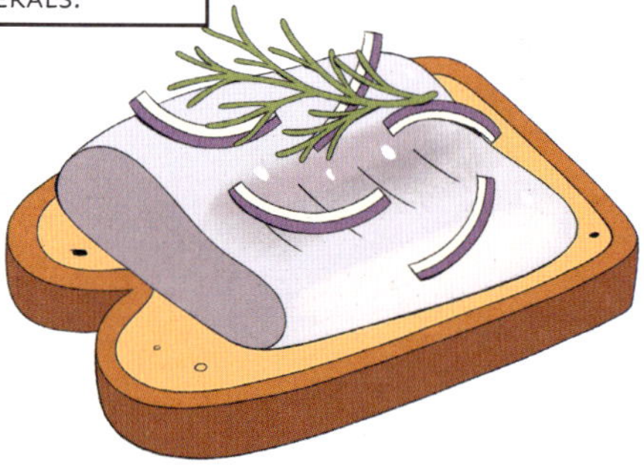

HERRING CAN BE EATEN STRAIGHT UP, ON BREAD, OR, LIKE WHITEFISH, AS A CHOPPED SALAD OR SCHMEAR.

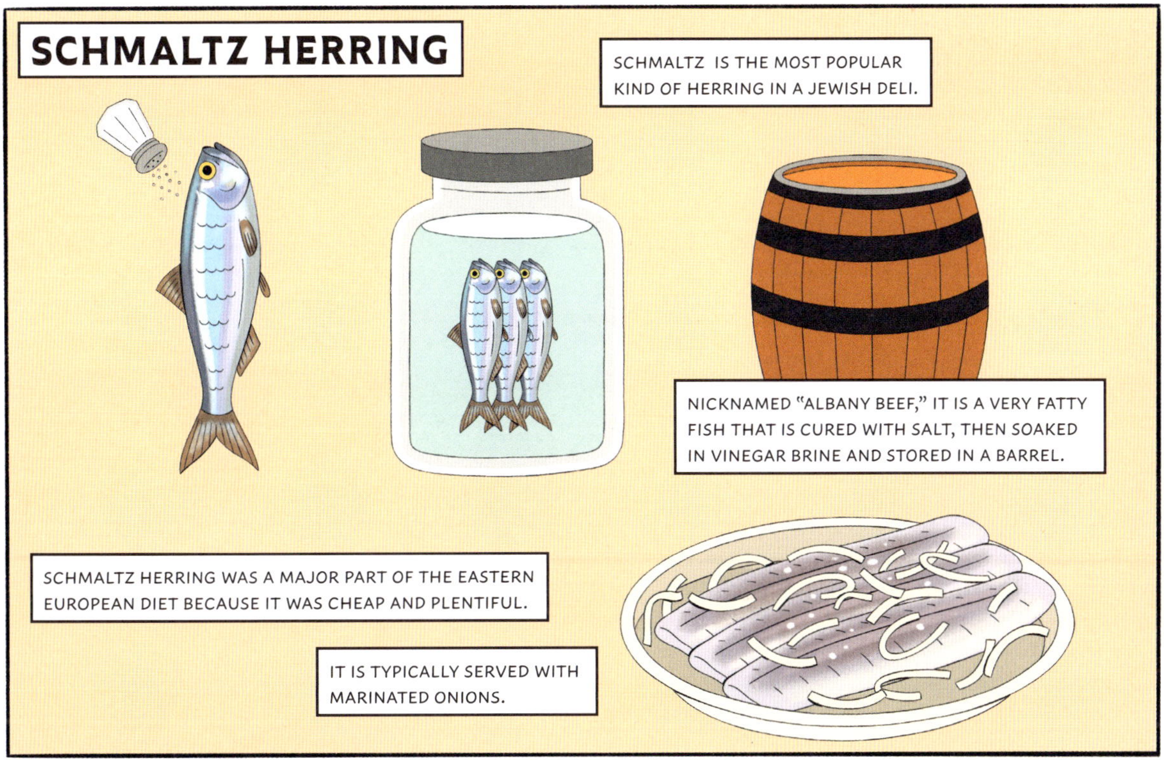
SCHMALTZ HERRING
SCHMALTZ IS THE MOST POPULAR KIND OF HERRING IN A JEWISH DELI.
NICKNAMED "ALBANY BEEF," IT IS A VERY FATTY FISH THAT IS CURED WITH SALT, THEN SOAKED IN VINEGAR BRINE AND STORED IN A BARREL.
SCHMALTZ HERRING WAS A MAJOR PART OF THE EASTERN EUROPEAN DIET BECAUSE IT WAS CHEAP AND PLENTIFUL.
IT IS TYPICALLY SERVED WITH MARINATED ONIONS.

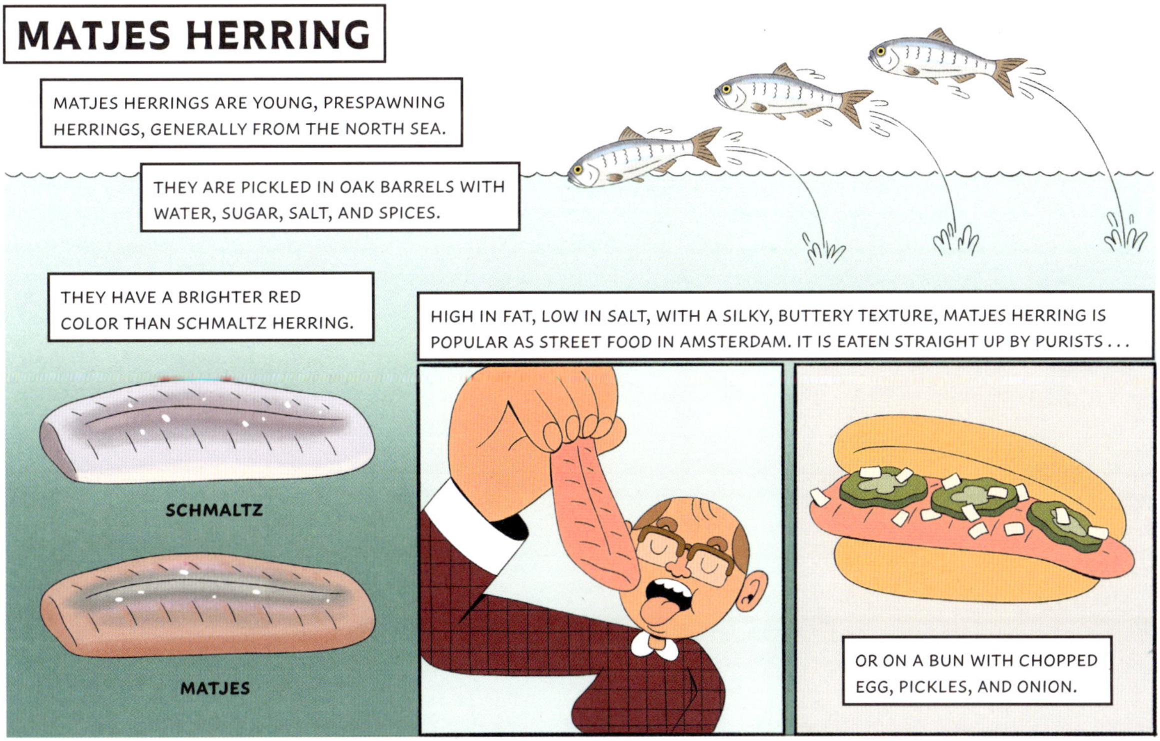
MATJES HERRING
MATJES HERRINGS ARE YOUNG, PRESPAWNING HERRINGS, GENERALLY FROM THE NORTH SEA.
THEY ARE PICKLED IN OAK BARRELS WITH WATER, SUGAR, SALT, AND SPICES.
THEY HAVE A BRIGHTER RED COLOR THAN SCHMALTZ HERRING.
SCHMALTZ
MATJES
HIGH IN FAT, LOW IN SALT, WITH A SILKY, BUTTERY TEXTURE, MATJES HERRING IS POPULAR AS STREET FOOD IN AMSTERDAM. IT IS EATEN STRAIGHT UP BY PURISTS . . .
OR ON A BUN WITH CHOPPED EGG, PICKLES, AND ONION.

Sablefish

SABLEFISH, OR BLACK COD (NOT RELATED TO COD), COMES FROM DEEP IN THE NORTHERN PACIFIC OCEAN.

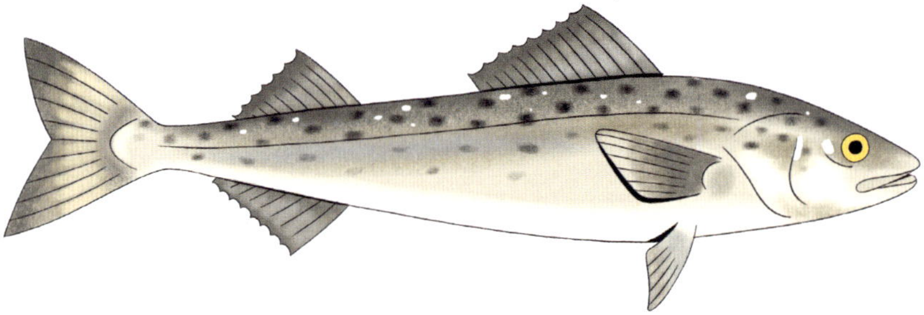

IT USED TO BE A PLENTIFUL AND CHEAP ALTERNATIVE TO STURGEON, BUT NOWADAYS SABLEFISH IS MORE EXPENSIVE BECAUSE OF THE HIGH DEMAND IN JAPAN.

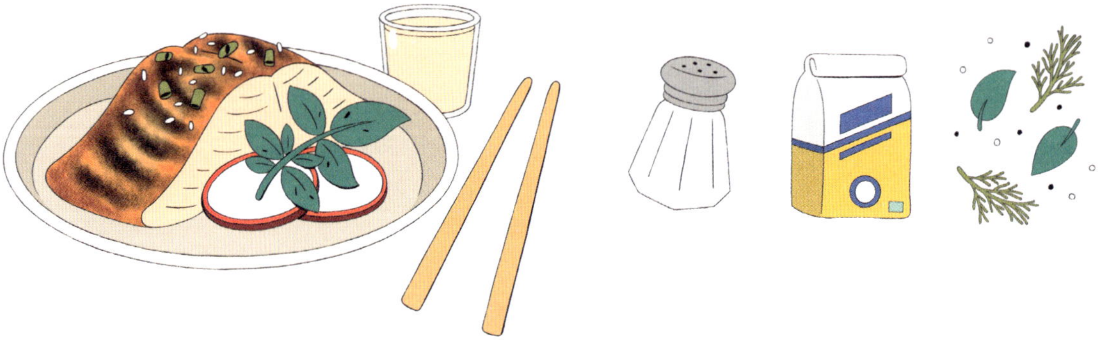

IT IS RICH AND FATTY LIKE SALMON, BUT HAS A MILDER FLAVOR.

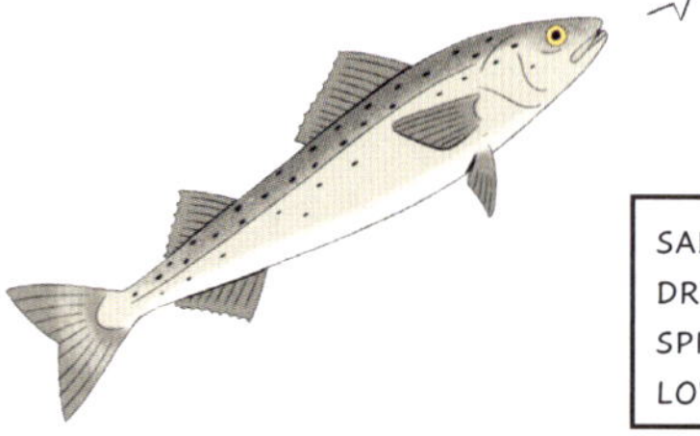

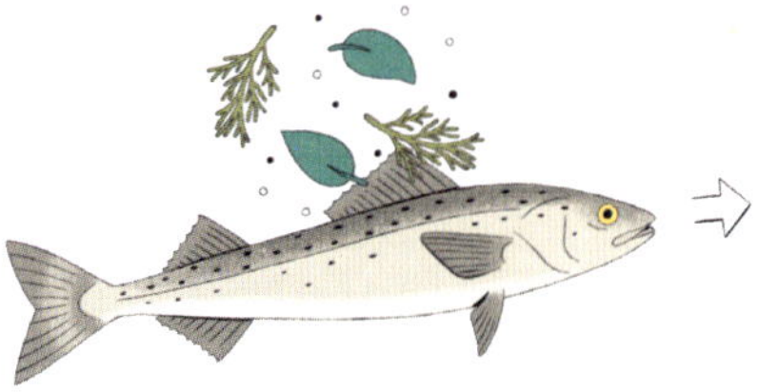

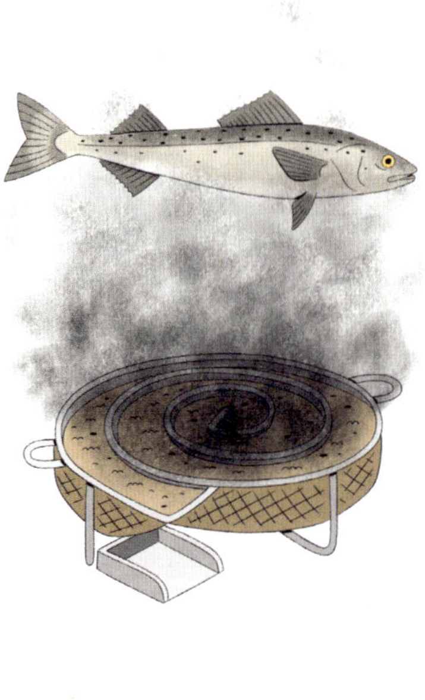

SABLEFISH IS PREPARED WITH A DRY CURE OF SALT, SUGAR, AND SPICES AND THEN SMOKED AT A LOW TEMPERATURE.

Caviar

CAVIAR (MOST LIKELY FROM THE MEDIEVAL GREEK *KHAVIARI*) IS FISH EGGS, OR ROE, CURED WITH SALT.

CAVIAR ORIGINALLY CAME ONLY FROM FEMALE STURGEON, BUT THE TERM HAS SINCE COME TO MEAN EGGS FROM MANY TYPES OF FISH, INCLUDING SALMON AND TROUT.

STURGEON

SALMON

TROUT

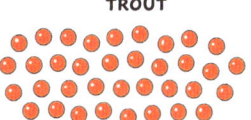

THE FIRST RECORD OF CAVIAR IS DOCUMENTED BY ARISTOTLE, THE ANCIENT GREEK PHILOSOPHER. HE DESCRIBES EATING AND ENJOYING STURGEON EGGS.

What a wise delicacy!

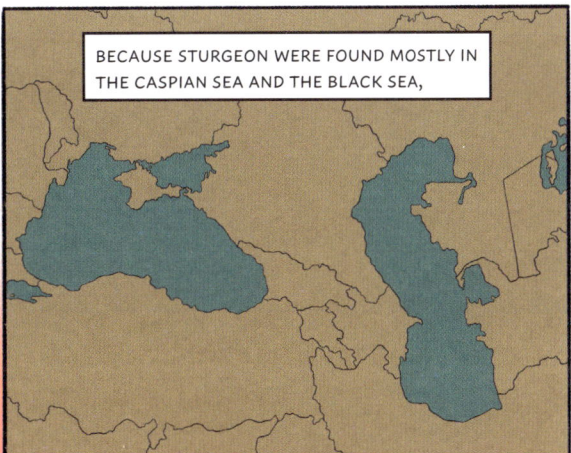

BECAUSE STURGEON WERE FOUND MOSTLY IN THE CASPIAN SEA AND THE BLACK SEA,

CAVIAR WAS ESPECIALLY POPULAR IN RUSSIA, WHERE IT ENTERED THE CULINARY CUSTOMS OF THE ORTHODOX CHURCH.

BY THE END OF THE NINETEENTH CENTURY, THE FRENCH WERE IMPORTING HIGH-QUALITY BELUGA CAVIAR FROM RUSSIA. IT WAS PRIZED BY ROYALTY AS A RARE AND EXPENSIVE DELICACY.

THE CAVIAR ORIGINALLY BROUGHT HERE BY GERMAN IMMIGRANTS WAS A MORE AFFORDABLE VARIETY.

AMERICA SOON BECAME A LEADING IMPORTER OF WHAT WAS CALLED RUSSIAN CAVIAR, ALTHOUGH MUCH OF IT WAS ACTUALLY HARVESTED FROM STURGEON IN THE ATLANTIC OCEAN .

A CAVIAR BOOM EVENTUALLY LED TO OVERFISHING. WILD STURGEON IN THE CASPIAN SEA BECAME RARE, MAKING BELUGA CAVIAR NEARLY IMPOSSIBLE TO FIND AND VERY EXPENSIVE.

SINCE THEN, CAVIAR HAS COME FROM SUS-TAINABLE FARM-RAISED STURGEON. IT IS ALSO MADE FROM THE ROE OF OTHER, MORE PLENTIFUL FISH, INCLUDING

PADDLEFISH, **HACKLEBACK**, **ATLANTIC SALMON**, AND **TROUT**.

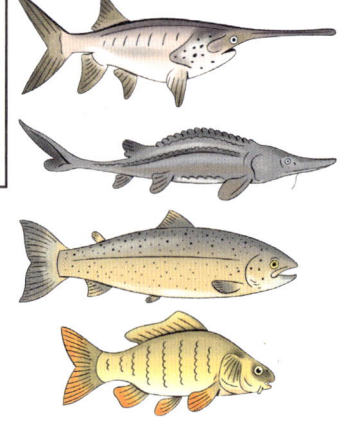

THIS HAS LED TO CHEAPER CAVIAR THAT CAN BE ENJOYED BY MORE PEOPLE, NOT JUST RICH KINGS.

HERE IS HOW CAVIAR IS MADE

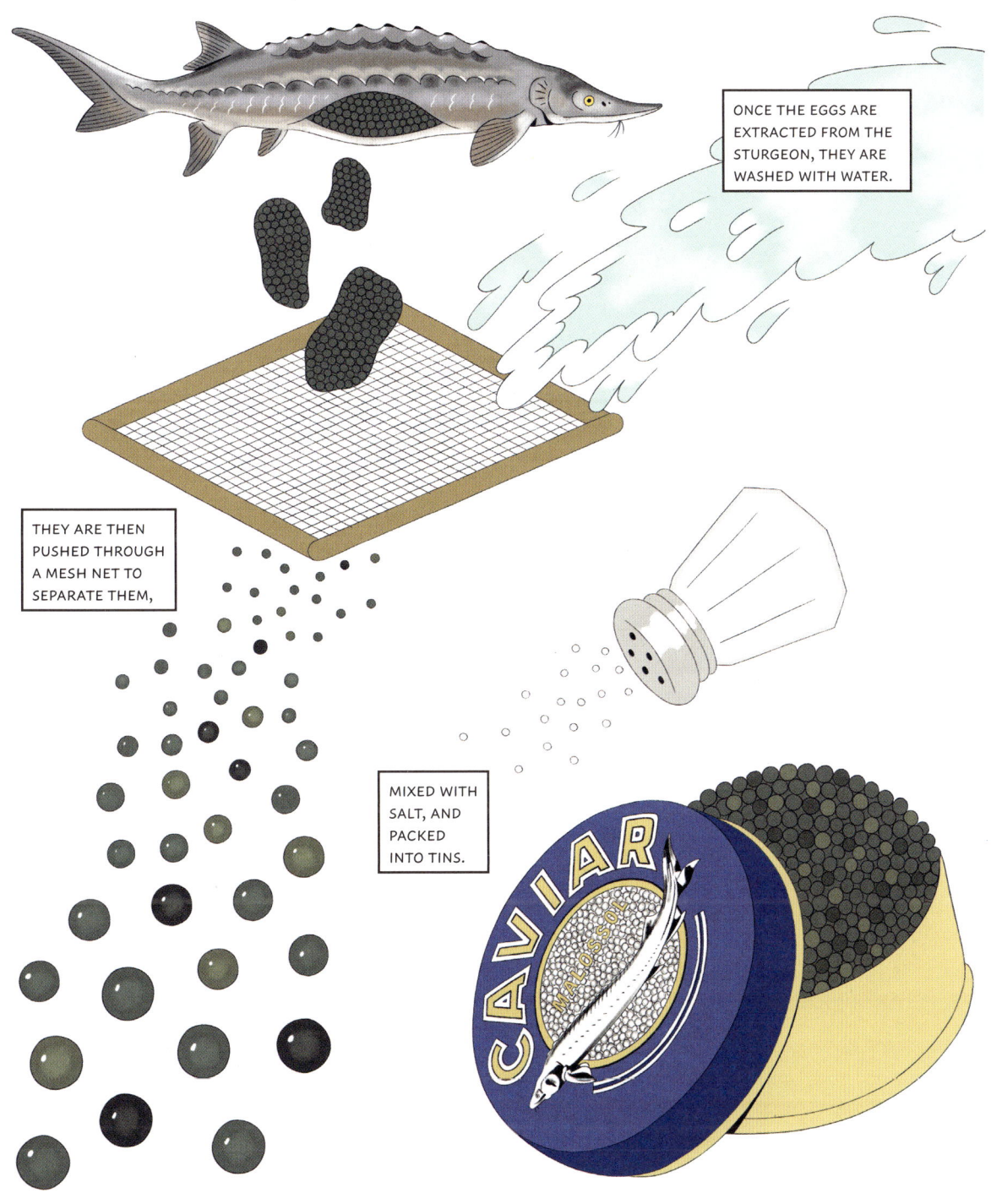

ONCE THE EGGS ARE EXTRACTED FROM THE STURGEON, THEY ARE WASHED WITH WATER.

THEY ARE THEN PUSHED THROUGH A MESH NET TO SEPARATE THEM,

MIXED WITH SALT, AND PACKED INTO TINS.

CAVIAR

MALOSSOL

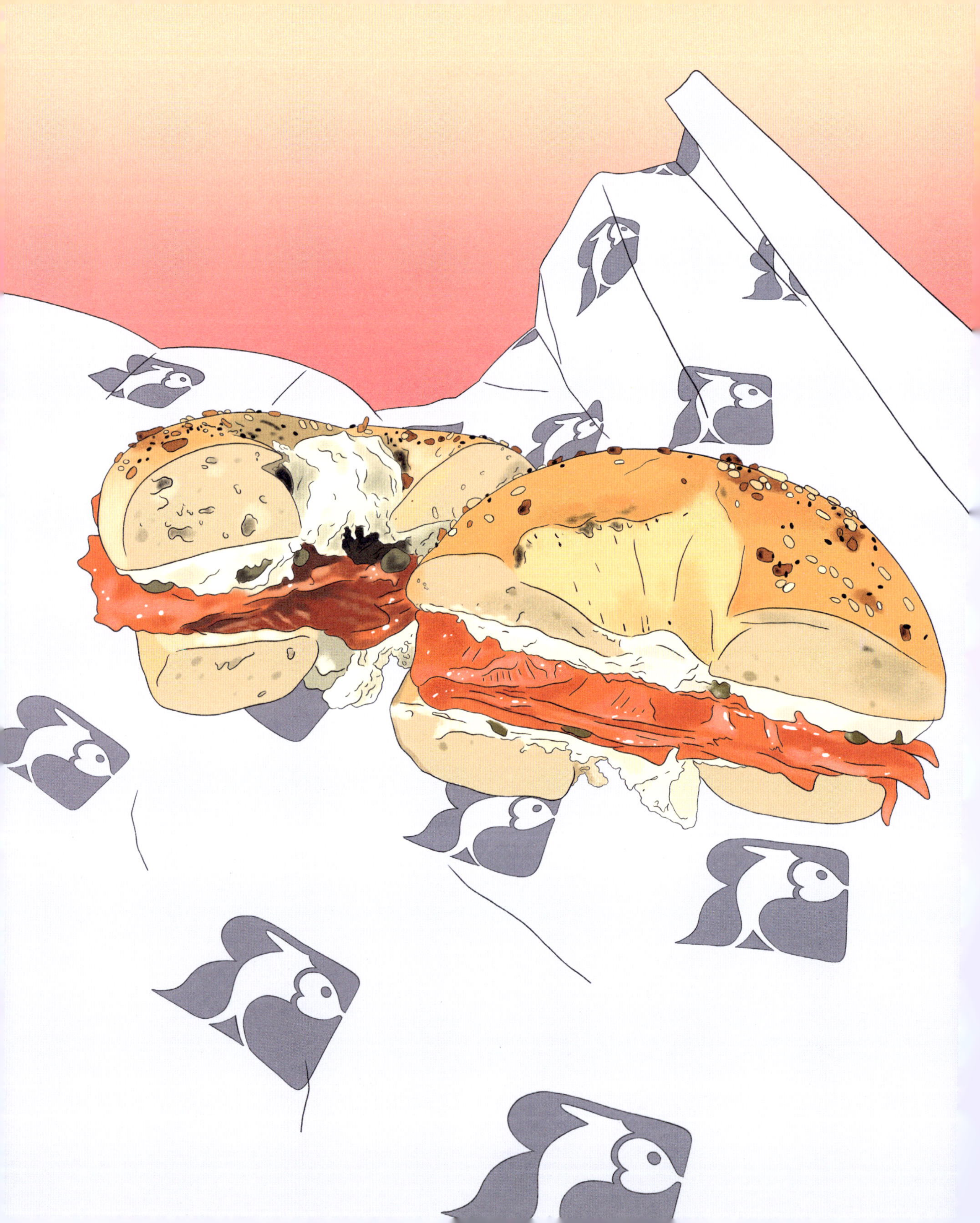

The Bagel and Lox Sandwich

Working on a book about Jewish deli food is really just an excuse to eat a ton of bagel and lox sandwiches, my favorite food in the world. For me, they evoke long celebratory hours: the brunch after a wedding or graduation, the table full of food when Grandpa comes into the city, the lazy hungover mornings in the park with a large iced coffee.

Before I dig into the Classic sandwich at Russ & Daughters, with Gaspé Nova and your choice of bagel and cream cheese, I'm struck by the proportions. Too often the story of bagel and smoked salmon sandwiches is one of "too much." The bagel is too big and doughy, or piled with too much salmon, or slathered in so much cream cheese that it's erupting from the hole. The Classic, however, is a confident sandwich, proportionate, with fine layers of translucent, unctuous salmon between reasonable schmears of cream cheese. It is a testament to a century of fine-tuning.

I suppose you could choose a different kind of salmon, but Gaspé Nova hits all the right notes in balance. It's rich and buttery, unbelievably smooth, with a hint of smokiness.

Like the pastrami on rye at Katz's, the point of this sandwich is to highlight the incredible quality of the main ingredient, and in this it succeeds brilliantly. The bagel provides just the right amount of chew, and the natural creaminess and slight tang of the cream cheese imbues the sandwich with additional richness and moistness to accentuate the starring role of the fish.

The trifecta of classic bagel sandwich accompaniments consists of tomato, red onion, and capers, which add acid and salt, but with the fish as good as it is at Russ & Daughters, these additions may seem like distractions. The same goes for optional extras such as cucumber, dill, or lemon—but to each their own taste. I find myself excited by the cream cheese varieties and sometimes go for the scallion option for an added texture. But here, and in general, when ingredients are top quality, the mantra that best applies is "Keep it simple."

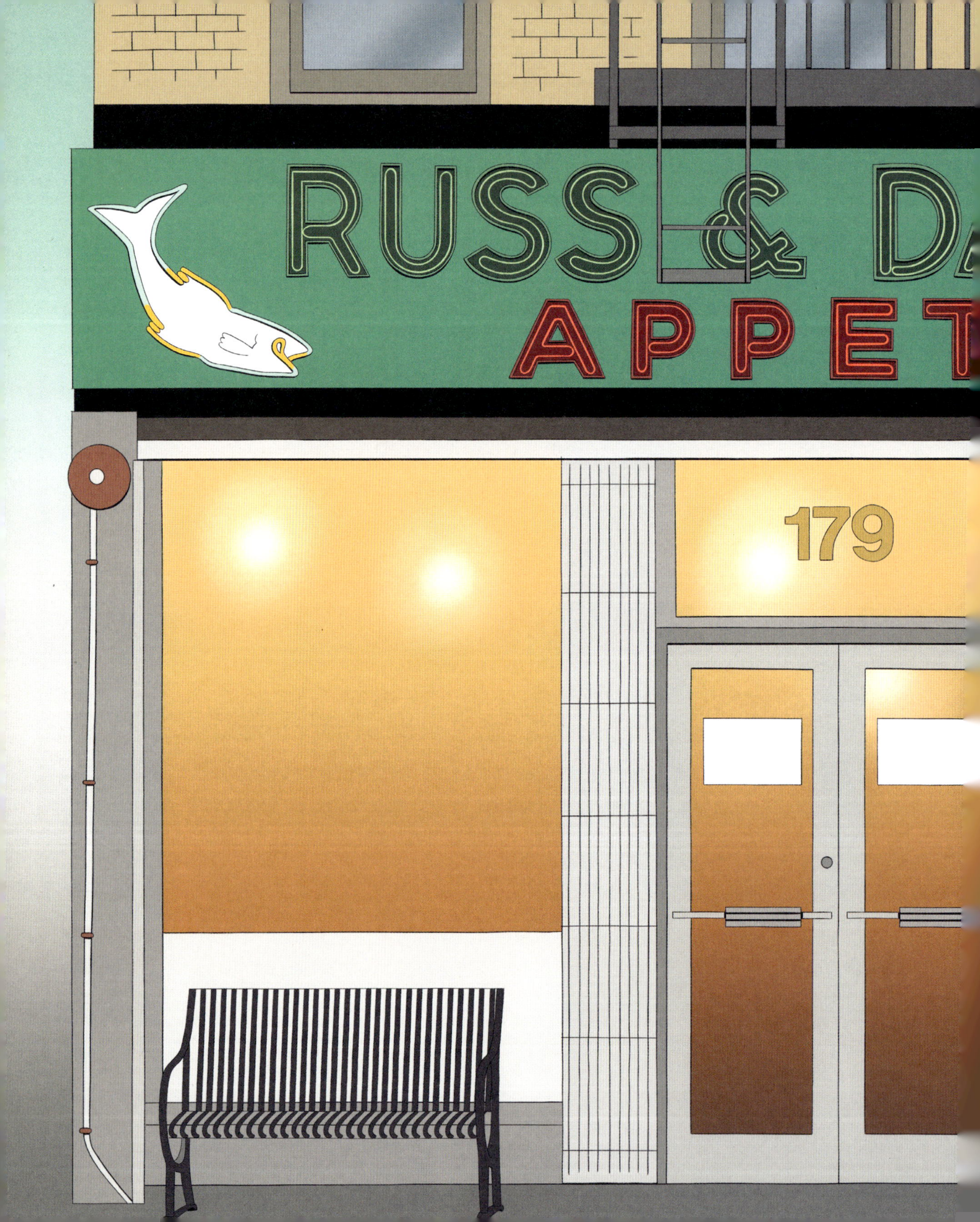
RUSS & DA
APPET
179

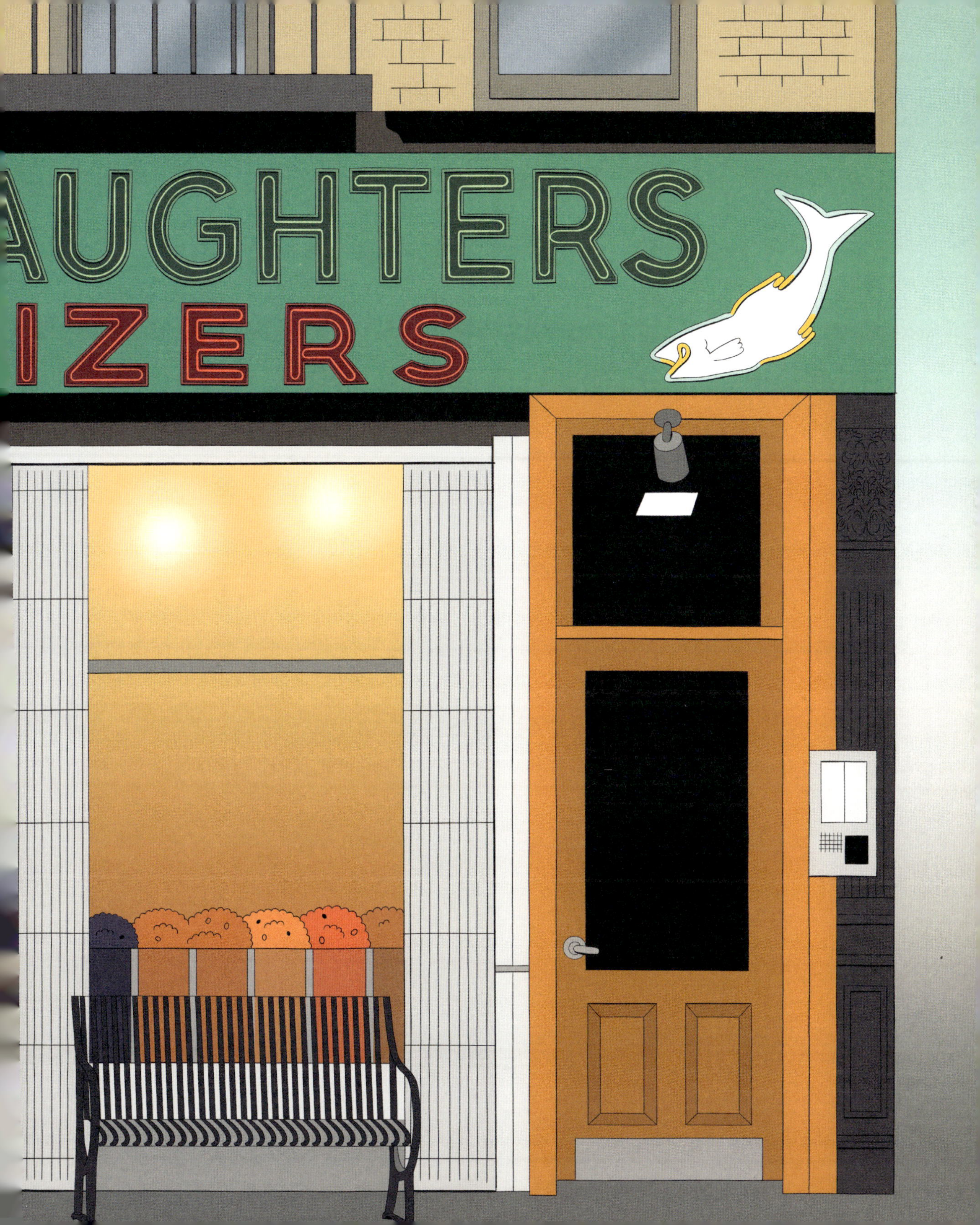
AUGHTERS
IZERS

RUSS & DAUGHTERS

The Shop
179 East Houston Street,
Manhattan, New York City

The Cafe
127 Orchard Street,
Manhattan, New York City

Brooklyn
141 Flushing Avenue,
Brooklyn, New York City

Joel Russ immigrated to the United States from Poland in 1907, with help from his sister. To pay her back, he sold schmaltz herring from a pushcart in the streets of the Lower East Side. He eventually opened up a candy store in Brooklyn. In 1914, he sold the candy store, returned to the Lower East Side, and opened J.R. Russ Cut Rate Appetizers on Orchard Street. In 1923, Russ moved the store to East Houston Street, where it remains today. Russ & Daughters sells fish, bagels, sweets, canned goods, and more, from the original appetizing store, a sit-down cafe on Orchard Street, and their Brooklyn counter.

Interview with Niki Russ Federman, Co-owner of Russ & Daughters

Could you explain in basic terms the distinction between a Jewish deli and an appetizing store?

It's no coincidence that Katz's Delicatessen and Russ & Daughters' appetizing store are one block apart from each other, because both places represent sister but distinct food traditions. These were born out of Jewish dietary laws and the arrival of Eastern European Jewish immigrants mostly to New York through Ellis Island. In kashrut law, meat and dairy cannot be purchased or eaten together, and so two different types of shops popped up. The delicatessen is for meat products, think corned beef and pastrami, and the appetizing store is where you go for fish and dairy, so think smoked fish and creamed cheese and bagels and herring.

Once the Jewish diaspora spread across America, the distinction between Jewish deli and appetizing [store] started to fade, and the deli became a catchall because people just wanted to go to one place. But we never strayed [from] being an appetizing store, making and preserving the appetizing tradition. Russ & Daughters is one of the last remaining true appetizing businesses, and it's emblematic of what the classic appetizing store is.

Why do you think so many appetizing stores have struggled to keep it going while Russ & Daughters has managed to hold steady?

First and foremost, it's our quality, because if we weren't known as the place with the best quality, we would not be able to survive more than one hundred years. And Russ & Daughters has stayed relevant and meaningful to each generation, both from within our family and to our customers. My father was raised to be the good Jewish son who became a professional—he became a lawyer. But after practicing law for many years, he chose to come back and run Russ & Daughters.

The first and second generations did this work in this new country so that their children and their grandchildren could do something "better." In our fourth generation, my cousin Josh and I, independently of one another, decided to make this our path. Everything we do is sort of guided by the intention or hope that someone in the fifth generation is going to step up and say that this is their path.

Now we can't guarantee that, but it's a hope. The younger generation has to step up to say, "I want to continue this legacy!" I think that something shifted when the public saw me and Josh choosing this path, and with Jake Dell, our contemporary at Katz's. It's inspired people who maybe thought they were supposed to be a lawyer but then decided they wanted to learn how to make brisket, as well as a crop of young people who have an interest in the tradition and want to do it in their own way.

For a new generation of customers, they need to see their peers involved and leading.

Yeah, absolutely. I can only speak for us, but we are guided by the desire to maintain the tradition, but to move it forward and keep it relevant. So we're doing these two seemingly incongruous things at the same time. How do you stay the same and also evolve?

What is your personal perfect order at Russ & Daughters?

My perfect order would be sitting down at Russ & Daughters' café and having the Anne Platter with a side of potato latkes. The Anne Platter, which is named in honor of my grandmother, has Gaspé Nova, sable, sturgeon, salmon roe, and a piece of smoked trout. It comes with

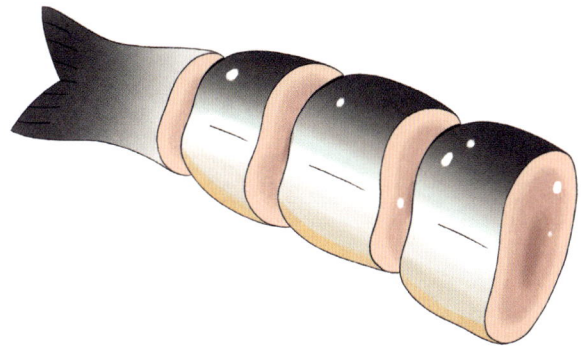

capers and onions and pickles, all the bagels and bialys, the bread basket. So eating that with a side of latkes and one of our homemade sodas. Plus a side of blintzes for dessert. That covers all the bases.

And for a newcomer flying solo?

The Anne Platter works for three or four people sitting down at a table. For one person, I would say, have the Classic Bagel and Lox Sandwich.

Is there a menu item that people tend to stay away from that you think is underrated?

I think that we've done a really great job of bringing herring back and making it exciting, especially now that there's so much interest in wild and sustainable fish. Herring is a superfood and checks all those boxes, and it happens to be delicious and inexpensive, so I'm a huge proponent.

What's your take on the future of Jewish food?

I live both in the past and the future. We do everything with the intention that Russ & Daughters is going to be around for another hundred years, and it should be because it holds so much meaning to so many people. It's a part of the very fabric of not just New York but the Jewish American consciousness and identity, and the immigrant story that so many Jewish Americans can tell about their own family.

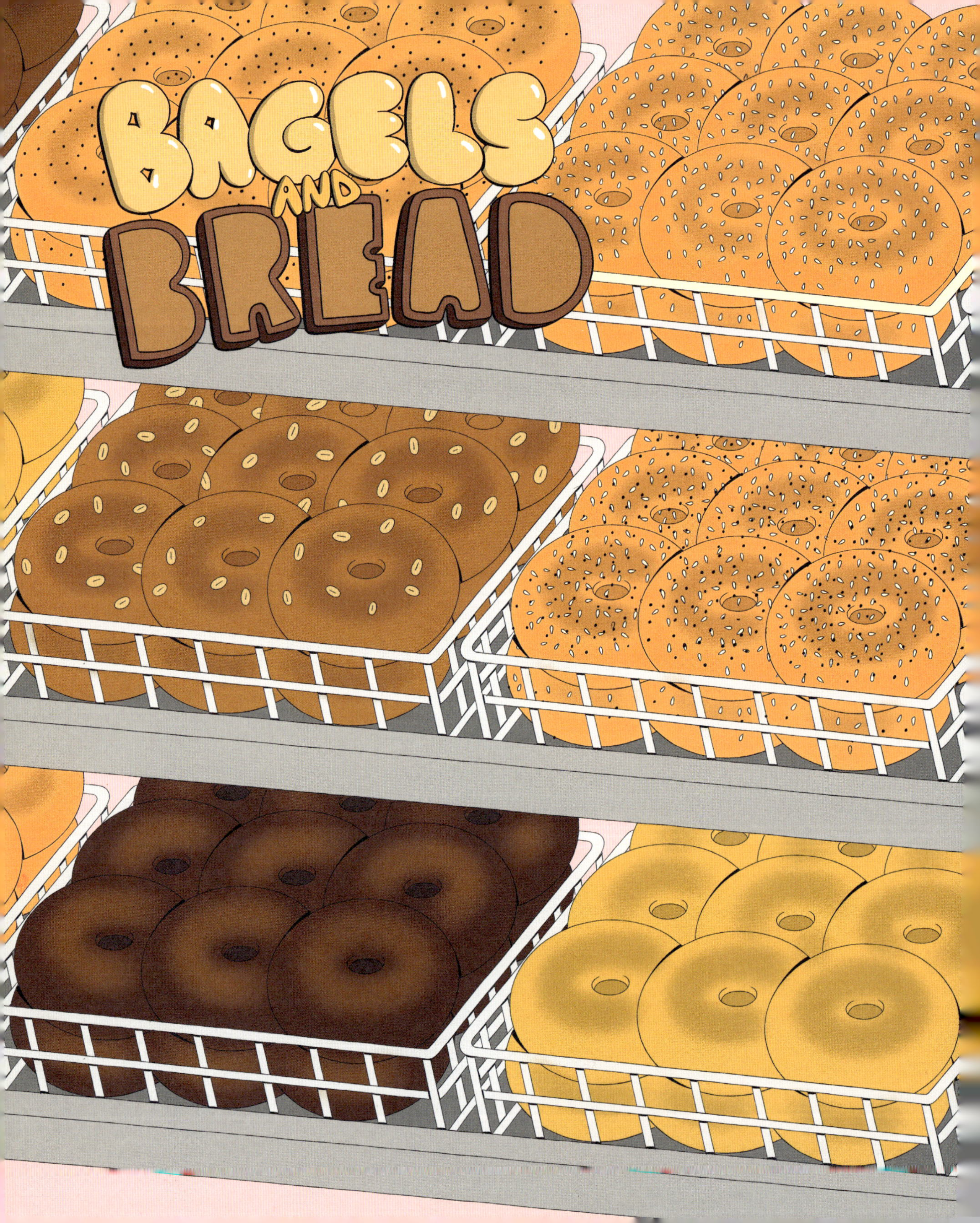
BAGELS
AND
BREAD

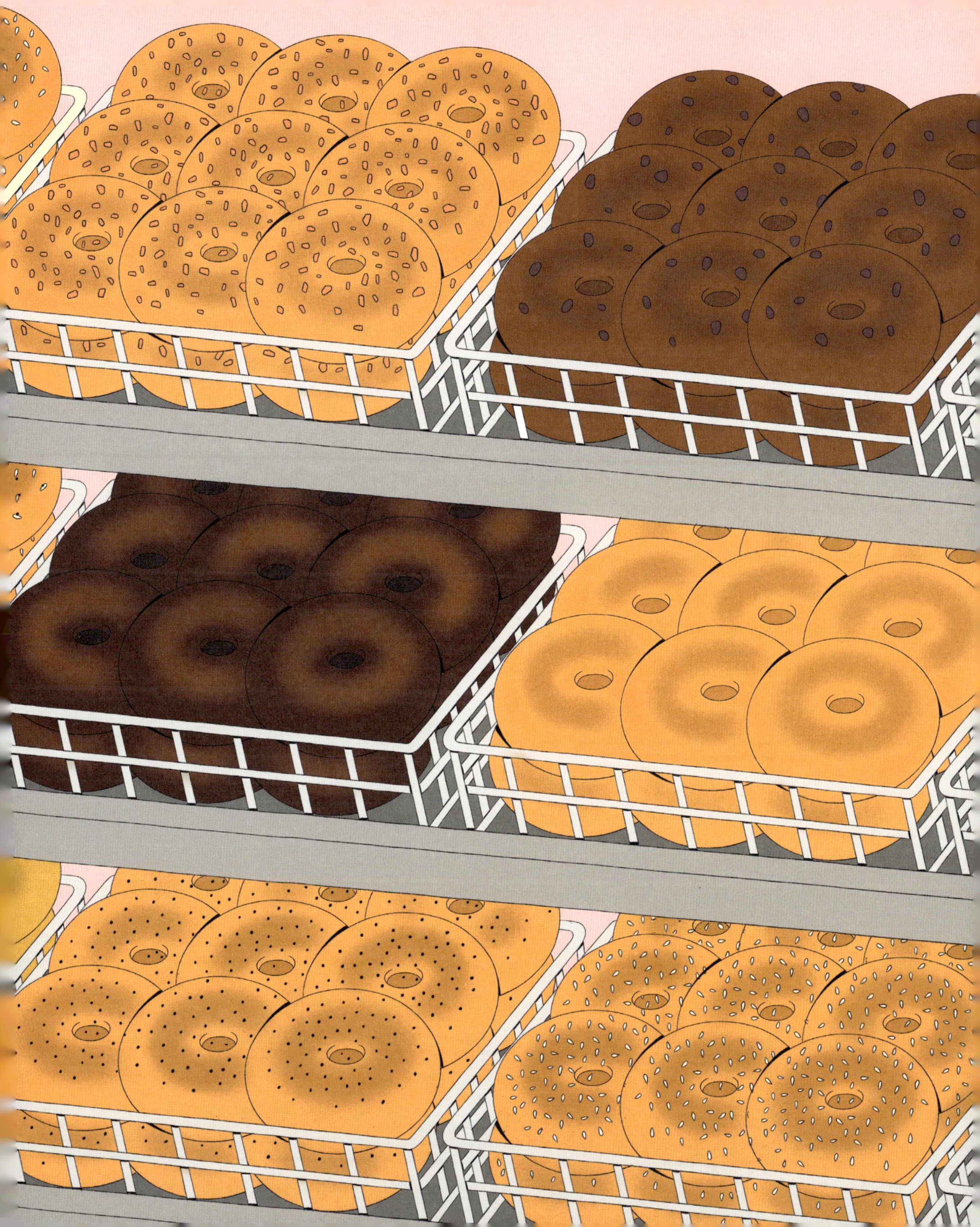

Bagels

THE BAGEL WAS BROUGHT TO THE UNITED STATES BY THE EASTERN EUROPEAN JEWS. BUT WHERE DID IT ORIGINATE?

THE BIRTH OF THE BAGEL IS HARD TO PLACE BECAUSE IT IS A VERY COMMON KIND OF PRODUCT (A SMALL BREAD) MADE WITH SIMPLE INGREDIENTS.

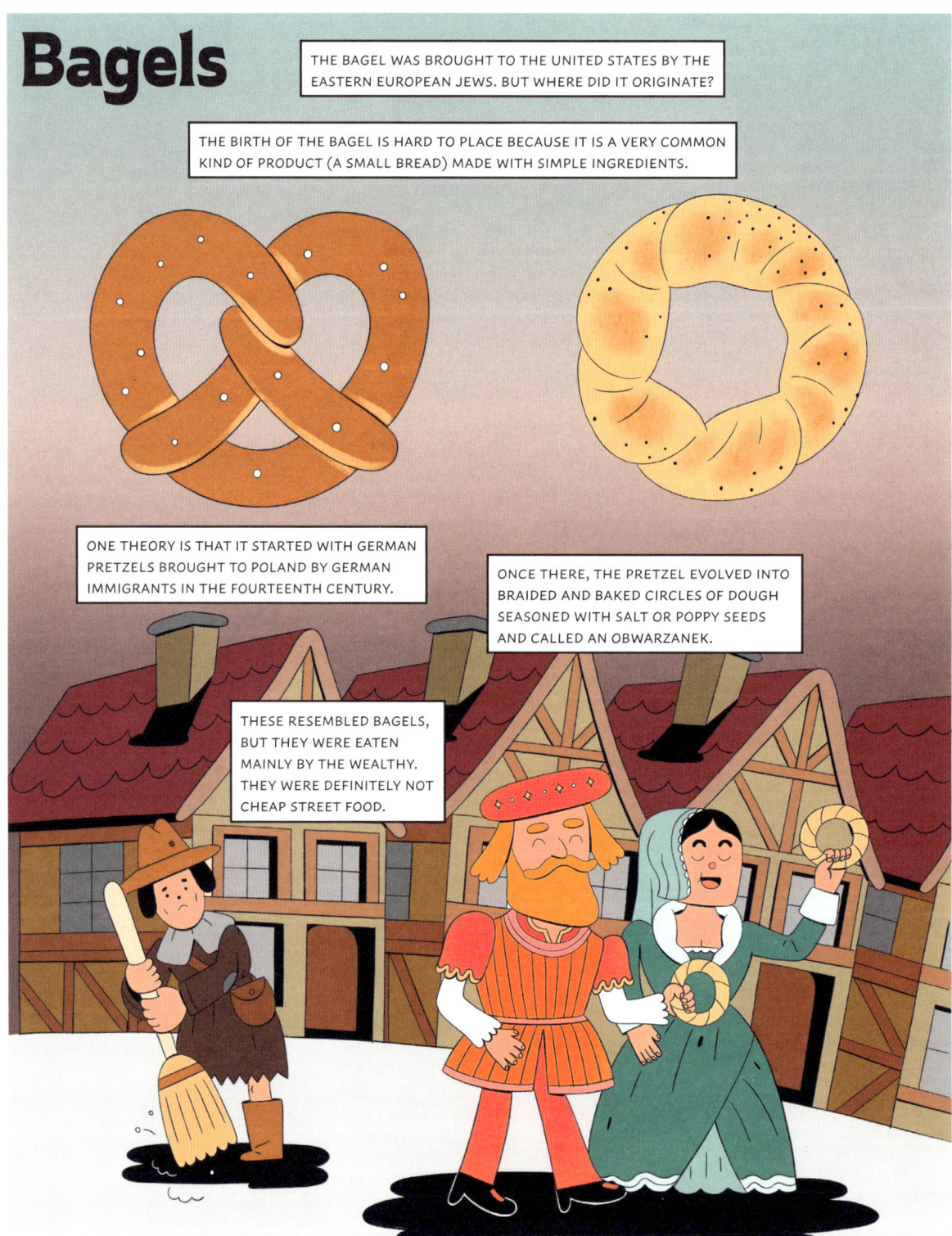

ONE THEORY IS THAT IT STARTED WITH GERMAN PRETZELS BROUGHT TO POLAND BY GERMAN IMMIGRANTS IN THE FOURTEENTH CENTURY.

ONCE THERE, THE PRETZEL EVOLVED INTO BRAIDED AND BAKED CIRCLES OF DOUGH SEASONED WITH SALT OR POPPY SEEDS AND CALLED AN OBWARZANEK.

THESE RESEMBLED BAGELS, BUT THEY WERE EATEN MAINLY BY THE WEALTHY. THEY WERE DEFINITELY NOT CHEAP STREET FOOD.

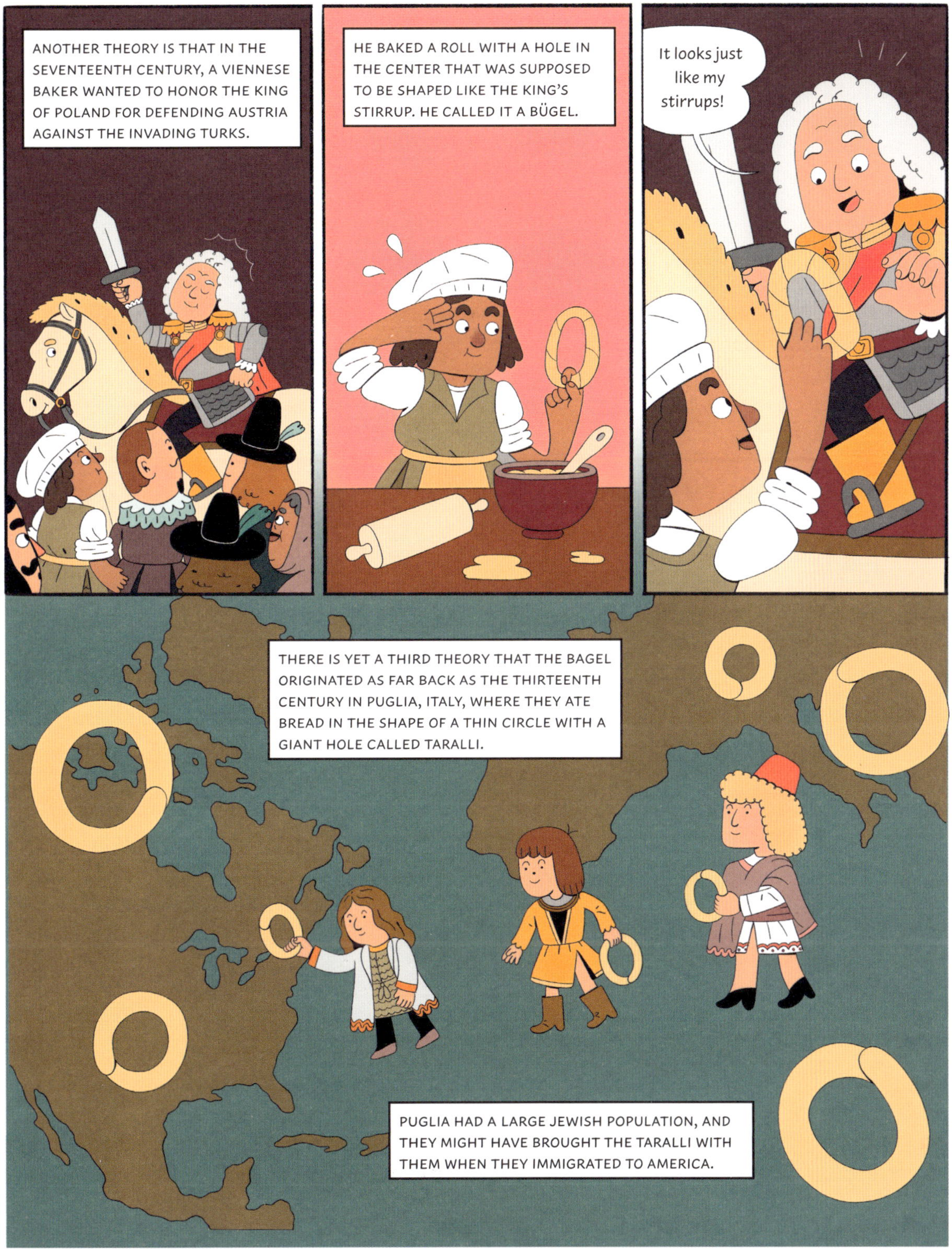
ANOTHER THEORY IS THAT IN THE SEVENTEENTH CENTURY, A VIENNESE BAKER WANTED TO HONOR THE KING OF POLAND FOR DEFENDING AUSTRIA AGAINST THE INVADING TURKS.
HE BAKED A ROLL WITH A HOLE IN THE CENTER THAT WAS SUPPOSED TO BE SHAPED LIKE THE KING'S STIRRUP. HE CALLED IT A BÜGEL.
It looks just like my stirrups!
THERE IS YET A THIRD THEORY THAT THE BAGEL ORIGINATED AS FAR BACK AS THE THIRTEENTH CENTURY IN PUGLIA, ITALY, WHERE THEY ATE BREAD IN THE SHAPE OF A THIN CIRCLE WITH A GIANT HOLE CALLED TARALLI.
PUGLIA HAD A LARGE JEWISH POPULATION, AND THEY MIGHT HAVE BROUGHT THE TARALLI WITH THEM WHEN THEY IMMIGRATED TO AMERICA.

WHEREVER THE BAGEL ORIGINATED, IT FIRST BECAME A DISTINCTLY JEWISH FOOD IN POLAND.

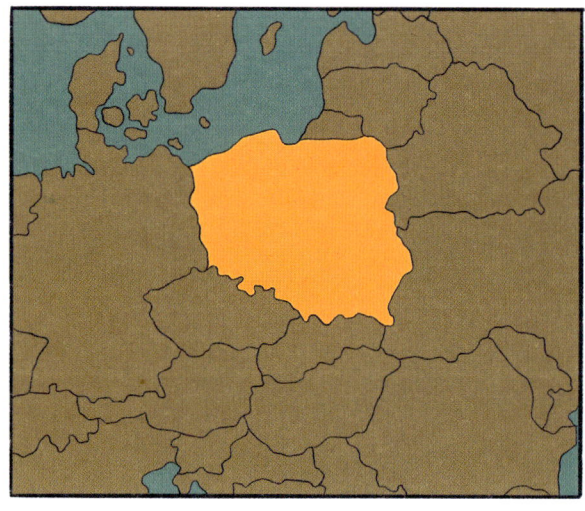

JEWS HAD PREVIOUSLY BEEN FORBIDDEN FROM BAKING BREAD, BUT A LAW WAS PASSED THAT ALLOWED THEM TO MAKE BREAD IF IT WAS BOILED, AND SO THEY TOOK TO MAKING BAGELS.

THE BAGEL'S HOLE WAS THERE TO ALLOW STREET SELLERS TO STRING MANY ONTO A POLE.

Bagels!
Fresh, boiled bagels!

IN THE UNITED STATES, THE BAGEL THRIVED AS JEWISH FARE.

IT WAS SOLD AS CHEAP, CONVENIENT STREET FOOD THAT WAS MEANT TO BE EATEN ON ITS OWN—NOT NECESSARILY AS A SANDWICH OR WITH ANY KIND OF SCHMEAR ON IT.

LIKE THE STORIES OF THE BAGEL'S ORIGIN, ITS RECIPE VARIES DEPENDING ON WHOM YOU ASK. THE BASIC COMMON DENOMINATORS ARE WATER, FLOUR, SALT, AND YEAST.

(ON THE EAST COAST, THE BAGEL DOUGH CAN ALSO BE MIXED WITH A SOURDOUGH STARTER.)

ONCE THE DOUGH IS MIXED AND THE GLUTEN HAS DEVELOPED, IT IS LEFT TO REST AND FERMENT.

IT THEN GETS DIVIDED INTO SMALLER SECTIONS, FOLLOWED BY ANOTHER PERIOD OF REST.

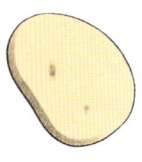

TIMING AND CLIMATE WILL AFFECT HOW THE DOUGH WILL REACT.

WHEN THE DOUGH IS READY, IT IS ROLLED INTO LONG LOGS.

THESE ARE THEN CUT INTO SMALLER PIECES AND FORMED INTO THE FAMILIAR ROUND BAGEL SHAPE. IT IS AT THIS POINT THAT TOPPINGS ARE ADDED.

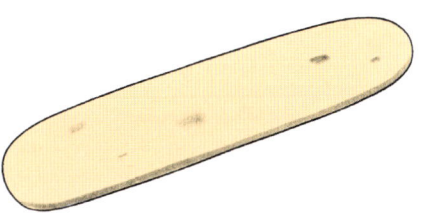

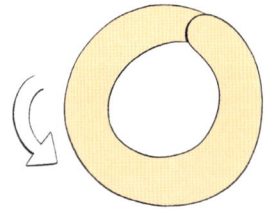

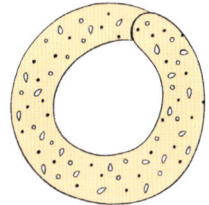

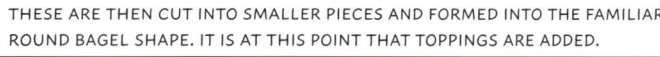

TYPICALLY, BAGELS ARE THEN BOILED IN WATER, BUT SOME BAKERIES WILL STEAM THEM INSTEAD. (PHILLY STYLE BAGELS, A BAKERY IN PHILADELPHIA, BOILS THEIR BAGELS IN A MIXTURE OF BEER AND WATER.)

VARIETIES OF BAGELS

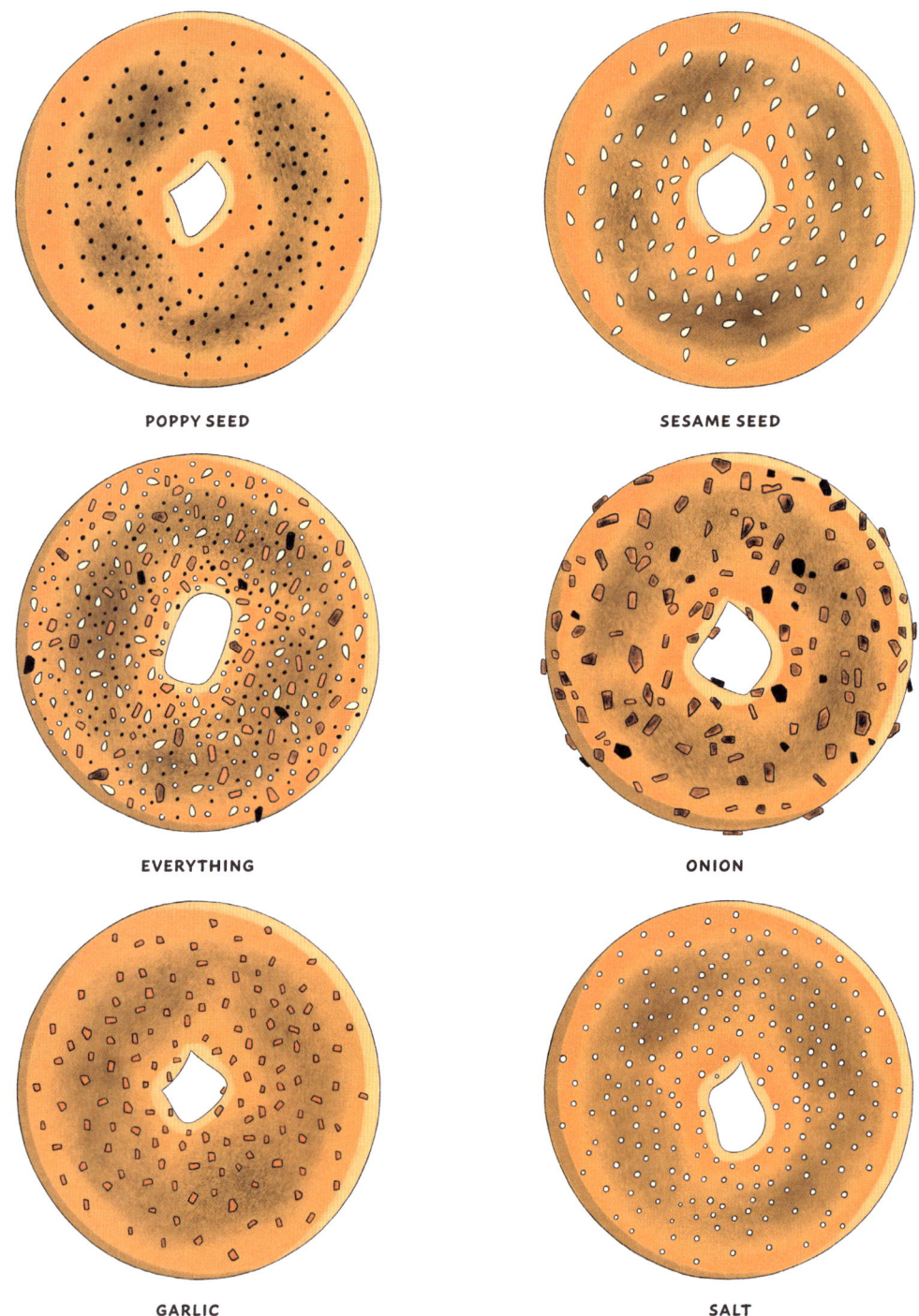

POPPY SEED

SESAME SEED

EVERYTHING

ONION

GARLIC

SALT

EGG

PUMPERNICKEL

WHEAT

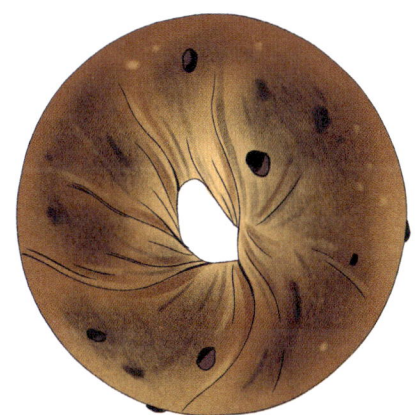

CINNAMON RAISIN

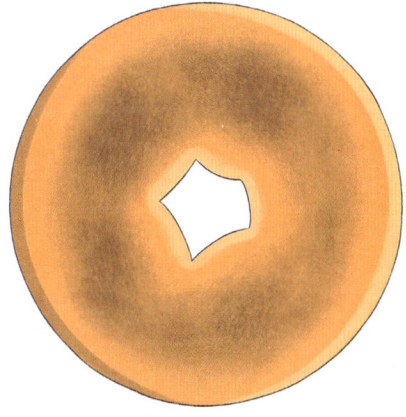

PLAIN

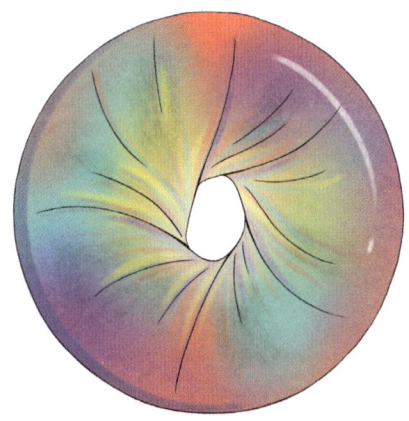

RAINBOW

MONTREAL-STYLE BAGELS

IN MONTREAL, THE BAGELS ARE SOMEWHAT DIFFERENT, BASED ON RECIPES BROUGHT OVER FROM JEWS IN RUSSIA.

THE DOUGH IS ROLLED THINNER, THE TEXTURE IS DENSER, AND THE BAGELS ARE BOILED IN WATER THAT CONTAINS HONEY, MALT, OR EVEN MAPLE SYRUP FOR A SWEETER TASTE.

THE MAIN DIFFERENCE, THOUGH, IS THAT MONTREAL-STYLE BAGELS ARE BAKED IN A WOOD-FIRED OVEN.

THEY ARE ALSO EATEN DIFFERENTLY, USUALLY DIPPED IN CREAM CHEESE, AS OPPOSED TO NEW YORK–STYLE BAGELS, WHICH ARE SLICED AND HAVE CREAM CHEESE SPREAD ON THEM.

THERE IS A LONG-STANDING DEBATE OVER WHICH BAGEL IS BETTER—NEW YORK OR MONTREAL—WITH EACH PARTY BOASTING OF ITS RESPECTIVE BAGEL'S SUPERIOR QUALITIES.

EVEN WITHIN EACH CITY, DISPUTES OVER WHICH BAGEL BAKERY IS BEST FUEL THIS INTENSE RIVALRY.

ESS-A-BAGEL

831 3rd Avenue,
Manhattan, New York City

Ess-a-Bagel's signature bagels frequently rank as among the best in New York.

Melanie Frost, Owner

My family started the business in 1976, over forty years ago. Before that, my uncle had a donut shop in Brooklyn. The landlord wasn't renewing the lease and my uncle had three kids to support, so he and my aunt combed the papers and found a bagel shop. They figured, "Donuts, bagels, they both have holes. We'll figure it out!" They found a baker who gave them a recipe and said, "Look,

this is using the most expensive flour and ingredients, but you're going to have the best bagels."

When they were first proofing the bagels, they discovered that they had risen too much. But they went with it and just put the bagels into the oven. They came out huge, and people just loved them. Crunchy on the outside, chewy on the inside. It's what we became known for.

Our bagels are hand-rolled and baked on the premises daily. They're made with all-natural ingredients, no preservatives, no added fat, no cholesterol. I really do think they're the best bagels. There's nothing like an Ess-a-Bagel straight out of the oven. Nothing!

FAIRMOUNT BAGEL

74 Fairmount Ouest Avenue,
Montreal, Quebec

The storied Fairmount Bagel was the first bagel bakery to open in Montreal.

Irwin Shlafman, Owner

In 1919, my grandfather left Russia. He was one of the many immigrants who jumped on any boat that was coming to the New World really not knowing where he was going to get off. He ended up in Montreal and tried to find a bagel bakery to work at, because that's what he was doing in Russia, but there weren't any. A friend that he came over with happened to be an oven builder, so the two of them found a quaint little spot here in the old part of the city, built an oven, and went into operation as the first bagel bakery in Montreal.

The difference between a Montreal bagel and New York bagel . . . many people will tell you many different

things. What I know is that automation was being introduced into the baking industry—be it bread, buns, or bagels—and some regions were more quick to adopt that and do away with the older styles of production. Here in Montreal, the technology thing didn't really adapt well to the bagel business, and my father continued rolling by hand and baking the bagel in a wood-fired oven.

From what I know, the recipes in New York and many places are lacking some of the ingredients that we still keep in our bagel, that my grandfather taught my father how to make and my father taught me. So we haven't changed anything. We still use whole eggs. We still use liquid molasses. We use extra ingredients that are difficult to weigh out and a pain to use. They're annoying!

Bialys

BIALYS ARE FROM BIALYSTOK, POLAND.

THEY WERE AN ESSENTIAL PART OF EVERY MEAL FOR JEWISH FAMILIES. WHILE SIMILAR TO BAGELS, BIALYS ARE NOT BOILED BEFORE BAKING, AND THEY HAVE NO CENTER HOLE.

INSTEAD, THERE IS A DEPRESSION IN THE MIDDLE THAT IS USUALLY FILLED WITH ONIONS, GARLIC, OR OTHER SEASONINGS. THE TEXTURE OF A BIALY IS ALMOST LIKE A PIZZA CRUST.

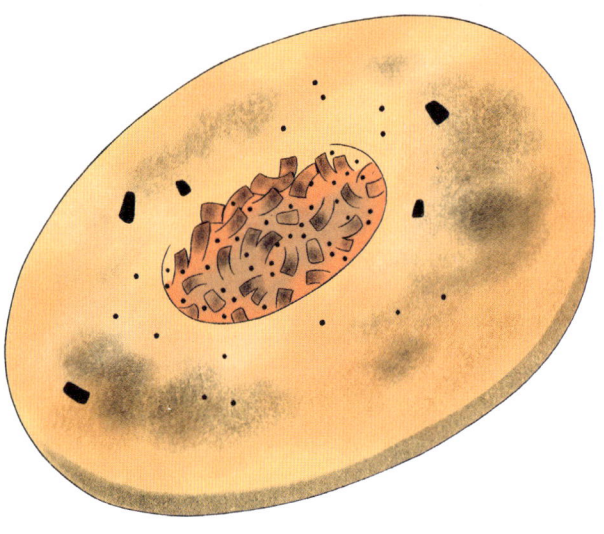

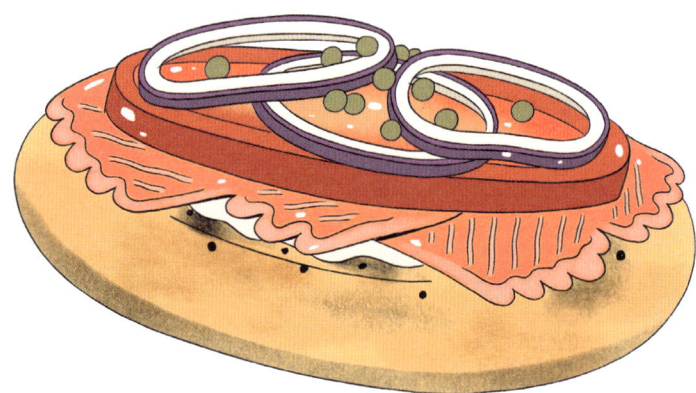

DESPITE THESE DIFFERENCES FROM THE BAGEL, A BIALY ALSO IS OFTEN PREPARED SLICED AND TOPPED WITH BUTTER OR CREAM CHEESE AND SMOKED FISH.

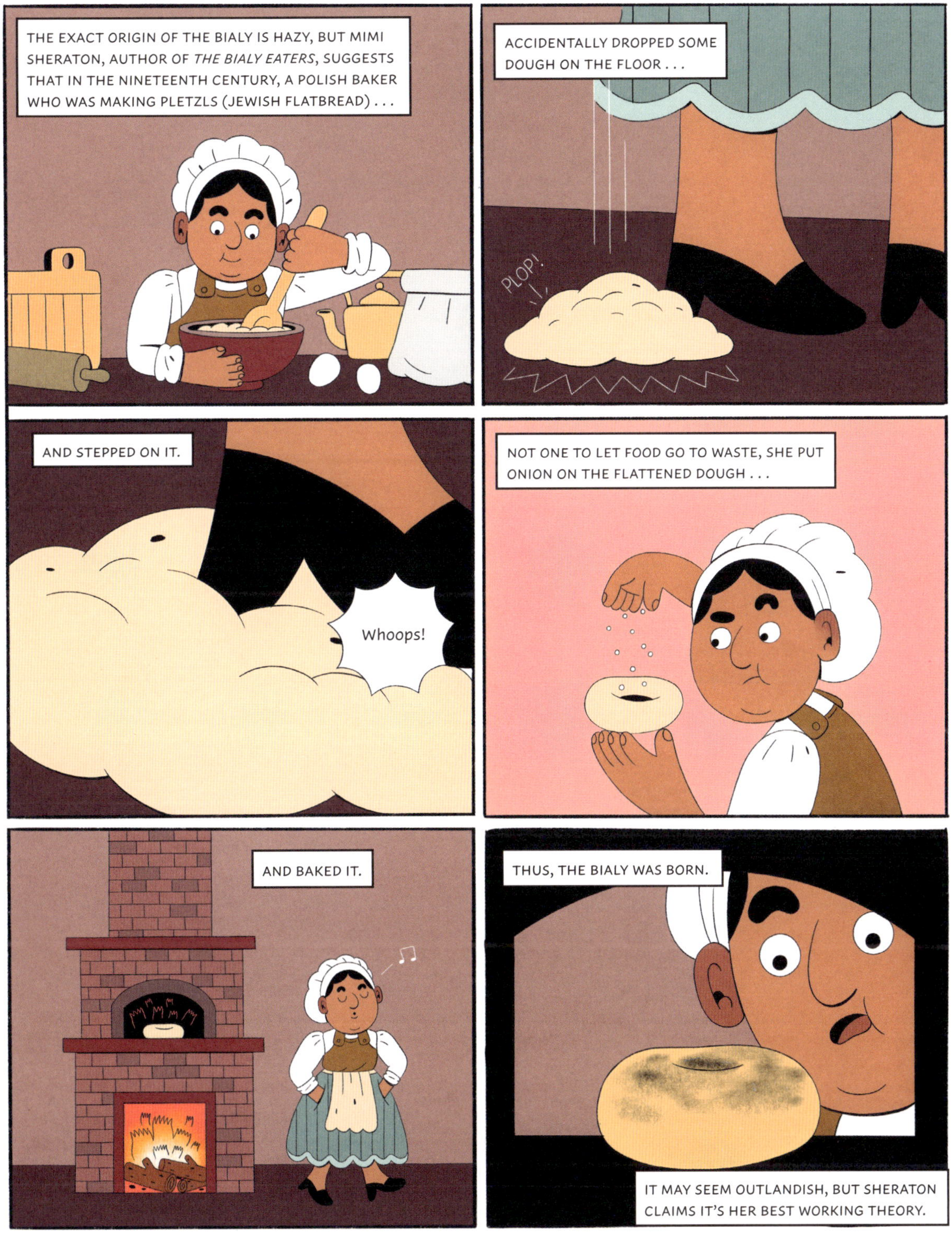
THE EXACT ORIGIN OF THE BIALY IS HAZY, BUT MIMI SHERATON, AUTHOR OF *THE BIALY EATERS*, SUGGESTS THAT IN THE NINETEENTH CENTURY, A POLISH BAKER WHO WAS MAKING PLETZLS (JEWISH FLATBREAD) . . .
ACCIDENTALLY DROPPED SOME DOUGH ON THE FLOOR . . .
PLOP!
AND STEPPED ON IT.
Whoops!
NOT ONE TO LET FOOD GO TO WASTE, SHE PUT ONION ON THE FLATTENED DOUGH . . .
AND BAKED IT.
THUS, THE BIALY WAS BORN.
IT MAY SEEM OUTLANDISH, BUT SHERATON CLAIMS IT'S HER BEST WORKING THEORY.

BIALY DOUGH IS A SIMPLE MIX OF WATER, FLOUR, SALT, AND YEAST.

YEAST

THE DOUGH IS KNEADED AND ROLLED OUT ON A FLOURY SURFACE SO THE OUTSIDE ISN'T SHINY LIKE A BAGEL, AND THEN SPLIT INTO INDIVIDUAL BALLS.

AN INDENTATION IS MADE IN THE CENTER, LEAVING A WIDE RIM AROUND IT.

AFTER THE INDENTATION IS FILLED WITH WHATEVER FILLING THE BAKER IS USING, THE DOUGH IS SPRINKLED WITH SALT AND POPPY SEEDS AND BAKED.

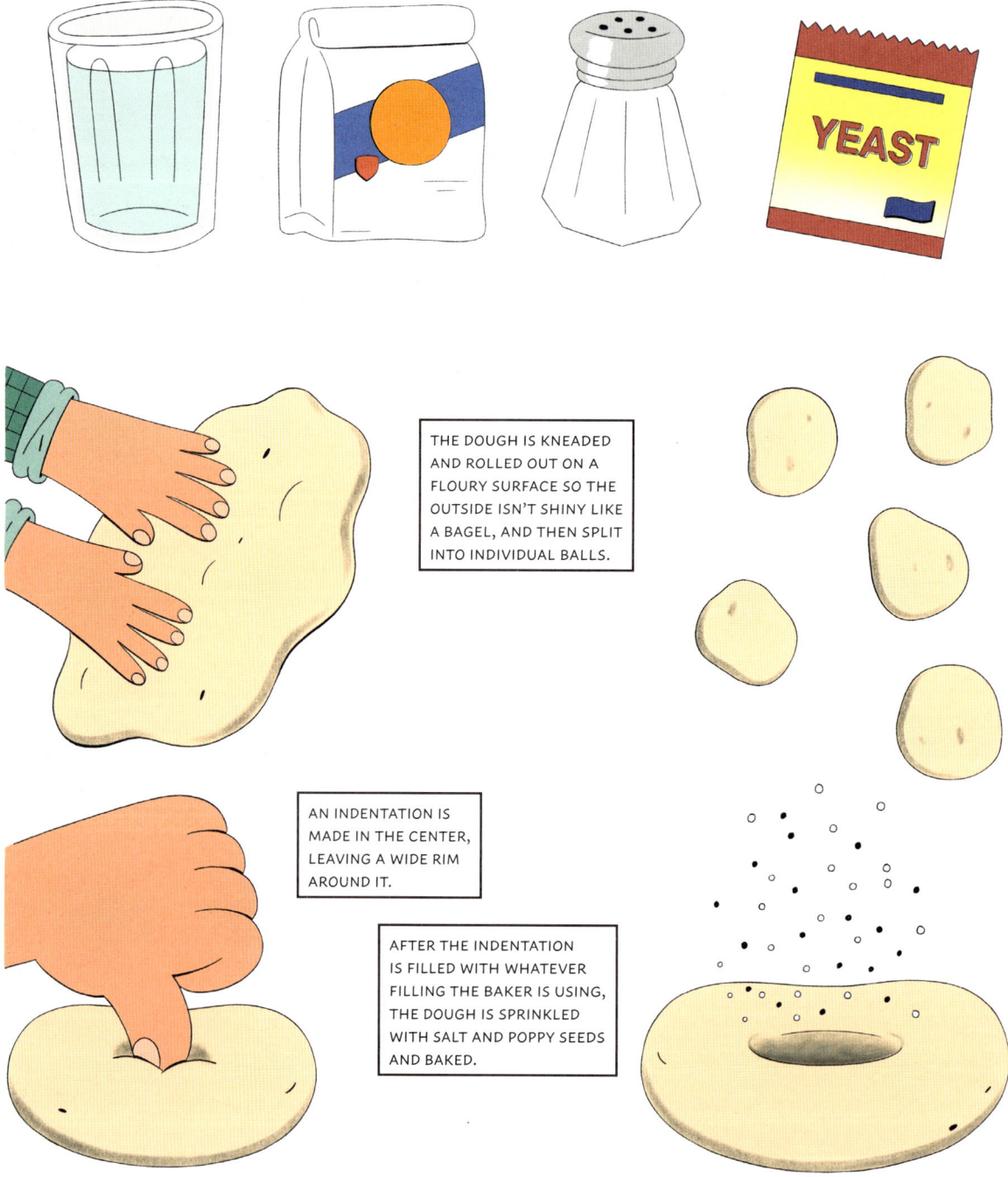

VARIETIES OF BIALYS

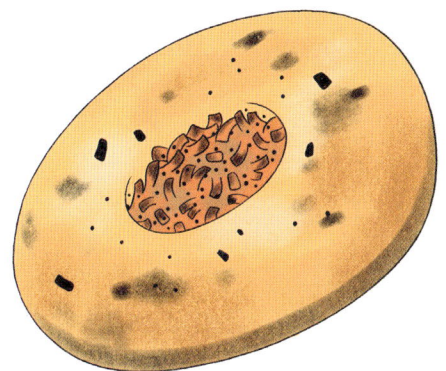

ONION + POPPY SEED

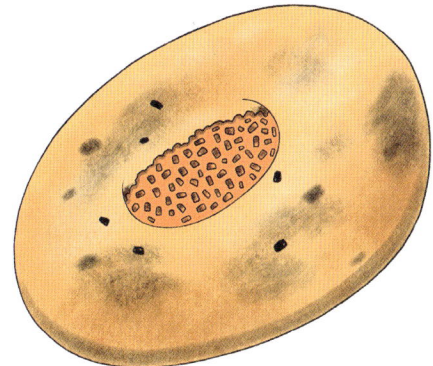

GARLIC

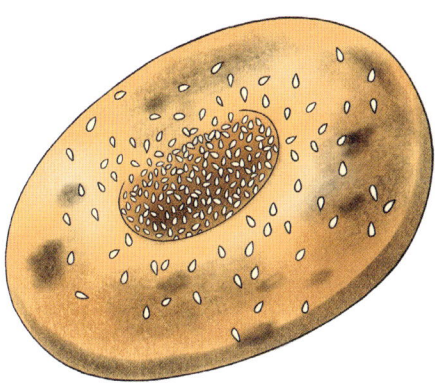

SESAME SEED

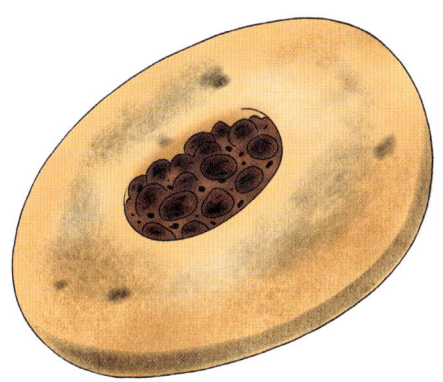

OLIVE

CHEESE

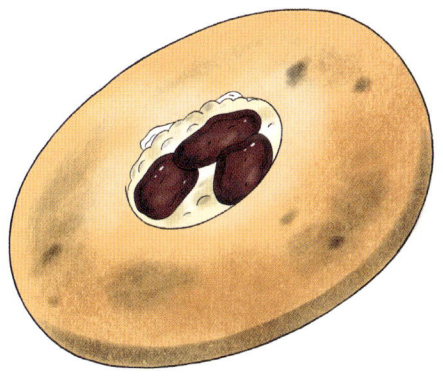

CREAM CHEESE + DATES

Rye

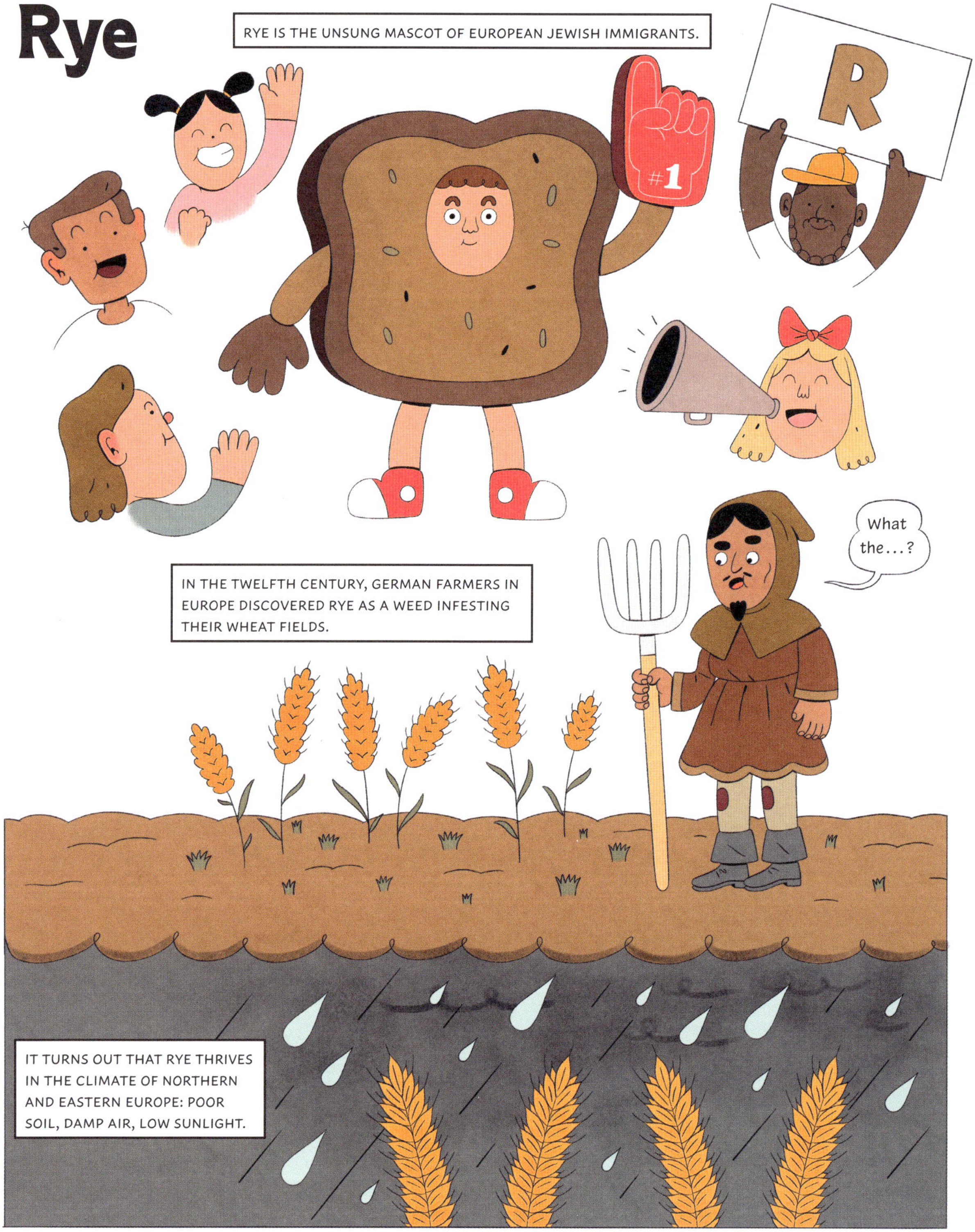
RYE IS THE UNSUNG MASCOT OF EUROPEAN JEWISH IMMIGRANTS.
R
#1
IN THE TWELFTH CENTURY, GERMAN FARMERS IN EUROPE DISCOVERED RYE AS A WEED INFESTING THEIR WHEAT FIELDS.
What the…?
IT TURNS OUT THAT RYE THRIVES IN THE CLIMATE OF NORTHERN AND EASTERN EUROPE: POOR SOIL, DAMP AIR, LOW SUNLIGHT.

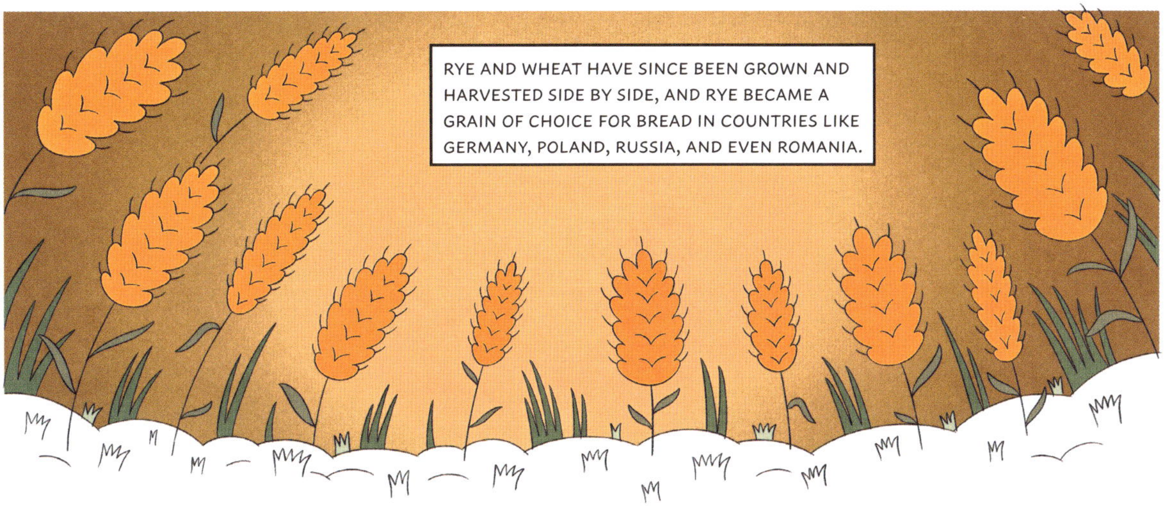
RYE AND WHEAT HAVE SINCE BEEN GROWN AND HARVESTED SIDE BY SIDE, AND RYE BECAME A GRAIN OF CHOICE FOR BREAD IN COUNTRIES LIKE GERMANY, POLAND, RUSSIA, AND EVEN ROMANIA.

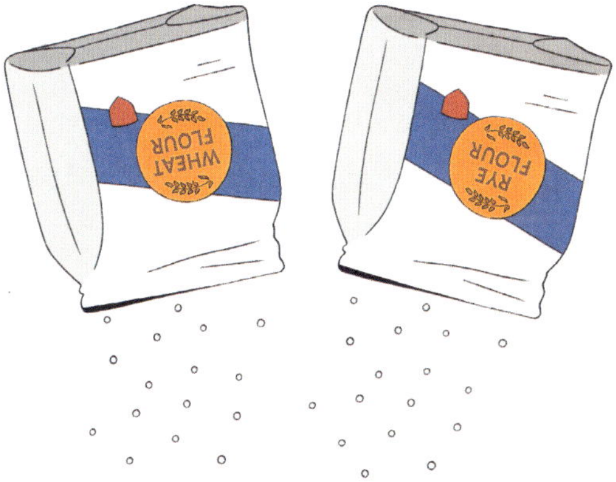
WHEAT FLOUR
RYE FLOUR

JEWISH BAKERS FAVORED A BREAD CALLED KORNBROT (YIDDISH FOR "RYE BREAD"); IT WAS MADE FROM A MIX OF WHEAT AND RYE FLOUR.

BECAUSE RYE WAS DARKER AND CHEAPER THAN WHEAT, IT WAS A MORE ACCESSIBLE INGREDIENT.

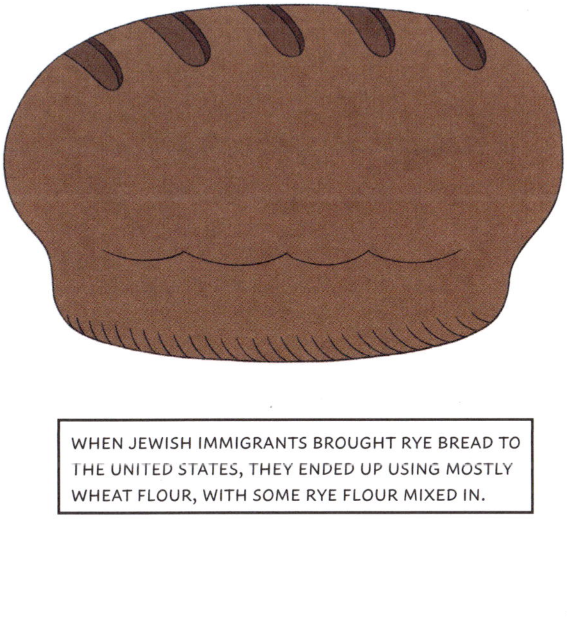

WHEN JEWISH IMMIGRANTS BROUGHT RYE BREAD TO THE UNITED STATES, THEY ENDED UP USING MOSTLY WHEAT FLOUR, WITH SOME RYE FLOUR MIXED IN.

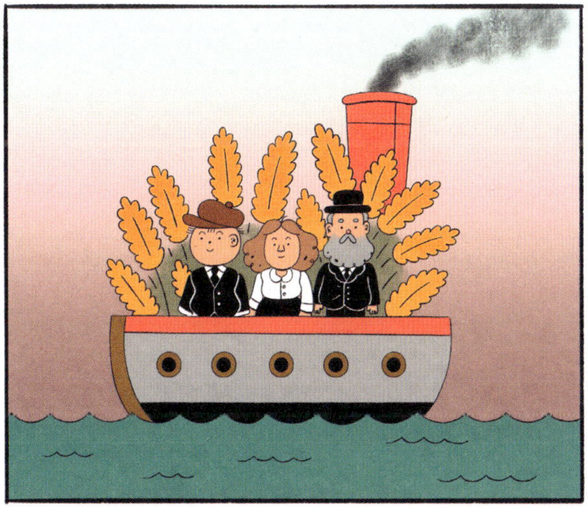

RYE BREAD INVOLVES THREE MAIN COMPONENTS: WHEAT FLOUR, RYE FLOUR, AND SOURDOUGH STARTER.

THESE ARE THE BASICS OF A NUMBER OF RYE-BASED PRODUCTS, INCLUDING BAGELS.

  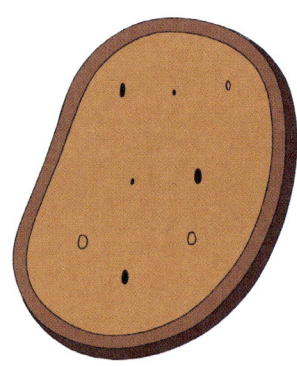

RYE BREAD HAS A COMPLEX FLAVOR THAT IS BOTH SOUR AND SWEET, MAKING IT THE PERFECT SANDWICH BREAD FOR BRISKET AND MUSTARD.

Do not put ketchup on rye bread!

Pumpernickel

PUMPERNICKEL, A TYPE OF RYE BREAD FROM GERMANY, HAS BY FAR THE STRANGEST ETYMOLOGY IN THIS ENTIRE BOOK.

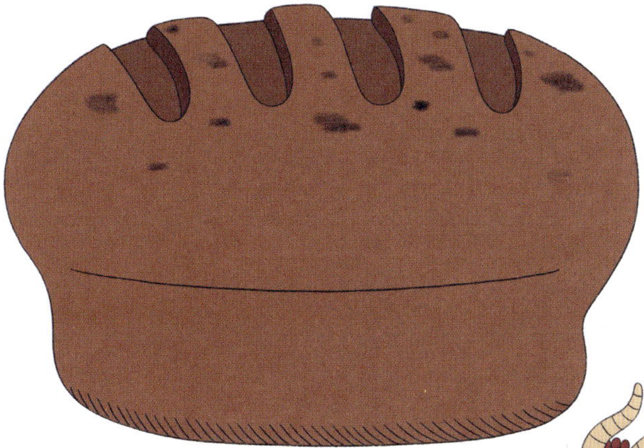

PUMPERN IS GERMAN FOR "FARTS," AND *NICKEL*, LIKE THE NAME NICHOLAS, REFERS TO DEVILISH CREATURES IN GERMAN MYTHOLOGY.

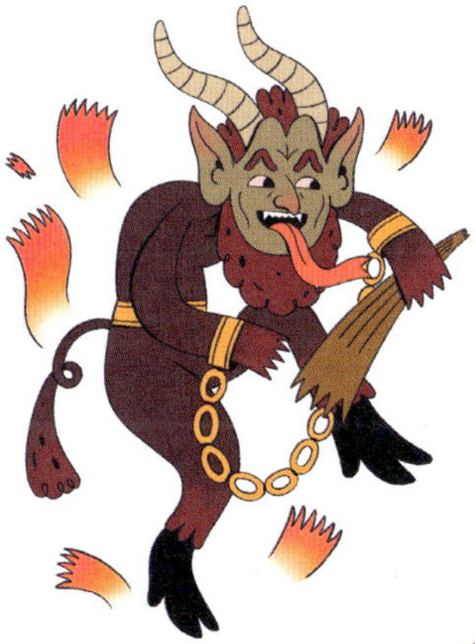

PUT TOGETHER, THE WORD ROUGHLY TRANSLATES TO "THE DEVIL'S FARTS"—POSSIBLY REFERRING TO THE GASEOUS EFFECT THE BREAD CAN HAVE ON ONE'S DIGESTIVE SYSTEM.

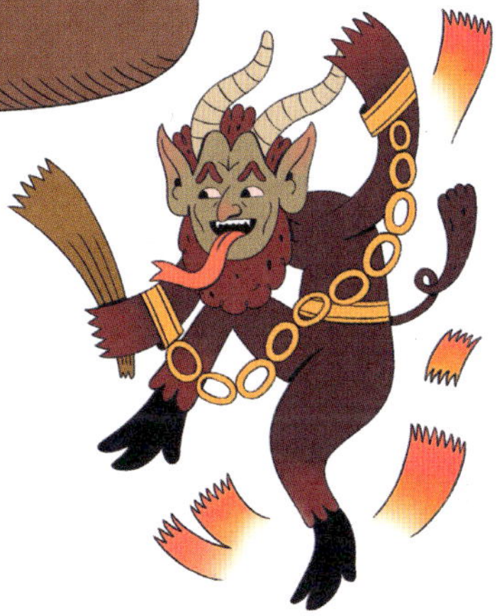

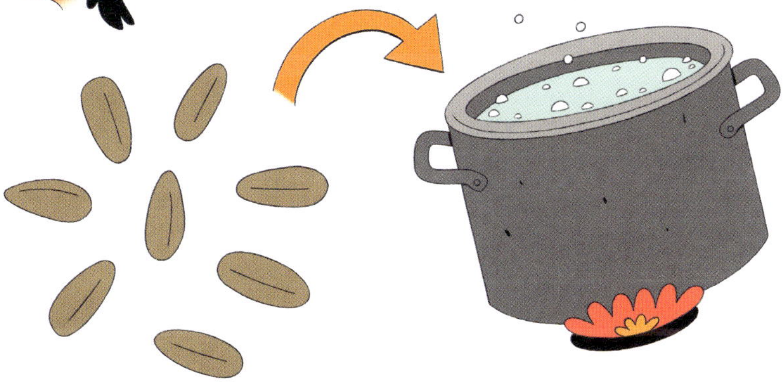

IN ADDITION TO THE RYE FLOUR, PUMPERNICKEL IS MADE WITH GROUND-UP, BOILED RYE BERRIES, WHICH GIVE IT AN EVEN STRONGER FLAVOR.

ALSO, BECAUSE PUMPERNICKEL IS BAKED FOR A LONGER TIME, IT'S A DARK COLOR.

SOME MORE MODERN RECIPES FOR PUMPERNICKEL INCLUDE MOLASSES AND COCOA POWDER FOR AN EVEN DARKER COLOR AND A MORE COMPLEX FLAVOR. IT CAN HAVE AN INTENSE SWEET AND EARTHY AROMA.

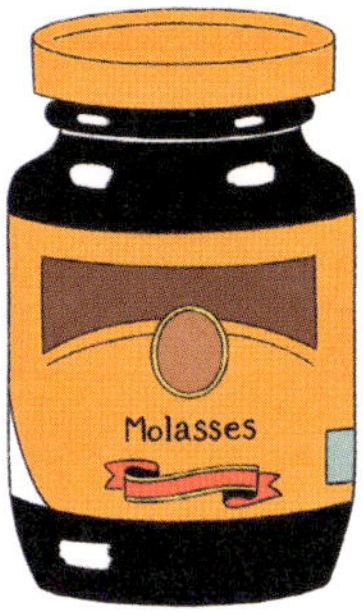
Molasses

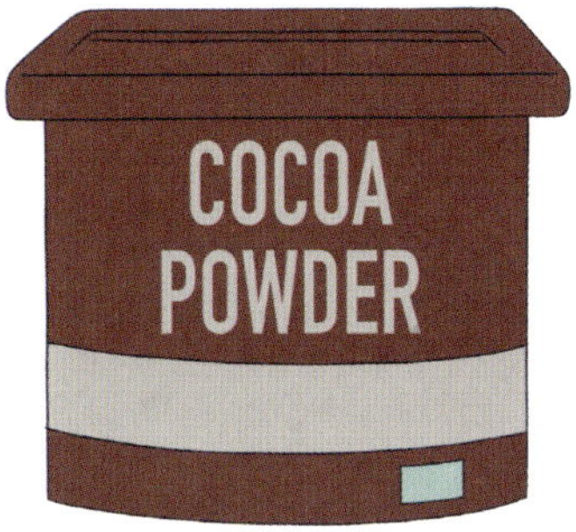
COCOA
POWDER

Challah

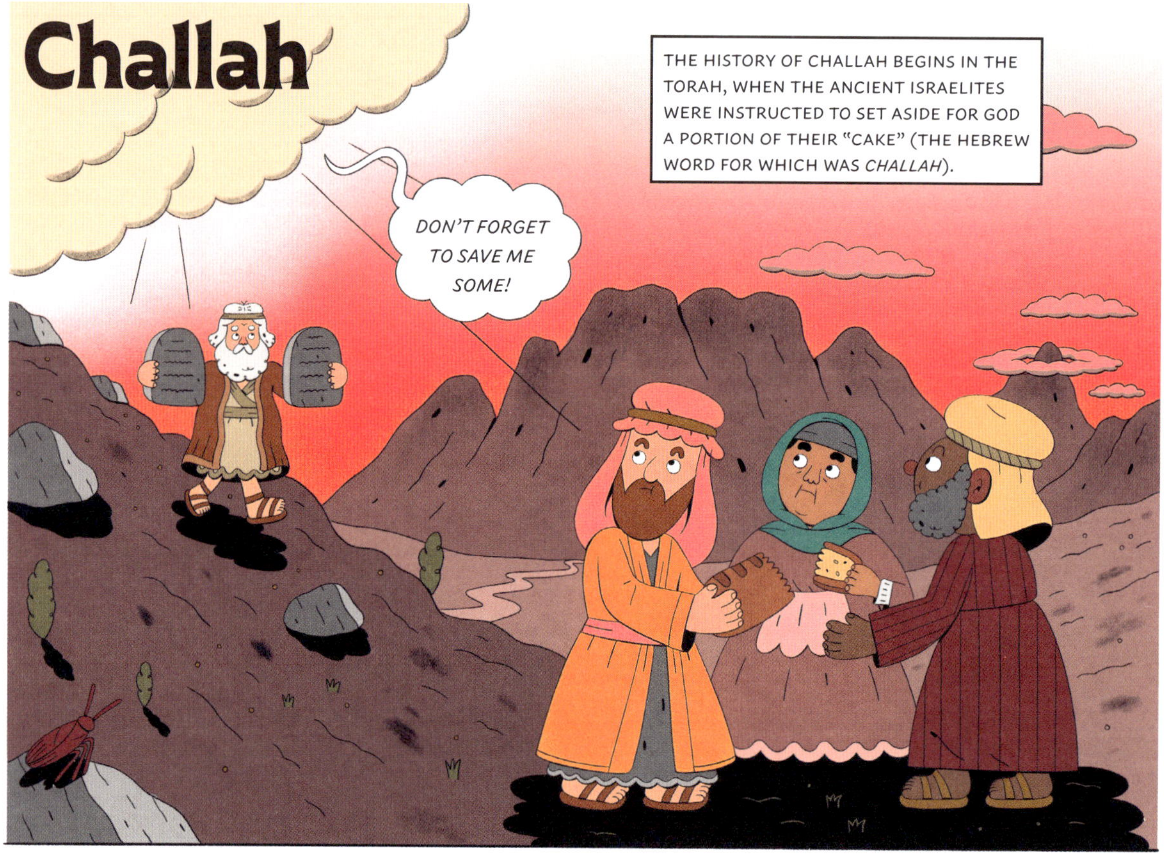
THE HISTORY OF CHALLAH BEGINS IN THE TORAH, WHEN THE ANCIENT ISRAELITES WERE INSTRUCTED TO SET ASIDE FOR GOD A PORTION OF THEIR "CAKE" (THE HEBREW WORD FOR WHICH WAS *CHALLAH*).
DON'T FORGET TO SAVE ME SOME!

CHALLAH BREAD HAS LONG BEEN OF GREAT SIGNIFICANCE IN JEWISH CULTURE. A STRAIGHT, BRAIDED LOAF IS THE SYMBOLIC BREAD OF CHOICE FOR THE WEEKLY SHABBAT BLESSING OVER BREAD (THE MOTZI BLESSING).

AND ROUND LOAVES ARE EATEN ON ROSH HASHANAH AND AFTER YOM KIPPUR TO SYMBOLIZE THE CYCLE OF THE SEASONS.

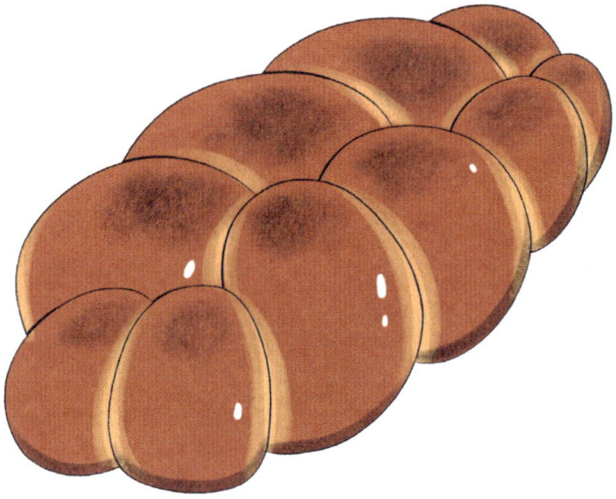

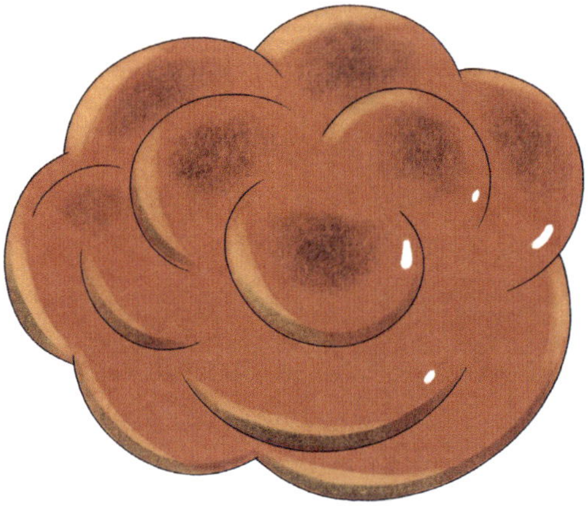

BEFORE THE MIDDLE AGES, CHALLAH MORE CLOSELY RESEMBLED FLAT BREAD. BUT THE CHALLAH THAT WE KNOW TODAY STARTED AS A GERMAN BREAD RECIPE IN THE FIFTEENTH CENTURY.

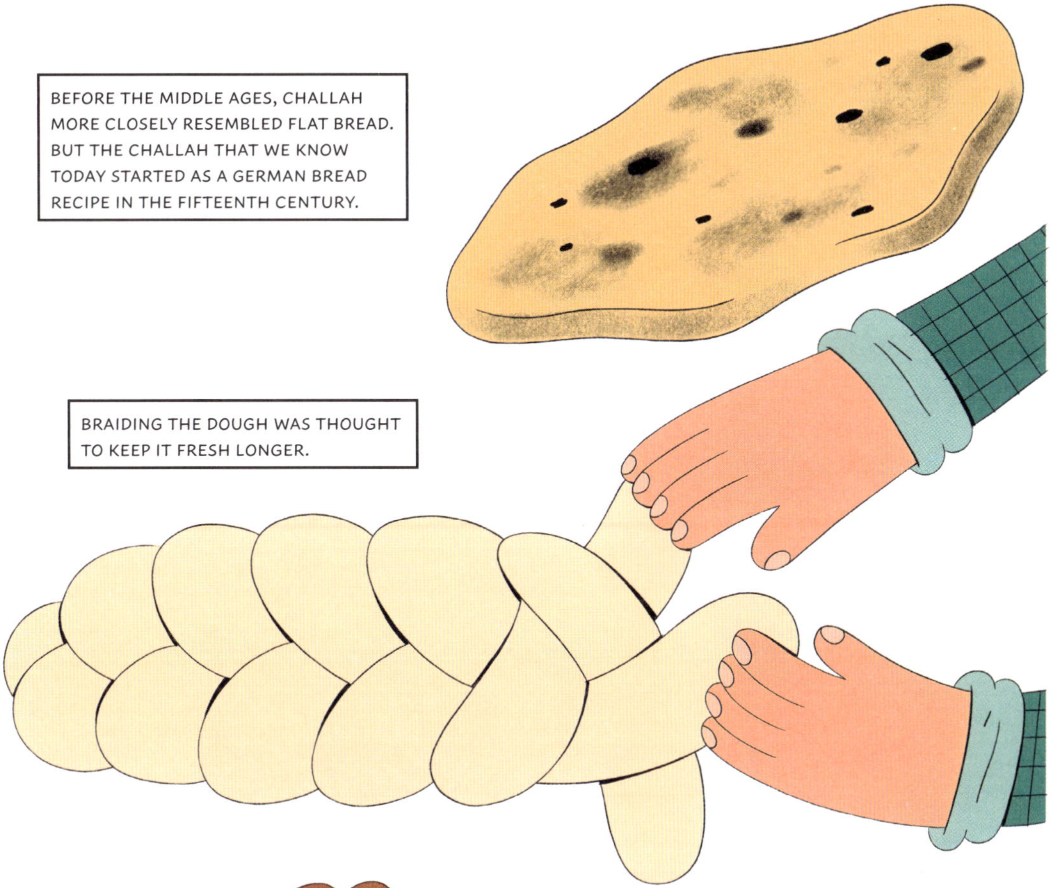

BRAIDING THE DOUGH WAS THOUGHT TO KEEP IT FRESH LONGER.

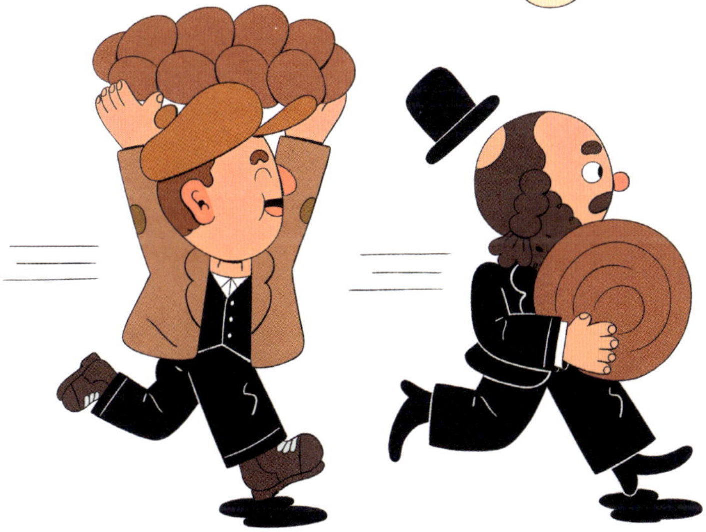

AS MEDIEVAL JEWS MIGRATED EASTWARD THROUGH EUROPE, THEY BROUGHT THEIR CHALLAH RECIPES WITH THEM.

LIKE OTHER BREADS, CHALLAH IS MADE WITH WATER, FLOUR, SUGAR, AND YEAST.

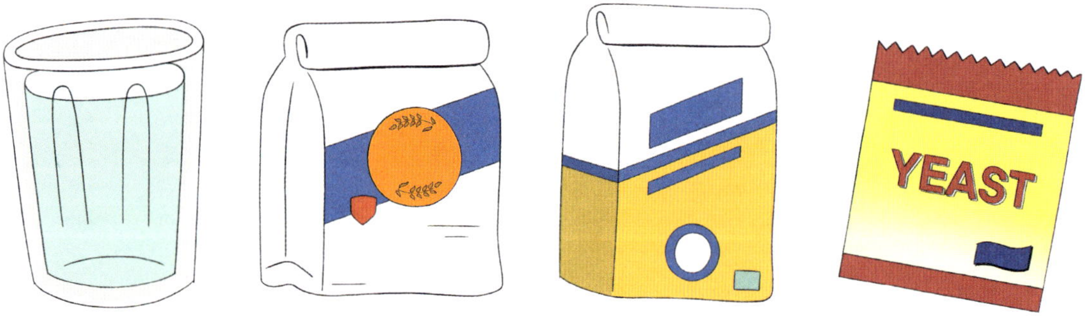
YEAST

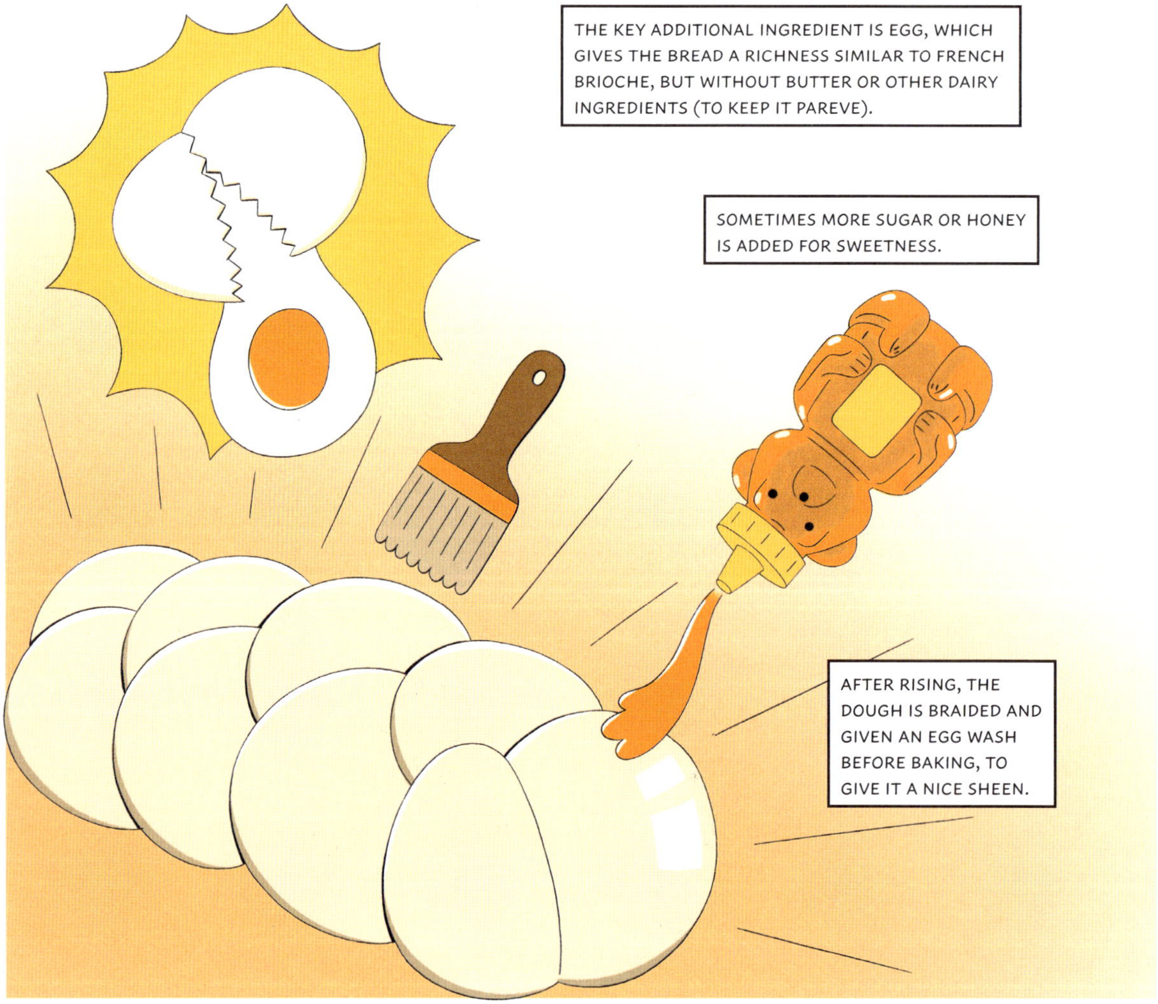
THE KEY ADDITIONAL INGREDIENT IS EGG, WHICH GIVES THE BREAD A RICHNESS SIMILAR TO FRENCH BRIOCHE, BUT WITHOUT BUTTER OR OTHER DAIRY INGREDIENTS (TO KEEP IT PAREVE).
SOMETIMES MORE SUGAR OR HONEY IS ADDED FOR SWEETNESS.
AFTER RISING, THE DOUGH IS BRAIDED AND GIVEN AN EGG WASH BEFORE BAKING, TO GIVE IT A NICE SHEEN.

VARIETIES OF CHALLAH SHAPES

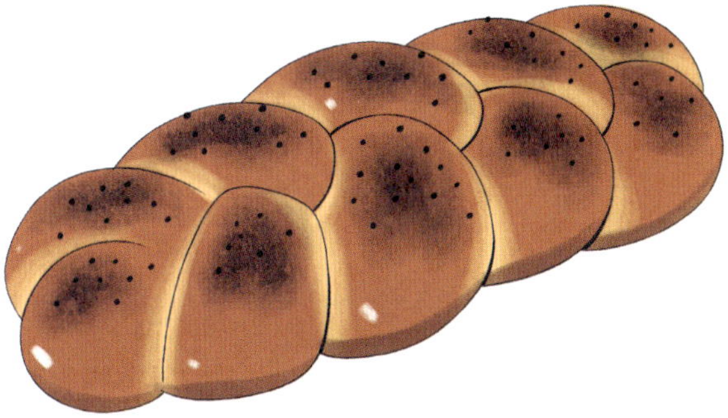

CLASSIC

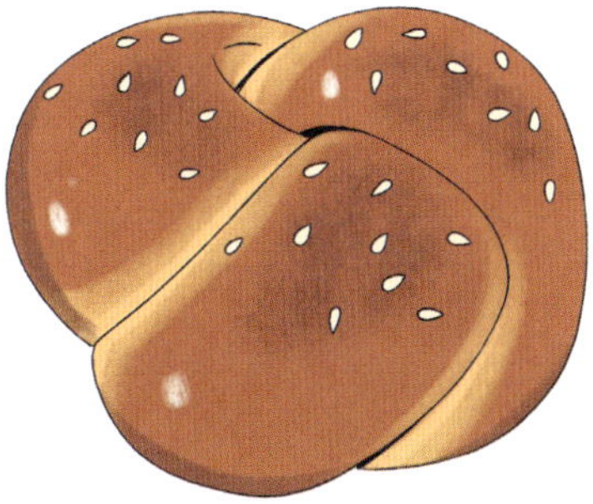

ROLL

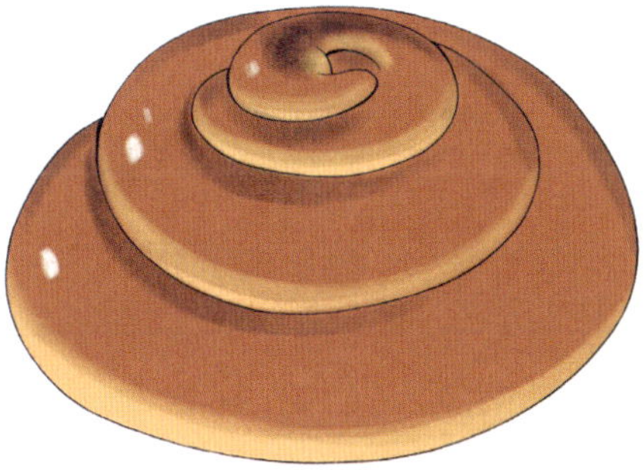

BUN

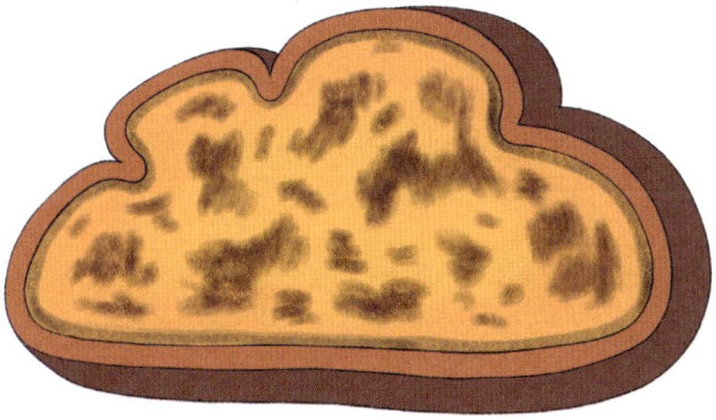

FRENCH TOAST

TECHNICALLY NOT A VARIETY, BUT CHALLAH IS THE ONLY BREAD YOU SHOULD USE TO MAKE FRENCH TOAST, SO IT DESERVES AN HONORABLE MENTION.

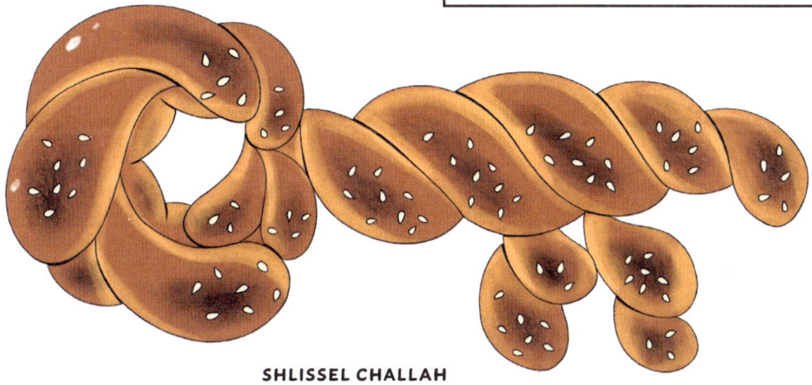

SHLISSEL CHALLAH

SHLISSEL IS YIDDISH FOR "KEY."

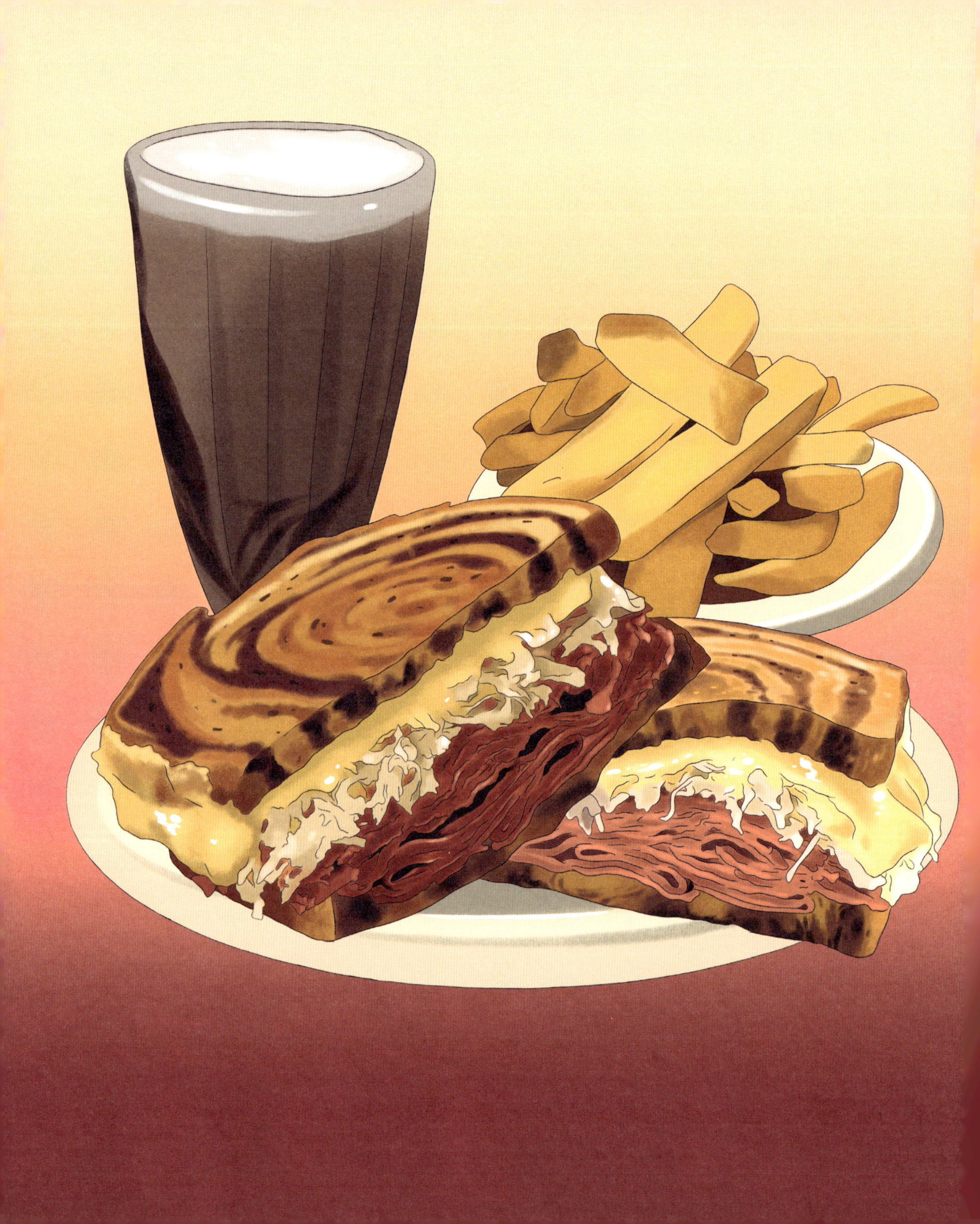

The Reuben Sandwich

The Reuben is a real conundrum. To put both cheese and mayonnaise on the same sandwich as corned beef is neither kosher nor European. And despite being around for about a century, the Reuben's rule-breaking ways resist considering it traditional. But the story of the Jewish deli is also one of adaptation and forging a path in new environments. I think of the Reuben as the original instance in which Eastern European Jewish food, which had been forged along the borders of so many European countries, became American. It was the first adaptation to a changing market and a harbinger of the future assimilation of so many Jewish immigrants.

But none of that would matter if the Reuben wasn't a delicious sandwich. I have speculated, while eating a particularly tasty version with a side of macaroni salad and half sour pickles, that I would have been one of those guys strutting into a turn-of-the-century Lower East Side deli and asking them to serve me some cheese with their meat.

The Reuben at Frankel's Delicatessen & Appetizing is ideal: a hot and sloppy dance of soft, fatty corned beef and sour tangy kraut, sweetened and moistened by dollops of Russian dressing that cascade around the edges and soak into the rye. A layer of melted Swiss cheese adds to the decadent experience, making for a salty, rich, heavy, restorative sandwich, perfect just as it's served.

But hey, if you're going to enjoy something that's already breaking rules, why not break some more? Replace the sauerkraut with coleslaw, the Russian dressing with Thousand Island, the Swiss with American. Replace the sauerkraut with coleslaw and the corned beef with turkey to make it a Rachel. Try it with pastrami. The Reuben is about making your own way in the world, rules be damned.

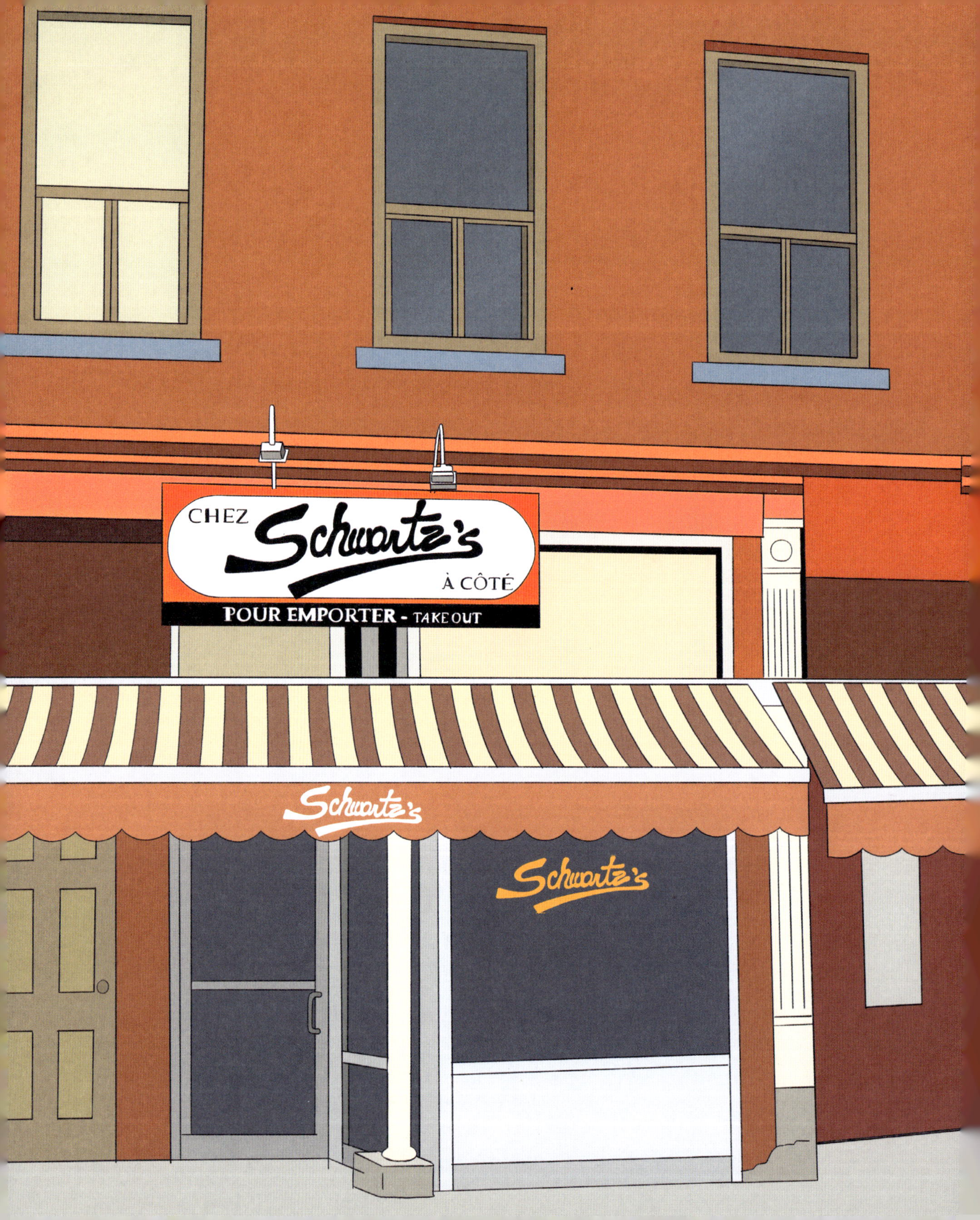
CHEZ Schwartz's À CÔTÉ
POUR EMPORTER - TAKEOUT
Schwartz's
Schwartz's

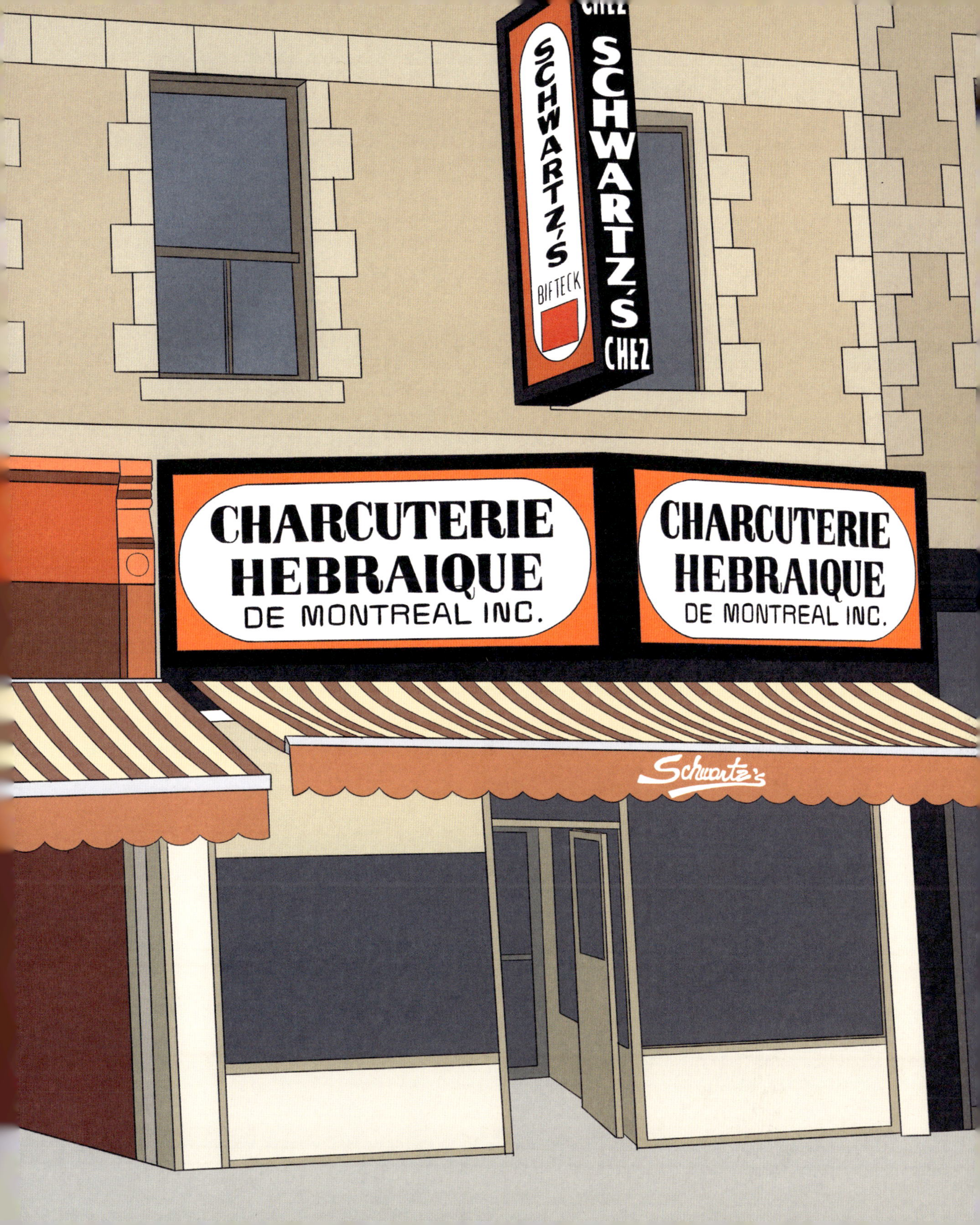
CHEZ SCHWARTZ'S
SCHWARTZ'S
BIFTECK
CHEZ
CHARCUTERIE HEBRAIQUE DE MONTREAL INC.
CHARCUTERIE HEBRAIQUE DE MONTREAL INC.
Schwartz's

SCHWARTZ'S DELI

3895 St. Laurent Boulevard,
Montreal, Quebec

Ruben Schwartz, a Jewish Romanian immigrant to Montreal, founded Schwartz's in 1928. At the time it was called Montreal Hebrew Delicatessen. The deli's name is practically synonymous with smoked meat, and it has become an international institution.

Interview with Frank Silva, General Manager of Schwartz's Deli

What's the perfect order at Schwartz's?
It's a medium fat [sandwich], french fries, pickle, and a black cherry [soda].

What's so good about the medium fat? Is that just the perfect amount for flavor?
Medium fat just melts in your mouth. It's all homemade here, the briskets. It's all natural. The french fries are homemade; we peel the potato, and we dice and fry it in vegetable oil, so nothing's frozen. With a nice, crunchy sour pickle and a sweet black cherry drink.

What's the key to perfect smoked meat, or is it a secret?
The key is basically not changing since 1928. The recipe is exactly the same. Everything is processed here at the deli. We don't have a freezer in the restaurant; everything's fresh.

Is that the key to the longevity of Schwartz's?
Absolutely. Give the customers what they want, what they're used to. They've been coming here forever, and they get the exact same thing every time.

Is there anything that's changed over the years?
Ownership. After Mr. Schwartz passed away in 1971, it was his business partner, Maurice Zbriger, and after that his lady friend [Armande Toupin Chartrand] for a while, and after that the accountant Hy Diamond, who sold it

to a business partner named Paul Nakis, who brought in Celine Dion as a partner, and that's the owner right now.

And nobody changed any recipes throughout all of that transition?

I've been here for thirty-eight years, so I've been here before most of these owners. And I run the place, so the owners basically just take in the cash, and they're all very happy. The staff run the show here.

Is there an item that people tend not to order but that you think they should try?

It's changed because Schwartz's at the very beginning was more of a steakhouse than a smoked meat house. Over the years it became a smoked meat house, so now people tend to order the steak a little less, but it's an excellent steak.

What is the best way to introduce someone to Jewish deli food—the smoked meat sandwich?

Yes, absolutely. You come here and you sit down and you have a sandwich that you'll never forget, and you'll keep coming back.

I read that you'll serve just the deckle of the brisket if ordered. Is that true?

Yes, we do. People come here and ask for a "corner," you know? That slice, that's just a nice big piece of meat. Now the ones that order that, of course they're the regulars. They've been coming here forever. A nice medium fat. We trim off the lean part, and it's heaven!

What does the future of Jewish deli look like?

Well, I think as long as you don't change—'cause, let's face it, not too many delis are around anymore—but if you stay consistent and hang on, it will be here forever. We just celebrated ninety years last year, and we're doing better than ever.

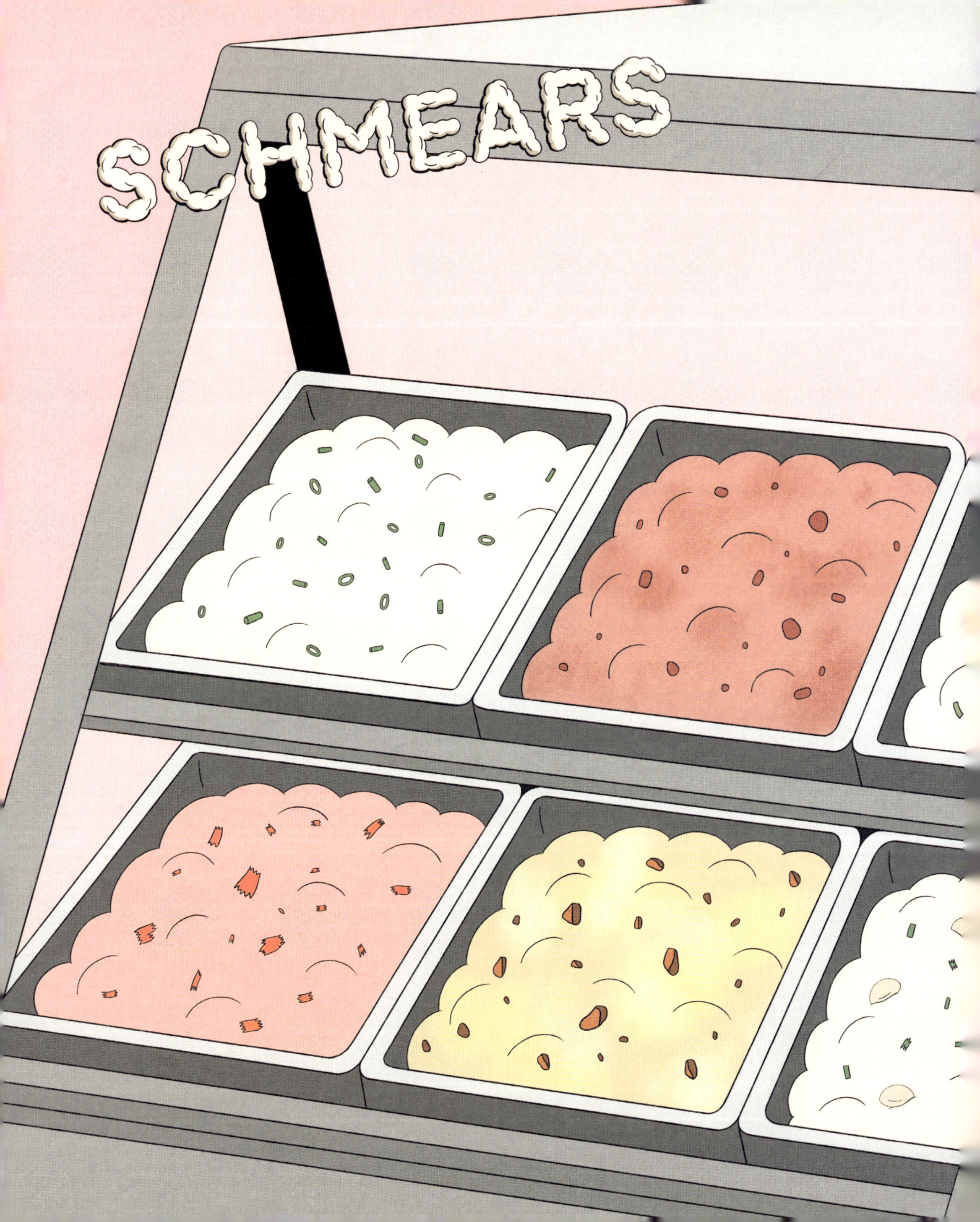
SCHMEARS

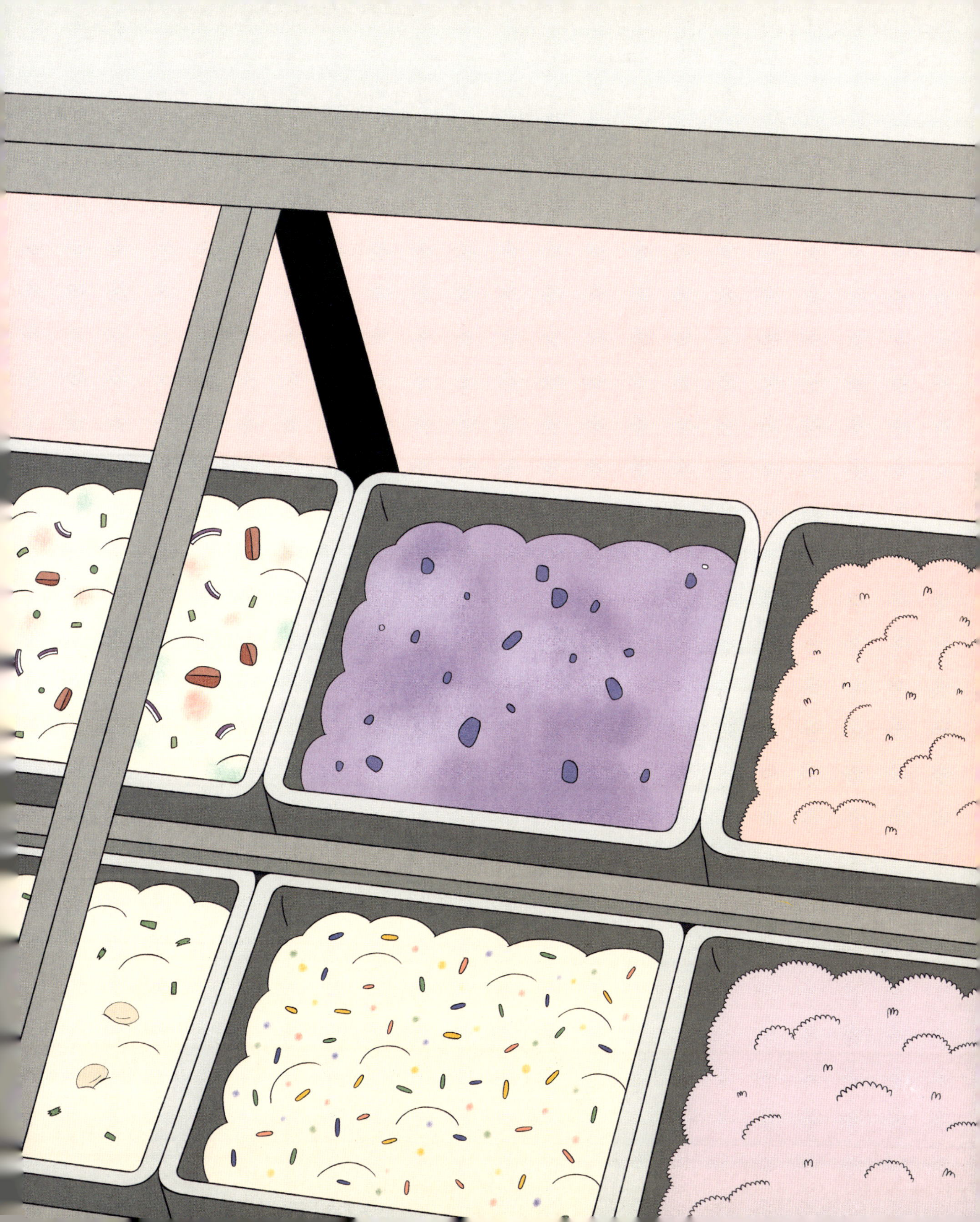

Cream Cheese

THE WORD *SCHMEAR* IS GERMAN FOR "SPREAD," BUT IT HAS BEEN ADOPTED INTO YIDDISH VERNACULAR. IT ORIGINALLY REFERRED TO CHEESE BUT NOW COVERS A VARIETY OF SPREADS FOR A BAGEL OR BIALY OR EVEN A PIECE OF RYE TOAST.

CREAMY, SPREADABLE CHEESE GOES BACK TO EARLY MODERN ENGLAND AND FRANCE. BUT CREAM CHEESE AS WE KNOW IT TODAY IS NOT ONLY AMERICAN IN ORIGIN—IT'S GENTILE.

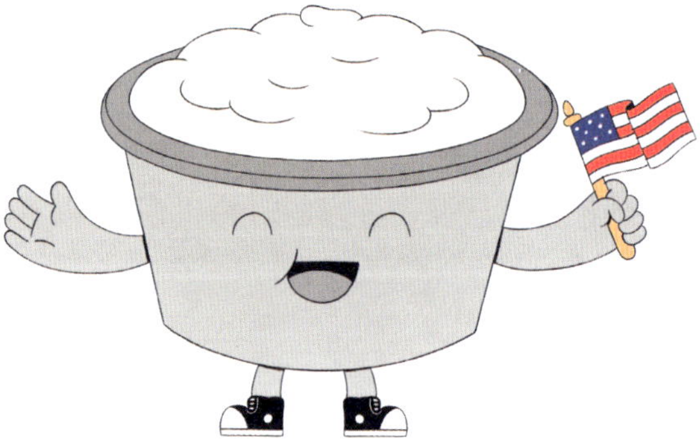

WHEN THE BRITISH COLONIZED NORTH AMERICA, THEY BROUGHT WITH THEM A TASTE FOR SOFT, SWEET CHEESES.

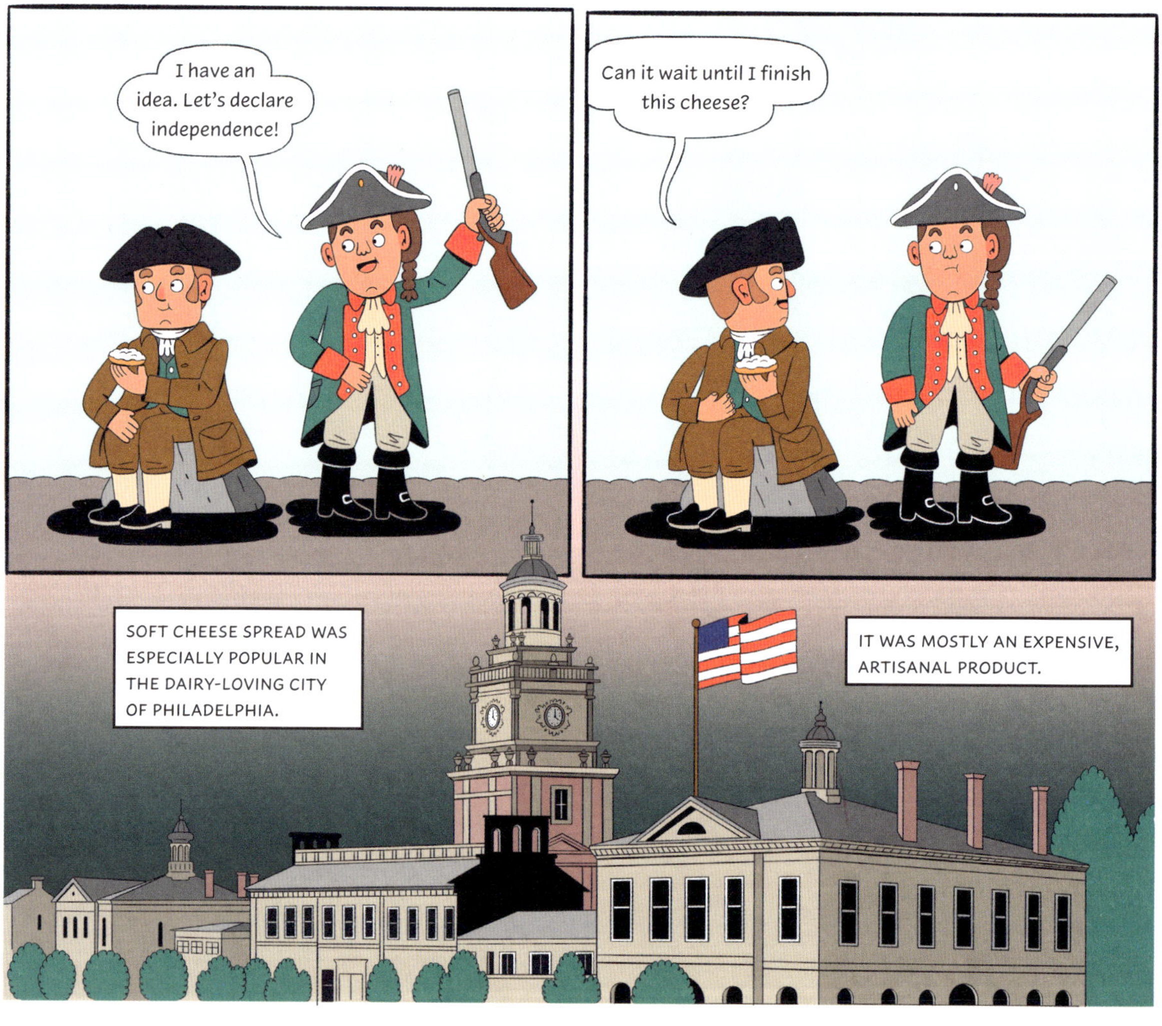
I have an idea. Let's declare independence!
Can it wait until I finish this cheese?
SOFT CHEESE SPREAD WAS ESPECIALLY POPULAR IN THE DAIRY-LOVING CITY OF PHILADELPHIA.
IT WAS MOSTLY AN EXPENSIVE, ARTISANAL PRODUCT.

IN THE LATE NINETEENTH CENTURY, A CHEESEMAKER IN UPSTATE NEW YORK NAMED WILLIAM LAWRENCE WAS TRYING TO RE-CREATE A VERSION OF A FANCY, SOFT FRENCH CHEESE CALLED NEUFCHÂTEL, TO CAPITALIZE ON THE GROWING DEMAND FOR EXPENSIVE EUROPEAN CHEESES.

HE ENDED UP ADDING MORE FAT TO IT FOR DELICATESSENS IN NEW YORK CITY TO SELL TO WEALTHY SHOPPERS.

Can you make it a little more decadent?

IT WAS MARKETED AS PHILADELPHIA CREAM CHEESE, BECAUSE THE CITY OF PHILADELPHIA WAS ASSOCIATED WITH THE HIGHEST-QUALITY CHEESES.

PHILADELPHIA

IN THE SAME WAY THAT JEWS IN EUROPE ADAPTED THE FOOD OF THEIR RESPECTIVE COUNTRIES TO THEIR OWN TASTES AND DIETARY LAWS, THEY TOOK AMERICAN CREAM CHEESE AND MADE IT INTO SOMETHING THEIR OWN.

THE CREAMY, FATTY SPREAD WAS THE PERFECT ACCOMPANIMENT TO THE SALTINESS OF LOX.

IT QUICKLY BECAME THE SPREAD OF CHOICE FOR BAGELS AND BIALYS.

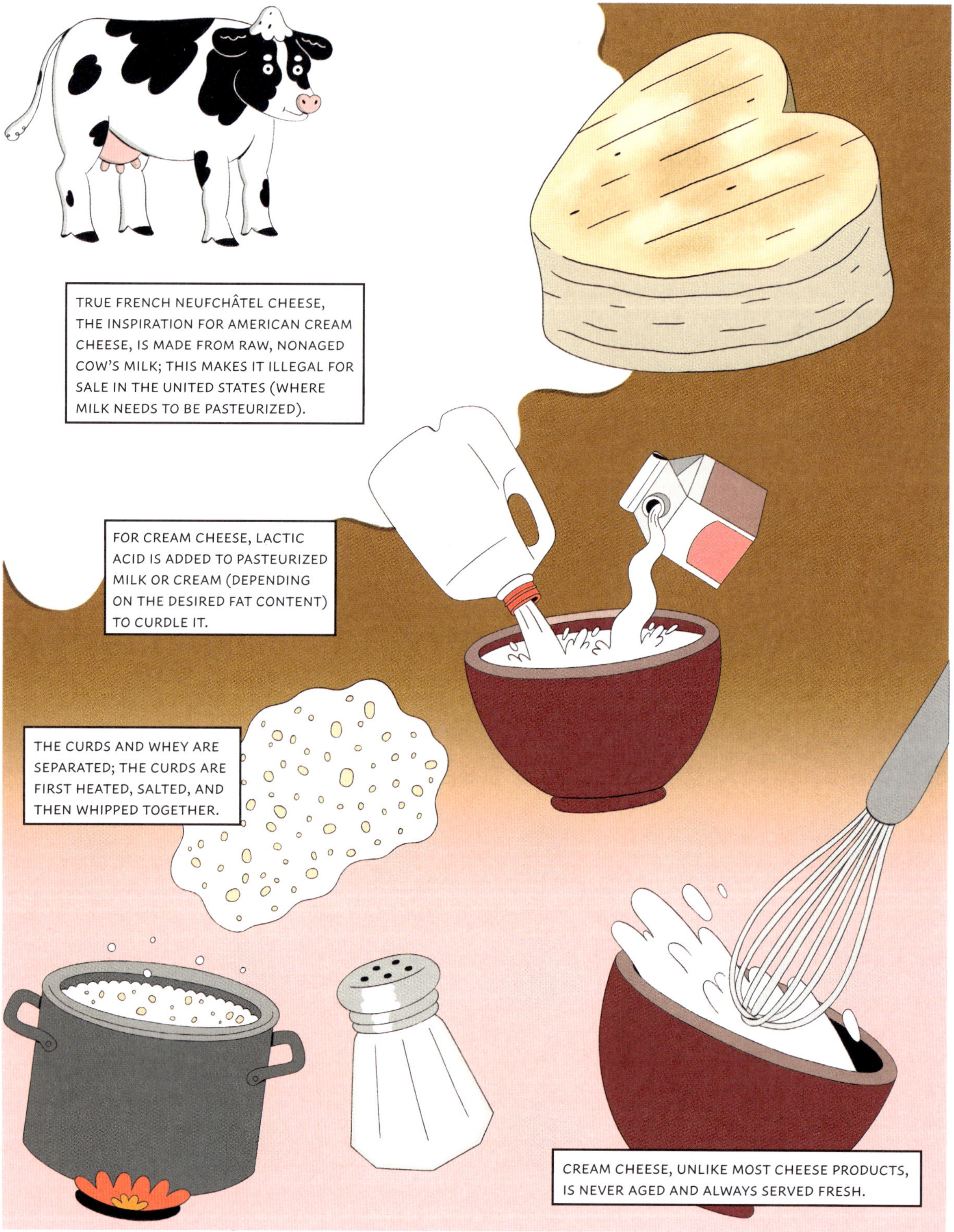
TRUE FRENCH NEUFCHÂTEL CHEESE, THE INSPIRATION FOR AMERICAN CREAM CHEESE, IS MADE FROM RAW, NONAGED COW'S MILK; THIS MAKES IT ILLEGAL FOR SALE IN THE UNITED STATES (WHERE MILK NEEDS TO BE PASTEURIZED).
FOR CREAM CHEESE, LACTIC ACID IS ADDED TO PASTEURIZED MILK OR CREAM (DEPENDING ON THE DESIRED FAT CONTENT) TO CURDLE IT.
THE CURDS AND WHEY ARE SEPARATED; THE CURDS ARE FIRST HEATED, SALTED, AND THEN WHIPPED TOGETHER.
CREAM CHEESE, UNLIKE MOST CHEESE PRODUCTS, IS NEVER AGED AND ALWAYS SERVED FRESH.

VARIETIES OF CREAM CHEESE

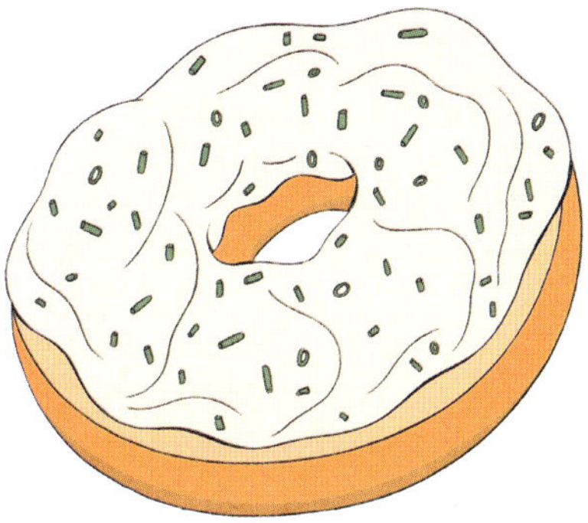

CHIVE

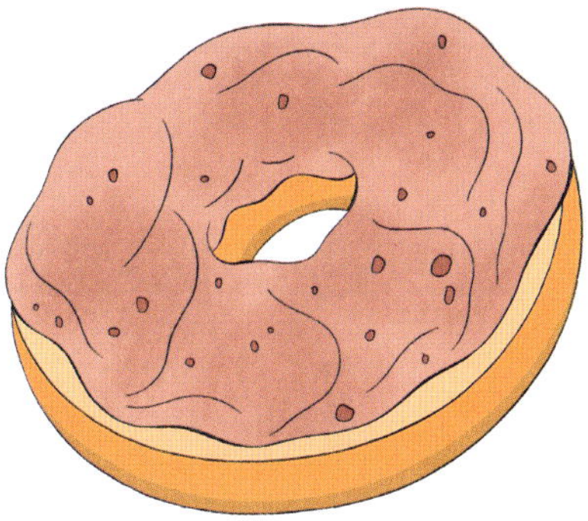

STRAWBERRY

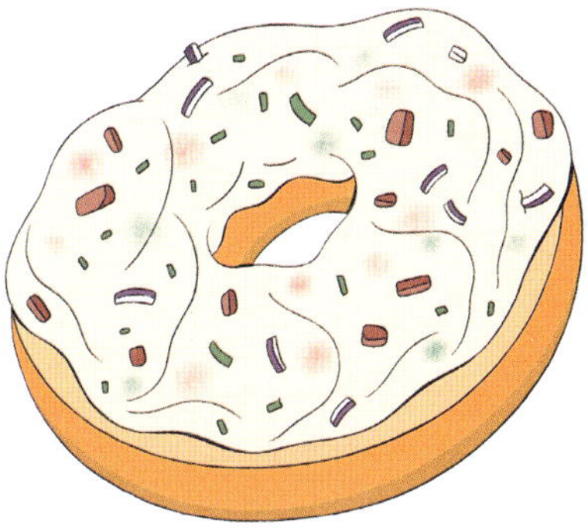

VEGETABLE

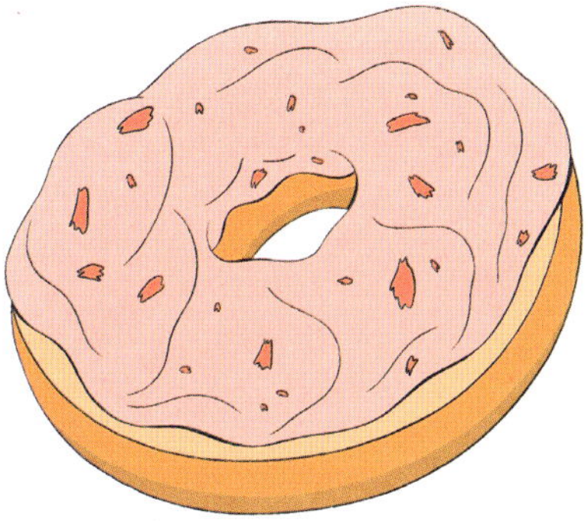

LOX

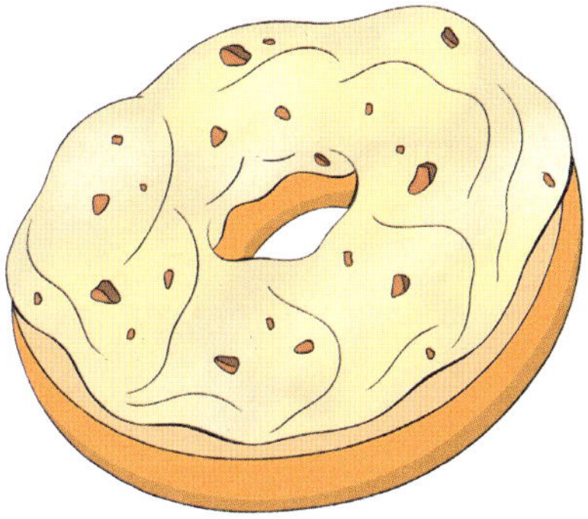

HONEY + NUTS

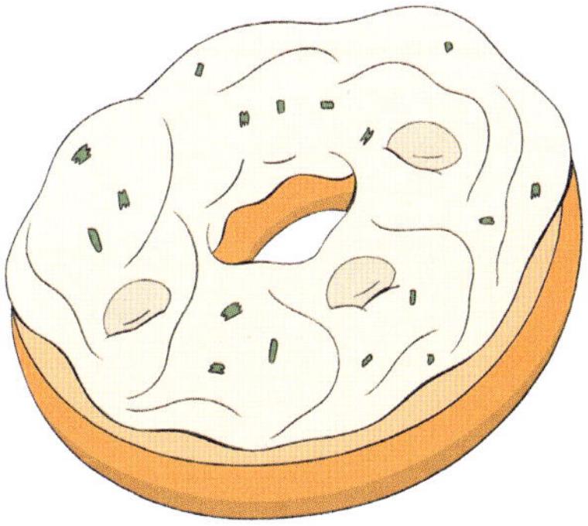

GARLIC HERB

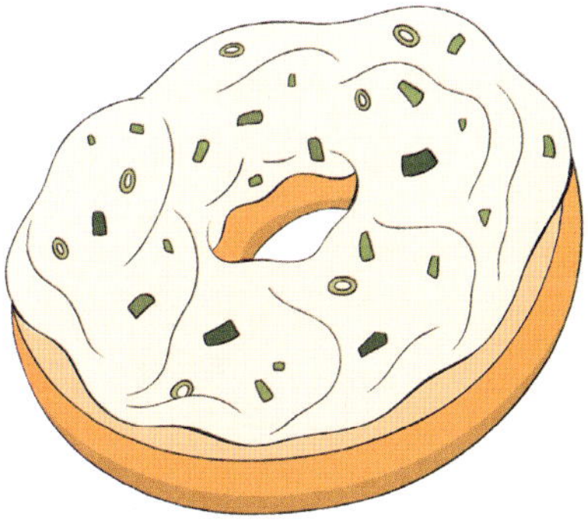

SCALLION

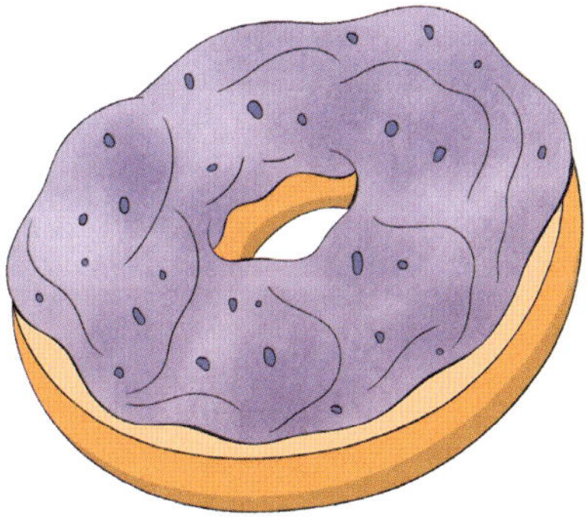

BLUEBERRY

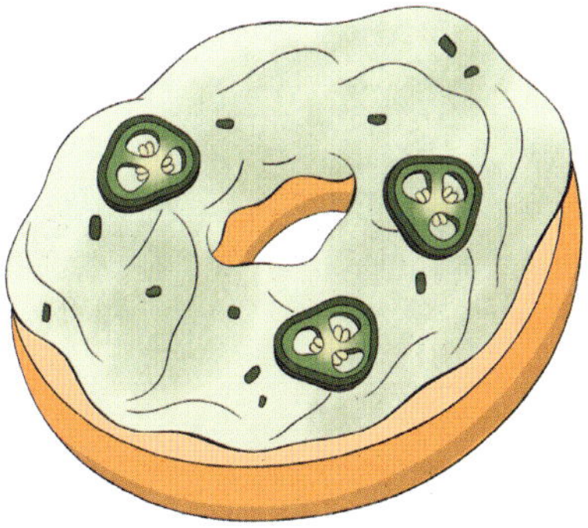

JALAPEÑO

Chopped Liver

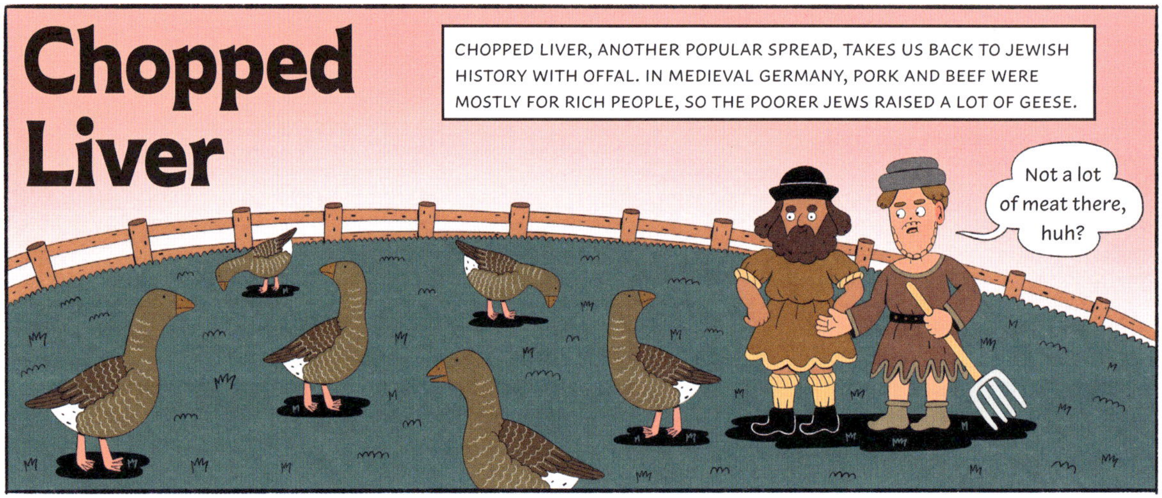
CHOPPED LIVER, ANOTHER POPULAR SPREAD, TAKES US BACK TO JEWISH HISTORY WITH OFFAL. IN MEDIEVAL GERMANY, PORK AND BEEF WERE MOSTLY FOR RICH PEOPLE, SO THE POORER JEWS RAISED A LOT OF GEESE.
Not a lot of meat there, huh?

BECAUSE THEY WERE TRYING TO BE RESOURCEFUL AND USE EVERY PART OF THE ANIMAL, AND BECAUSE THE UPPER CLASSES TENDED NOT TO BUY OFFAL, GOOSE LIVER BECAME A POPULAR ITEM WITH ASHKENAZI JEWS.

ONCE AGAIN, THE IMMIGRANTS BROUGHT IT TO THE UNITED STATES, WHERE THEY COULD AFFORD TO USE BEEF AND CHICKEN LIVERS AS WELL.

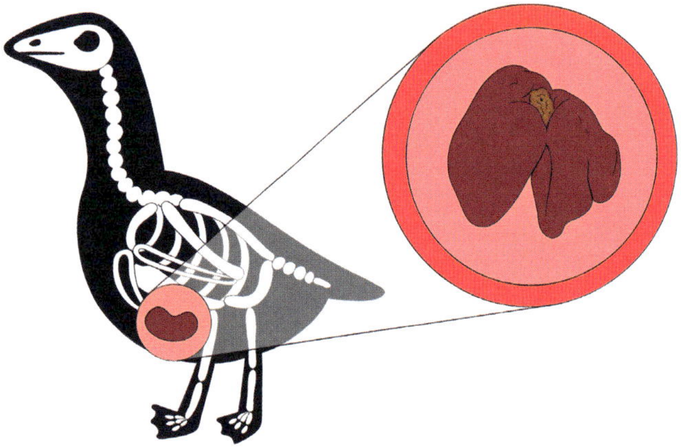

AS GOOSE LIVER BECAME MORE EXPENSIVE, CHICKEN LIVERS BECAME THE MOST POPULAR BASE FOR CHOPPED LIVER.

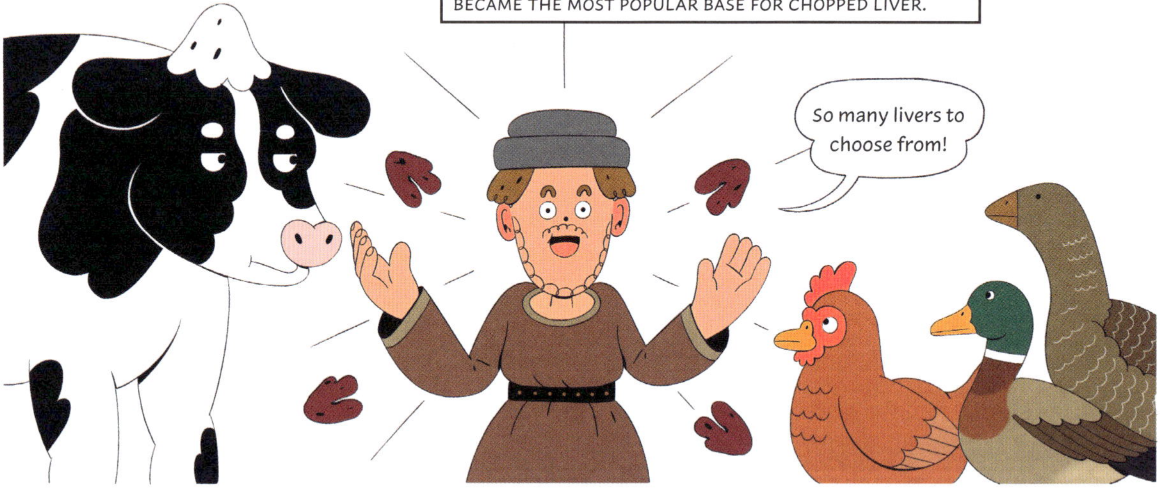
So many livers to choose from!

HERE IS HOW CHOPPED LIVER IS MADE

FIRST, THE LIVERS ARE COOKED.

TO MAKE SURE THEY ARE KOSHER, THEY ARE BROILED ON AN OPEN RACK WHILE ALL THE BLOOD DRIPS INTO A PAN BELOW.

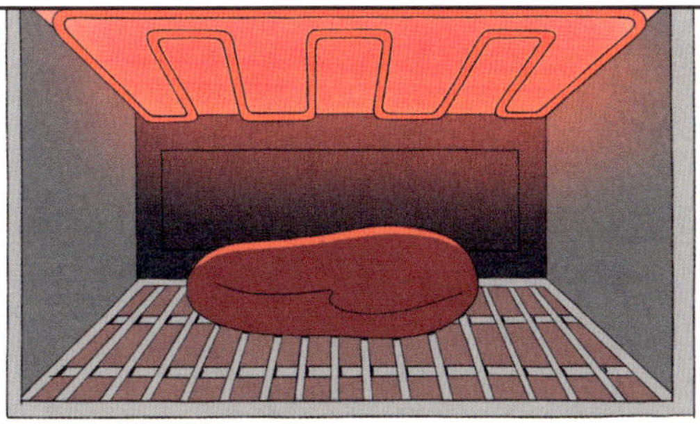

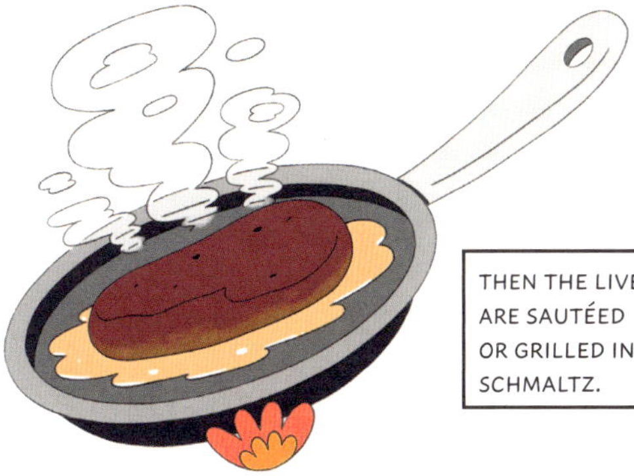

THEN THE LIVERS ARE SAUTÉED OR GRILLED IN SCHMALTZ.

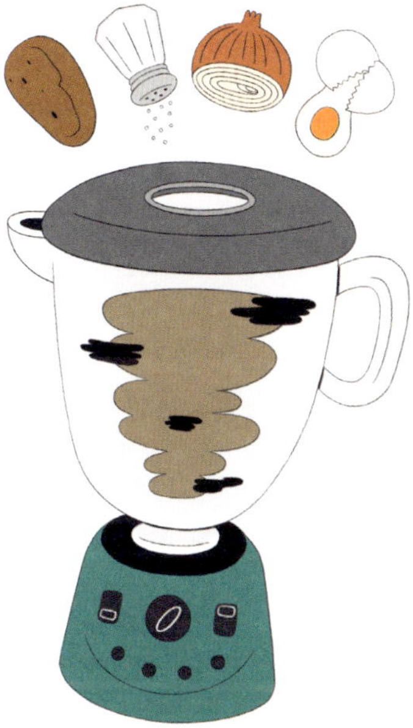

THE COOKED LIVERS ARE CHOPPED OR GROUND AND MIXED WITH MORE SCHMALTZ AND OTHER INGREDIENTS AND SEASONINGS, USUALLY ONIONS AND EGGS.

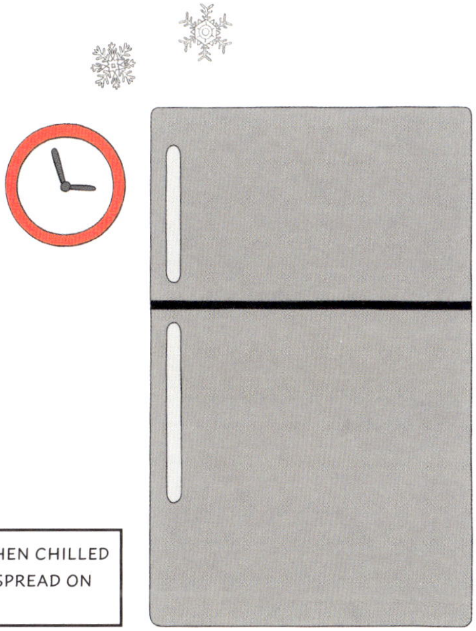

THE MIXTURE IS THEN CHILLED AND SERVED AS A SPREAD ON BREAD OR MATZO.

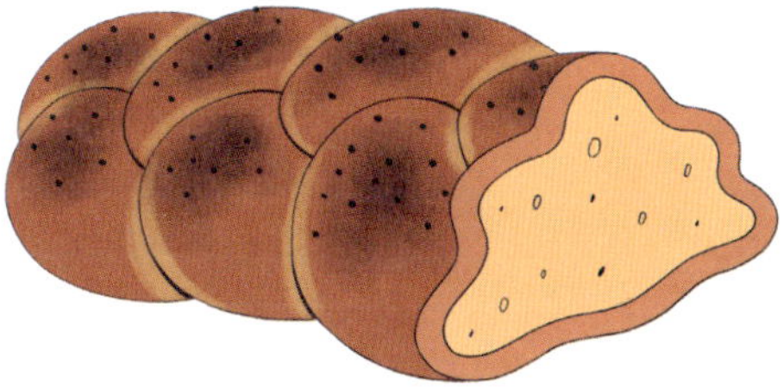

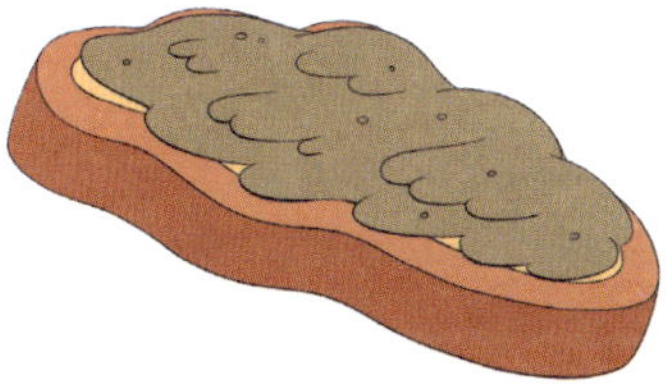

Schmaltz

SCHMALTZ IS YIDDISH FOR "FAT"—MORE PRECISELY, RENDERED CHICKEN FAT. IT IS ANOTHER PERFECT EXAMPLE OF JEWISH ADAPTABILITY AND RESOURCEFULNESS.

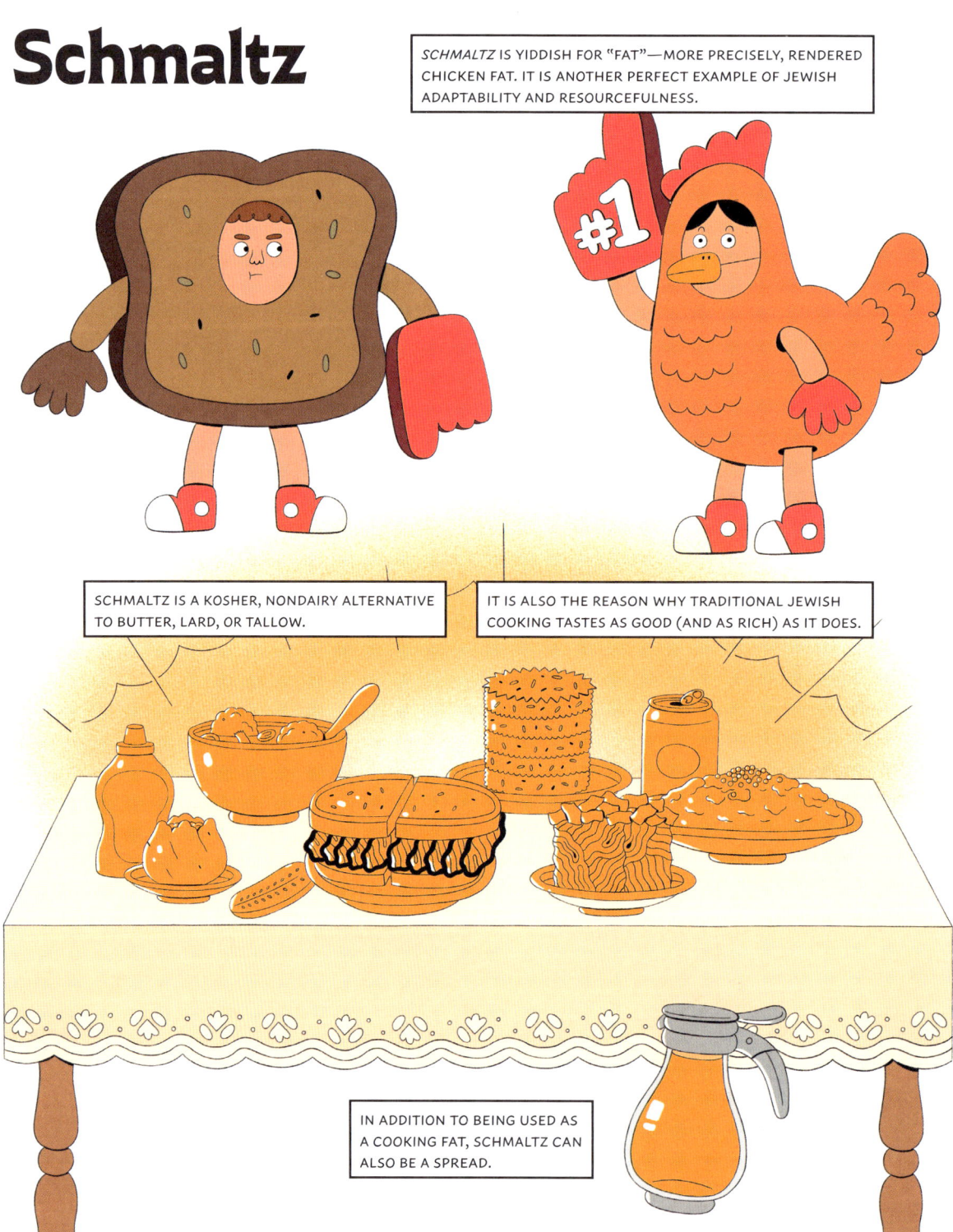

SCHMALTZ IS A KOSHER, NONDAIRY ALTERNATIVE TO BUTTER, LARD, OR TALLOW.

IT IS ALSO THE REASON WHY TRADITIONAL JEWISH COOKING TASTES AS GOOD (AND AS RICH) AS IT DOES.

IN ADDITION TO BEING USED AS A COOKING FAT, SCHMALTZ CAN ALSO BE A SPREAD.

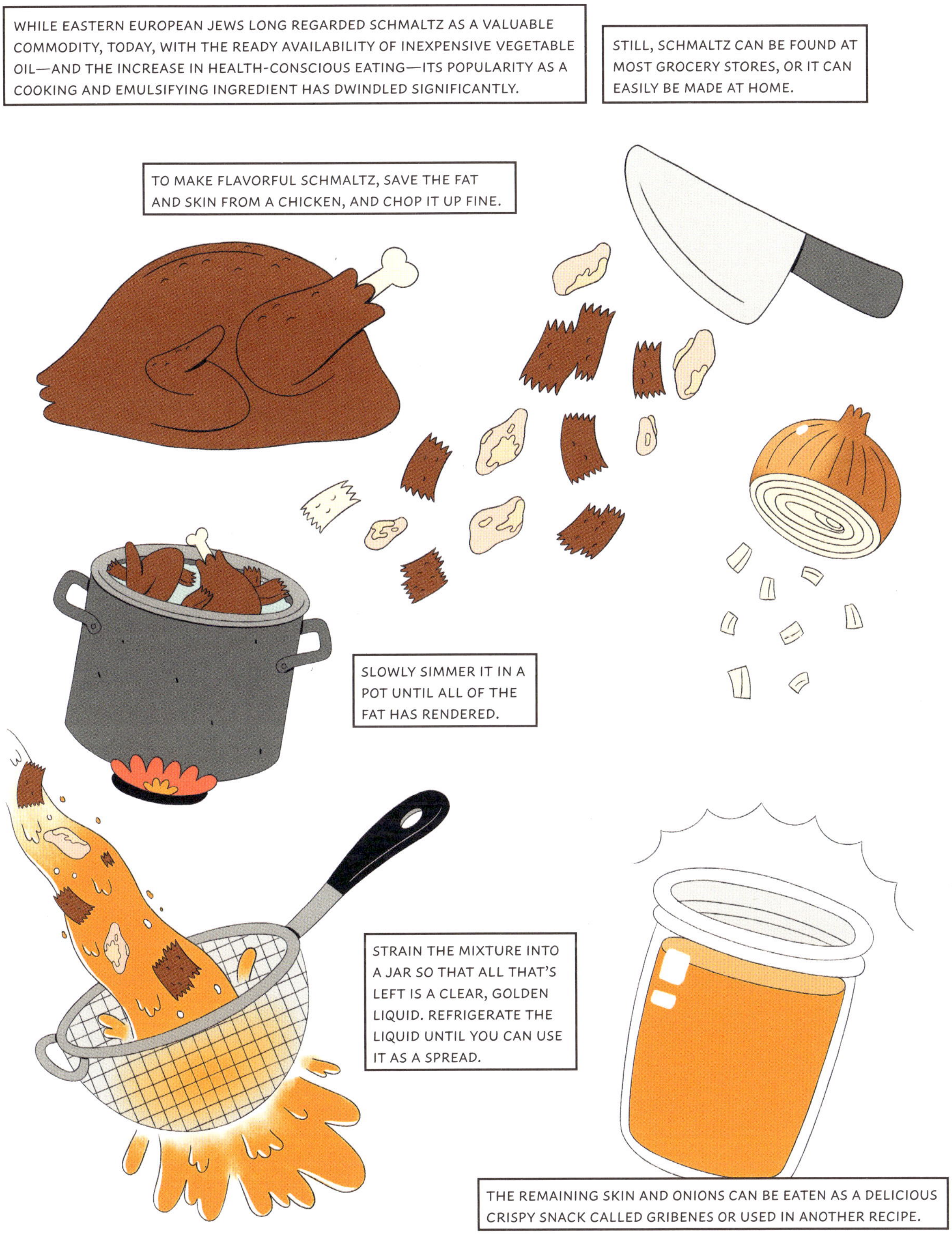
WHILE EASTERN EUROPEAN JEWS LONG REGARDED SCHMALTZ AS A VALUABLE COMMODITY, TODAY, WITH THE READY AVAILABILITY OF INEXPENSIVE VEGETABLE OIL—AND THE INCREASE IN HEALTH-CONSCIOUS EATING—ITS POPULARITY AS A COOKING AND EMULSIFYING INGREDIENT HAS DWINDLED SIGNIFICANTLY.
STILL, SCHMALTZ CAN BE FOUND AT MOST GROCERY STORES, OR IT CAN EASILY BE MADE AT HOME.
TO MAKE FLAVORFUL SCHMALTZ, SAVE THE FAT AND SKIN FROM A CHICKEN, AND CHOP IT UP FINE.
SLOWLY SIMMER IT IN A POT UNTIL ALL OF THE FAT HAS RENDERED.
STRAIN THE MIXTURE INTO A JAR SO THAT ALL THAT'S LEFT IS A CLEAR, GOLDEN LIQUID. REFRIGERATE THE LIQUID UNTIL YOU CAN USE IT AS A SPREAD.
THE REMAINING SKIN AND ONIONS CAN BE EATEN AS A DELICIOUS CRISPY SNACK CALLED GRIBENES OR USED IN ANOTHER RECIPE.

Mustard

MUSTARD IS AN ANCIENT CONDIMENT.

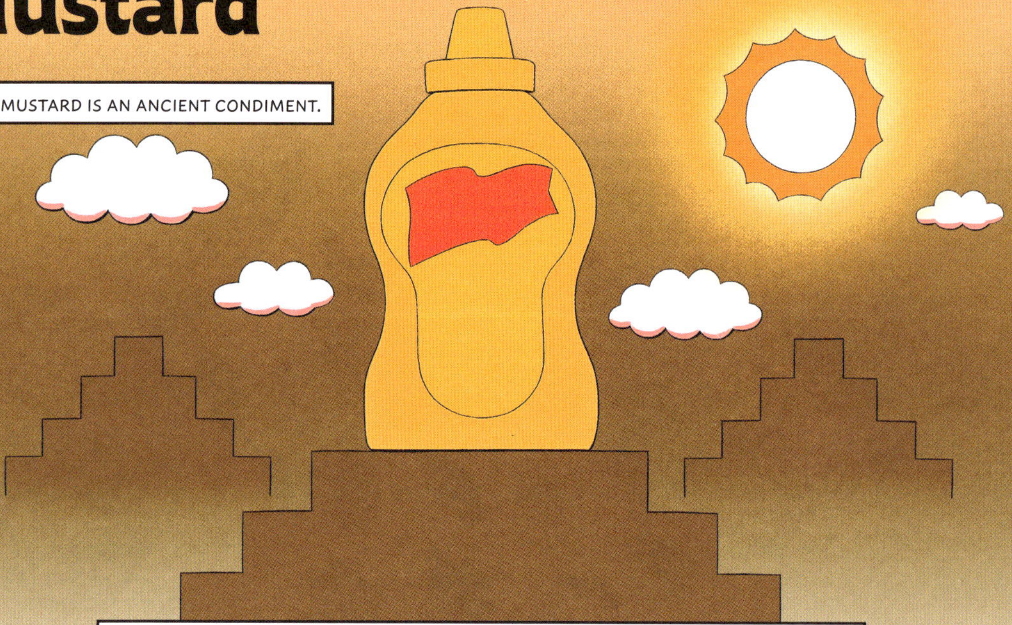

THE ROMANS CRUSHED SEEDS FROM THE MUSTARD PLANT AND MIXED THEM WITH WINE TO FORM A PASTE (*MUST* IS THE FRENCH WORD FOR UNFERMENTED GRAPE JUICE).

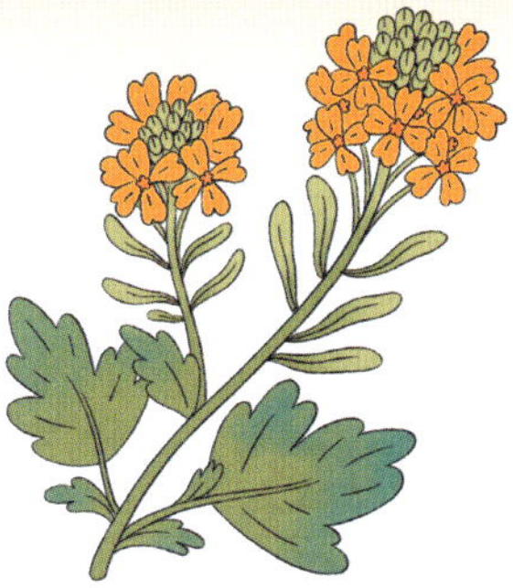

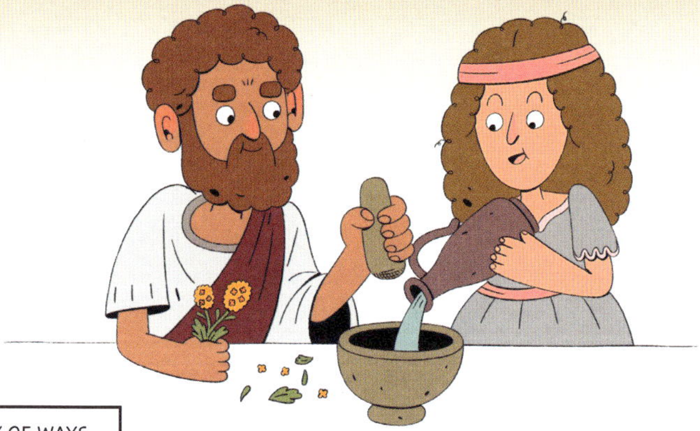

MUSTARD TODAY IS PREPARED IN A GREAT VARIETY OF WAYS, BUT ALWAYS WITH SEEDS FROM THE MUSTARD PLANT, WATER, AND A TYPE OF ACID—VINEGAR, FOR EXAMPLE.

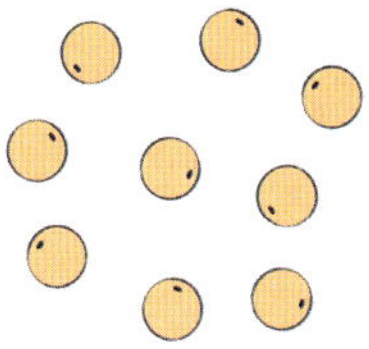

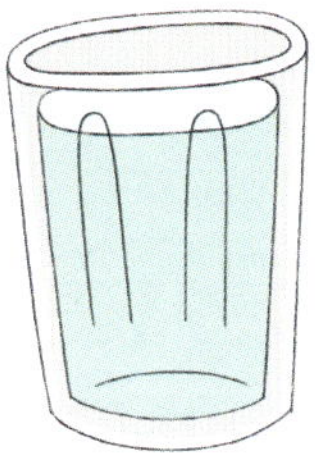

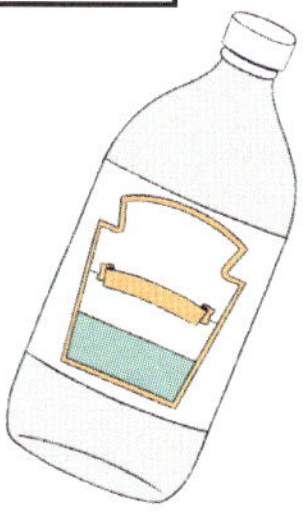

WHAT YOU WILL FIND ON THE TABLE OF A TYPICAL JEWISH DELI IS A BROWN, SPICY MUSTARD.

VARIETIES OF MUSTARD

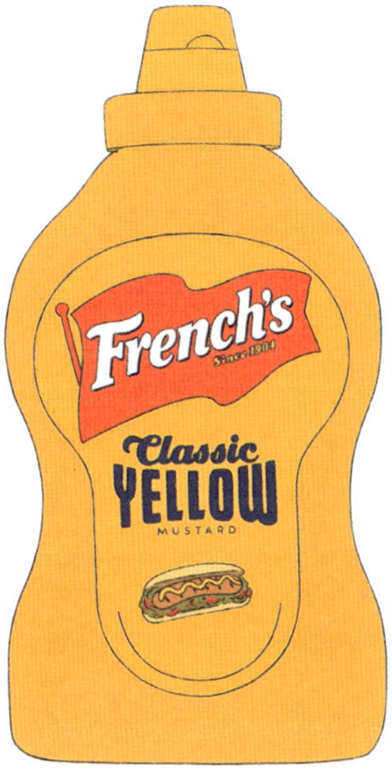
French's
Classic
YELLOW
MUSTARD

FRENCH'S CLASSIC YELLOW MUSTARD

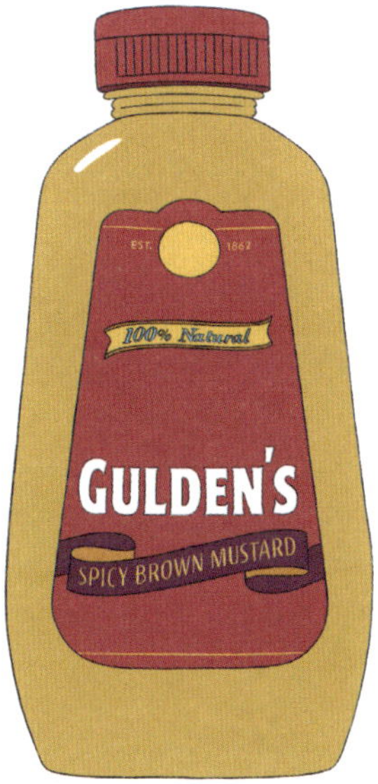
100% Natural
GULDEN'S
SPICY BROWN MUSTARD

GULDEN'S SPICY BROWN MUSTARD

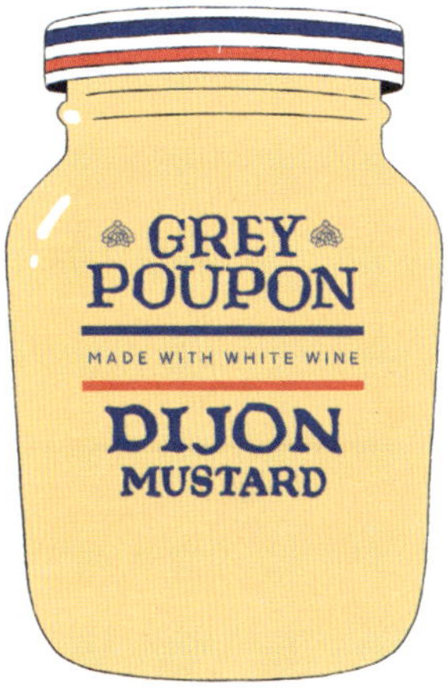
GREY
POUPON
MADE WITH WHITE WINE
DIJON
MUSTARD

GREY POUPON DIJON MUSTARD

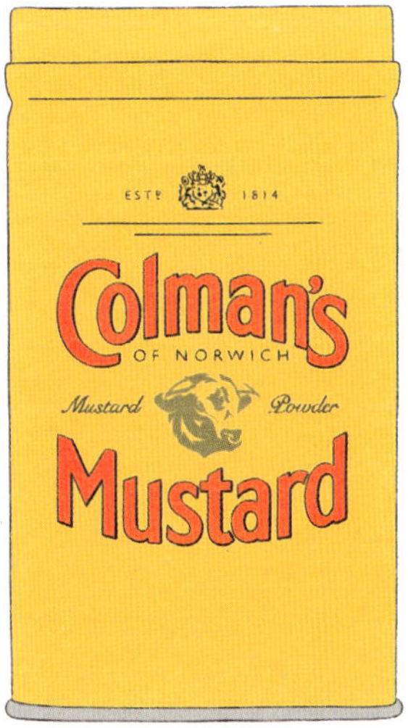
ESTD 1814
Colman's
OF NORWICH
Mustard Powder
Mustard

COLMAN'S DRY MUSTARD

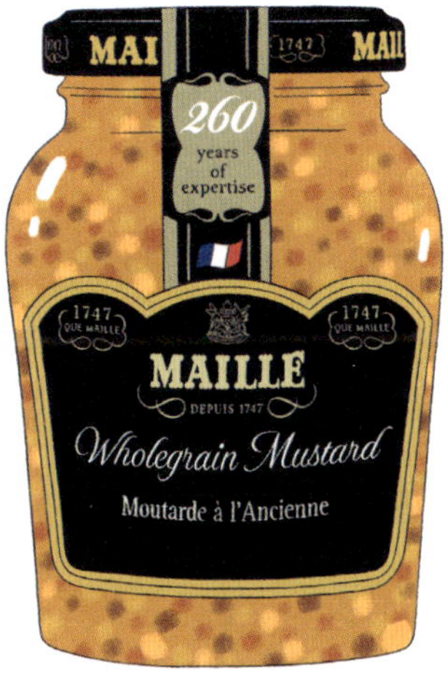
260
years
of
expertise
1747
1747
MAILLE
DEPUIS 1747
Wholegrain Mustard
Moutarde à l'Ancienne

MAILLE WHOLEGRAIN MUSTARD

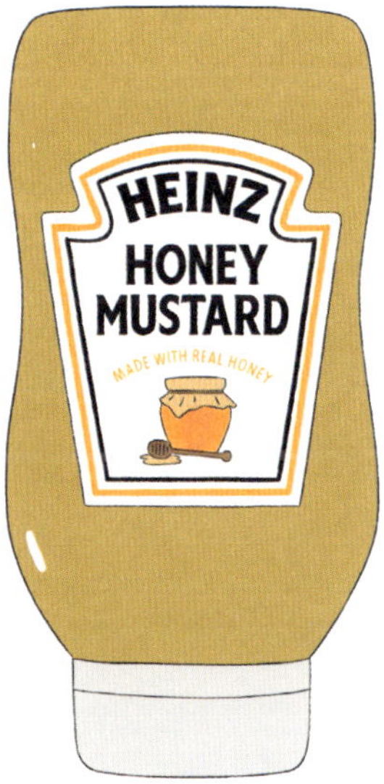
HEINZ
HONEY
MUSTARD
MADE WITH REAL HONEY

HEINZ HONEY MUSTARD

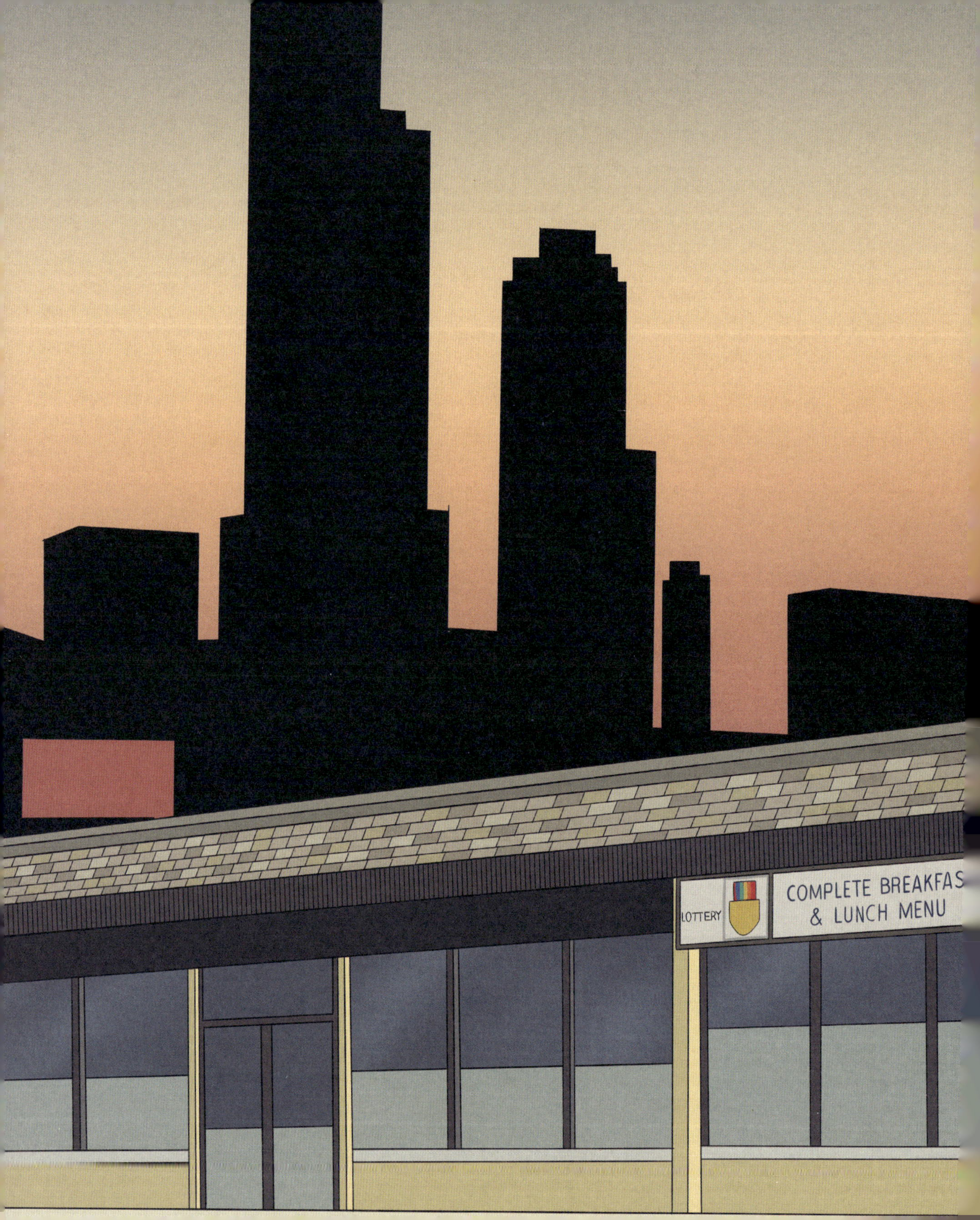
LOTTERY
COMPLETE BREAKFAS
& LUNCH MENU

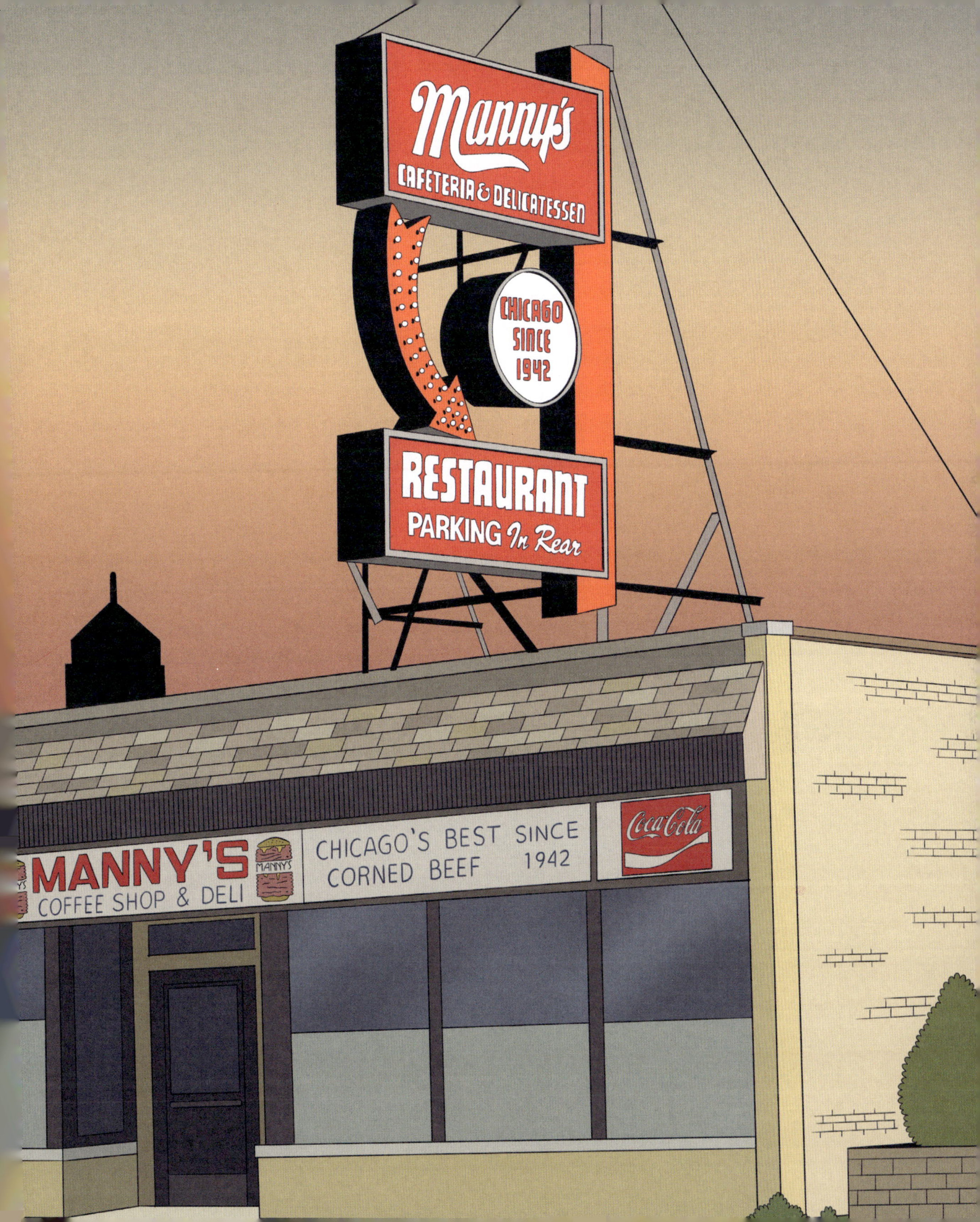
Manny's
CAFETERIA & DELICATESSEN
CHICAGO SINCE 1942
RESTAURANT
PARKING In Rear
MANNY'S
COFFEE SHOP & DELI
CHICAGO'S BEST CORNED BEEF
SINCE 1942
Coca-Cola

MANNY'S CAFETERIA & DELICATESSEN

1141 South Jefferson Street,
Chicago, Illinois

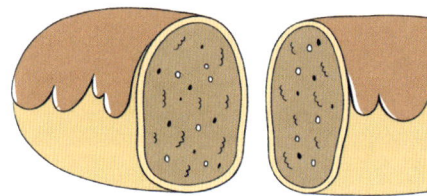

After World War II, Russian brothers Jack and Charlie Raskin opened a cafeteria in Chicago that served food inspired by their Jewish grandmother's cooking. When the brothers split up to run separate businesses, Jack changed the name of the cafeteria from Sonny's to Manny's—named for his son, Emmanuel—so that he would have to replace only the *s* and the *o* on the sign. In 1964, the cafeteria moved to its current location on Jefferson Street, where Manny worked as a cook. Manny's is the oldest delicatessen in Chicago. It still serves up food from the Old World to new generations of mavens, preserving Jewish culinary culture in a city that should be teeming with delis—given its history as a bastion of meat production and its population of Ashkenazi Jews—but has instead become a relative deli wasteland.

Interview with Dan Raskin, Owner of Manny's Cafeteria and Delicatessen

What do you think is the perfect order at Manny's?
Oh, that's hard.

What about *your* order?
It's really hard to get a full taste of all of our items because I think we do so many things really well. We're not just about the big sandwiches. The things that I would definitely recommend for someone to try are the combo corned beef and pastrami sandwich with a potato pancake and a matzo ball soup.

Do you think that's the best way to introduce someone to Jewish food who's unfamiliar?
Yes, and then the next thing I would tell them to try is one of our knishes.

Is there an item that people tend to stay away from but that you think they should try?
Kishke.

What is that?
It's a matzo meal stuffing inside a natural beef casing. Not very many places still make it with natural casing, but we still make it like that. You can get kishke at some places on other people's menus, but it's usually got vegetables or it's in a plastic casing. We still make ours the old-fashioned way, how we always made it—with natural beef casing—and it's really good.

Is there an advantage to the cafeteria-style setup here at Manny's?
I think it exposes people to see what all of our items are instead of just looking at the menu. People like to pick foods with their eyes and not just off a menu.

Has Manny's always done it that way?
Yes.

What do you think keeps Manny's going? Are people coming because of generational traditions?
I think it's that, and I think the big thing that keeps us going is that we're family-owned, and I *want* to keep it going. A lot of businesses get to the point that nobody in the family wants to take them over, and they don't make it past that.

Do you think there's a future for the Jewish deli?
I do, but I don't think the future of Jewish deli is what old-school Jewish deli is. There are all sorts of restaurants

that have some Jewish items on their menus, but to survive they don't [operate] as a Jewish deli.

Because of the obscurity?

I just think it's the whole package. They need to have other items on their menu that draw in people who don't know deli food, and they also have things on their menu that are just better margin items. A lot of the new delis that are opening up have a whole hamburger section on their menu. That's not Jewish deli. They need to expand their menus past what the traditional deli is, and I don't think it's a bad thing. I think it's good that some people are doing this. I hope that more people open Jewish delis in Chicago. You don't want more competition, but I do think it helps because people talk about deli and then they go try multiple places.

It gets people excited.

To get the bar business, and to get the general public who are not educated on deli, which is obviously the majority of people, you need to have other items. You've seen it in some other restaurants that people wouldn't think have Jewish items on there, like Au Cheval, which is a big hamburger place in Chicago. They have Jewish roots; the owner's a Jewish person. They have matzo ball soup on their menu, but they have a fried bologna sandwich, so it's not a strictly Jewish restaurant at all. I think the future of Jewish foods is that they're incorporated into other menus and enrich them.

The people who are passionate about the food are going to do whatever they can to sneak it in.

Right. I think if you ask a guy who owns twenty restaurants why he didn't open a Jewish deli, he's gonna say there's no margin in Jewish deli. So he opens other restaurants and has some Jewish deli items in there. I think that's been a trend for twenty years.

SOUPS AND SIDES

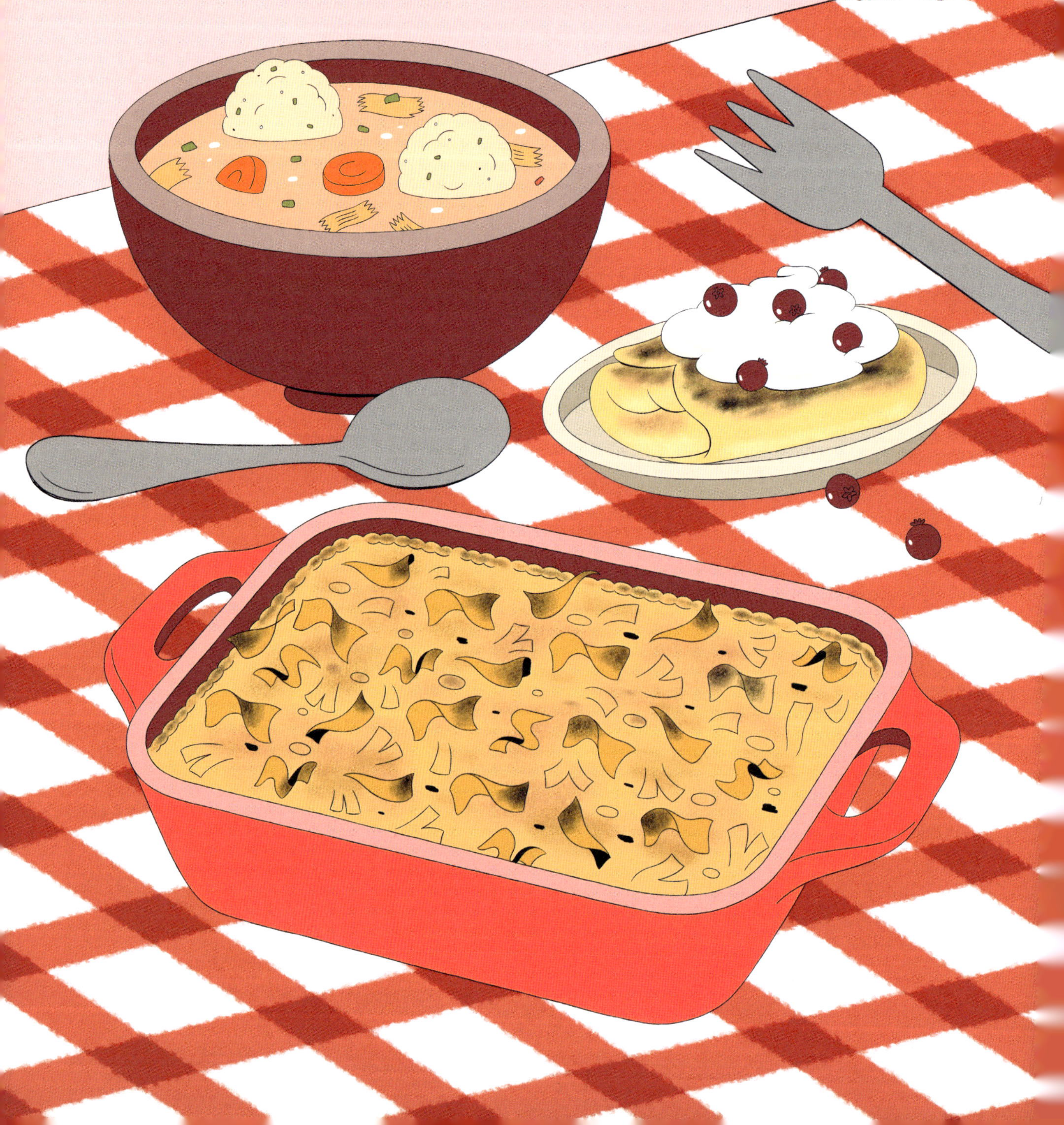

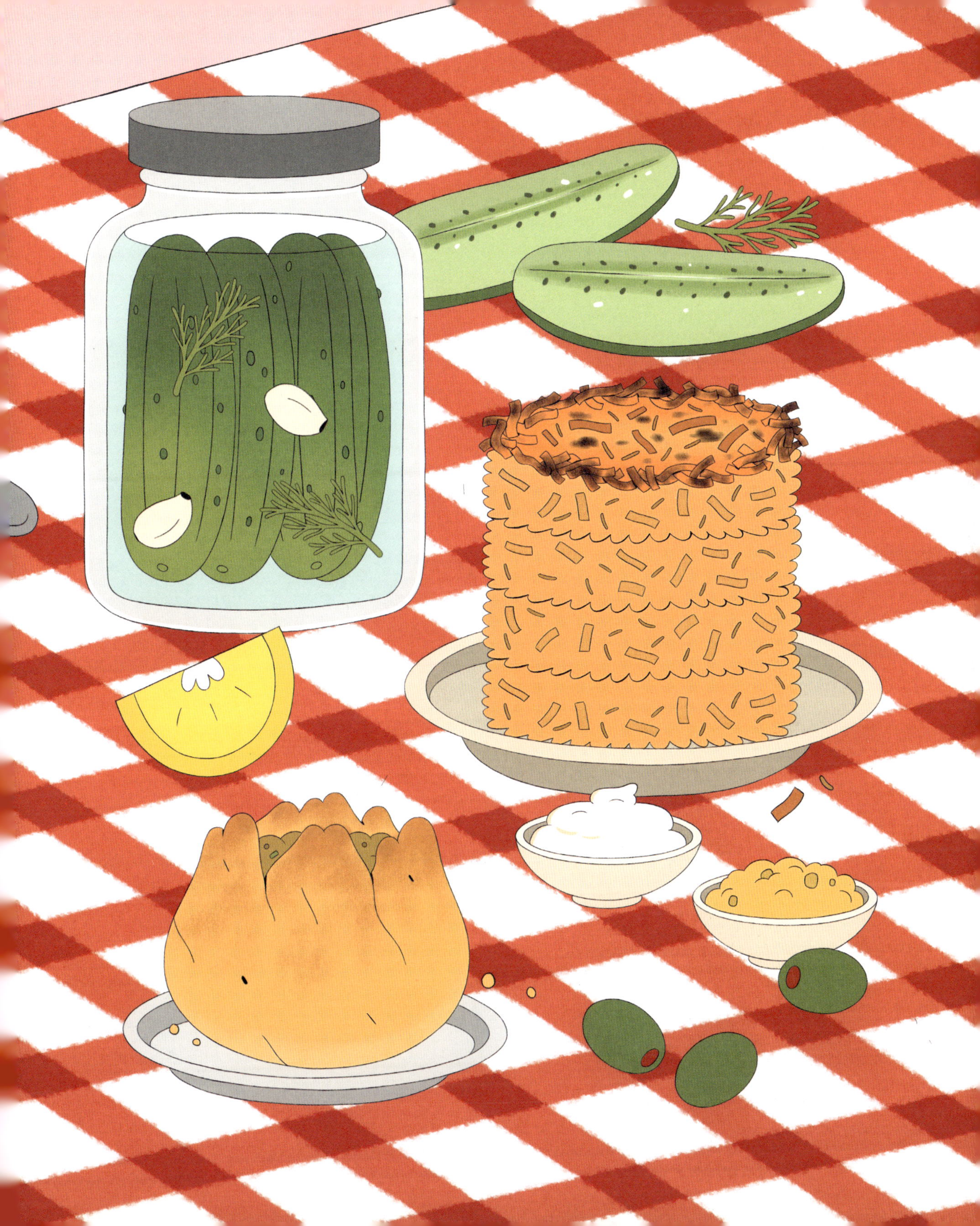

Matzo Ball Soup

MATZO BALLS ARE ANOTHER EXAMPLE OF THE POOR JEWISH IMMIGRANT'S RELUCTANCE TO LET ANYTHING GO TO WASTE, INCLUDING THE CRUMBS LEFT OVER FROM MATZO.

BEFORE THERE WERE MATZO BALLS, THERE WERE KNÖDEL, OR IN POLISH, KNOEDELA, DUMPLINGS MADE OUT OF BREAD OR POTATOES.

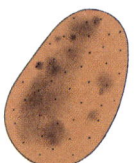

JEWISH FAMILIES ADAPTED THE RECIPE AND USED LEFTOVER MATZO MEAL INSTEAD OF BREAD OR POTATO, WITH SCHMALTZ AS THE BINDING FAT.

What are you doing? Those are perfectly good matzo crumbs you're throwing away!

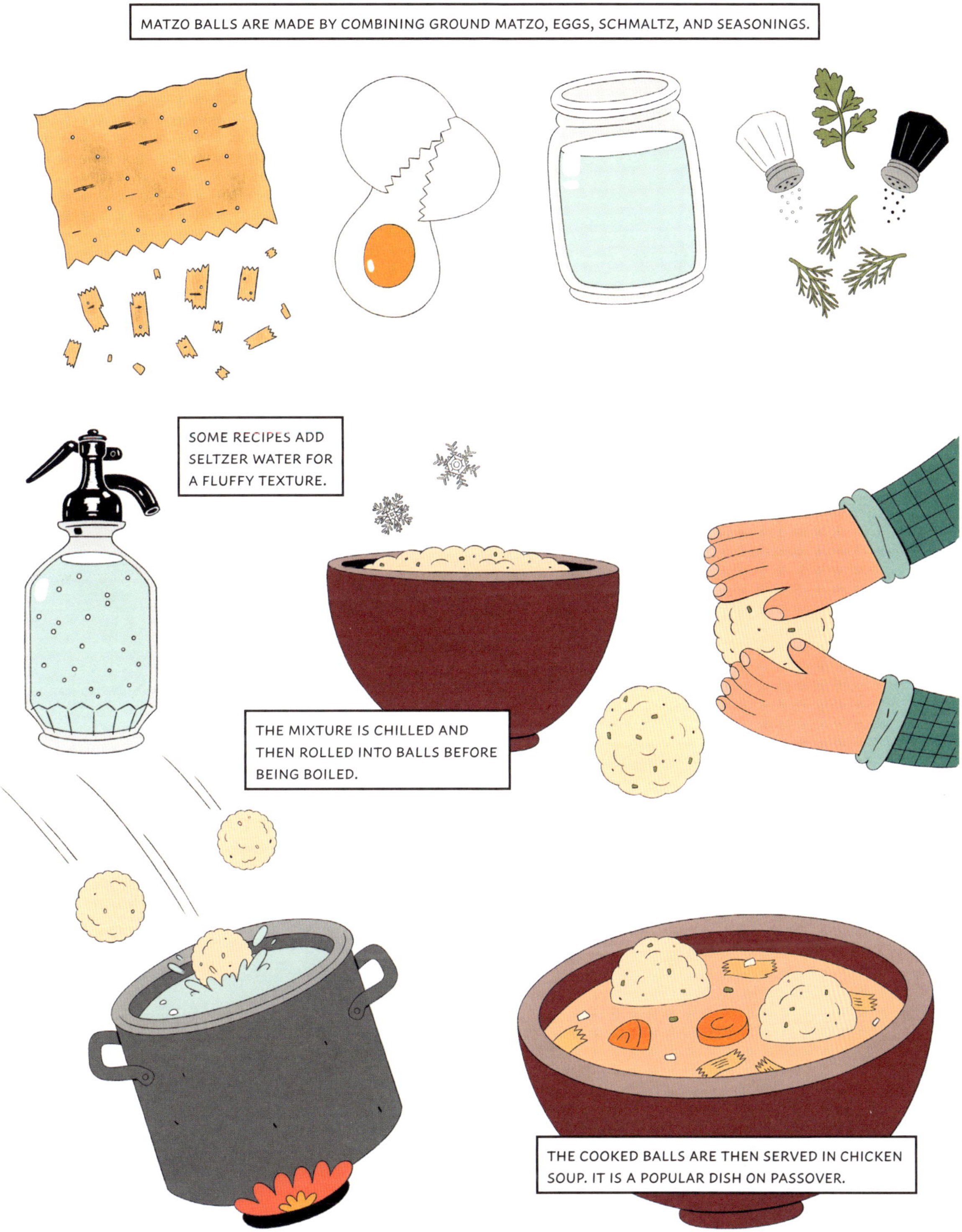
MATZO BALLS ARE MADE BY COMBINING GROUND MATZO, EGGS, SCHMALTZ, AND SEASONINGS.
SOME RECIPES ADD SELTZER WATER FOR A FLUFFY TEXTURE.
THE MIXTURE IS CHILLED AND THEN ROLLED INTO BALLS BEFORE BEING BOILED.
THE COOKED BALLS ARE THEN SERVED IN CHICKEN SOUP. IT IS A POPULAR DISH ON PASSOVER.

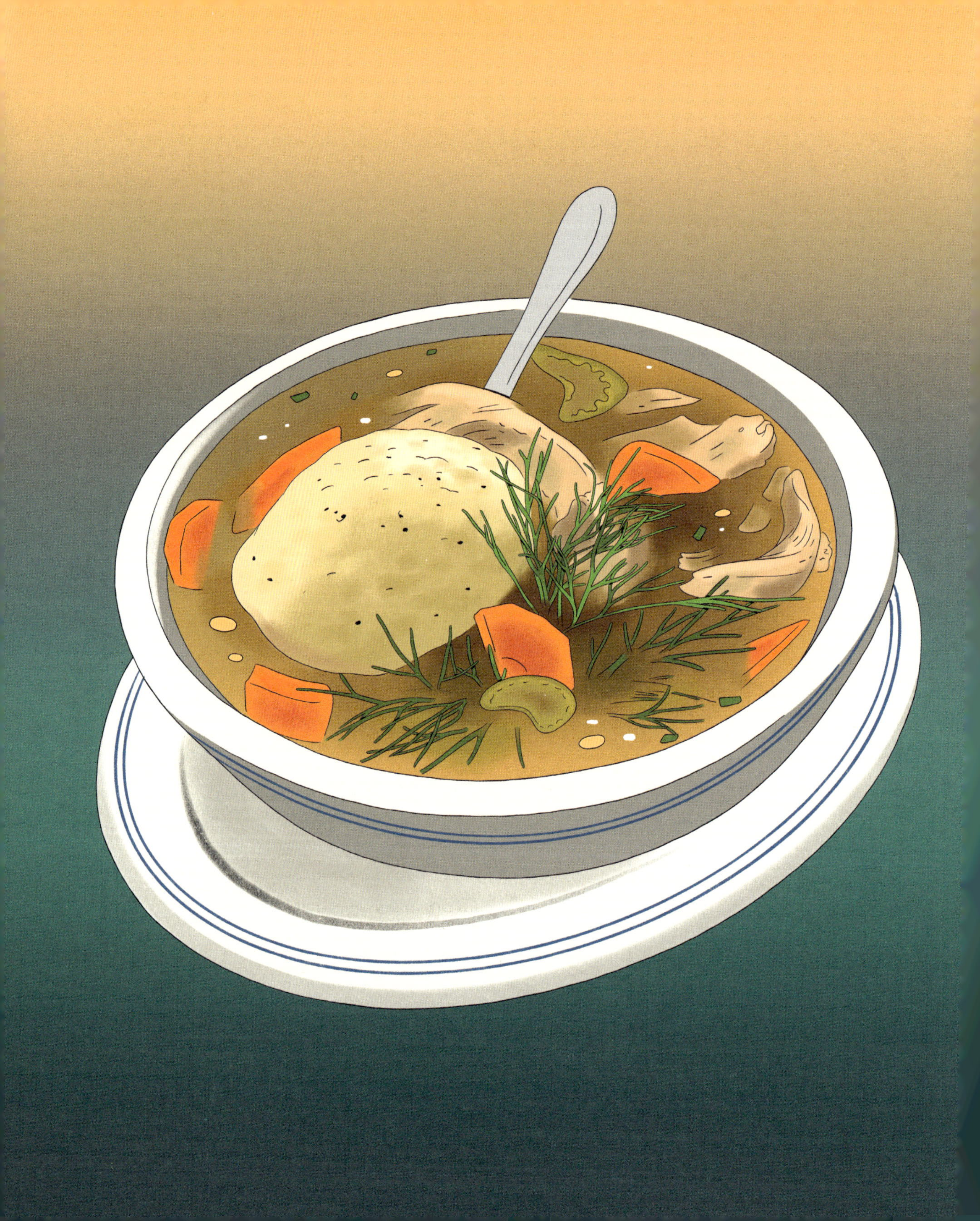

An Ode to Matzo Ball Soup

Matzo ball soup serves as an ambassador of Jewish food, welcoming newcomers with a big, warm hug. A number of the business owners I talked to list it as their number one item for introducing customers to the world of deli. It's unassuming, hot, and healing. Without the matzo ball, it's chicken soup, recognized across cultures as good-for-the-soul comfort food in its most basic form. But with the matzo ball, the soup becomes something more complex and even contentious. Should the balls be dense and chewy or light and fluffy? Three small balls or one giant one? It's an especially personal dish, unique to each family, full of intimate variations from generations of tinkering.

In a deli, you're most likely to find a bowl with one big matzo ball, whereas the homemade soups served at Passover will likely have two or three smaller balls. I find that the latter allows the broth to better penetrate the matzo balls, which should, I think, be just dense enough to hold their shape, but light enough to stay airy and fluffy without coming apart when you spoon a chunk from them. There's something intensely satisfying about a perfectly shaped and tender sphere soaked in salty broth, melting in your mouth, herbaceous and savory.

My love of matzo ball soup is congruent with my love of dill, schmaltz, and salt. The only thing worse than a too-dense matzo ball is one that is too bland. They must be simmered in something salty, with dill and parsley adding freshness to balance the rich fatty schmaltz that holds it all together.

There's nothing flashy about matzo ball soup, but its simple perfection will always be there as a warming companion for your latkes, sandwich, or blintzes, cast as a side dish but deserving the spotlight.

Like the bagel debate, the texture of a perfect matzo ball is highly contested. Whether it should be light and fluffy or small, dense, and chewy is left up to personal choice AND FAMILY TRADITION. All matzo balls are welcome!

Borscht

IT WOULD NOT HAVE BEEN POSSIBLE FOR SO MANY JEWS TO EMIGRATE FROM EASTERN EUROPE WITHOUT BRINGING BORSCHT WITH THEM.

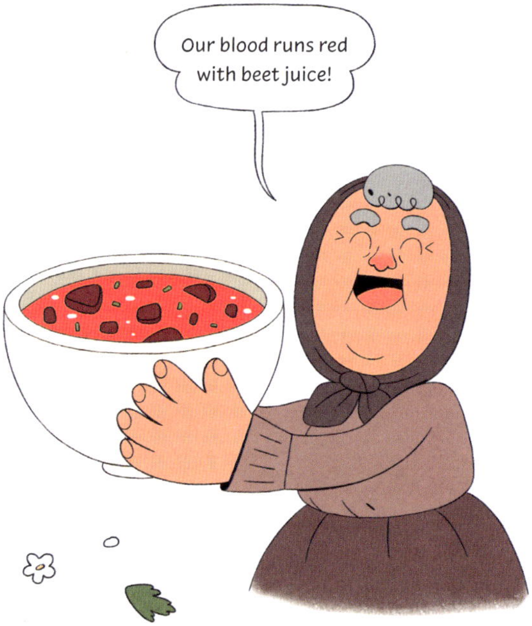
Our blood runs red with beet juice!

IN THE EARLY MIDDLE AGES, SOUP IN EASTERN EUROPE WAS MADE FROM A PLANT CALLED COW PARSNIP, A MEMBER OF THE CARROT FAMILY.

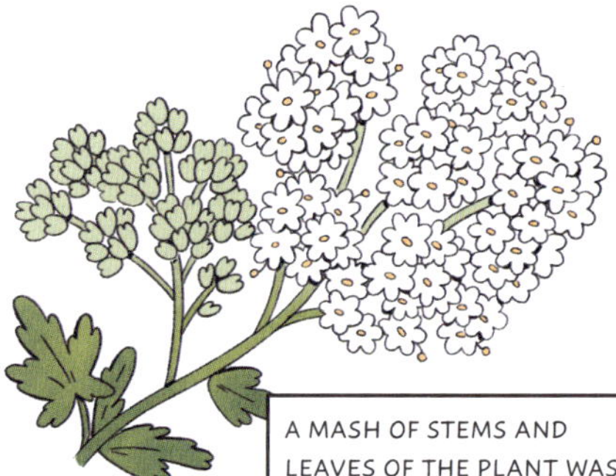

A MASH OF STEMS AND LEAVES OF THE PLANT WAS FIRST FERMENTED AND THEN MIXED WITH CHICKEN BROTH TO MAKE A SOUR SOUP.

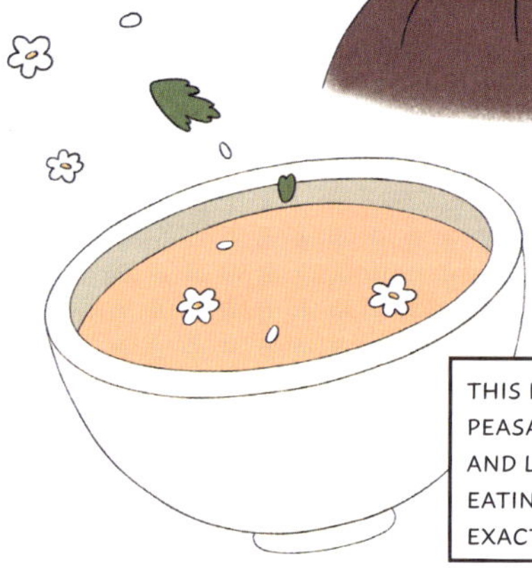

THIS IS WHAT JEWISH PEASANTS IN POLAND AND LITHUANIA WERE EATING, AND IT WAS NOT EXACTLY A DELICACY.

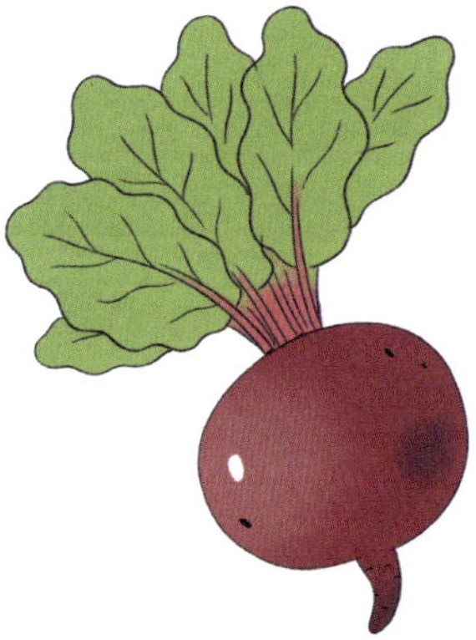

IN THE SEVENTEENTH CENTURY, AS BEETS GREW MORE POPULAR IN THE REGION, THEY EVENTUALLY BECAME THE MAIN INGREDIENT IN BORSCHT.

FOR THE ASHKENAZI JEWS, HOT BORSCHT HAD AN HONORED PLACE ON THE PASSOVER TABLE. IT IS NOW THE MOST COMMON TYPE OF BORSCHT IN THE UNITED STATES.

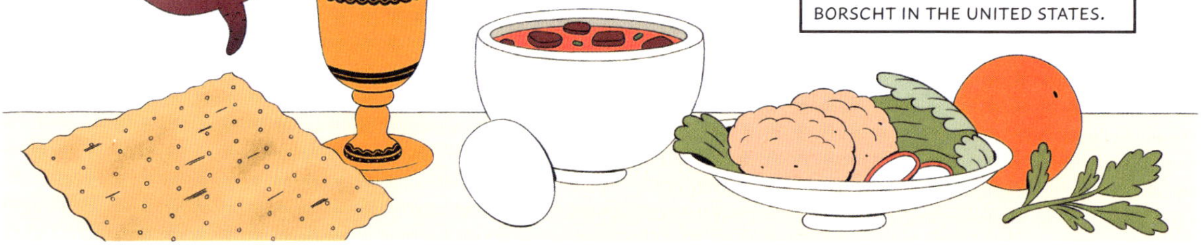

BORSCHT WAS USUALLY PREPARED BY FIRST MAKING BEET SOUR, WHICH IS FERMENTED BEETROOT JUICE.

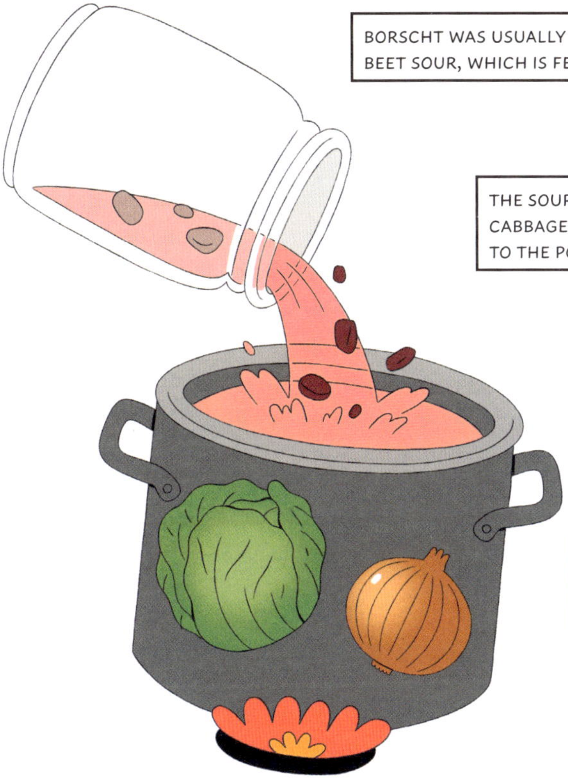

THE SOUR WAS BOILED IN WATER, WITH CABBAGE AND OTHER VEGETABLES ADDED TO THE POT.

CHICKEN BROTH WAS SOMETIMES ADDED AS WELL.

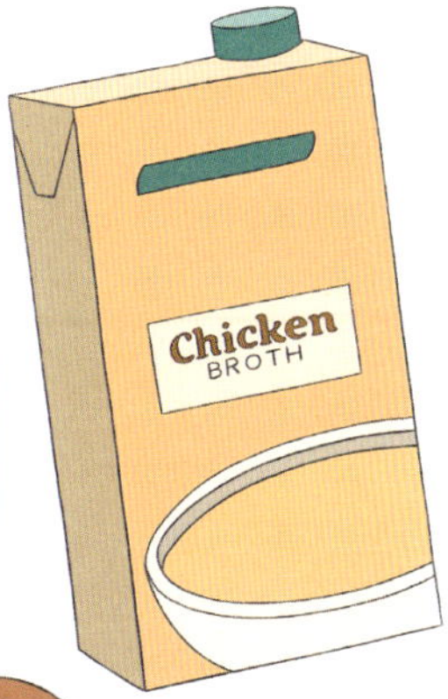
Chicken
BROTH

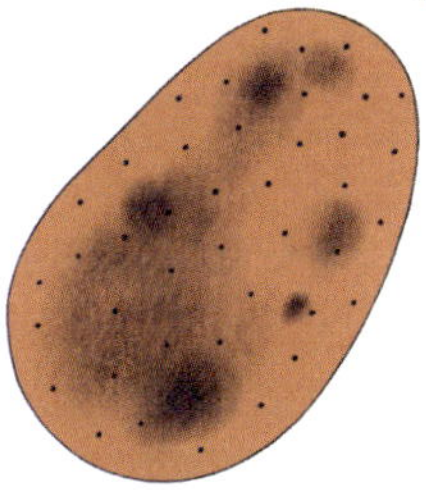

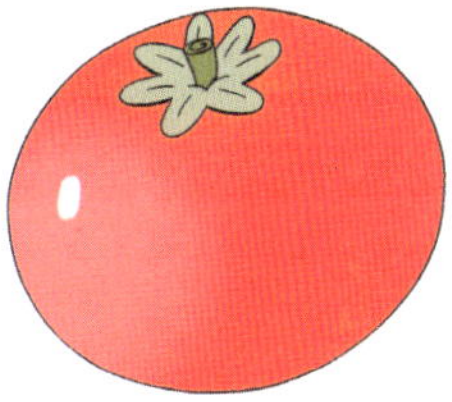

UKRAINIAN IMMIGRANTS WOULD ALSO THROW IN POTATOES AND TOMATOES.

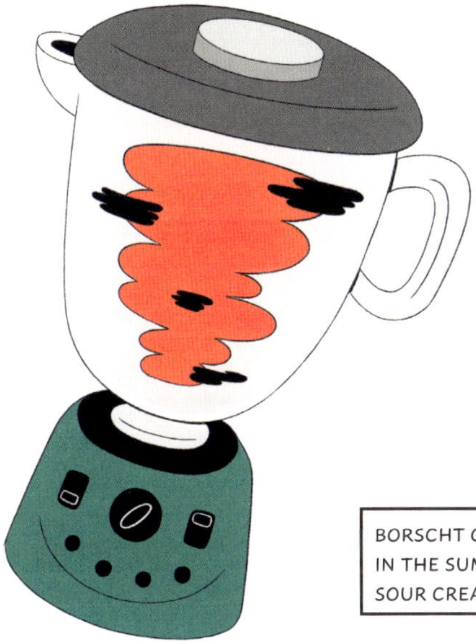

A SIMPLER RECIPE TODAY INVOLVES BOILING BEETS WITH ONIONS, POTATOES, AND SOME ROOT VEGETABLES, ADDING SALT AND OTHER SEASONINGS, AND THEN PUREEING EVERYTHING. BEET PIECES OR SHREDS CAN ALSO BE ADDED TO THE SOUP.

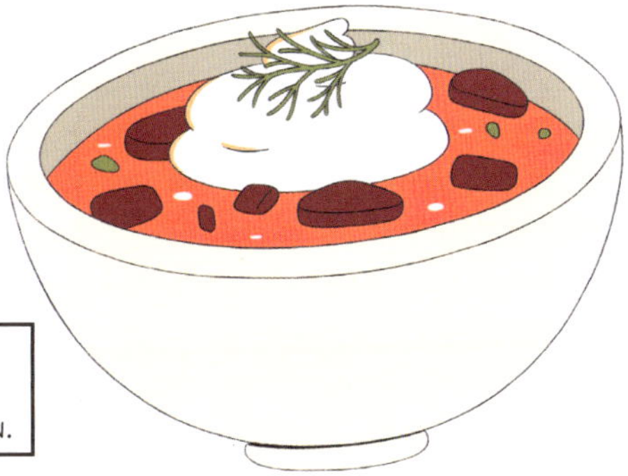

BORSCHT CAN BE SERVED COLD IN THE SUMMER, WITH SOME SOUR CREAM AND DILL MIXED IN.

Kugel

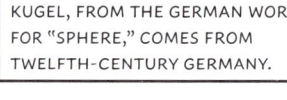

KUGEL, FROM THE GERMAN WORD FOR "SPHERE," COMES FROM TWELFTH-CENTURY GERMANY.

THE WORD MAY ALSO DERIVE FROM THE ROUND RING-SHAPED CAKES FROM GERMANY CALLED GUGELHUPF.

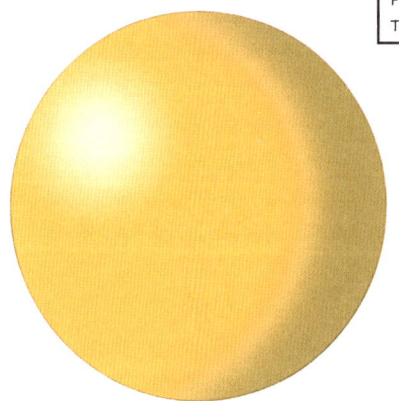

AN EARLY VERSION OF THE DISH WAS A STEAMED SAVORY PUDDING MADE FROM SUET, FLOUR, AND BREAD CRUMBS.

OBSERVANT JEWISH FAMILIES DO NOT COOK ON SHABBAT. INSTEAD, BEFORE SUNDOWN ON FRIDAY, THEY MIGHT PREPARE A LARGE MEAT STEW CALLED CHOLENT TO SIMMER ON LOW HEAT OVERNIGHT.

(IN THE SHTETL [SMALL VILLAGE] OF THE OLD COUNTRY, THIS WOULD BE DONE IN THE COMMUNITY BAKER'S OVEN.)

BY LUNCHTIME ON SATURDAY, AS WORSHIPPERS RETURNED HOME FROM SYNAGOGUE, THE SLOW-COOKED STEW WOULD BE READY WITHOUT ANY MORE PREPARATION.

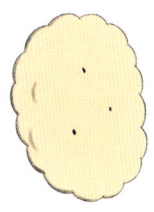
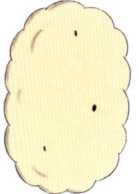
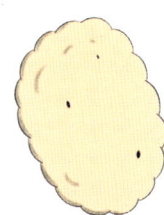

BECAUSE GERMAN JEWS ENJOYED STEAMED PUDDINGS, THEY BEGAN TO ADD ROUND DUMPLINGS TO THE CHOLENT.

THE DUMPLING BATTER—AN EGG AND BREAD MIXTURE—WAS STEAMED IN A KUGELTOPF, A SMALL CLAY POT, AND THEN FINISHED IN THE STEW. THE RESULT WAS MORE OF A PUDDING THAN A DUMPLING.

AS SUGAR BECAME A MORE PROMINENT FEATURE OF THE EUROPEAN DIET, THE DISH WAS OFTEN MORE SWEET THAN SAVORY.

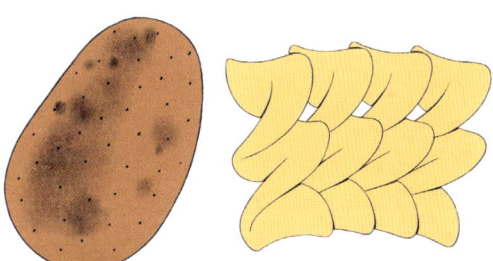

POTATOES OR NOODLES WERE ALSO ADDED TO THE RECIPE.

IT WAS NOT UNTIL JEWISH IMMIGRANTS BROUGHT KUGEL TO THE UNITED STATES, WHERE THEY SUDDENLY HAD OVENS IN THEIR HOMES, THAT IT BECAME A BAKED DISH.

THERE ARE MANY VARIETIES OF KUGEL, BUT THEY ARE ALL MADE WITH SOME COMBINATION OF EGG, FAT, AND A STARCH.

THE MOST COMMON KUGEL IN THE JEWISH AMERICAN DELI—AND DIET—IS A BAKED, USUALLY SWEET, NOODLE CASSEROLE.

SOUR CREAM
COTTAGE CHEESE

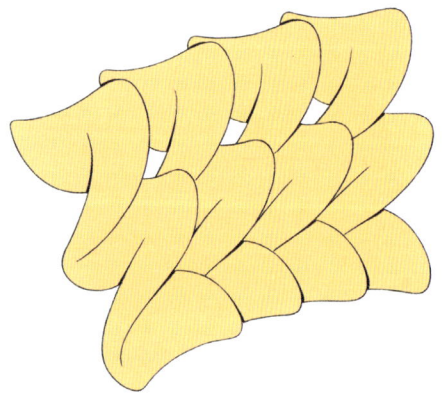

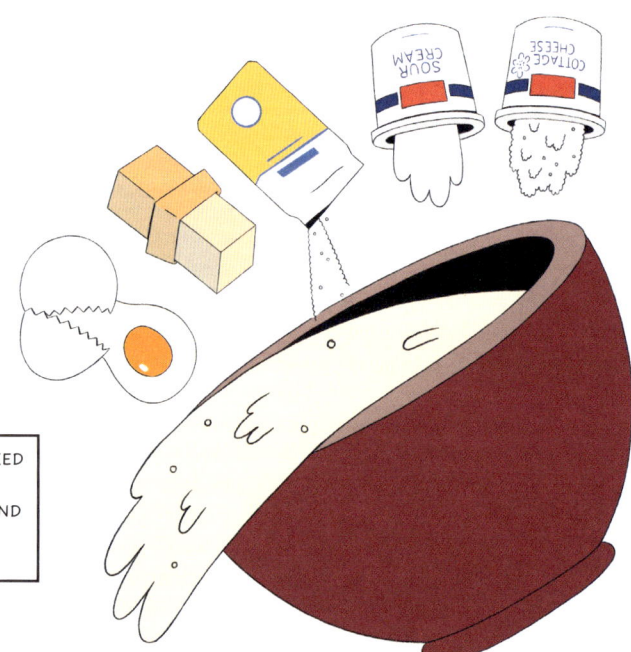

NOODLE KUGEL IS MADE BY COMBINING COOKED EGG NOODLES WITH A CREAMY SAUCE MADE FROM EGGS, BUTTER, SUGAR, SOUR CREAM, AND COTTAGE CHEESE. IT CAN ALSO BE FLAVORED WITH CINNAMON AND RAISINS.

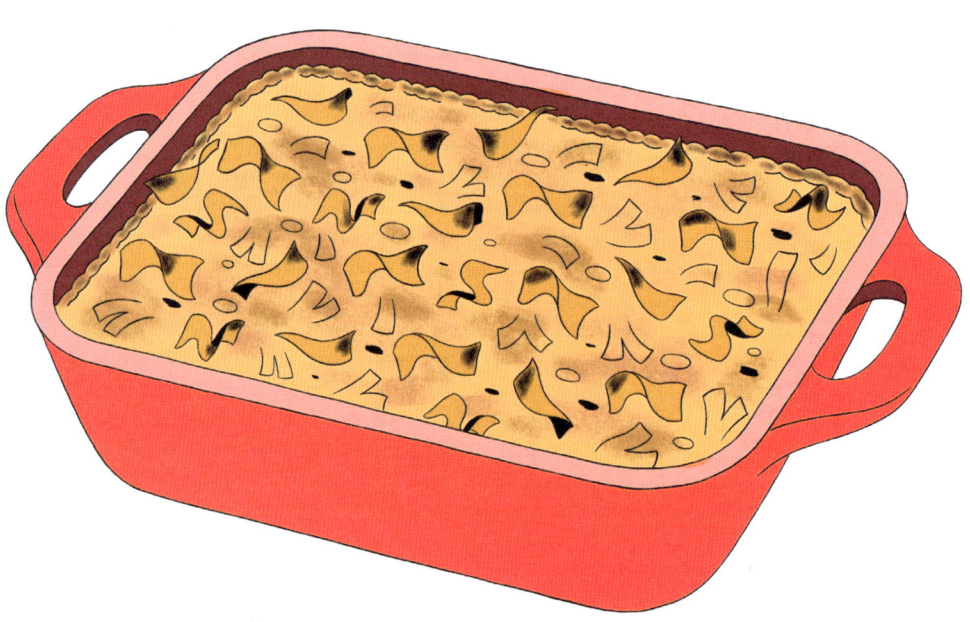

VARIETIES OF KUGEL

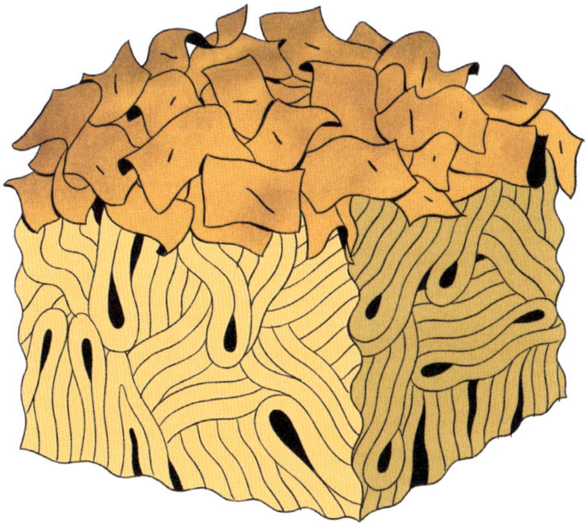

CLASSIC

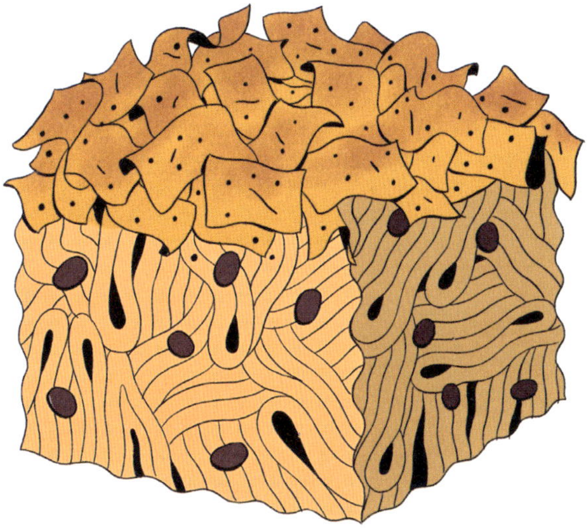

CINNAMON RAISIN

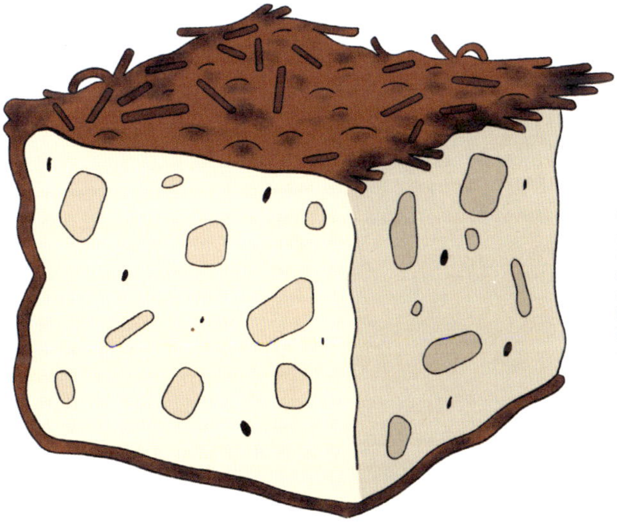

POTATO

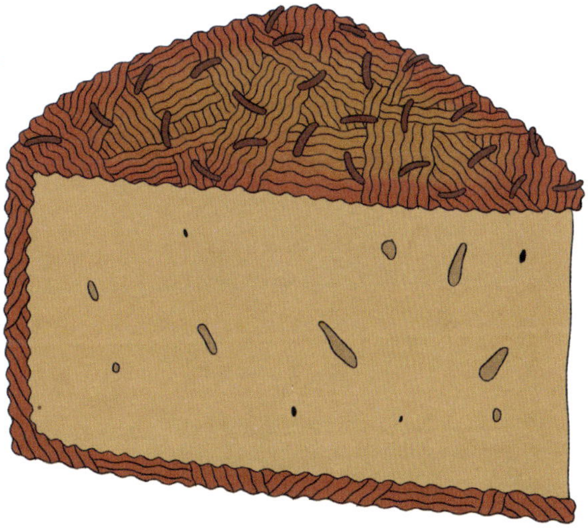

YERUSHALMI KUGEL

JERUSALEM STYLE WITH BLACK PEPPER AND CARAMELIZED NOODLES

Blintzes

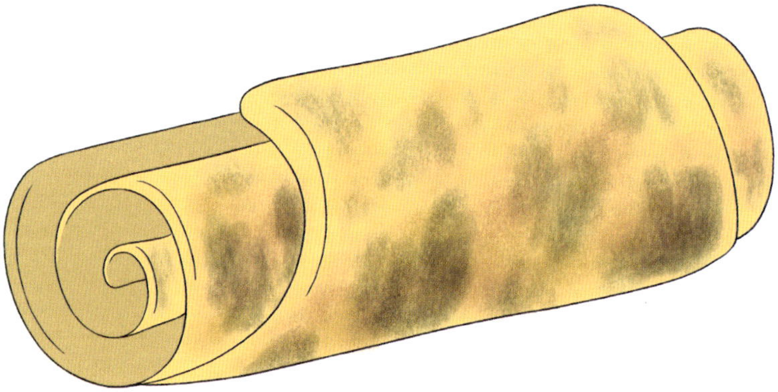

BLINTZES DERIVE FROM A HUNGARIAN DISH CALLED PALACSINTA, A SWEET, ROLLED-UP PANCAKE. THE NAME COMES FROM *BLINTSE*, THE YIDDISH WORD FOR "PANCAKE."

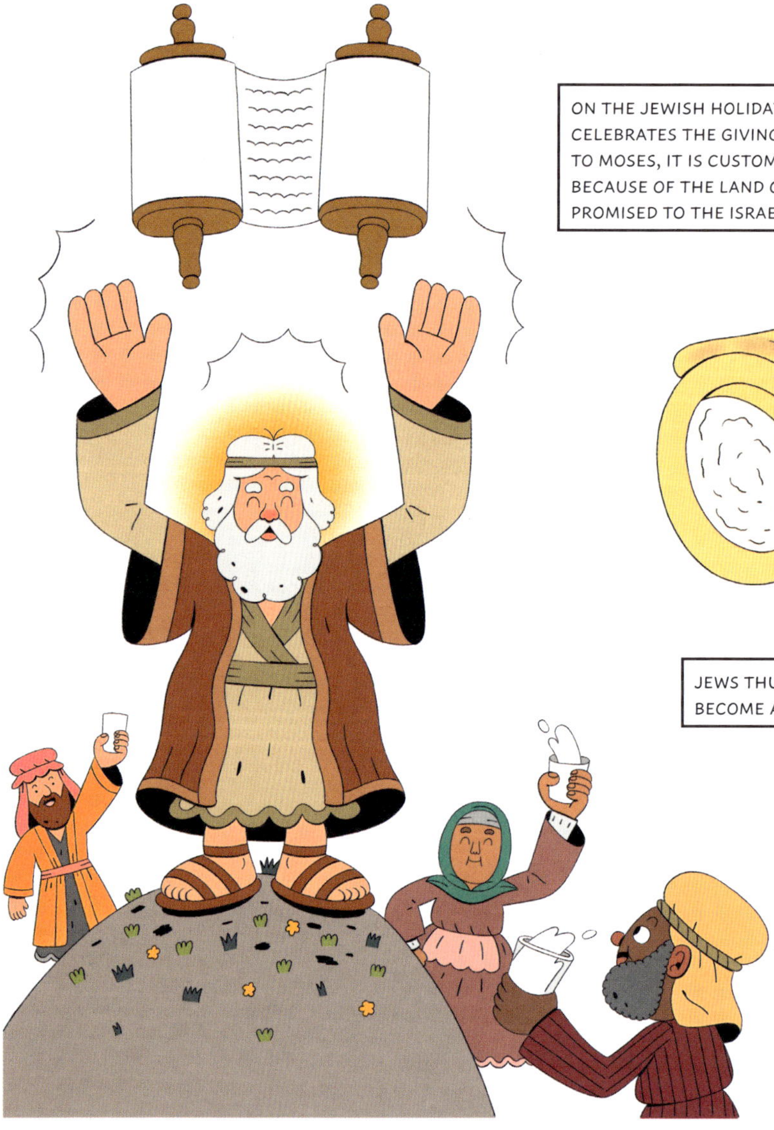

ON THE JEWISH HOLIDAY SHAVUOT, WHICH CELEBRATES THE GIVING OF THE TORAH TO MOSES, IT IS CUSTOMARY TO EAT DAIRY, BECAUSE OF THE LAND OF MILK AND HONEY PROMISED TO THE ISRAELITES.

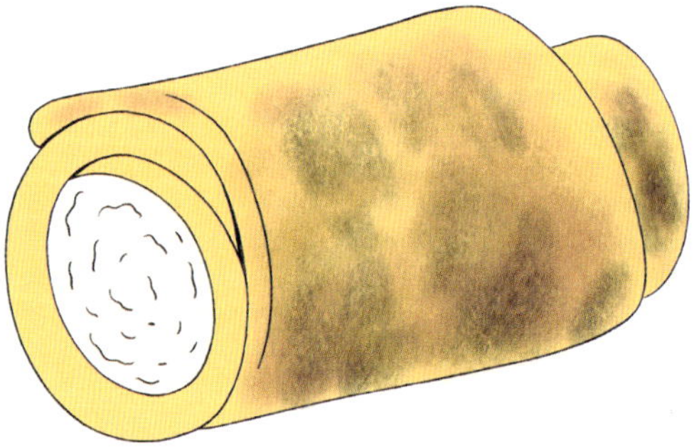

JEWS THUS ADAPTED THE PALACSINTA TO BECOME A VESSEL FOR A SWEET DAIRY FILLING.

THE CLASSIC JEWISH CHEESE BLINTZ COMES FROM UKRAINE.

A THIN BATTER IS MADE OUT OF WATER, MILK, EGGS, AND FLOUR.

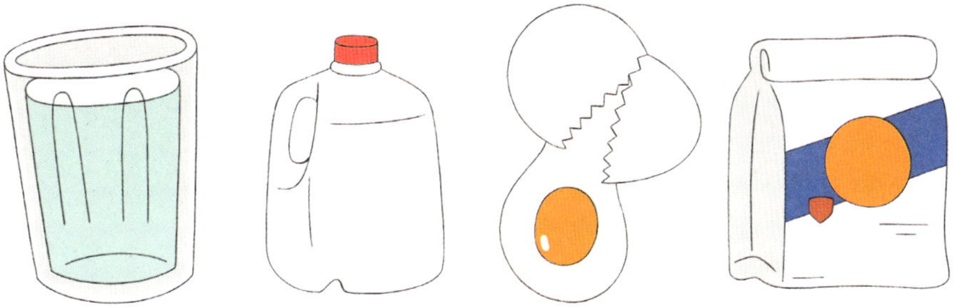

THE DIFFERENCE BETWEEN BLINTZES AND CREPES IS THAT BLINTZES ARE COOKED ON ONLY ONE SIDE, SO THE INSIDE REMAINS SOFT.

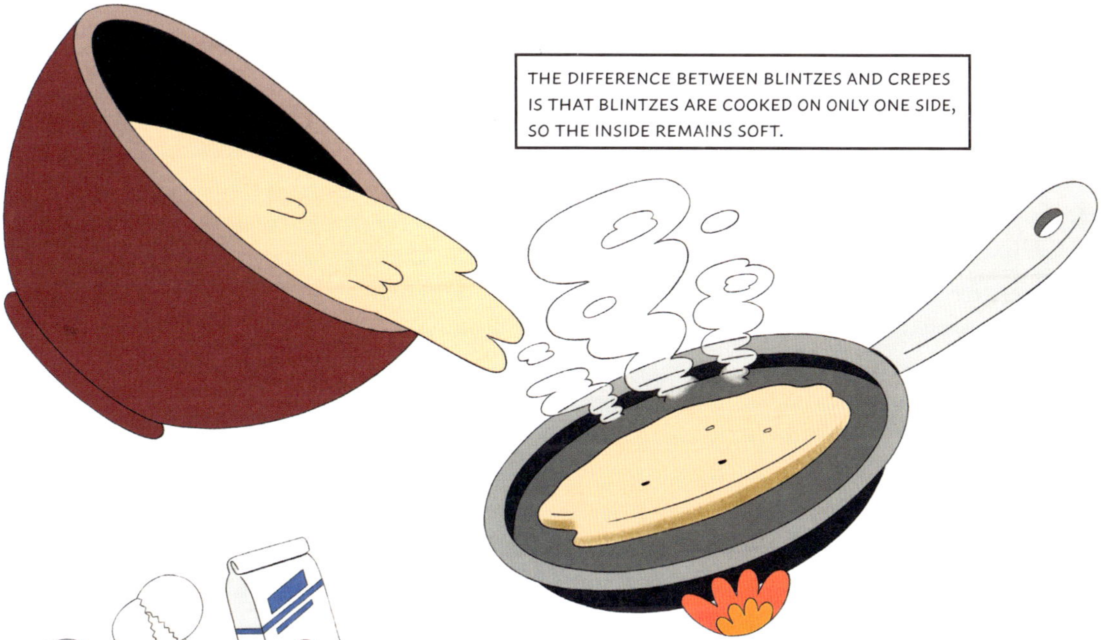

AS SOON AS THE PANCAKE IS PANFRIED (IN BUTTER), IT IS TOPPED WITH A MIXTURE MADE OF FARMER CHEESE, EGG, AND SUGAR.

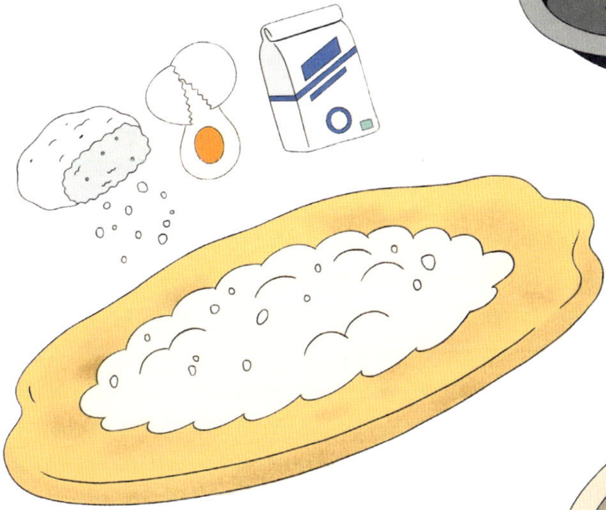

IT IS THEN ROLLED UP INTO A TUBE AND FRIED AGAIN BEFORE BEING TOPPED WITH SOUR CREAM AND FRESH BERRIES.

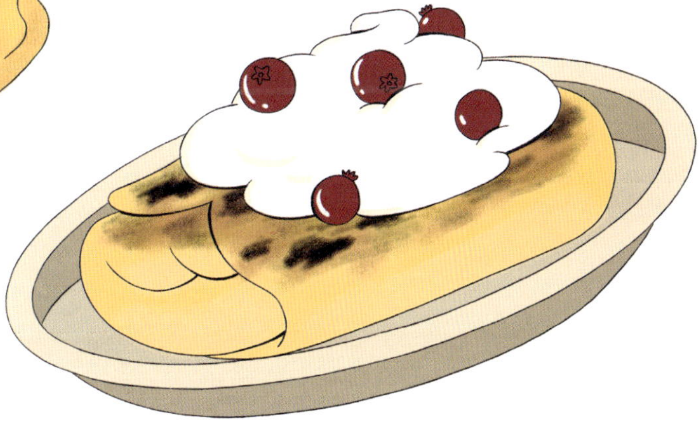

Knishes

EVERY CULTURE HAS ITS VERSION OF THE KNISH:

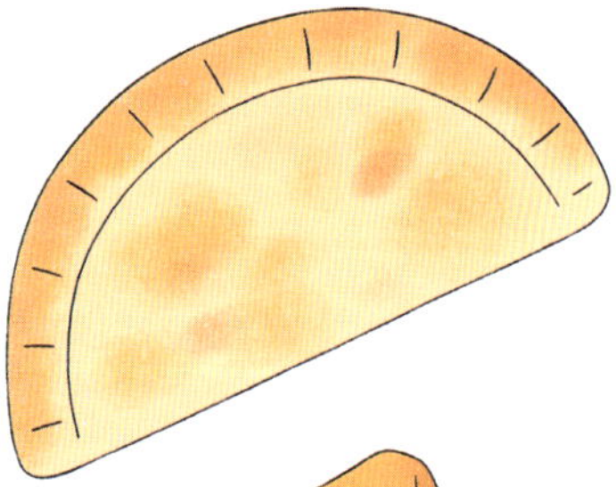

SPANISH EMPANADAS,

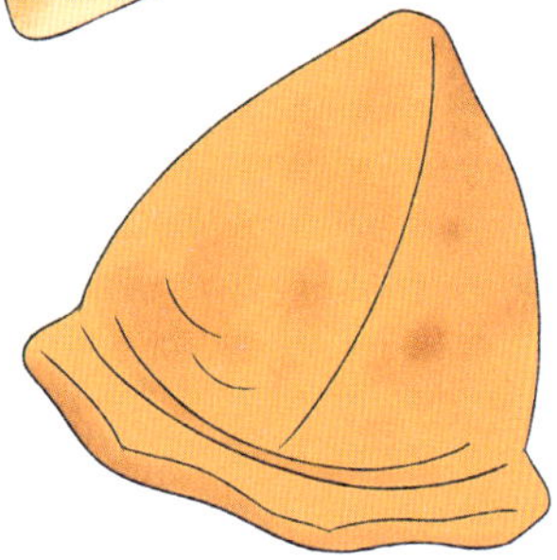

INDIAN SAMOSAS,

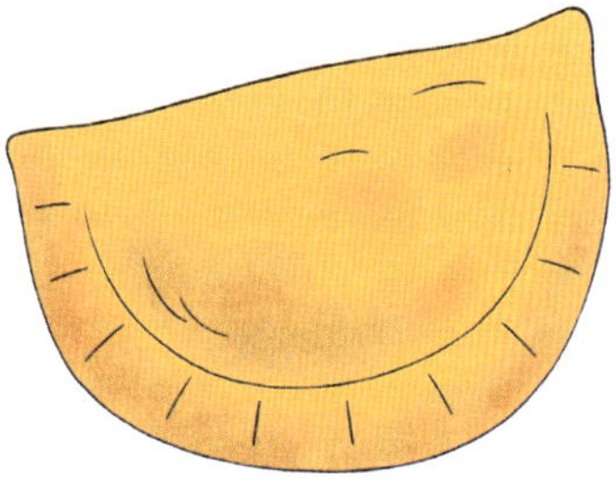

JAMAICAN PATTIES,

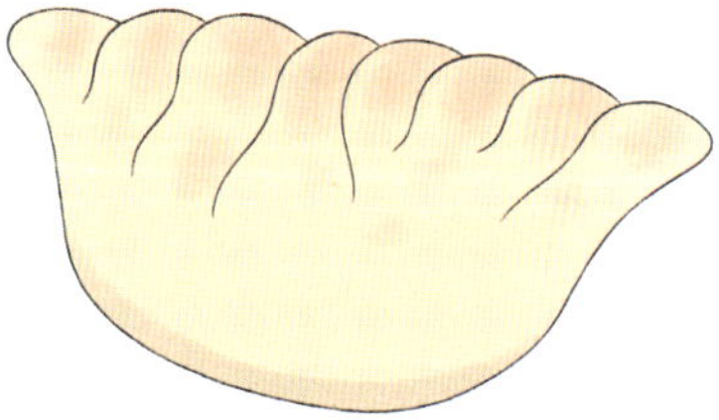

CHINESE DUMPLINGS,

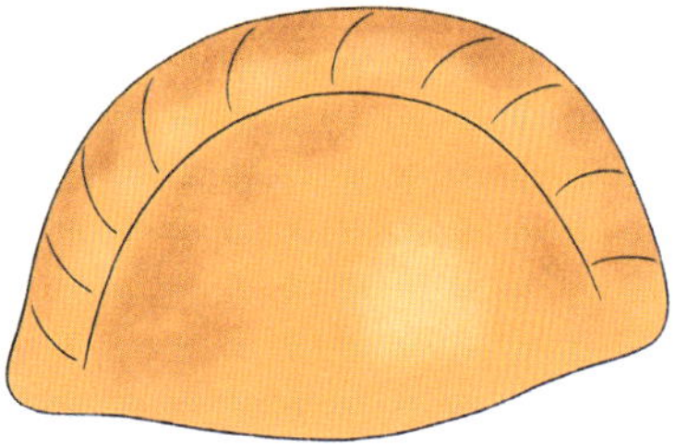

BRITISH PASTIES . . .

THEY ARE ALL DOUGH POCKETS WITH FILLING.

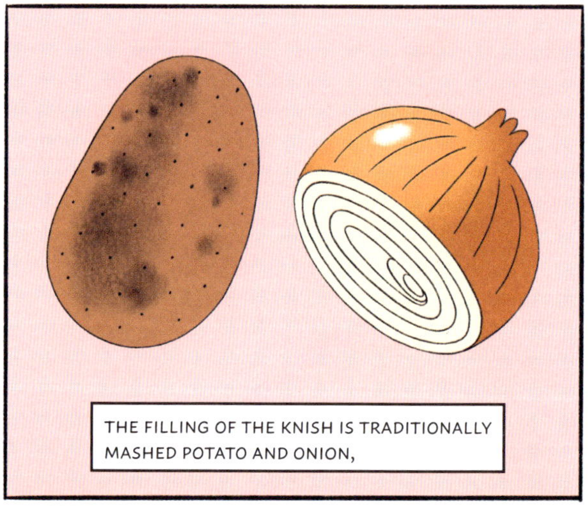
THE FILLING OF THE KNISH IS TRADITIONALLY MASHED POTATO AND ONION,

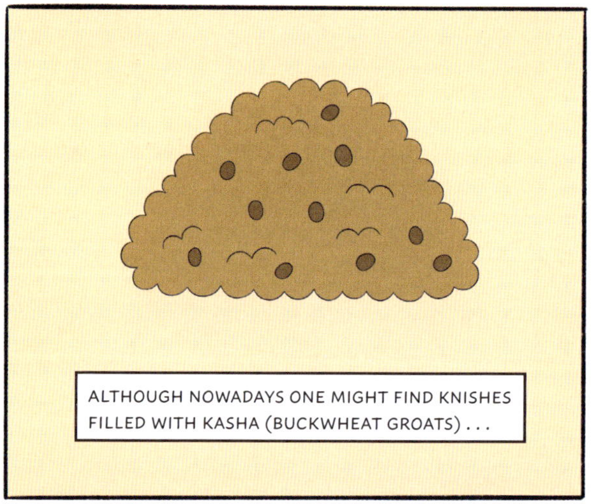
ALTHOUGH NOWADAYS ONE MIGHT FIND KNISHES FILLED WITH KASHA (BUCKWHEAT GROATS) . . .

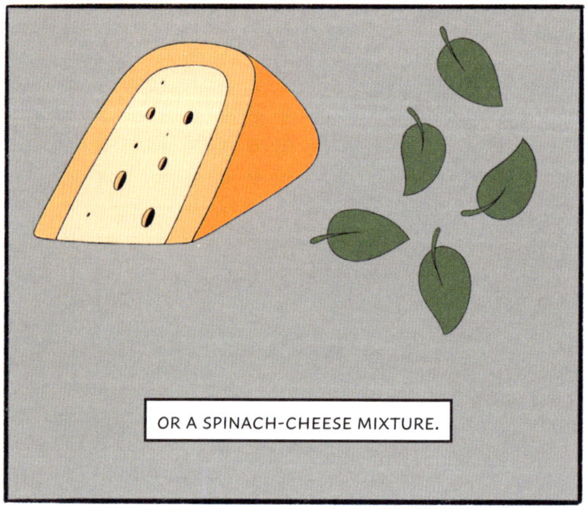
OR A SPINACH-CHEESE MIXTURE.

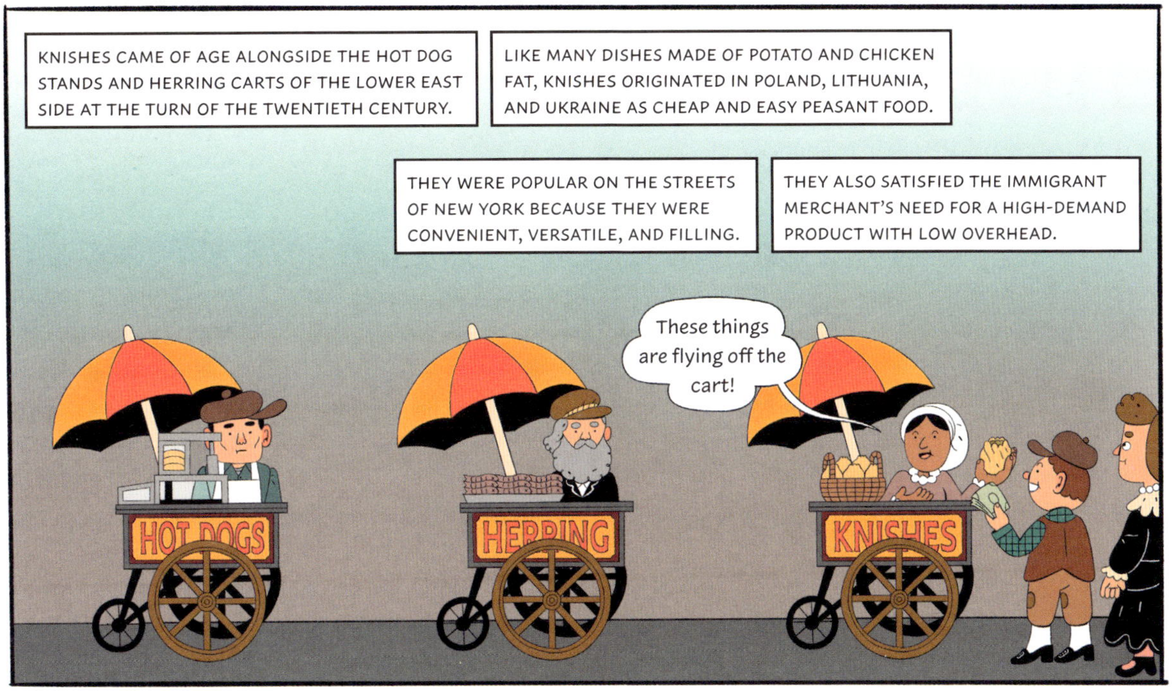
KNISHES CAME OF AGE ALONGSIDE THE HOT DOG STANDS AND HERRING CARTS OF THE LOWER EAST SIDE AT THE TURN OF THE TWENTIETH CENTURY.
LIKE MANY DISHES MADE OF POTATO AND CHICKEN FAT, KNISHES ORIGINATED IN POLAND, LITHUANIA, AND UKRAINE AS CHEAP AND EASY PEASANT FOOD.
THEY WERE POPULAR ON THE STREETS OF NEW YORK BECAUSE THEY WERE CONVENIENT, VERSATILE, AND FILLING.
THEY ALSO SATISFIED THE IMMIGRANT MERCHANT'S NEED FOR A HIGH-DEMAND PRODUCT WITH LOW OVERHEAD.
HOT DOGS
HERRING
These things are flying off the cart!
KNISHES

KNISHERIES BEGAN TO POP UP ALL OVER NEW YORK, BECOMING AS MUCH A PART OF THE CITY'S CULINARY CULTURE AS BAGELS AND BIALYS.

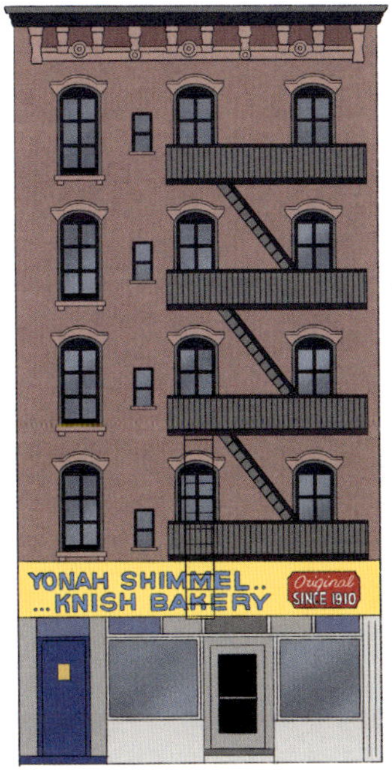
YONAH SHIMMEL.. ...KNISH BAKERY
Original SINCE 1910

HOWEVER, THEIR POPULARITY HAS NOT SURVIVED AS WELL AS THE BAGEL'S.

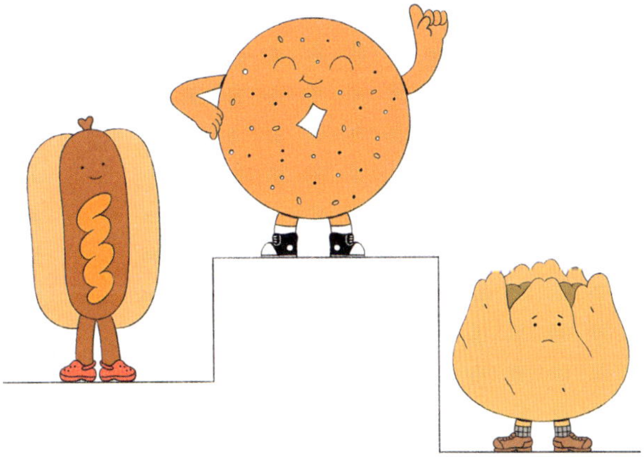

THE STREET CARTS, OF COURSE, ARE ALL GONE. STILL, GREAT KNISHES CAN BE FOUND AROUND THE CITY; YOU JUST HAVE TO KNOW WHERE TO LOOK.

A CLASSIC OLD-SCHOOL KNISH IS MADE FROM A DOUGH OF FLOUR, OIL, VINEGAR, AND SELTZER.

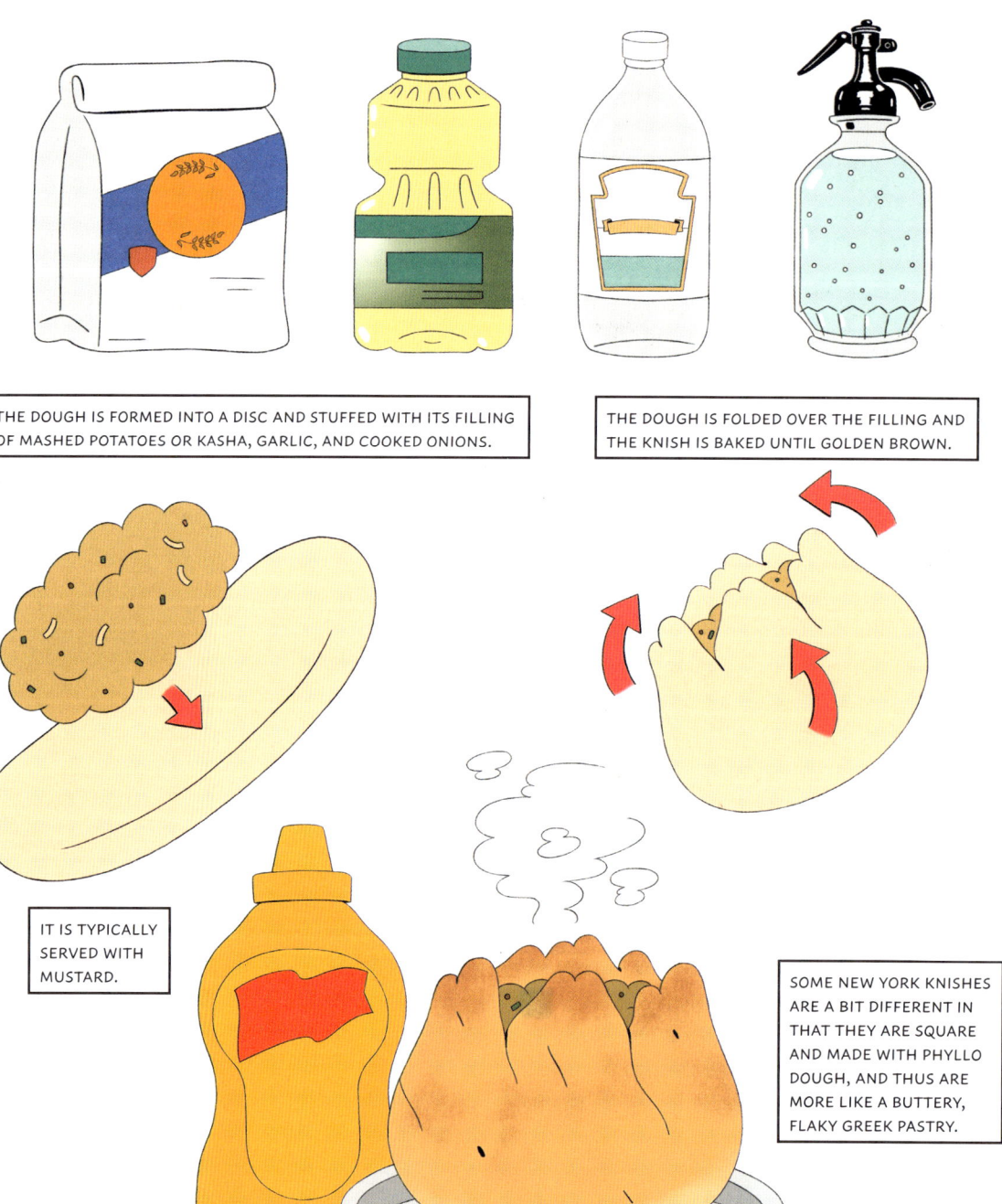

THE DOUGH IS FORMED INTO A DISC AND STUFFED WITH ITS FILLING OF MASHED POTATOES OR KASHA, GARLIC, AND COOKED ONIONS.

THE DOUGH IS FOLDED OVER THE FILLING AND THE KNISH IS BAKED UNTIL GOLDEN BROWN.

IT IS TYPICALLY SERVED WITH MUSTARD.

SOME NEW YORK KNISHES ARE A BIT DIFFERENT IN THAT THEY ARE SQUARE AND MADE WITH PHYLLO DOUGH, AND THUS ARE MORE LIKE A BUTTERY, FLAKY GREEK PASTRY.

VARIETIES OF KNISHES

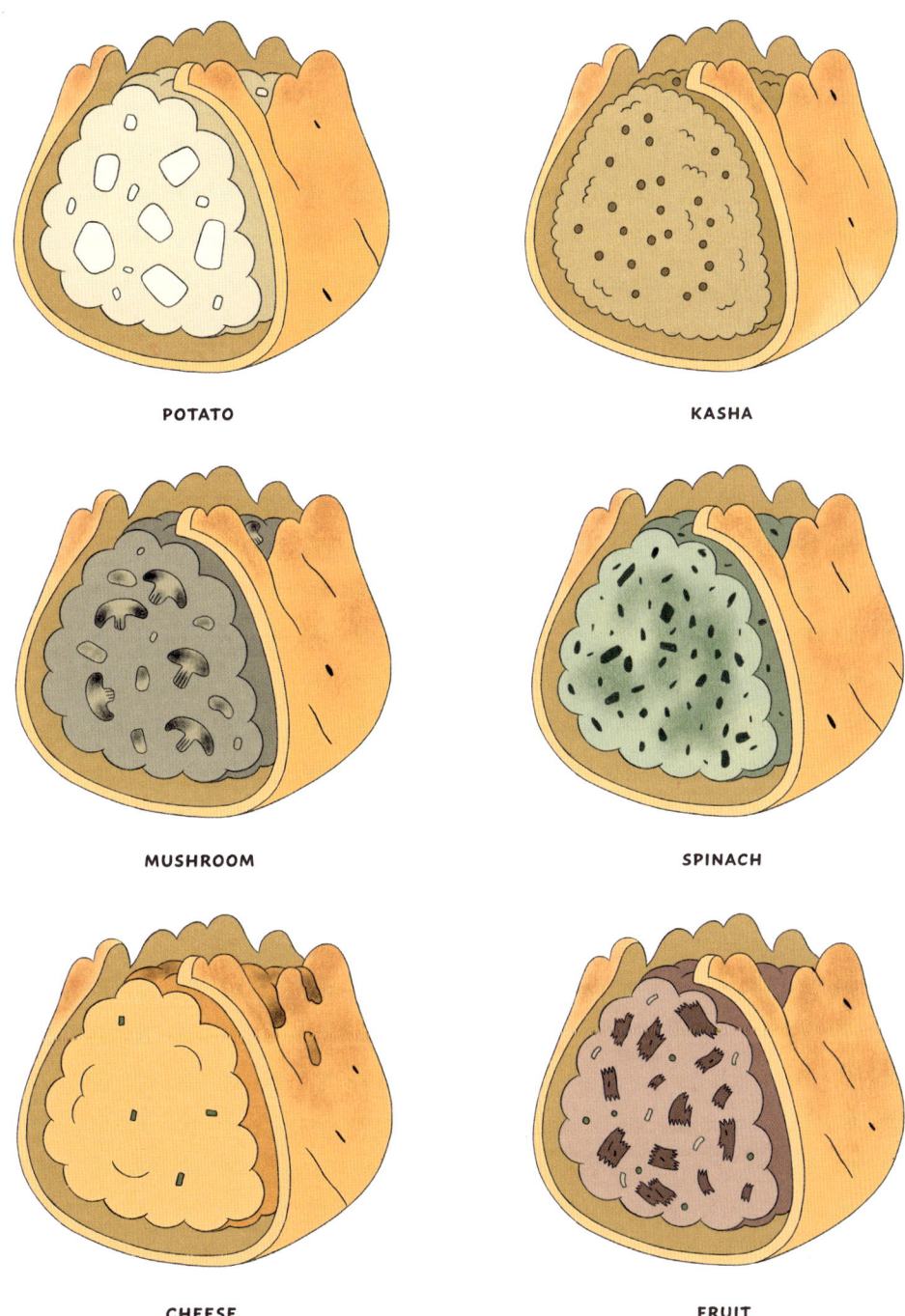

POTATO

KASHA

MUSHROOM

SPINACH

CHEESE

FRUIT

Pickles

THE PICKLING OF CUCUMBERS HAS BEEN AROUND FOREVER.

LIKE OTHER JEWISH DISHES WE HAVE EXAMINED—CORNED BEEF, HERRING, LOX, AND MORE—KOSHER DILL PICKLES INVOLVE SOAKING SOMETHING IN A SALTY BRINE FOR A PERIOD OF TIME.

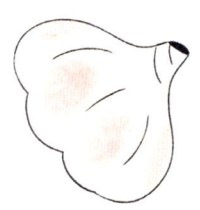

GARLIC AND DILL—AN HERB THAT THRIVES LIKE RYE IN THE COLD, WET, EASTERN EUROPEAN CLIMATE—IN THE BRINE GIVE THESE PICKLES THEIR CHARACTERISTIC FLAVOR.

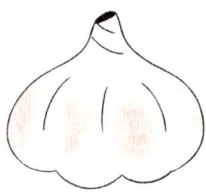

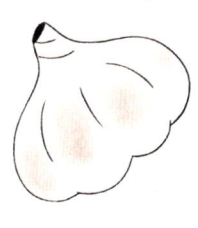

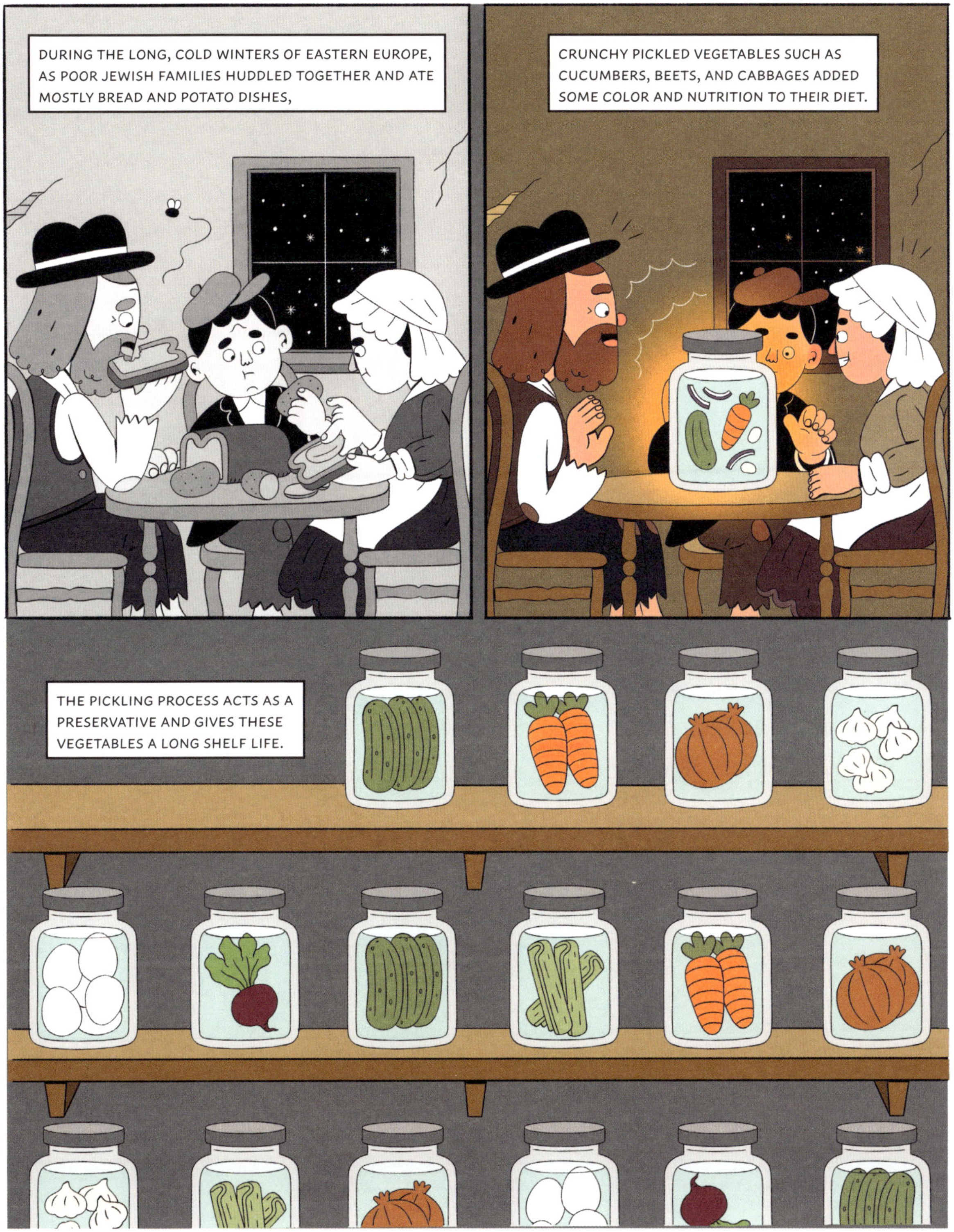
DURING THE LONG, COLD WINTERS OF EASTERN EUROPE, AS POOR JEWISH FAMILIES HUDDLED TOGETHER AND ATE MOSTLY BREAD AND POTATO DISHES,
CRUNCHY PICKLED VEGETABLES SUCH AS CUCUMBERS, BEETS, AND CABBAGES ADDED SOME COLOR AND NUTRITION TO THEIR DIET.
THE PICKLING PROCESS ACTS AS A PRESERVATIVE AND GIVES THESE VEGETABLES A LONG SHELF LIFE.

KOSHER DILL PICKLES ARE SO NAMED NOT BECAUSE THEY ARE KOSHER—ALTHOUGH THEY GENERALLY ARE—BUT BECAUSE THEY ARE ASSOCIATED WITH BEING BROUGHT FROM EUROPE BY JEWISH IMMIGRANTS, WHO THEN SERVED THEM IN THEIR DELIS.

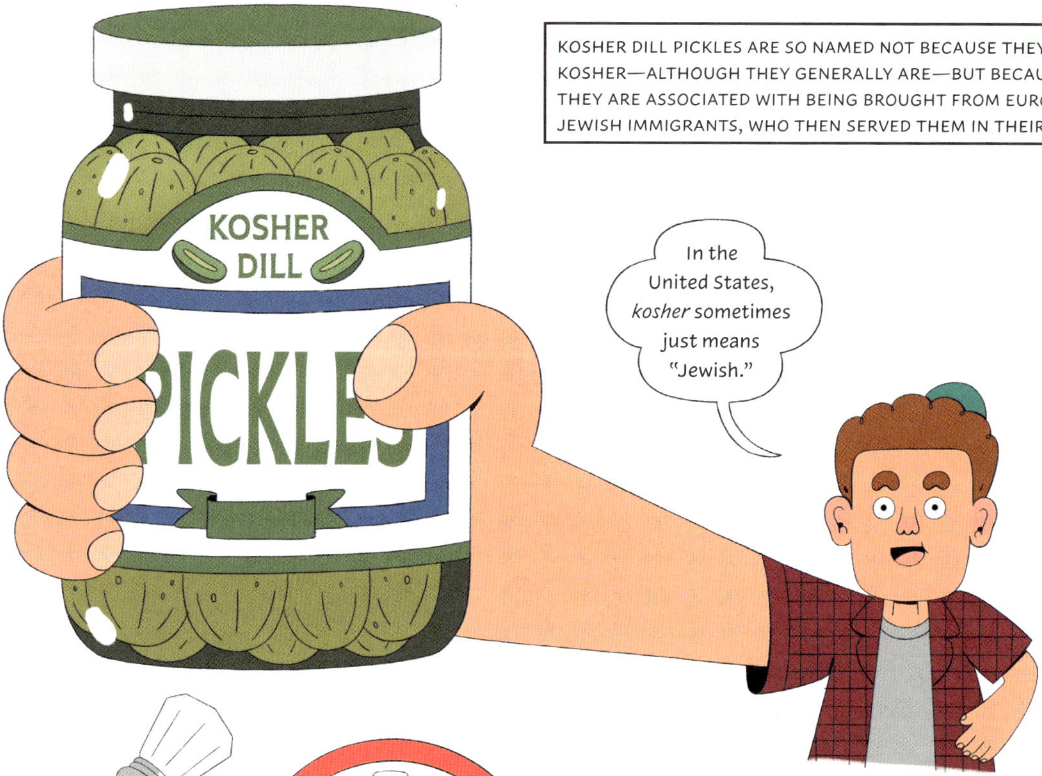
KOSHER
DILL
PICKLES
In the United States, *kosher* sometimes just means "Jewish."

KOSHER DILLS ARE A UNIQUE KIND OF PICKLE IN THAT THEY ARE FERMENTED IN A SALT BRINE WITH NO VINEGAR; THIS IS WHAT *KOSHER* HAS COME TO MEAN WHEN IT COMES TO PICKLES.

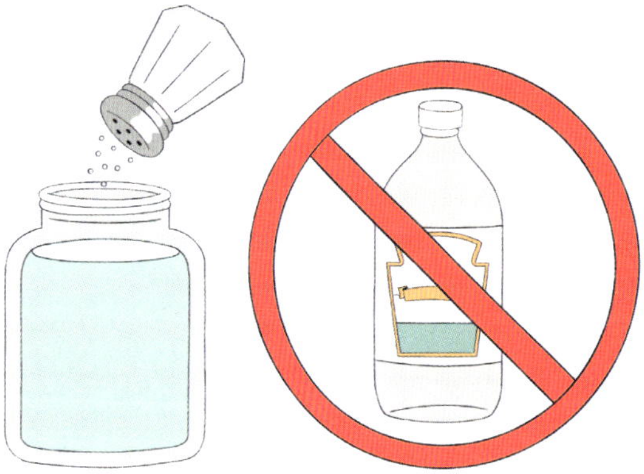

IF A PICKLE IS SPECIFICALLY *NOT* KOSHER, IT MEANS IT WAS PICKLED IN A VINEGAR BRINE.

NOT ONLY WAS VINEGAR TOO EXPENSIVE FOR THE POOR ASHKENAZI JEWS IN EASTERN EUROPE, BUT THE VINEGAR WOULD HAVE BEEN DERIVED FROM NONKOSHER WINE.

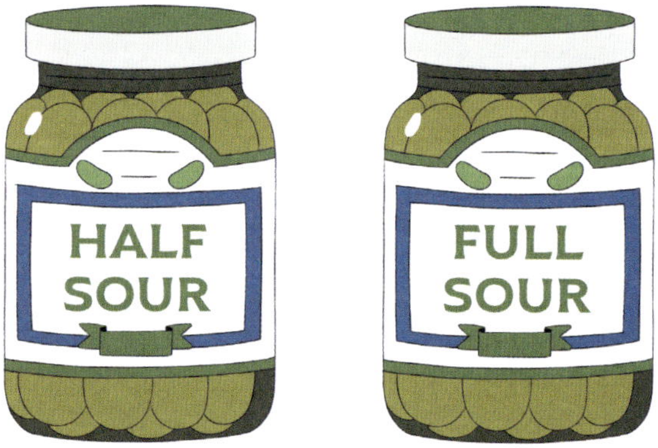
HALF SOUR
FULL SOUR

DELI PICKLES—LIKE THE PICKLES ONCE SOLD BY STREET CART VENDORS—COME IN TWO VARIETIES: HALF SOUR AND FULL SOUR.

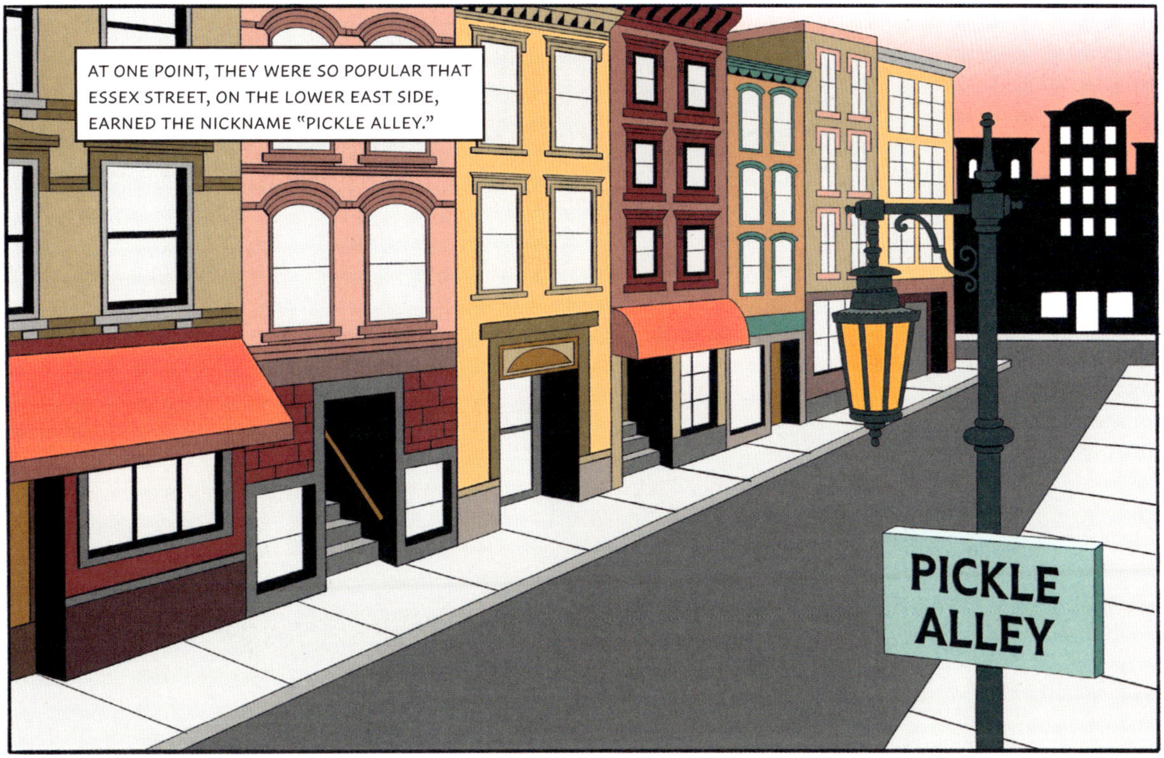
AT ONE POINT, THEY WERE SO POPULAR THAT ESSEX STREET, ON THE LOWER EAST SIDE, EARNED THE NICKNAME "PICKLE ALLEY."
PICKLE ALLEY

THE MAIN DIFFERENCE BETWEEN HALF SOUR AND FULL SOUR PICKLES IS THE AMOUNT OF TIME THEY SPEND FERMENTING. THE LONGER THEY ARE IN THE BRINE, THE MORE SOUR (AND LESS CRUNCHY) THEY BECOME.

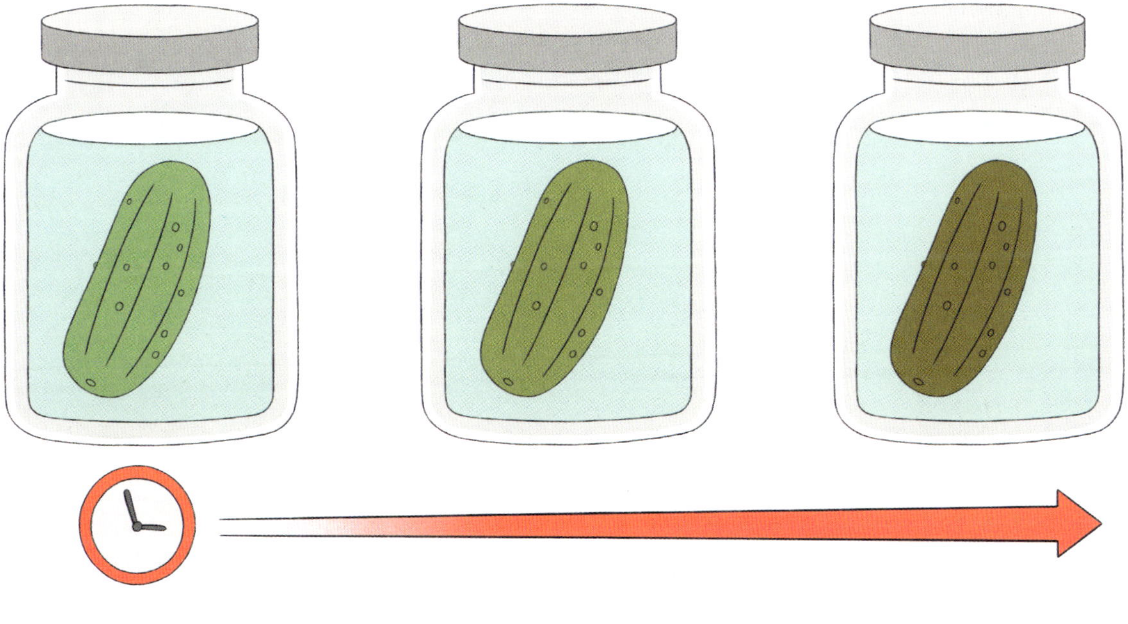

TO MAKE DILL PICKLES

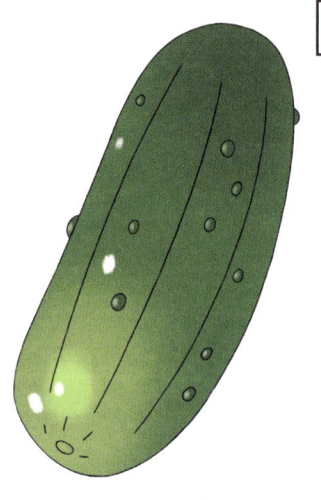

KIRBY CUCUMBERS (THE MOST COMMON KIND USED FOR PICKLING) ARE WASHED AND PACKED INTO A JAR OR BARREL.

A BRINE MADE OF SALT DISSOLVED IN WATER IS POURED OVER THE CUCUMBERS.

DILL SPRIGS ARE ADDED, ALONG WITH HERBS AND SEASONINGS SUCH AS:

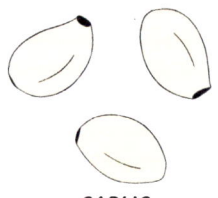

GARLIC

DILL SEED

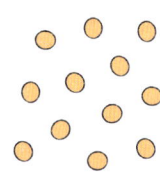

MUSTARD SEED

FENNEL SEED

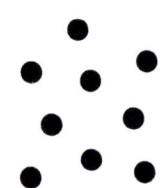

BLACK PEPPERCORNS

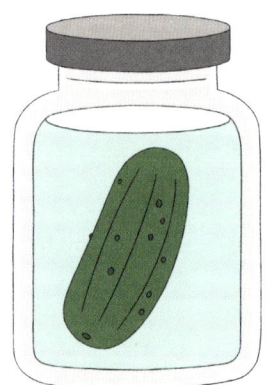

THE BARREL OR JAR IS COVERED, AND THE PICKLES FERMENT FOR SIX TO EIGHT WEEKS— SOMETIMES LONGER.

DILL PICKLES ARE BRIGHT AND ACIDIC, THE PERFECT COMPANION TO SOFT, FATTY MEAT AND SPICY MUSTARD.

VARIETIES OF PICKLES

FULL SOUR

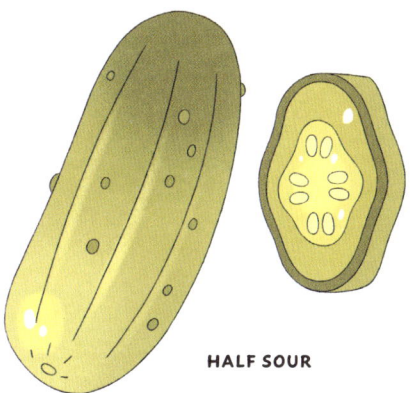

HALF SOUR

KOSHER DILL

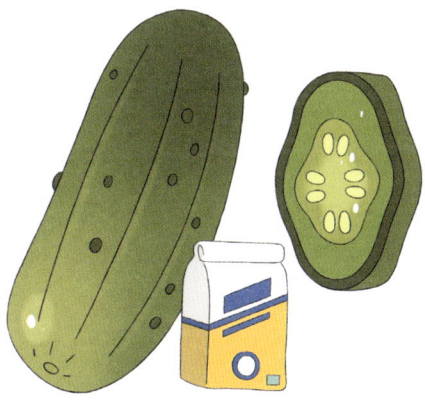

BREAD & BUTTER

GHERKIN

HUNGARIAN

Latkes

LATKES ARE AMONG THE A-LIST CELEBRITIES OF JEWISH FOOD.

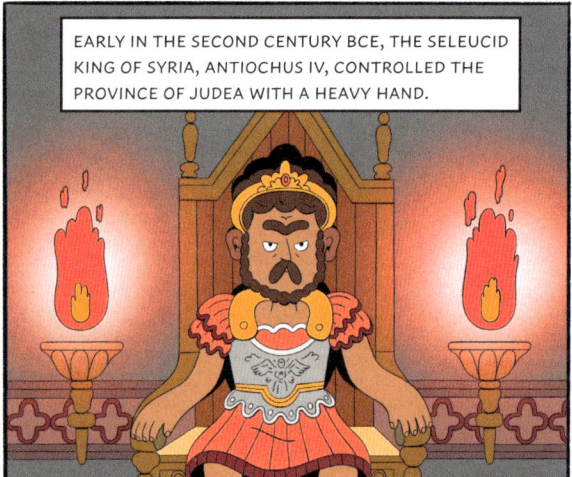

EARLY IN THE SECOND CENTURY BCE, THE SELEUCID KING OF SYRIA, ANTIOCHUS IV, CONTROLLED THE PROVINCE OF JUDEA WITH A HEAVY HAND.

HE FORBADE THE JEWISH PEOPLE TO PRACTICE THEIR RELIGION AND COMMANDED THEM TO WORSHIP OTHER GODS.

HIS SOLDIERS KILLED MANY PEOPLE AND DESECRATED THE TEMPLE IN JERUSALEM BY FILLING IT WITH IDOLS AND PIGS.

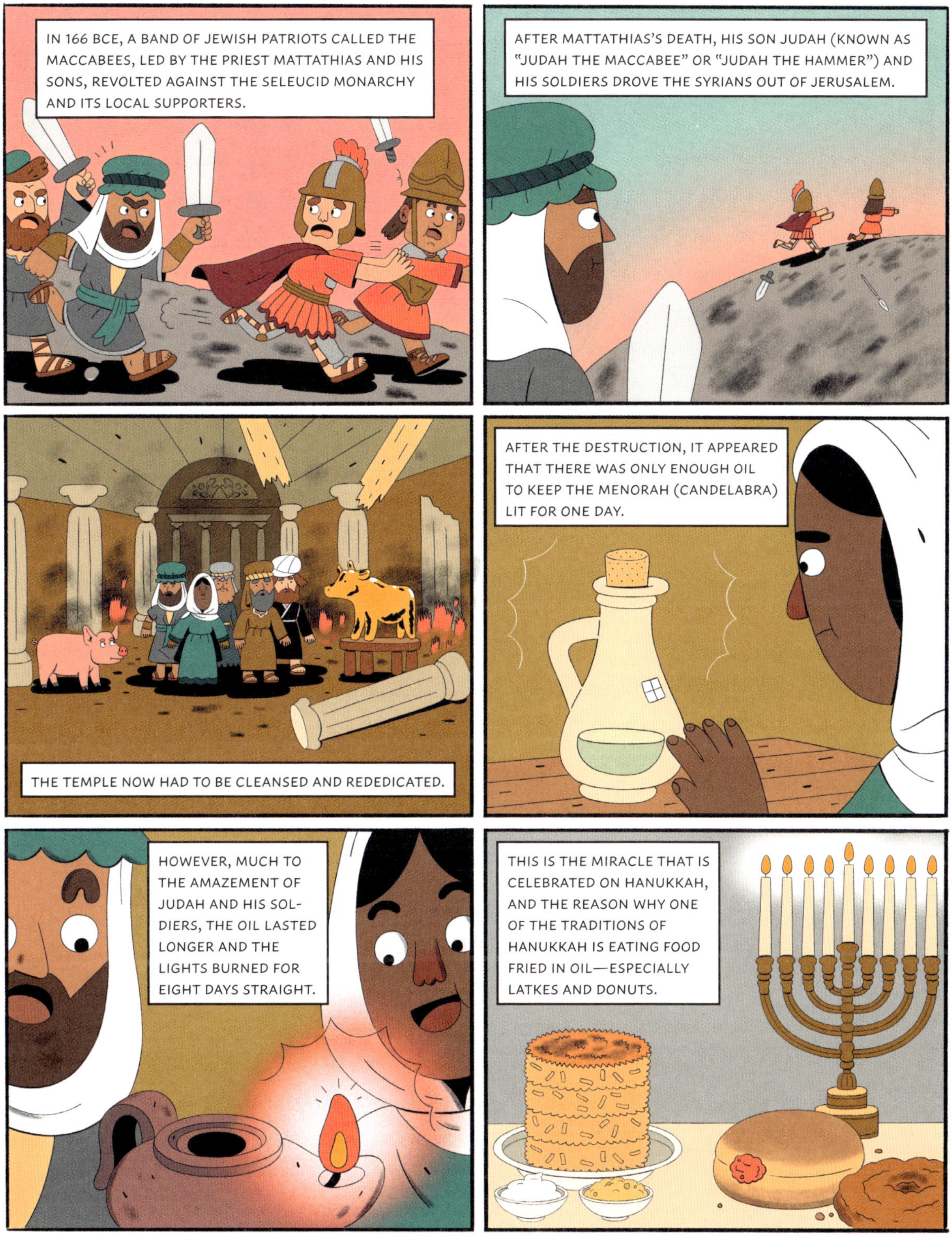
IN 166 BCE, A BAND OF JEWISH PATRIOTS CALLED THE MACCABEES, LED BY THE PRIEST MATTATHIAS AND HIS SONS, REVOLTED AGAINST THE SELEUCID MONARCHY AND ITS LOCAL SUPPORTERS.
AFTER MATTATHIAS'S DEATH, HIS SON JUDAH (KNOWN AS "JUDAH THE MACCABEE" OR "JUDAH THE HAMMER") AND HIS SOLDIERS DROVE THE SYRIANS OUT OF JERUSALEM.
THE TEMPLE NOW HAD TO BE CLEANSED AND REDEDICATED.
AFTER THE DESTRUCTION, IT APPEARED THAT THERE WAS ONLY ENOUGH OIL TO KEEP THE MENORAH (CANDELABRA) LIT FOR ONE DAY.
HOWEVER, MUCH TO THE AMAZEMENT OF JUDAH AND HIS SOLDIERS, THE OIL LASTED LONGER AND THE LIGHTS BURNED FOR EIGHT DAYS STRAIGHT.
THIS IS THE MIRACLE THAT IS CELEBRATED ON HANUKKAH, AND THE REASON WHY ONE OF THE TRADITIONS OF HANUKKAH IS EATING FOOD FRIED IN OIL—ESPECIALLY LATKES AND DONUTS.

ANOTHER STORY THAT RELATES HANUKKAH TO LATKES IS FROM THE BOOK OF JUDITH IN THE HEBREW BIBLE. JUDITH, A GREAT HERO OF THE JEWISH PEOPLE, WENT TO THE TENT OF THE ASSYRIAN GENERAL HOLOFERNES, WHO LUSTED AFTER THE BEAUTIFUL WIDOW.

SHE PLIED HIM WITH WINE AND FRIED CHEESE PANCAKES UNTIL HE FELL ASLEEP, AT WHICH POINT SHE CUT OFF HIS HEAD.

More cheese pancakes, my lord?

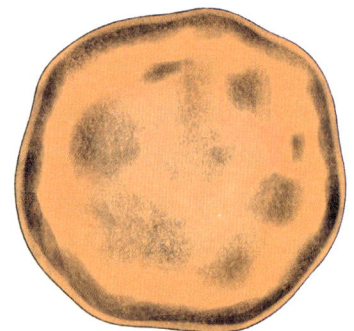

THIS IS WHY MEDIEVAL JEWS CELEBRATED HANUKKAH WITH CHEESE LATKES.

IN EASTERN EUROPE, WHERE POTATOES WERE CHEAP AND ABUNDANT, THEY REPLACED THE CHEESE IN THE PANCAKE.

Enough cheese! We gotta do something with all these potatoes.

AND SCHMALTZ REPLACED THE OLIVE OIL OF THE MEDITERRANEAN.

THERE ARE MANY WAYS TO MAKE POTATO LATKES; THICKNESS IS THE GREATEST VARIABLE.

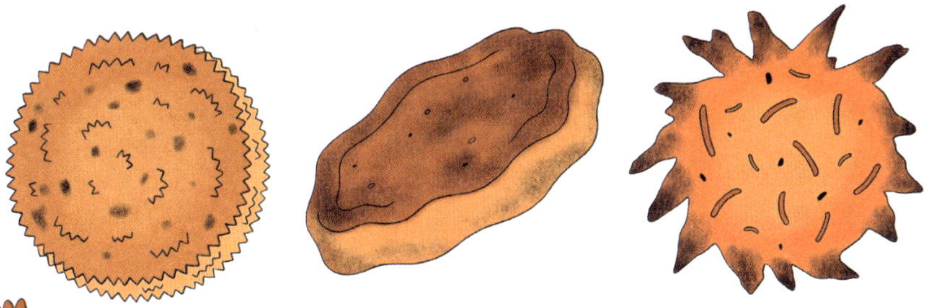

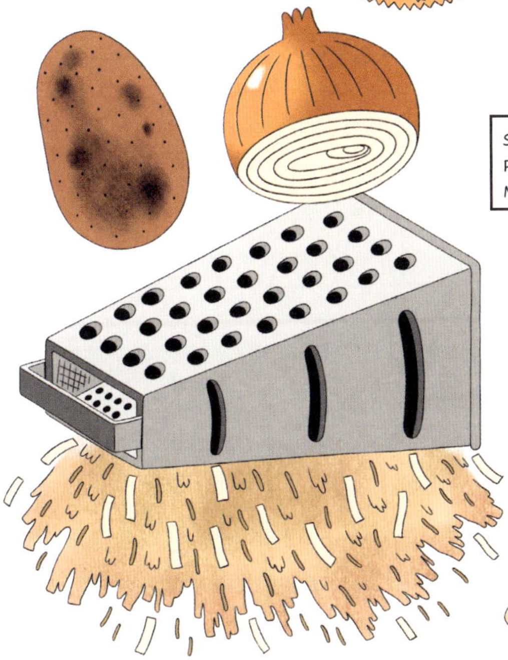

SHREDDED POTATOES AND ONIONS ARE PRESSED AND DRAINED TO REMOVE AS MUCH MOISTURE AS POSSIBLE.

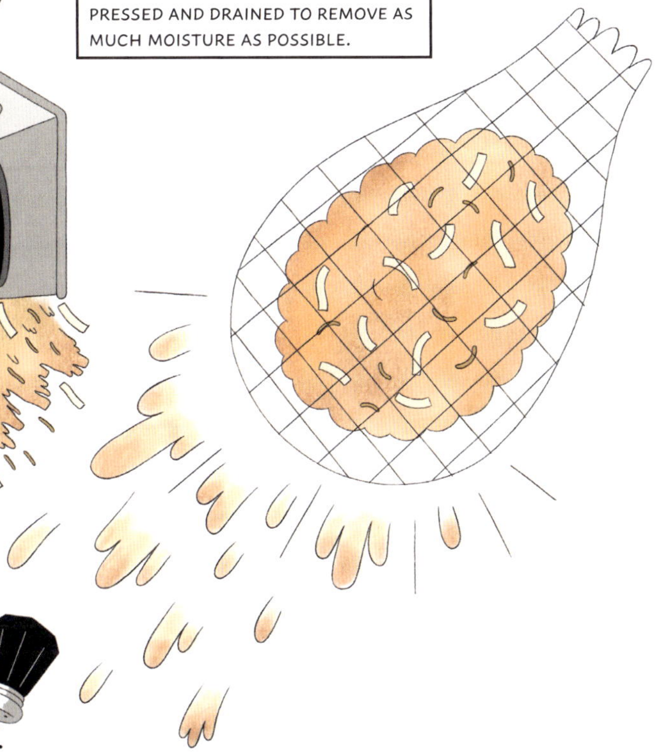

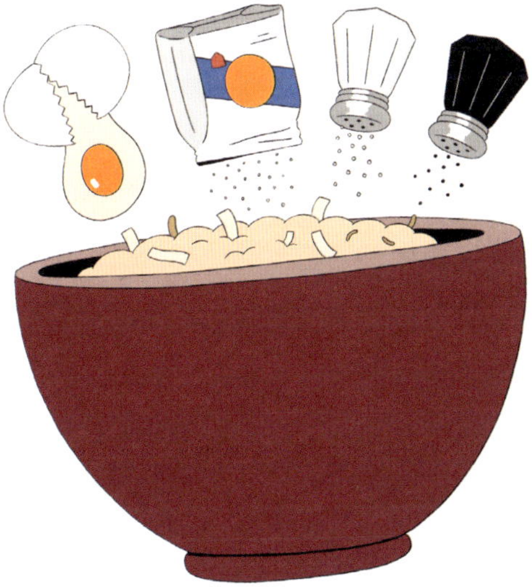

THEY ARE THEN MIXED WITH EGG, FLOUR (OR MATZO MEAL), SALT, AND PEPPER INTO A THICK BATTER.

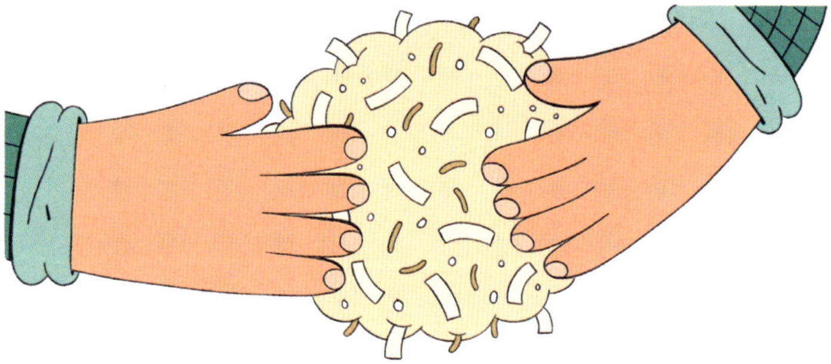

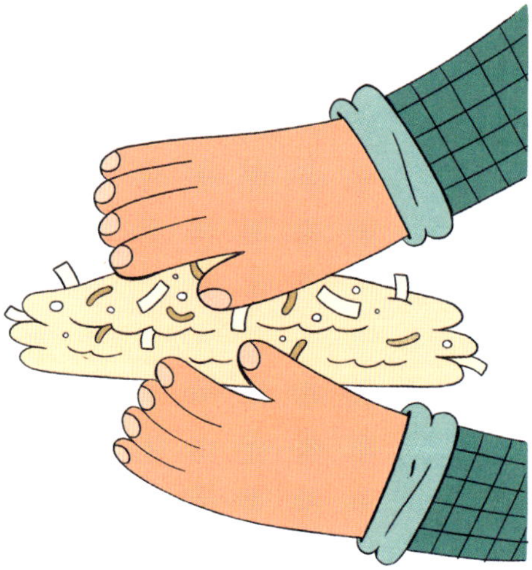

THE BATTER POTATO MIXTURE IS SHAPED INTO INDIVIDUAL PATTIES, WHICH ARE FRIED IN SCHMALTZ OR OIL.

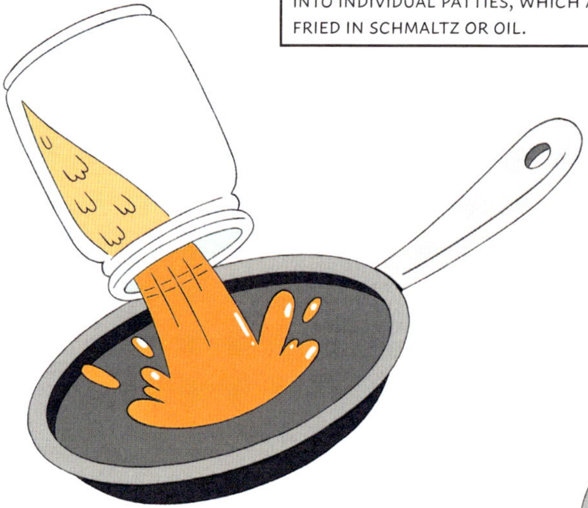

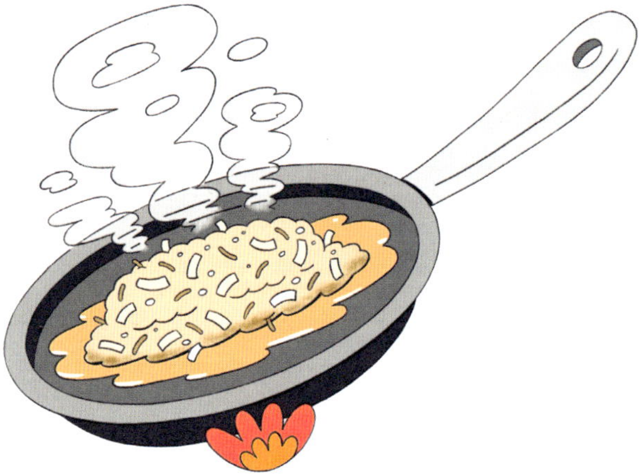

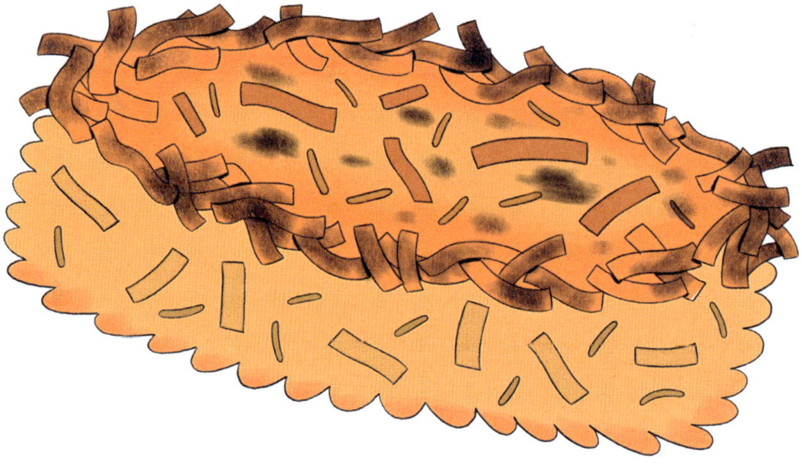

YOU CAN ALSO ADD SMOKED FISH, CAVIAR, POMEGRANATE SEEDS . . . GET CREATIVE!

LATKE TOPPINGS

SOUR CREAM

APPLE SAUCE

CAVIAR

EGG

POMEGRANATE

FISH

Eggs

EGGS ARE CONSIDERED PAREVE. THIS MAKES THEM NOT ONLY KOSHER BUT ALSO VERSATILE IN HOW THEY CAN BE USED IN JEWISH COOKING. SCRAMBLED EGGS WITH SCHMALTZ AND ONIONS ARE PERFECTLY FINE—AND ABSOLUTELY DELICIOUS.

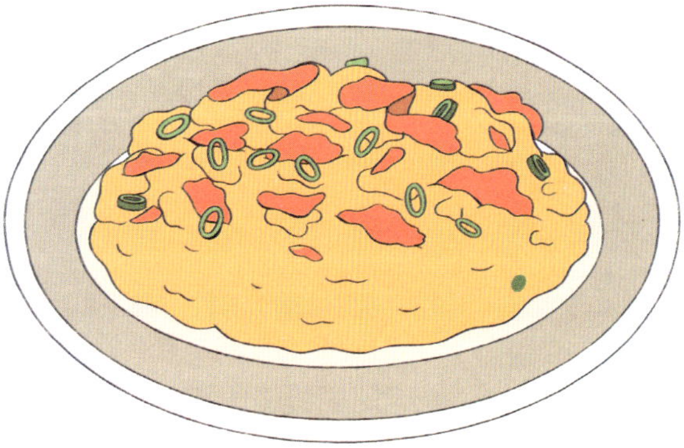

LOX AND EGGS

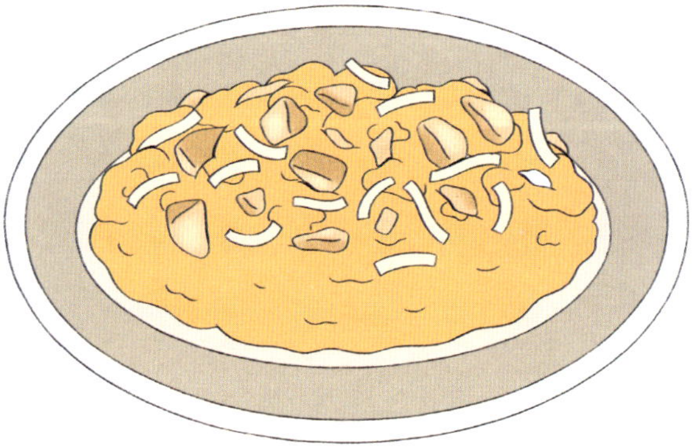

STURGEON AND EGGS

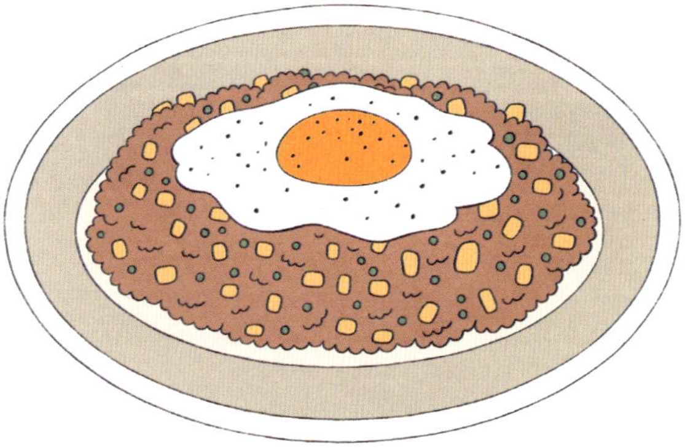

CORNED BEEF HASH

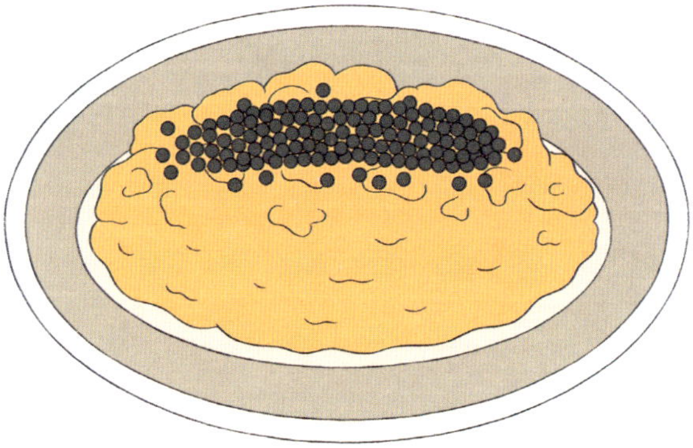

EGGS AND CAVIAR

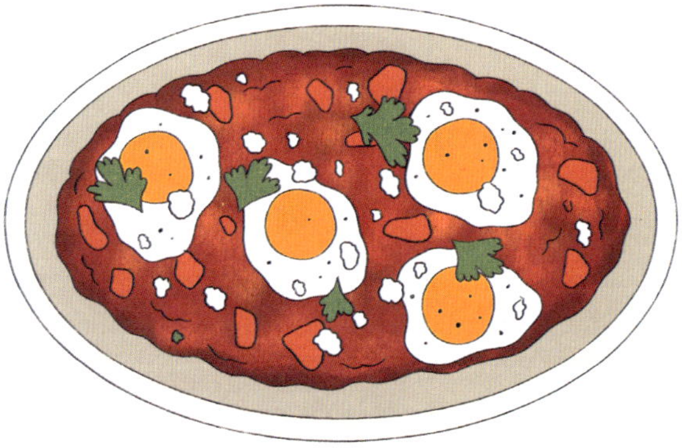

SHAKSHUKA

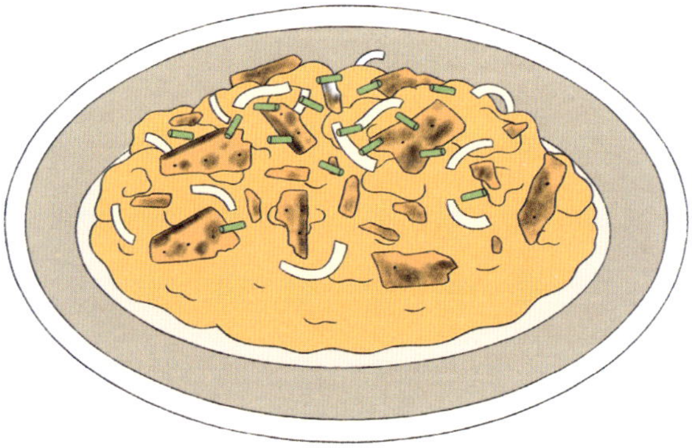

MATZO BREI

MATZO BREI

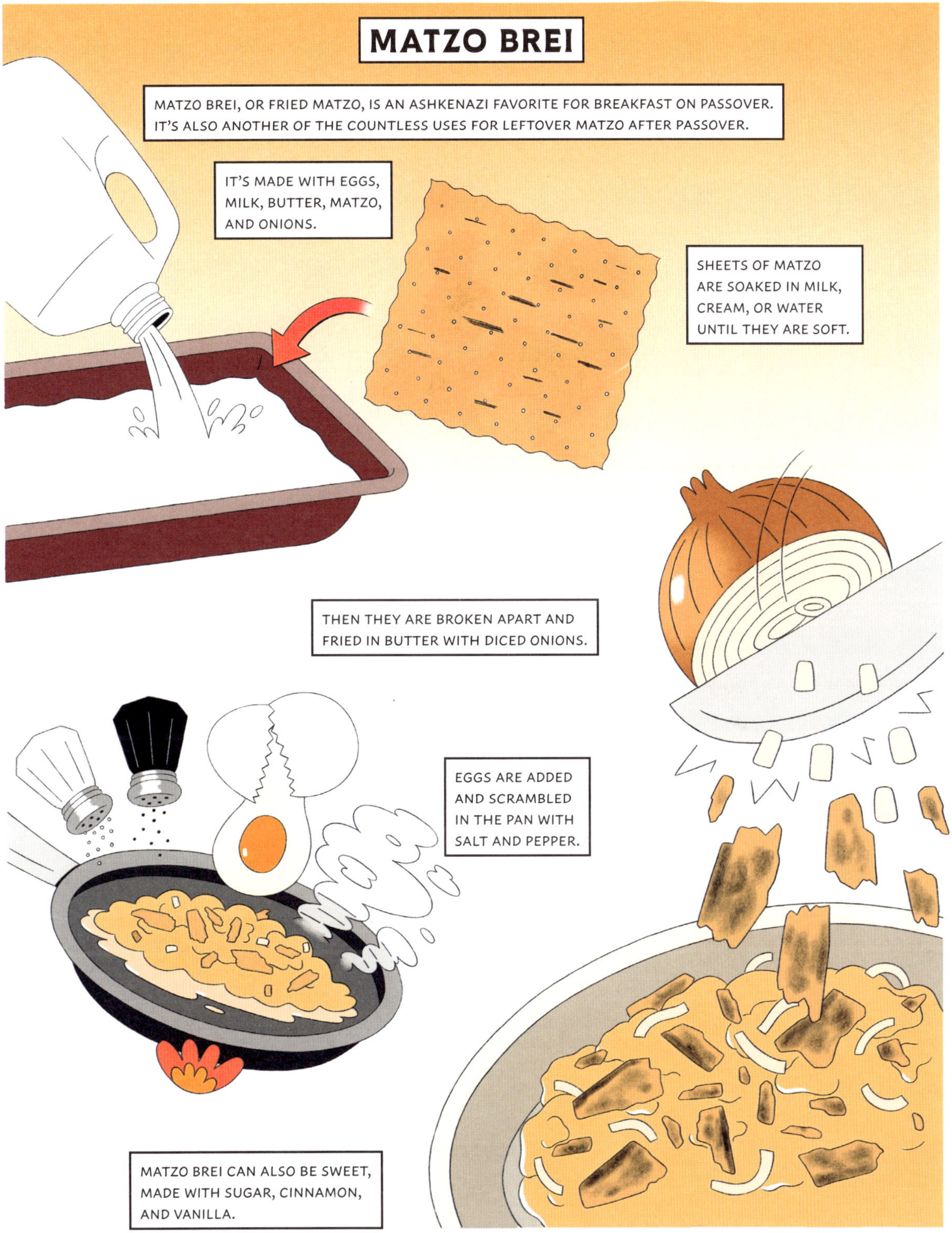
MATZO BREI, OR FRIED MATZO, IS AN ASHKENAZI FAVORITE FOR BREAKFAST ON PASSOVER. IT'S ALSO ANOTHER OF THE COUNTLESS USES FOR LEFTOVER MATZO AFTER PASSOVER.
IT'S MADE WITH EGGS, MILK, BUTTER, MATZO, AND ONIONS.
SHEETS OF MATZO ARE SOAKED IN MILK, CREAM, OR WATER UNTIL THEY ARE SOFT.
THEN THEY ARE BROKEN APART AND FRIED IN BUTTER WITH DICED ONIONS.
EGGS ARE ADDED AND SCRAMBLED IN THE PAN WITH SALT AND PEPPER.
MATZO BREI CAN ALSO BE SWEET, MADE WITH SUGAR, CINNAMON, AND VANILLA.

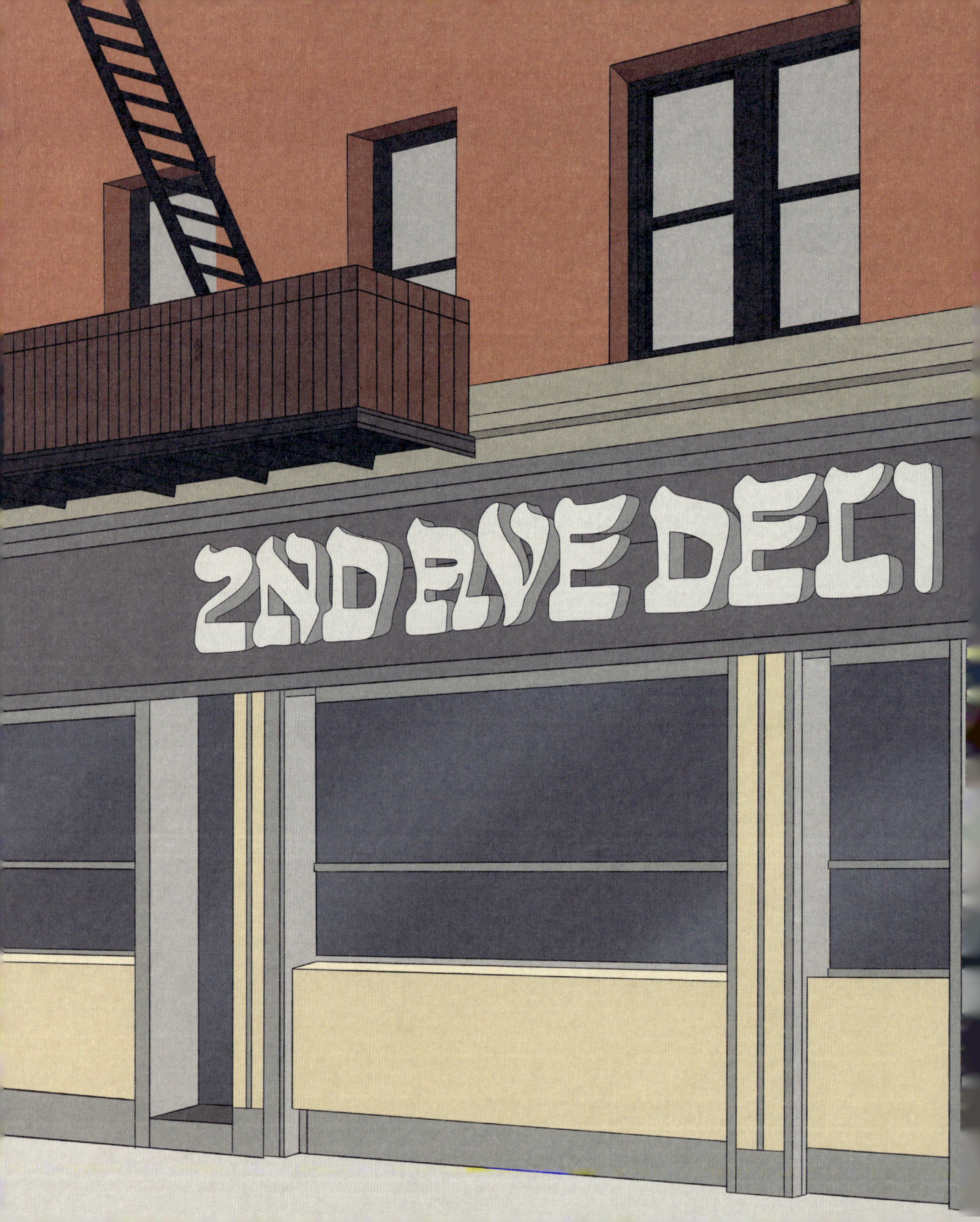
2ND AVE DELI

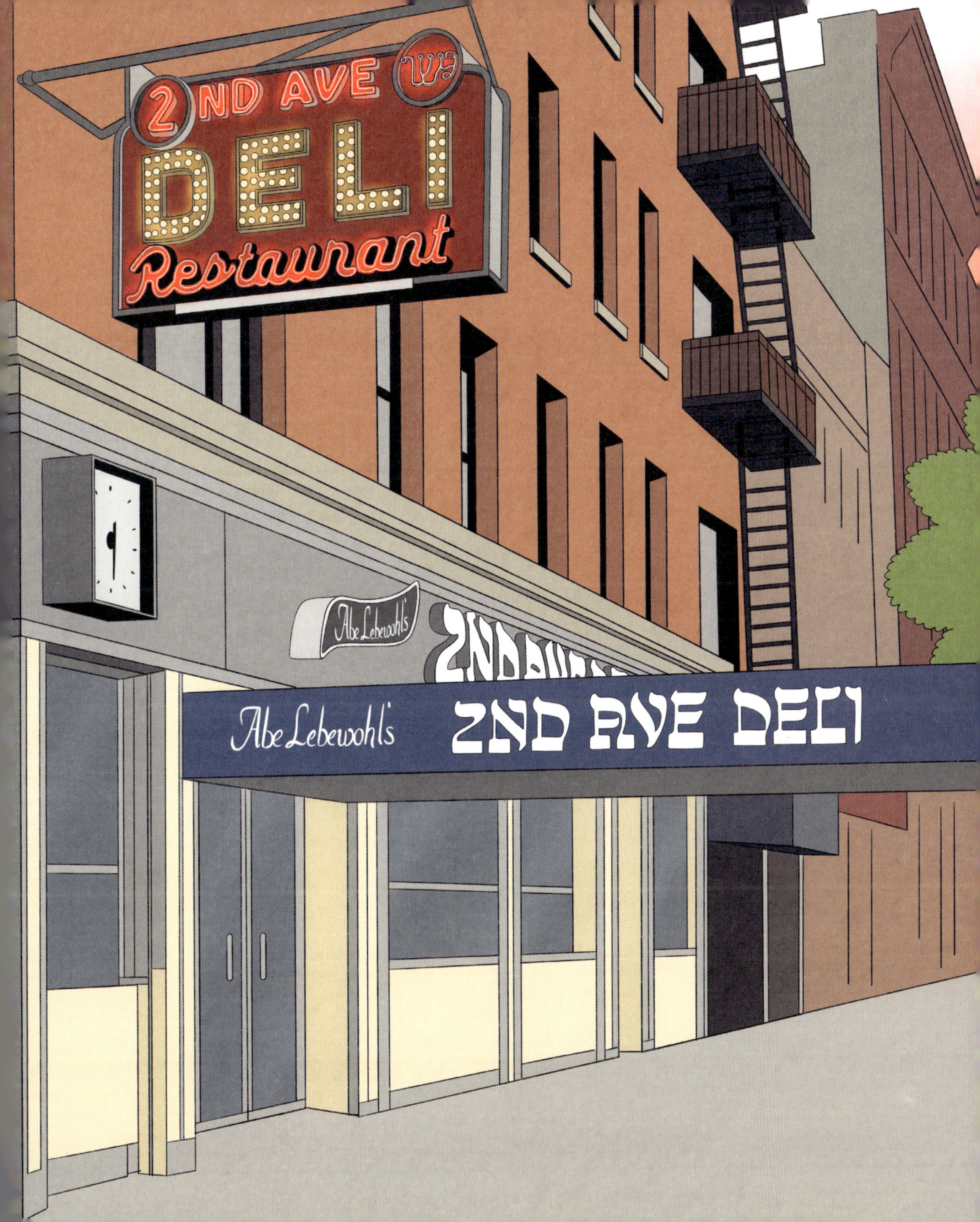

2ND AVE
DELI
Restaurant
Abe Lebewohl's
2ND AVE DELI

2ND AVE DELI

2nd Ave Deli has two locations in Manhattan:
1442 1st Avenue
162 East 33rd Street

The 2nd Ave Deli was founded in 1954 by Abe Lebewohl, a Ukrainian Holocaust survivor who immigrated to the United States with his family and worked a series of restaurant jobs. After he purchased a small cafe on Second Avenue and Tenth Street in the East Village, Lebewohl worked to expand the cafe into a cultural hub. Right in the middle of the Yiddish theater district, 2nd Ave Deli quickly became a gathering place for artists and musicians of all types, enjoying decades of Hollywood patronage and wild success as one of New York City's premiere delicatessens. In 2006, the original deli closed, but with the help of Abe's brother and two nephews, two new locations took its place, one on Thirty-Third Street and one on First Avenue.

Interview with Josh Lebewohl, Co-owner of the 2nd Ave Deli

How has the 2nd Ave Deli has made it this far?

It's really, really good. Everything we make is delicious. It's all homemade. It's a place people feel at home.

What is the perfect order?

I would say the classic order would be our famous matzo ball soup—Jewish penicillin. It flies off the shelf even in the summer, but you can imagine how much we sell in the cold months.

A lot of people say that matzo ball soup is the best way to introduce someone to Jewish food in general.

I'll give you the classic order and then expand upon it.

OK, great.

Add the pastrami sandwich. Plus, I'm a dessert person, so I'll probably have some babka or rugelach for dessert. And I would just suggest the same thing when you try any cuisine for the first time: either go with someone who knows what they're talking about, or let the waiter guide you. It's really just trying all the delicious foods, whether it's pastrami, corned beef from the deli counter, stuffed cabbage, chicken soup, gefilte fish, some old-world classics.

Is there an item that people tend to stay away from that you think is worth trying?

There are a couple of items that are both really delicious that I always find it very funny to give to people without telling them what they are. Definitely tongue, and p'tcha (jellied calves' feet). With p'tcha, we serve it one of two ways, depending on how it's congealed: jellied or in soup

198

form so it's bone broth. I remember serving it to a friend who, had she known that it was calves' feet, wouldn't have eaten it, but she was like, "Oh my god, I'll have a second."

What's your take on the future of the Jewish deli? What will happen to the deli in the next decade or so?

Hopefully grow! I think it's always going to be one of those things where it's going to grow and change with the times. We opened a speakeasy bar a couple of years ago on the second floor of our Upper East Side restaurant. It's somewhere where you can get delicious, slightly elevated food and maybe a cocktail with it. When you look at the menu, you've got pastrami deviled eggs, so it's still unmistakably 2nd Ave Deli, but with a bit of a twist.

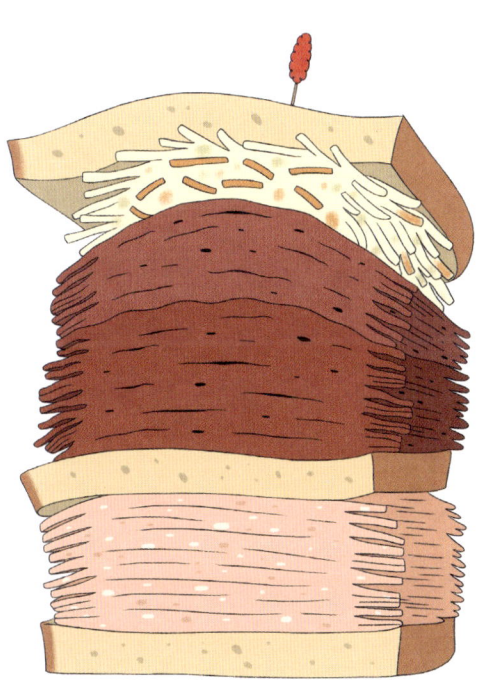

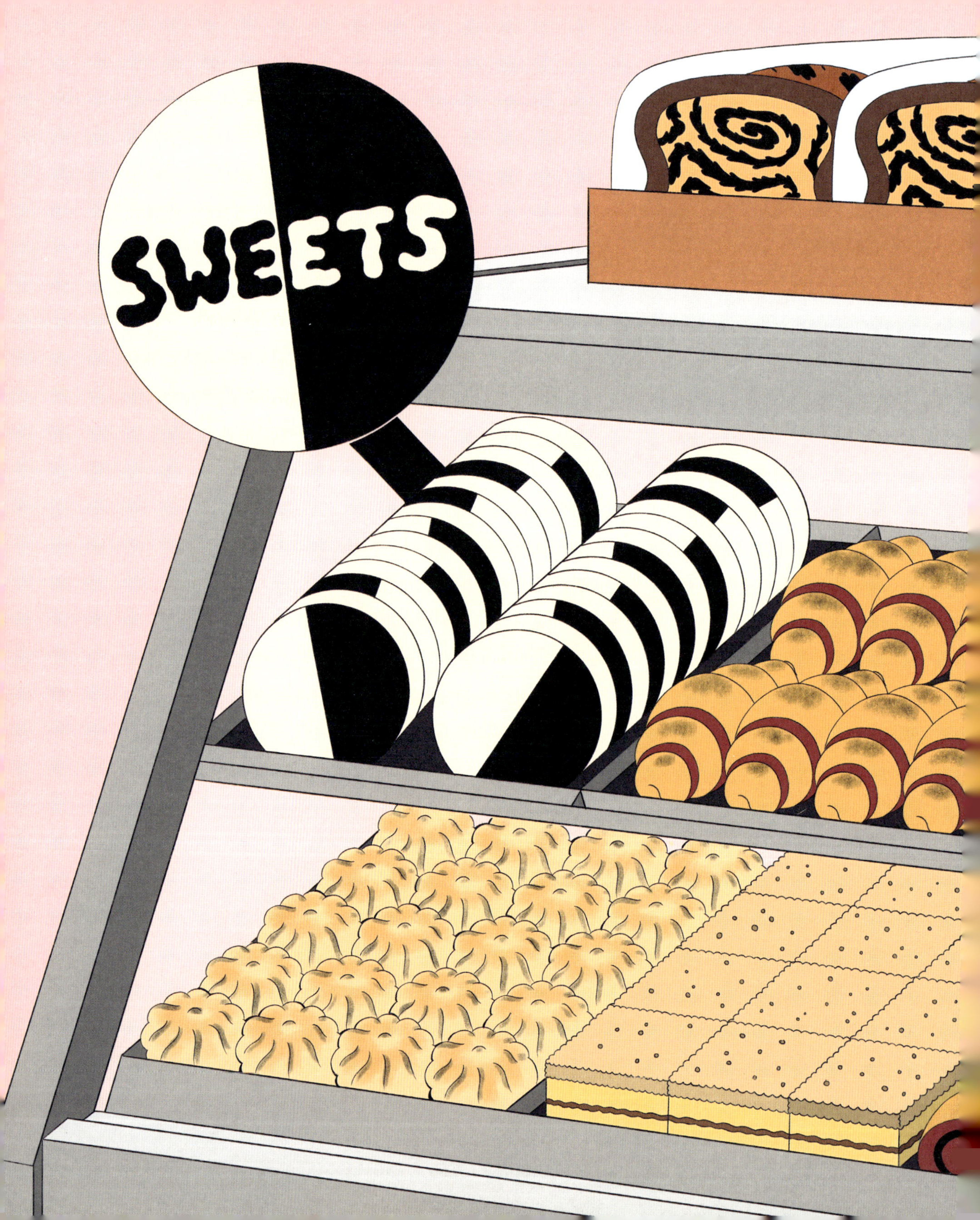
SWEETS

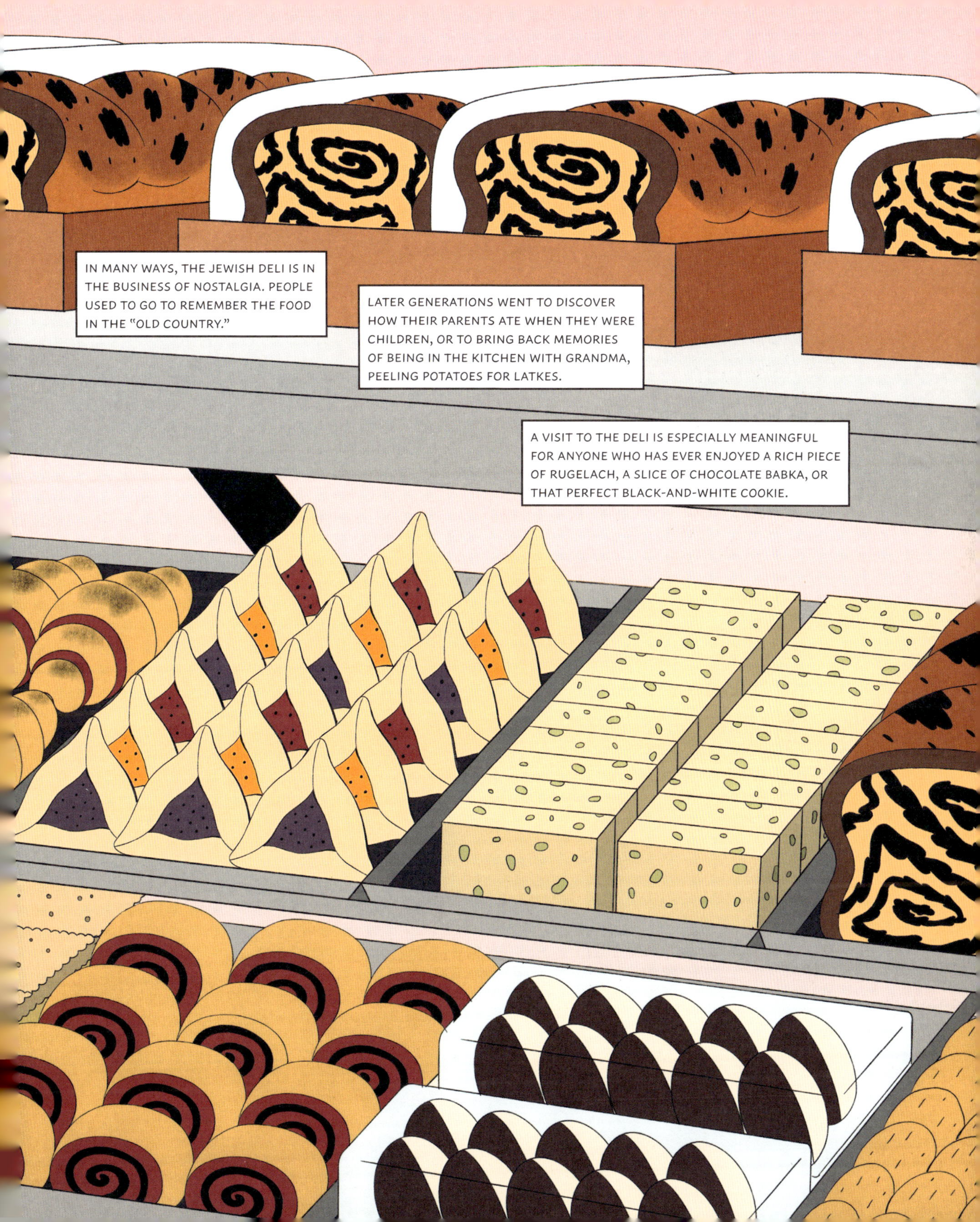
IN MANY WAYS, THE JEWISH DELI IS IN THE BUSINESS OF NOSTALGIA. PEOPLE USED TO GO TO REMEMBER THE FOOD IN THE "OLD COUNTRY."
LATER GENERATIONS WENT TO DISCOVER HOW THEIR PARENTS ATE WHEN THEY WERE CHILDREN, OR TO BRING BACK MEMORIES OF BEING IN THE KITCHEN WITH GRANDMA, PEELING POTATOES FOR LATKES.
A VISIT TO THE DELI IS ESPECIALLY MEANINGFUL FOR ANYONE WHO HAS EVER ENJOYED A RICH PIECE OF RUGELACH, A SLICE OF CHOCOLATE BABKA, OR THAT PERFECT BLACK-AND-WHITE COOKIE.

The Black-and-White Cookie

GET READY FOR A MIND-BLOWING REVELATION: A TRUE BLACK-AND-WHITE COOKIE IS NOT A COOKIE.

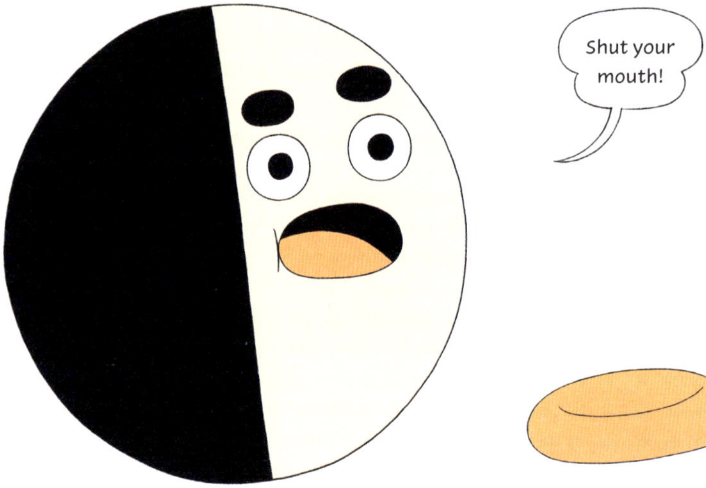
Shut your mouth!

IT'S A DROP CAKE, SO CALLED BECAUSE IT BEGINS WITH A THICK BATTER WITH EXTRA FLOUR THAT'S DROPPED ONTO A BAKING SHEET BEFORE GOING INTO THE OVEN.

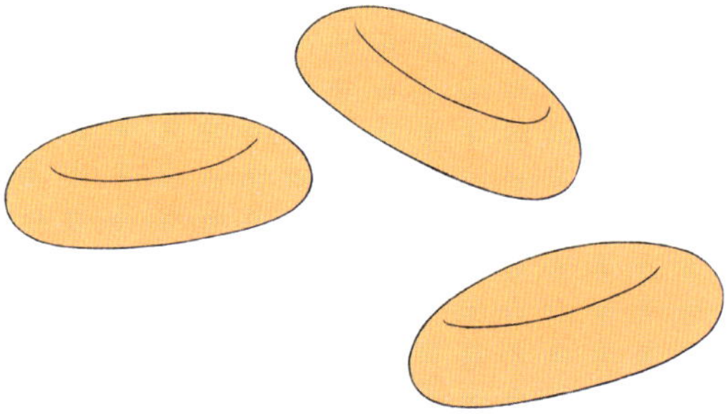

IT IS RELATED TO COOKIES OF THE EIGHTEENTH CENTURY, WHICH WERE ACTUALLY JUST LITTLE CAKES.

THE RECIPE FOR THIS THICK, CAKEY "COOKIE" WAS BROUGHT TO THE UNITED STATES BY BAVARIAN IMMIGRANTS AT THE TURN OF THE TWENTIETH CENTURY.

THE FIRST AMERICAN SIGHTING WAS IN UTICA, IN UPSTATE NEW YORK, AT HEMSTROUGHT'S BAKERY. THEY WERE CALLED HALF-MOONS.

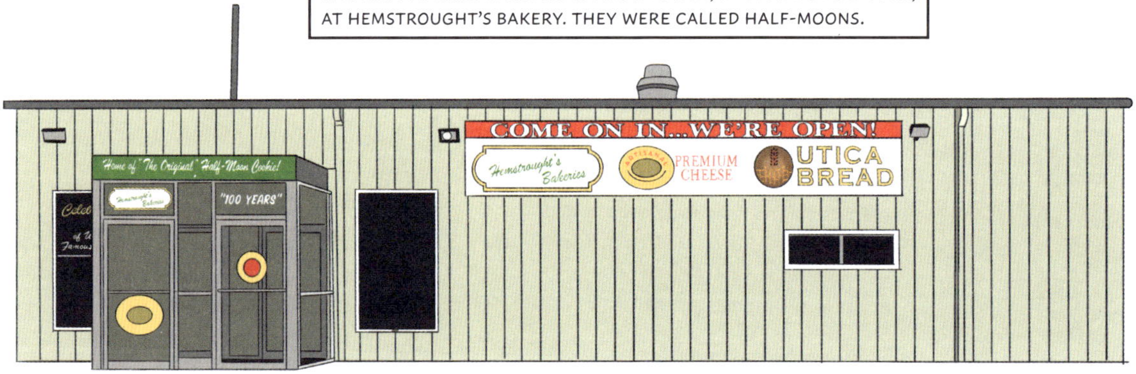
COME ON IN...WE'RE OPEN!
Hemstrought's Bakeries
PREMIUM CHEESE
UTICA BREAD
Home of "The Original" Half-Moon Cookie!
"100 YEARS"

Glaser's
BAKE SHOP

GLASER'S BAKE SHOP IN MANHATTAN ALSO CLAIMS TO HAVE INVENTED THE BLACK-AND-WHITE COOKIE AT AROUND THE SAME TIME.

DESPITE ALL THE RUMORS, THE BLACK-AND-WHITE COOKIE IS NEITHER A PLEA FOR RACIAL JUSTICE NOR A SYMBOL OF SOCIAL HARMONY. THE CONTRASTING ICING WAS MERELY AN EYE-CATCHING MARKETING STRATEGY.

B&W COOKIE!

THE BLACK-AND-WHITE COOKIE IS, IN FACT, MORE NEW YORKER THAN JEWISH, ALTHOUGH TO MOST PEOPLE IT SEEMS JEWISH SIMPLY BECAUSE IT IS FROM NEW YORK.

THESE TREATS ARE FOUND IN JEWISH DELIS BUT ALSO IN ALL KINDS OF FOOD MARKETS, BAKERIES, AND BODEGAS.

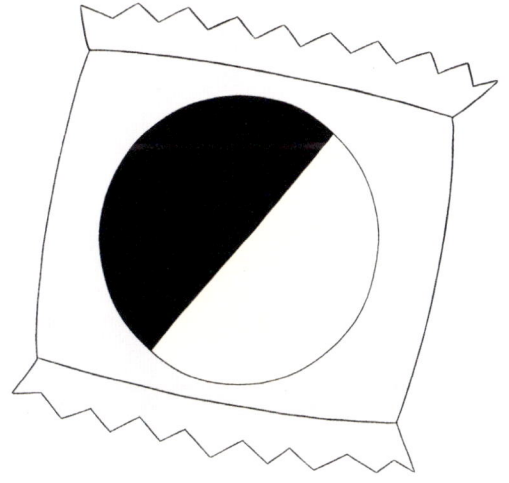

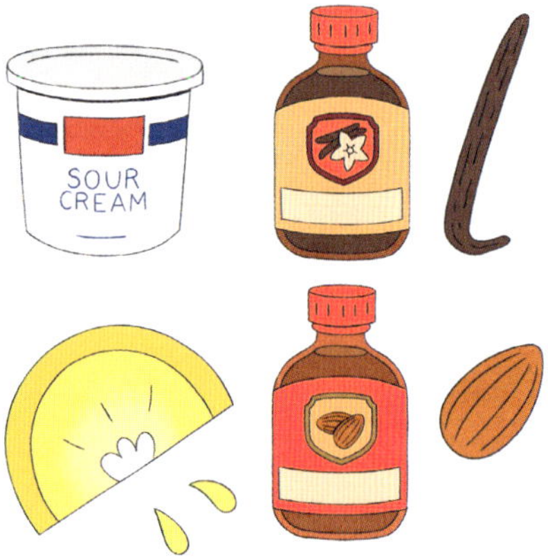
SOUR CREAM

THE COOKIE STARTS WITH A MIXTURE OF SOUR CREAM, VANILLA, LEMON JUICE, AND ALMOND EXTRACT.

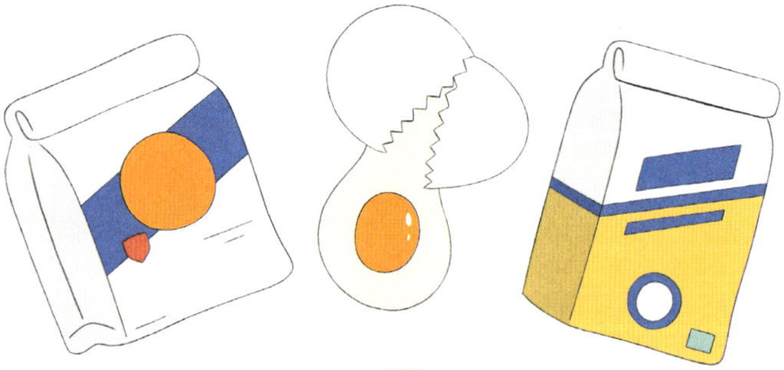

THESE ARE COMBINED WITH FLOUR, EGGS, AND SUGAR,

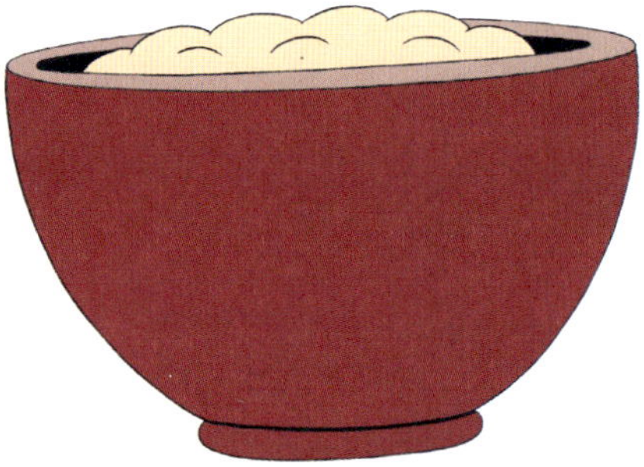

AND THE BATTER IS DOLLOPED ONTO A SHEET AND BAKED INTO SPRINGY CAKES.

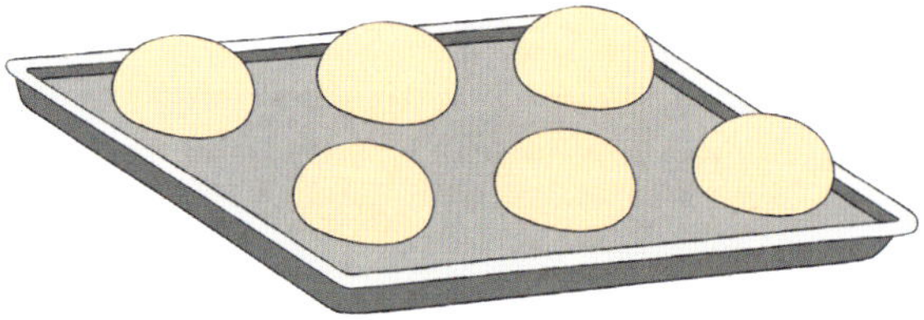

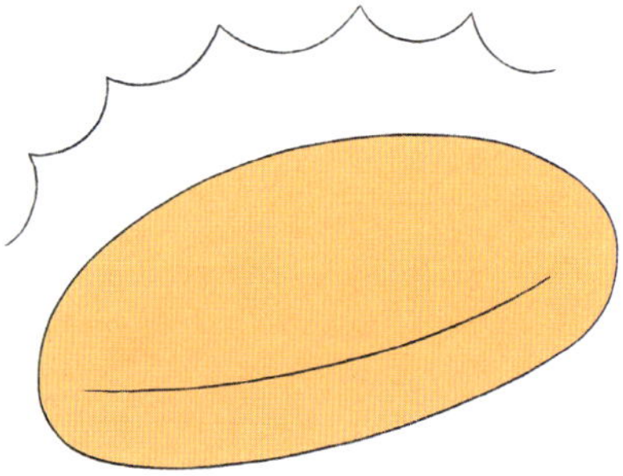

SOME PLACES USE FONDANT FOR THE BLACK-AND-WHITE TOPPING, BUT THE MORE TRADITIONAL METHOD IS TO SPREAD CHOCOLATE AND VANILLA ICING WITH A SPATULA.

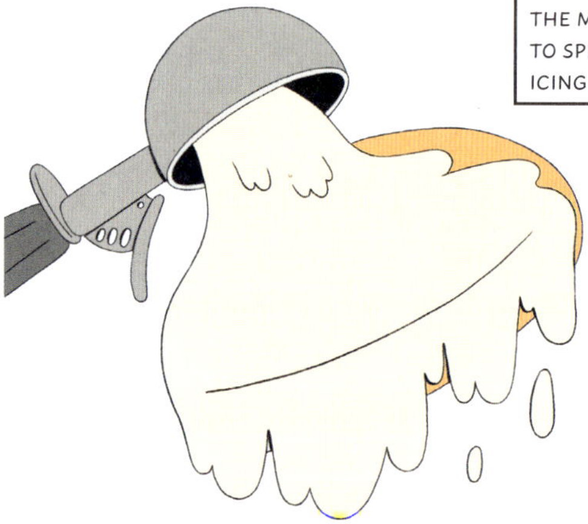

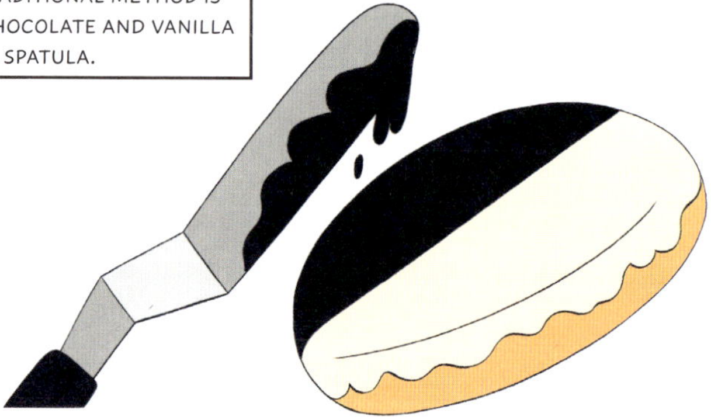

My Black-and-White Cookie Tour

I ran around New York eating a bellyaching number of black-and-white cookies and encountered a much wider variety than I had expected.

The fact that they are secretly cakes, disguised as "cookies," adds to their elusive appeal.

For their near ubiquity and iconic dessert status, it's oddly difficult to pin down any universal or ideal qualities, which vary with personal taste and who is making them.

My delicious research confirmed that they range in scale from bite-size to as big as your face, and in thickness from a cracker to a deck of playing cards.

I believe that a black-and-white cookie should be shared by two people, split in half perpendicular to the icing's dividing line, allowing each person to get a taste of both flavors. So I prefer the bigger variety.

The cake should be moist and slightly dense, sticky to the touch, and not too sweet, with a hint of something extra like lemon or almond. The best black-and-white cookie I ever ate was slightly chewier at the rim, almost like an expertly fried pancake.

The icing is where I found the most variety on my cookie tour, ranging from hard and brittle (making the cookie feel cheap and candy-coated) to a soft melty glaze (which can be a little messy). The perfect texture lies somewhere in the middle—the icing should be able to bend with the cookie but still make a clean break.

The black-and-white icings should taste like chocolate and vanilla, respectively—not uniformly of sugar as is the case with mass-produced varieties. And as far as I'm concerned, the more chocolaty, the better.

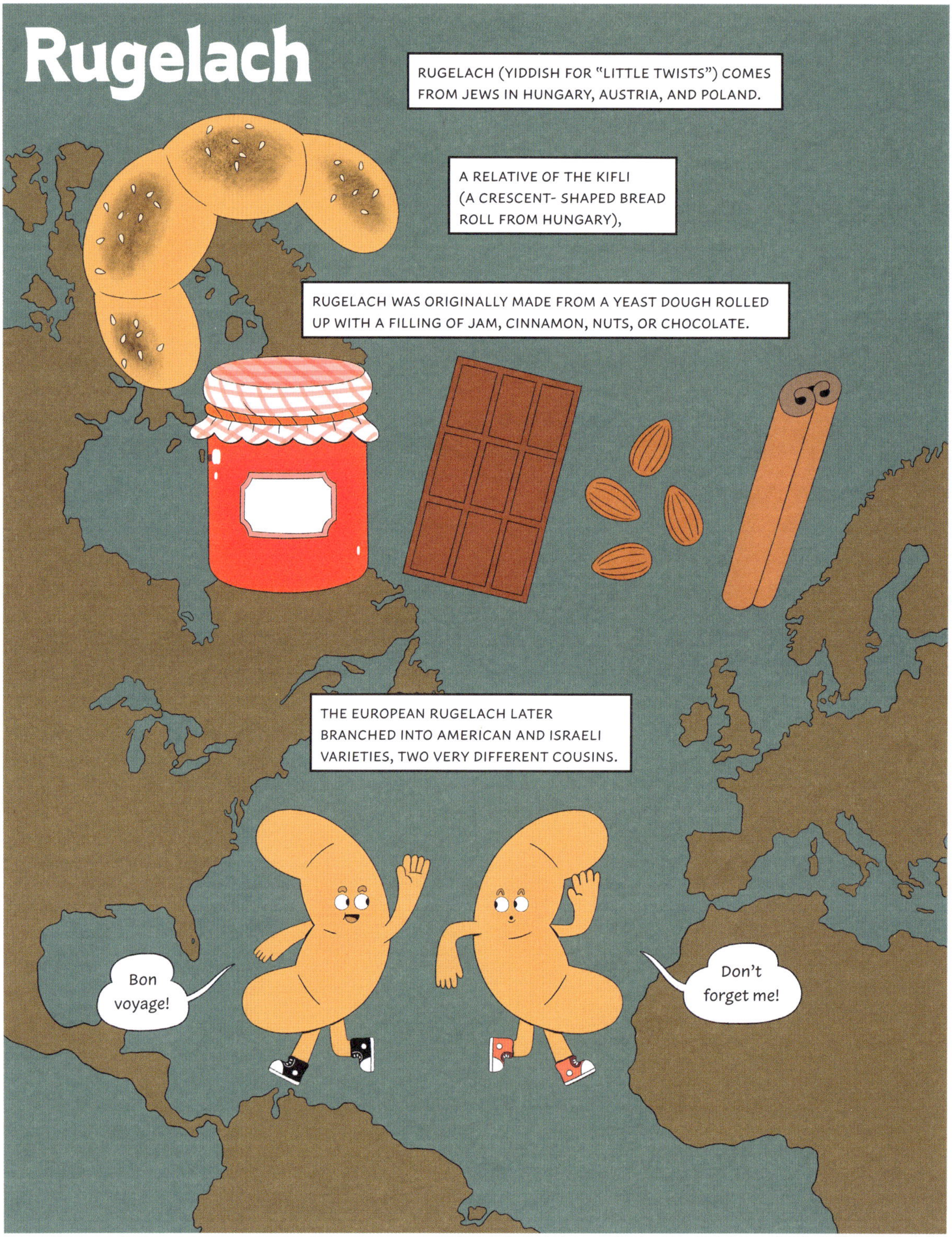
Rugelach
RUGELACH (YIDDISH FOR "LITTLE TWISTS") COMES FROM JEWS IN HUNGARY, AUSTRIA, AND POLAND.
A RELATIVE OF THE KIFLI (A CRESCENT- SHAPED BREAD ROLL FROM HUNGARY),
RUGELACH WAS ORIGINALLY MADE FROM A YEAST DOUGH ROLLED UP WITH A FILLING OF JAM, CINNAMON, NUTS, OR CHOCOLATE.
THE EUROPEAN RUGELACH LATER BRANCHED INTO AMERICAN AND ISRAELI VARIETIES, TWO VERY DIFFERENT COUSINS.
Bon voyage!
Don't forget me!

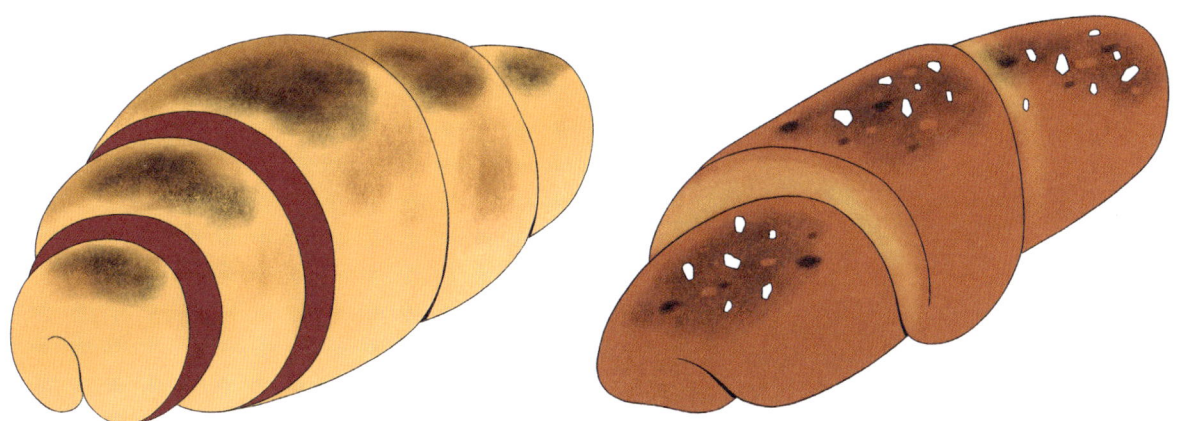

IN THE UNITED STATES, THE YEAST DOUGH WAS REPLACED WITH A DOUGH MADE WITH SOUR CREAM OR CREAM CHEESE, CHANGING THE TEXTURE AND ADDING A BIT OF TANG TO THE FLAVOR.

IN ISRAEL, RUGELACH HAS A MULTILAYERED DOUGH MADE WITH BUTTER; WHEN BAKED, IT RESEMBLES A FLAKY CROISSANT. A MIDDLE EASTERN INFLUENCE LED TO VERY SWEET FILLINGS, SUCH AS HALVAH (A FUDGE MADE OUT OF SESAME PASTE).

SOMETIMES, MARGARINE OR VEGETABLE SHORTENING IS SUBSTITUTED FOR THE DAIRY SO THAT THE RUGELACH WILL BE PAREVE.

Babka

BABKA (FROM THE SLAVIC *BABA* FOR "GRANDMOTHER") IS A LARGE, BREADY BROTHER TO RUGELACH.

IT TOO HAILS FROM UKRAINE AND POLAND.

IT IS A SWEET (BUT NOT TOO SWEET), YEASTY LOAF TYPICALLY FILLED WITH CINNAMON, RAISINS, NUTS, OR CHEESE. A CHOCOLATE VERSION HAS BECOME ESPECIALLY POPULAR IN THE UNITED STATES.

BABKA IS SAID TO HAVE BEEN INVENTED IN THE EARLY NINETEENTH CENTURY BY GRANDMOTHERS TAKING LEFTOVER CHALLAH PIECES AND TWISTING THEM TOGETHER.

Can't let these perfectly good scraps go to waste!

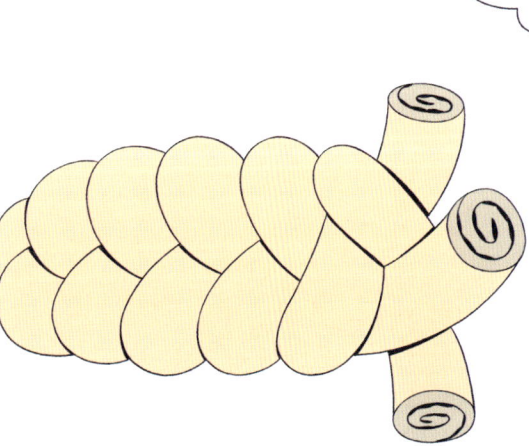

JEWISH AMERICAN BABKA USES A DOUGH NOT UNLIKE THAT OF CHALLAH, AND IT TOO IS BRAIDED.

ISRAELI BABKA, LIKE ISRAELI RUGELACH, HAS A BUTTER-BASED DOUGH AND A FLAKY CROISSANT TEXTURE.

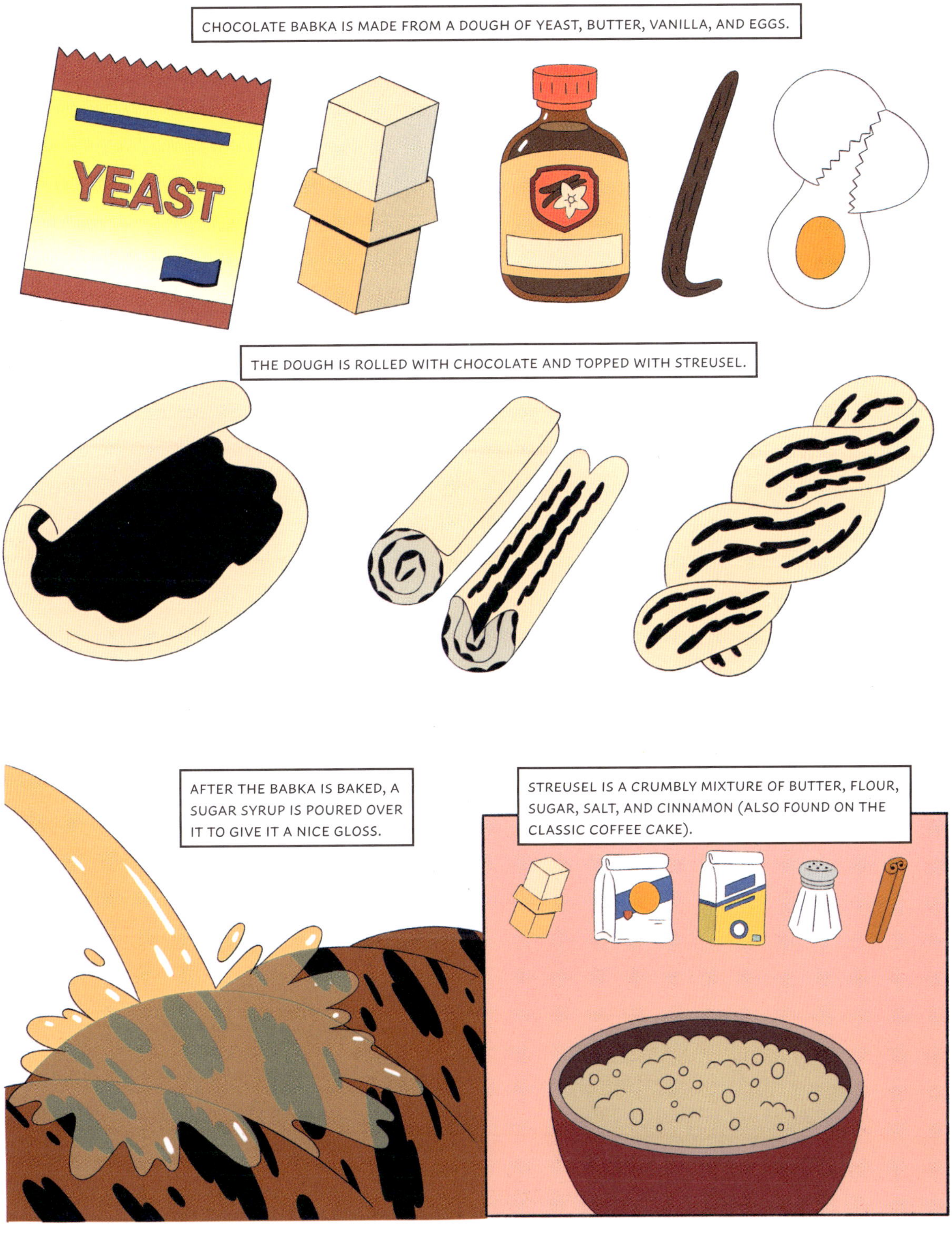
CHOCOLATE BABKA IS MADE FROM A DOUGH OF YEAST, BUTTER, VANILLA, AND EGGS.
YEAST
THE DOUGH IS ROLLED WITH CHOCOLATE AND TOPPED WITH STREUSEL.
AFTER THE BABKA IS BAKED, A SUGAR SYRUP IS POURED OVER IT TO GIVE IT A NICE GLOSS.
STREUSEL IS A CRUMBLY MIXTURE OF BUTTER, FLOUR, SUGAR, SALT, AND CINNAMON (ALSO FOUND ON THE CLASSIC COFFEE CAKE).

Hamantaschen

HAMANTASCHEN, WHICH STARTED OUT AS MOHNTASCHEN (FROM THE GERMAN *MOHN*, MEANING "POPPY SEED," AND *TASCHEN*, MEANING "POCKETS"), HAVE A HEROIC BIBLICAL ANCESTRY.

THEY ARE TREATS THAT CELEBRATE THE JEWISH HOLIDAY OF PURIM.

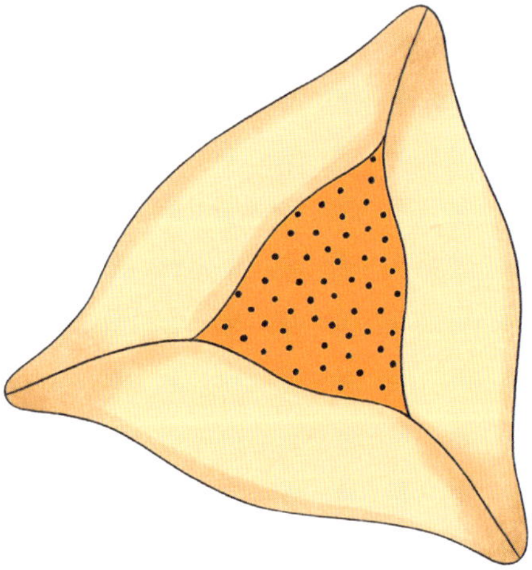

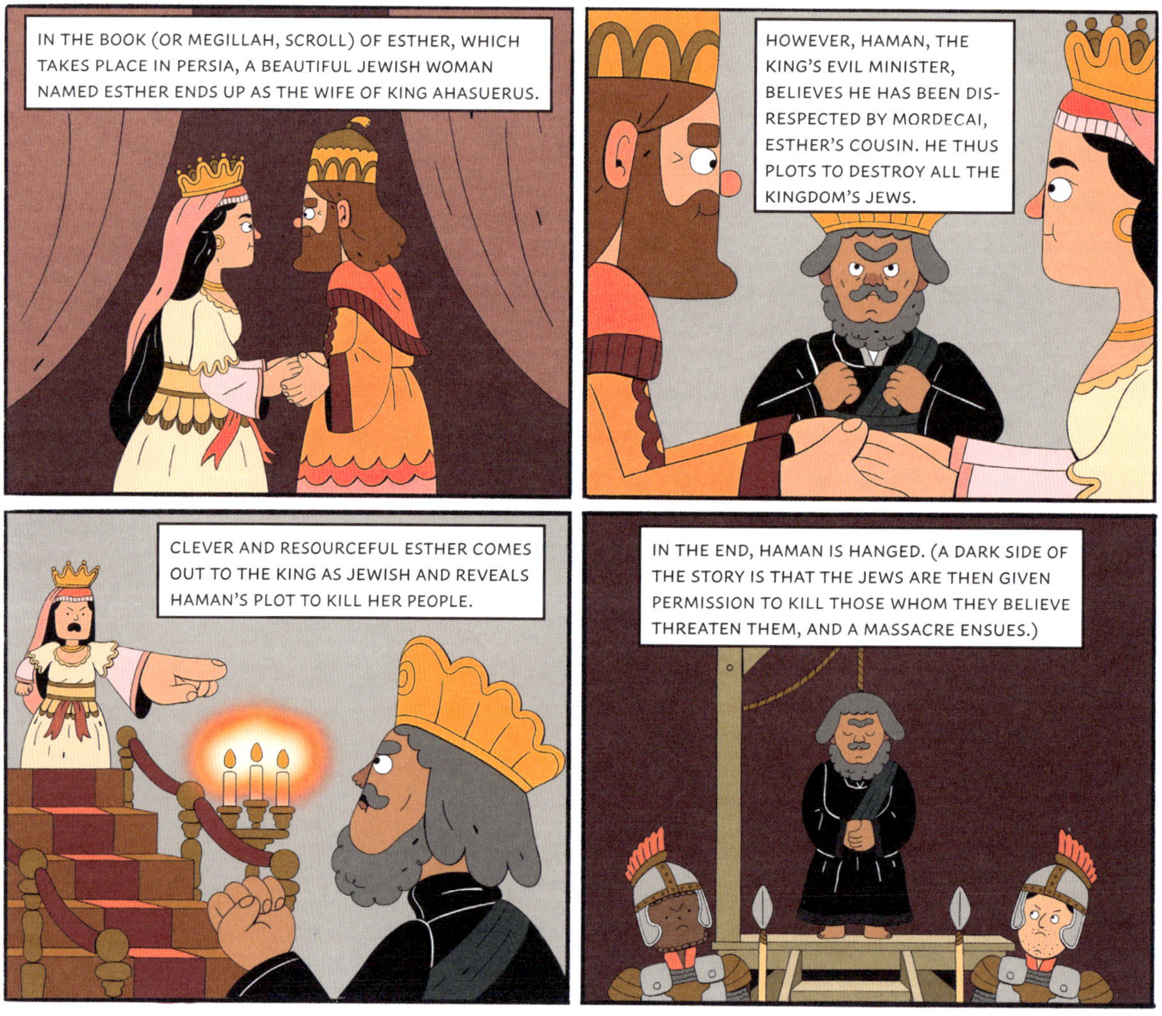
IN THE BOOK (OR MEGILLAH, SCROLL) OF ESTHER, WHICH TAKES PLACE IN PERSIA, A BEAUTIFUL JEWISH WOMAN NAMED ESTHER ENDS UP AS THE WIFE OF KING AHASUERUS.
HOWEVER, HAMAN, THE KING'S EVIL MINISTER, BELIEVES HE HAS BEEN DISRESPECTED BY MORDECAI, ESTHER'S COUSIN. HE THUS PLOTS TO DESTROY ALL THE KINGDOM'S JEWS.
CLEVER AND RESOURCEFUL ESTHER COMES OUT TO THE KING AS JEWISH AND REVEALS HAMAN'S PLOT TO KILL HER PEOPLE.
IN THE END, HAMAN IS HANGED. (A DARK SIDE OF THE STORY IS THAT THE JEWS ARE THEN GIVEN PERMISSION TO KILL THOSE WHOM THEY BELIEVE THREATEN THEM, AND A MASSACRE ENSUES.)

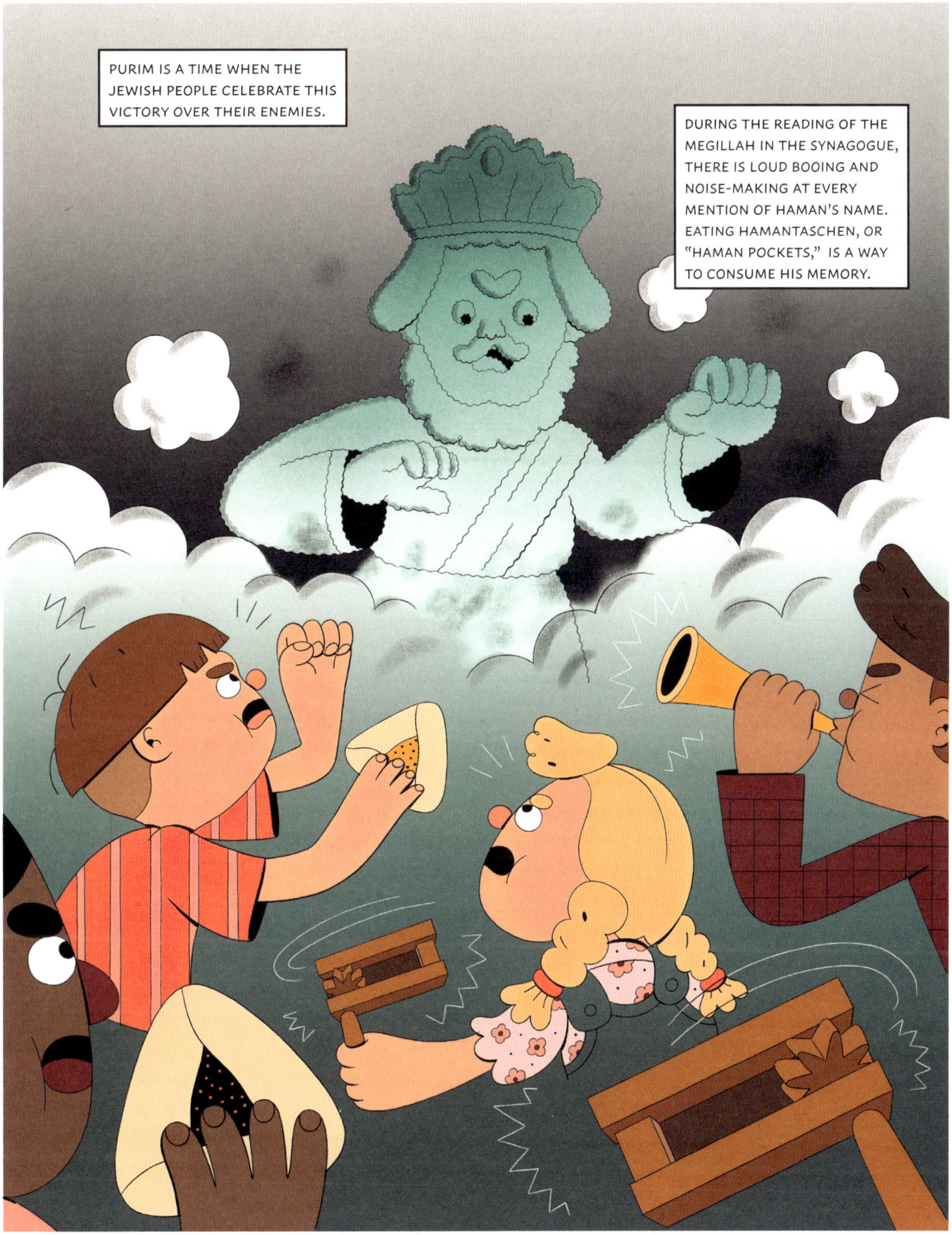
PURIM IS A TIME WHEN THE JEWISH PEOPLE CELEBRATE THIS VICTORY OVER THEIR ENEMIES.
DURING THE READING OF THE MEGILLAH IN THE SYNAGOGUE, THERE IS LOUD BOOING AND NOISE-MAKING AT EVERY MENTION OF HAMAN'S NAME. EATING HAMANTASCHEN, OR "HAMAN POCKETS," IS A WAY TO CONSUME HIS MEMORY.

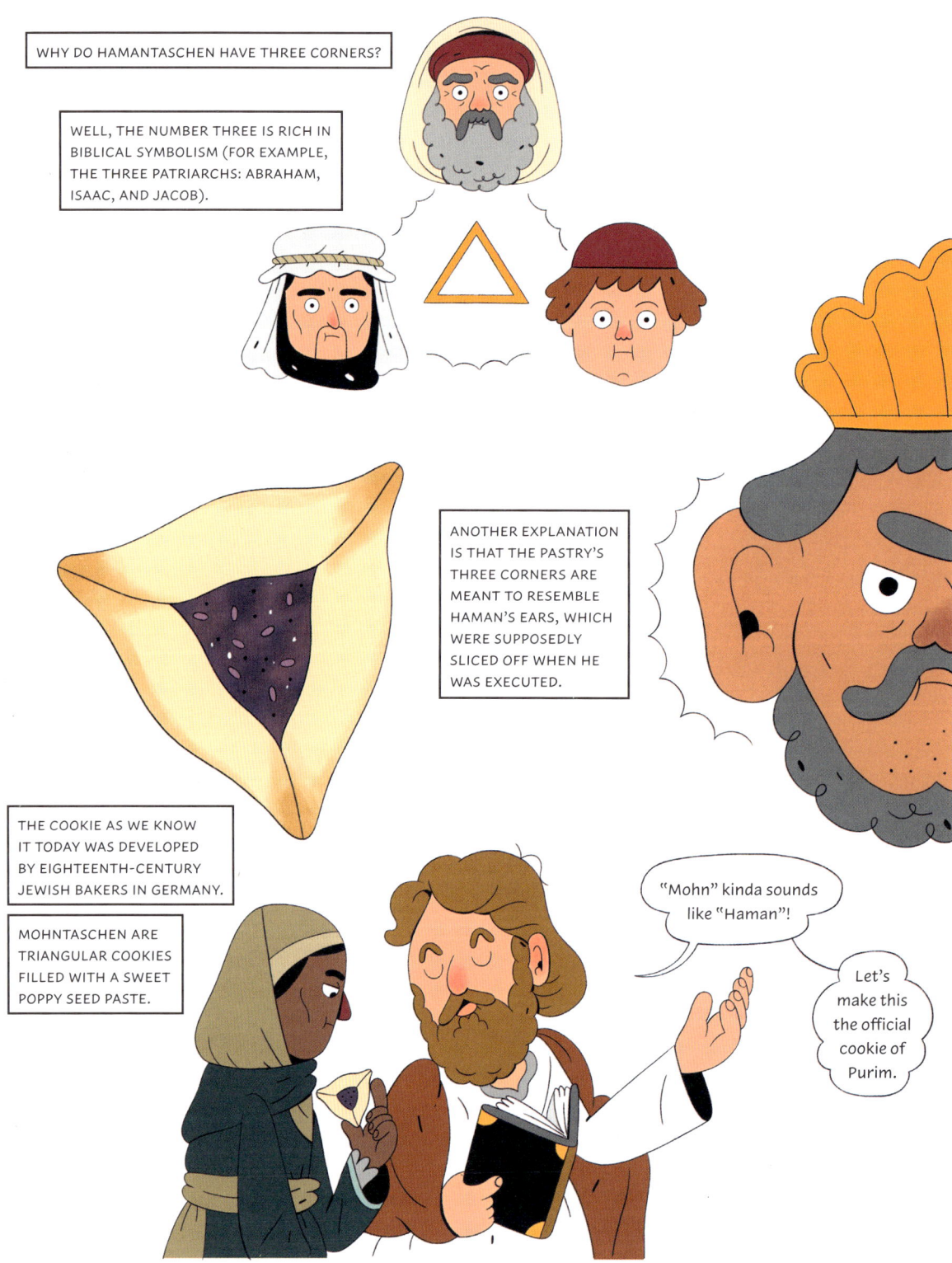

WHY DO HAMANTASCHEN HAVE THREE CORNERS?

WELL, THE NUMBER THREE IS RICH IN BIBLICAL SYMBOLISM (FOR EXAMPLE, THE THREE PATRIARCHS: ABRAHAM, ISAAC, AND JACOB).

ANOTHER EXPLANATION IS THAT THE PASTRY'S THREE CORNERS ARE MEANT TO RESEMBLE HAMAN'S EARS, WHICH WERE SUPPOSEDLY SLICED OFF WHEN HE WAS EXECUTED.

THE COOKIE AS WE KNOW IT TODAY WAS DEVELOPED BY EIGHTEENTH-CENTURY JEWISH BAKERS IN GERMANY.

MOHNTASCHEN ARE TRIANGULAR COOKIES FILLED WITH A SWEET POPPY SEED PASTE.

"Mohn" kinda sounds like "Haman"!

Let's make this the official cookie of Purim.

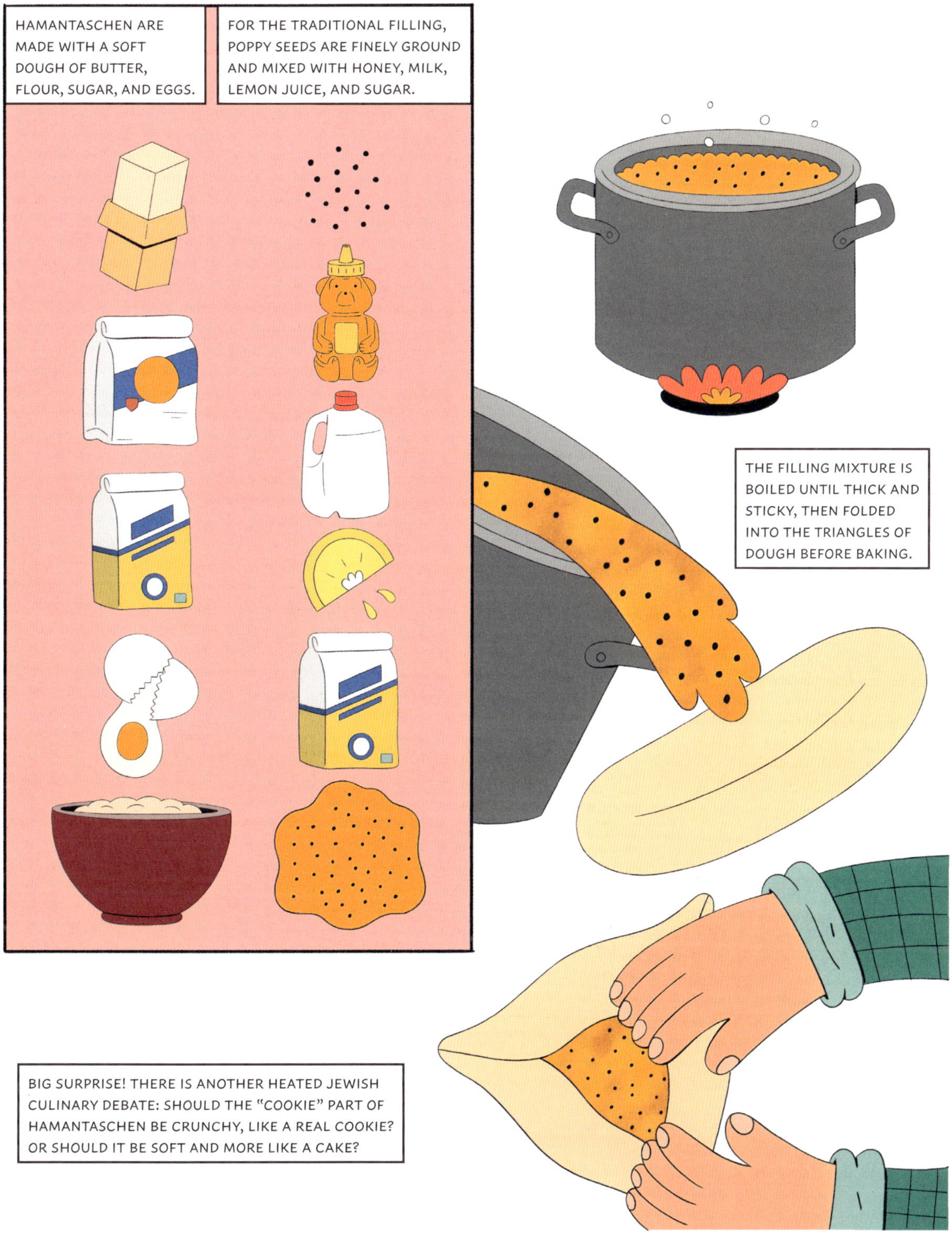
HAMANTASCHEN ARE MADE WITH A SOFT DOUGH OF BUTTER, FLOUR, SUGAR, AND EGGS.
FOR THE TRADITIONAL FILLING, POPPY SEEDS ARE FINELY GROUND AND MIXED WITH HONEY, MILK, LEMON JUICE, AND SUGAR.
THE FILLING MIXTURE IS BOILED UNTIL THICK AND STICKY, THEN FOLDED INTO THE TRIANGLES OF DOUGH BEFORE BAKING.
BIG SURPRISE! THERE IS ANOTHER HEATED JEWISH CULINARY DEBATE: SHOULD THE "COOKIE" PART OF HAMANTASCHEN BE CRUNCHY, LIKE A REAL COOKIE? OR SHOULD IT BE SOFT AND MORE LIKE A CAKE?

Halvah

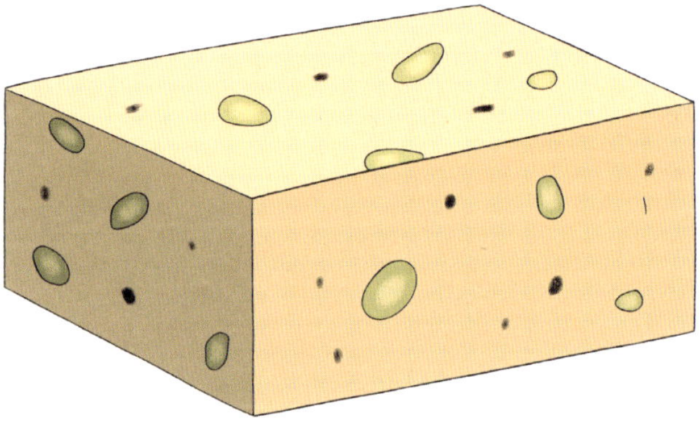

HALVAH (FROM *HALWA*, ARABIC FOR "SWEET") IS A SIMPLE CANDY MADE FROM SESAME-SEED PASTE. ITS ORIGINS MAY GO AS FAR BACK AS 3000 BCE.

THE HALVAH YOU FIND IN JEWISH DELIS IS TRADITIONALLY MADE WITH SESAME TAHINI. IT WAS BROUGHT FROM THE MIDDLE EAST BY WAY OF THE OTTOMAN EMPIRE TO ROMANIA, WHERE THE ASHKENAZI JEWS ADOPTED IT AND THEN CARRIED IT TO THE UNITED STATES.

HALVAH BECAME ESPECIALLY POPULAR IN NEW YORK THANKS TO UKRAINIAN IMMIGRANT NATHAN RADUTZKY.

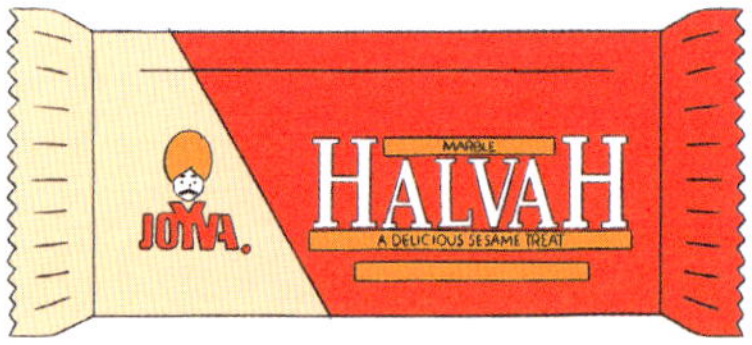
JOYVA
MARBLE
HALVAH
A DELICIOUS SESAME TREAT

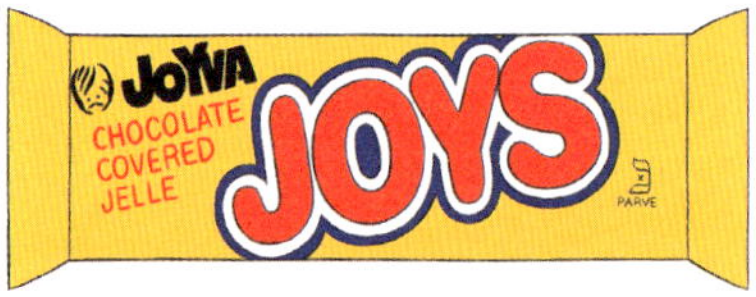
JOYVA
CHOCOLATE COVERED JELLE
JOYS
PARVE

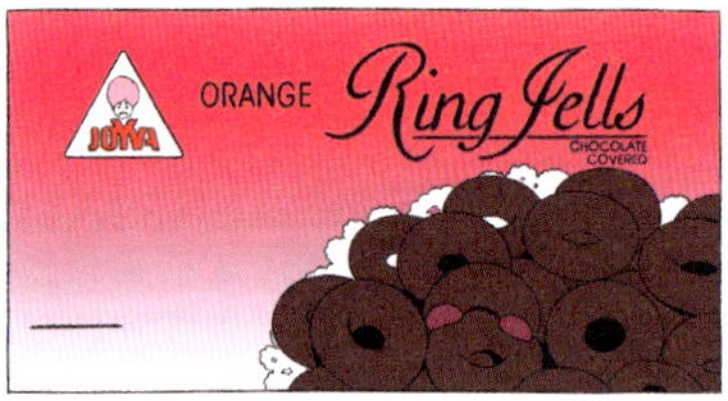
JOYVA
ORANGE
Ring Jells
CHOCOLATE COVERED

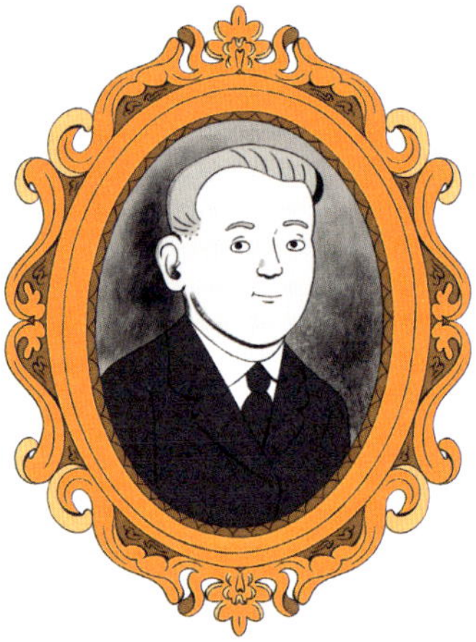

HE SOLD IT FROM A PUSHCART AND THEN STARTED A BUSINESS CALLED INDEPENDENT HALVAH AND CANDIES, WHICH LATER BECAME JOYVA.

THE SIMPLE RECIPE MAKES HALVAH A MARKETABLE KOSHER CONFECTION WITH A LONG SHELF LIFE. ITS DISTINCTIVE PASTY TEXTURE AND SOMEWHAT BITTERSWEET TASTE, HOWEVER, MAKE IT AN ACQUIRED TASTE.

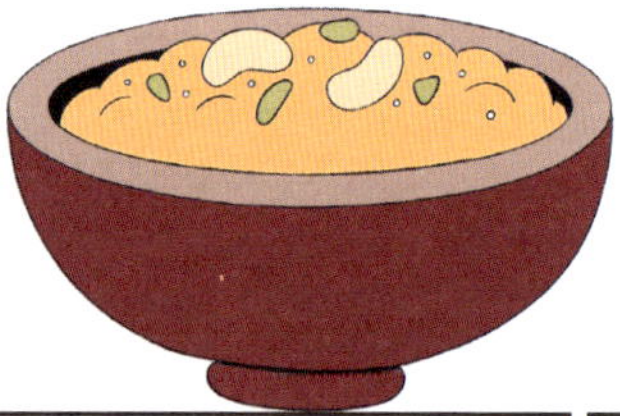

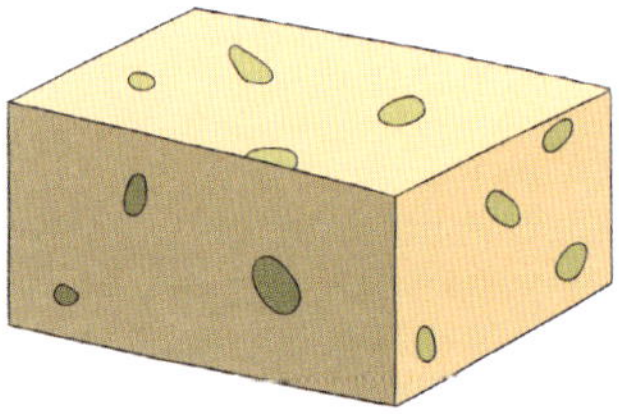

THERE ARE TWO MAIN KINDS OF HALVAH. ONE IS FLOUR-BASED, MADE FROM SEMOLINA, AND IS POPULAR IN INDIA.

THE OTHER VARIETY, FAMILIAR TO JEWISH AND ARAB AMERICANS, IS MADE FROM A "BUTTER" PRODUCED BY GRINDING SESAME SEEDS.

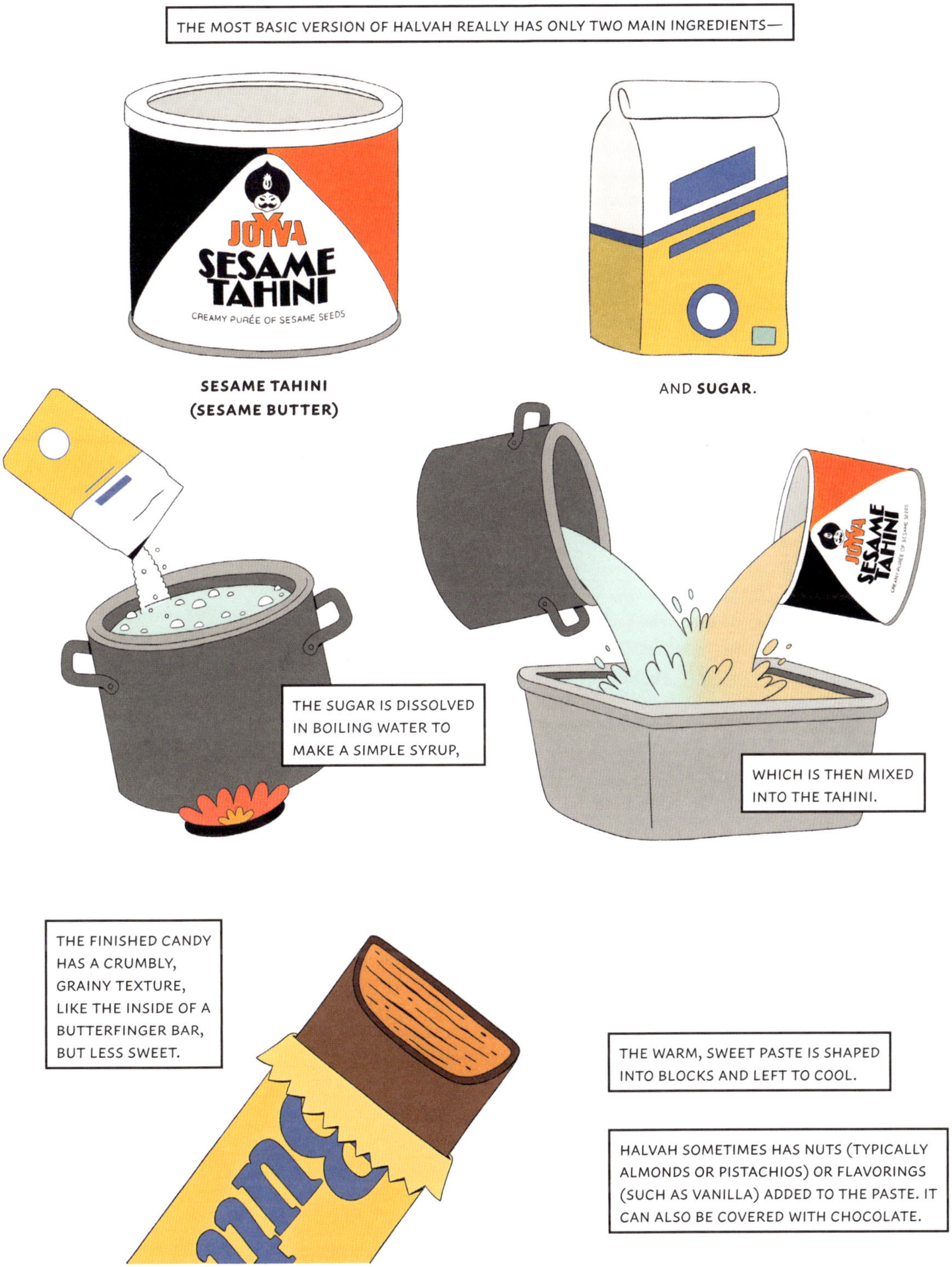
THE MOST BASIC VERSION OF HALVAH REALLY HAS ONLY TWO MAIN INGREDIENTS—
JOYVA
SESAME TAHINI
CREAMY PURÉE OF SESAME SEEDS
SESAME TAHINI (SESAME BUTTER)
AND SUGAR.
THE SUGAR IS DISSOLVED IN BOILING WATER TO MAKE A SIMPLE SYRUP,
WHICH IS THEN MIXED INTO THE TAHINI.
THE FINISHED CANDY HAS A CRUMBLY, GRAINY TEXTURE, LIKE THE INSIDE OF A BUTTERFINGER BAR, BUT LESS SWEET.
THE WARM, SWEET PASTE IS SHAPED INTO BLOCKS AND LEFT TO COOL.
HALVAH SOMETIMES HAS NUTS (TYPICALLY ALMONDS OR PISTACHIOS) OR FLAVORINGS (SUCH AS VANILLA) ADDED TO THE PASTE. IT CAN ALSO BE COVERED WITH CHOCOLATE.

Macaroons

MACAROONS (FROM THE FRENCH *MACARON* BY WAY OF THE ITALIAN *MACARONE*, "FILLED PASTA") ARE ONE OF THE FEW ITEMS IN JEWISH CULINARY CULTURE TO COME FROM ITALY.

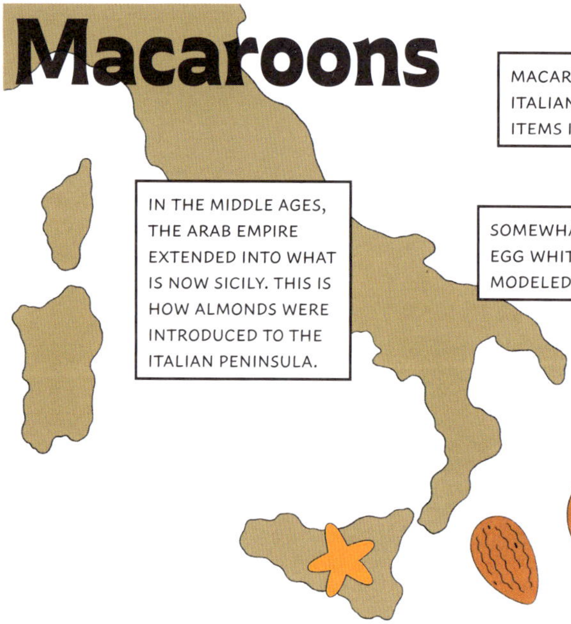

IN THE MIDDLE AGES, THE ARAB EMPIRE EXTENDED INTO WHAT IS NOW SICILY. THIS IS HOW ALMONDS WERE INTRODUCED TO THE ITALIAN PENINSULA.

SOMEWHAT LATER, COOKIES MADE FROM CRUSHED ALMONDS AND EGG WHITES WERE BAKED AT AN ITALIAN MONASTERY, REPORTEDLY MODELED TO RESEMBLE THE MONKS' BELLY BUTTONS.

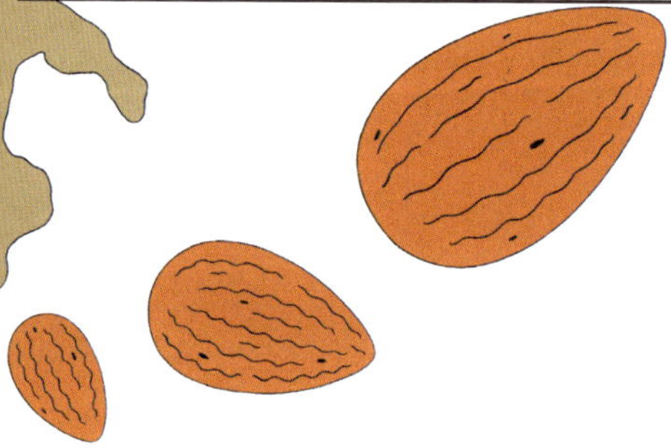

ITALIAN JEWS TOOK TO THE COOKIE BECAUSE, LIKE MATZO, IT HAS NO LEAVENING AND SO COULD BE EATEN DURING THE EIGHT DAYS OF THE PASSOVER HOLIDAY.

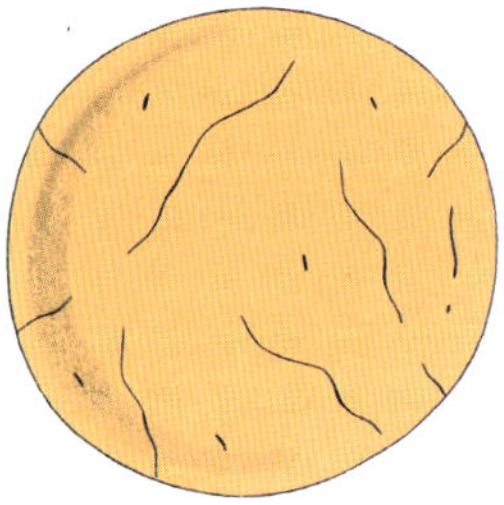

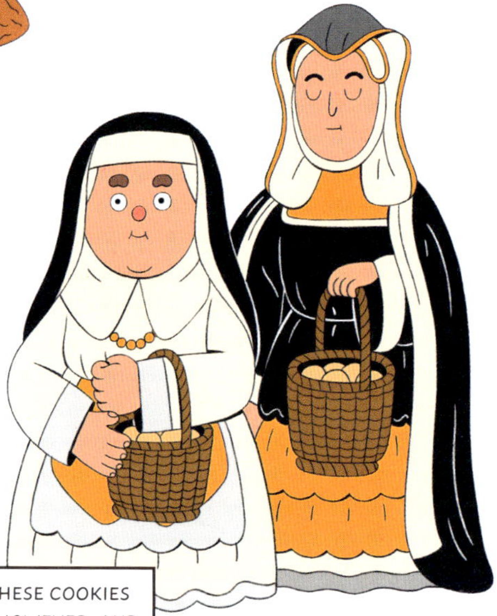

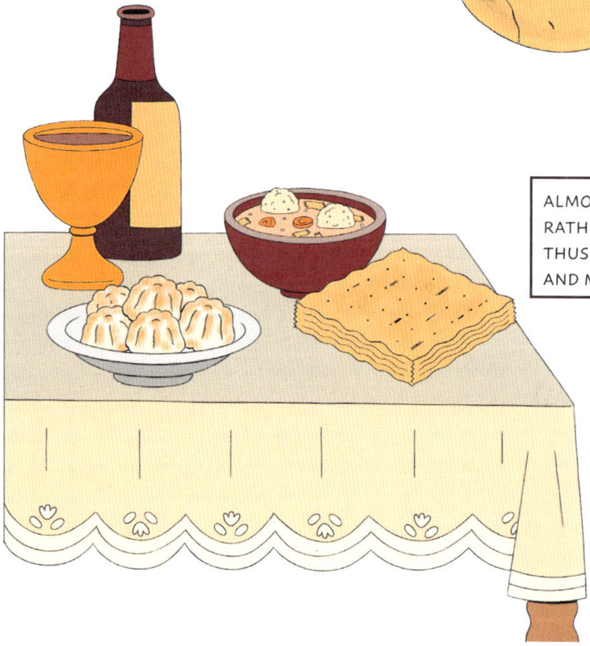

ALMONDS MADE THESE COOKIES RATHER BRITTLE, HOWEVER, AND THUS DIFFICULT TO TRANSPORT AND MARKET.

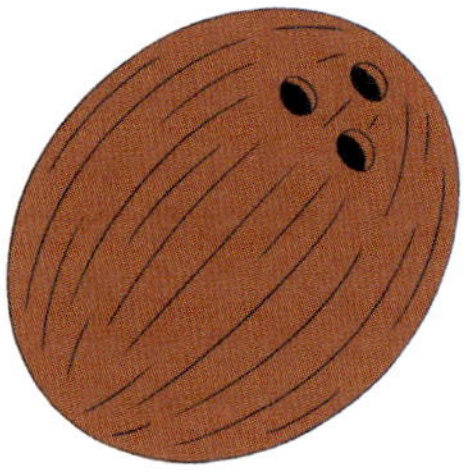

SO AMERICAN BAKERS USED COCONUT INSTEAD, WHICH GAVE THE COOKIE A SOFTER, CHEWIER TEXTURE.

TO MAKE MACAROONS, EGG WHITES ARE WHIPPED UNTIL THEY ARE WHITE AND FROTHY,

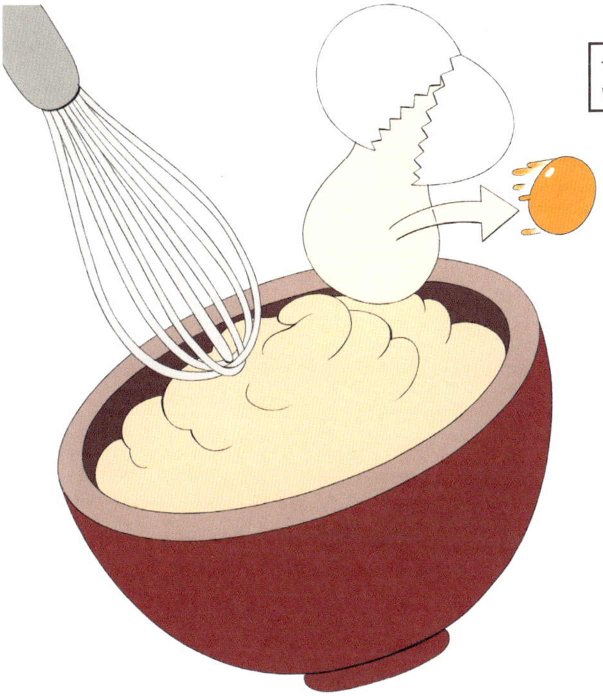

AND THEN THEY'RE FOLDED INTO A MIXTURE OF SUGAR, CONDENSED MILK, AND VANILLA.

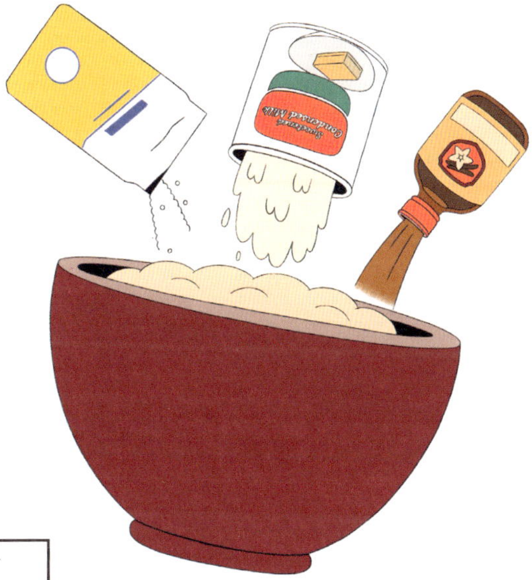

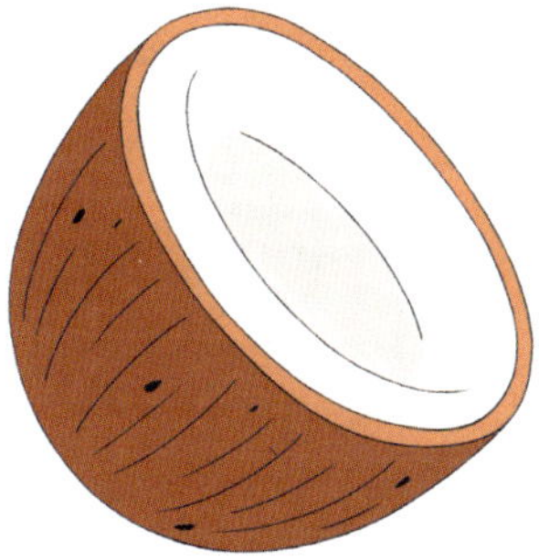

SHREDDED COCONUT (OR SOMETIMES ALMOND PASTE) IS ADDED TO THE BATTER, WHICH IS THEN BAKED INTO COOKIES.

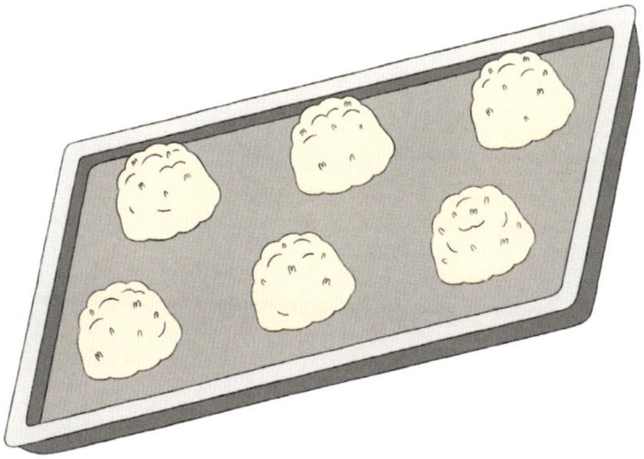

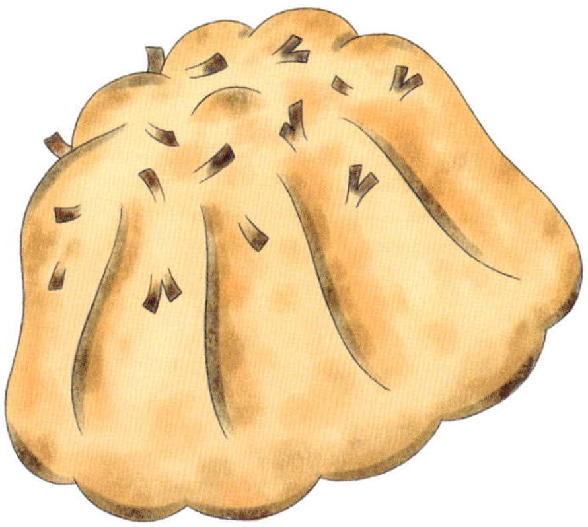

Coffee Cake

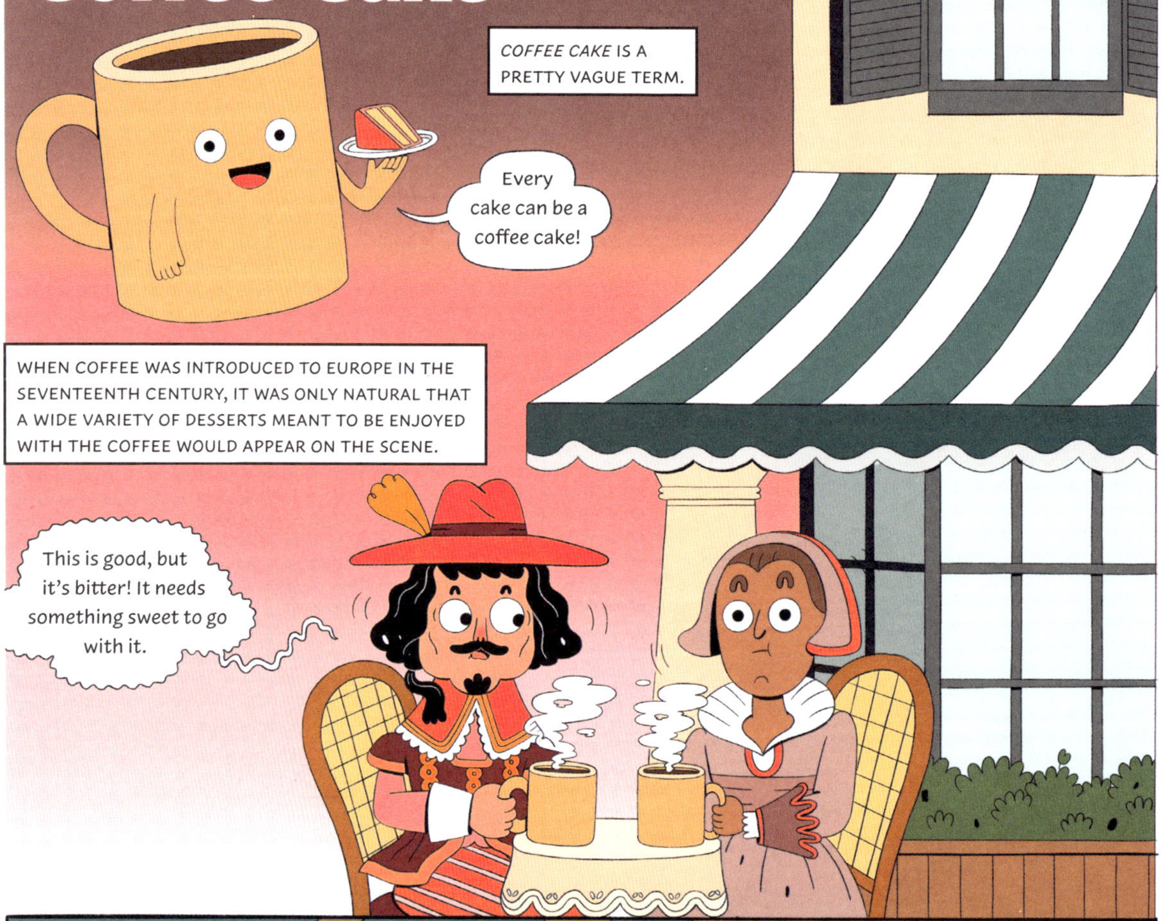
COFFEE CAKE IS A PRETTY VAGUE TERM.
Every cake can be a coffee cake!
WHEN COFFEE WAS INTRODUCED TO EUROPE IN THE SEVENTEENTH CENTURY, IT WAS ONLY NATURAL THAT A WIDE VARIETY OF DESSERTS MEANT TO BE ENJOYED WITH THE COFFEE WOULD APPEAR ON THE SCENE.
This is good, but it's bitter! It needs something sweet to go with it.

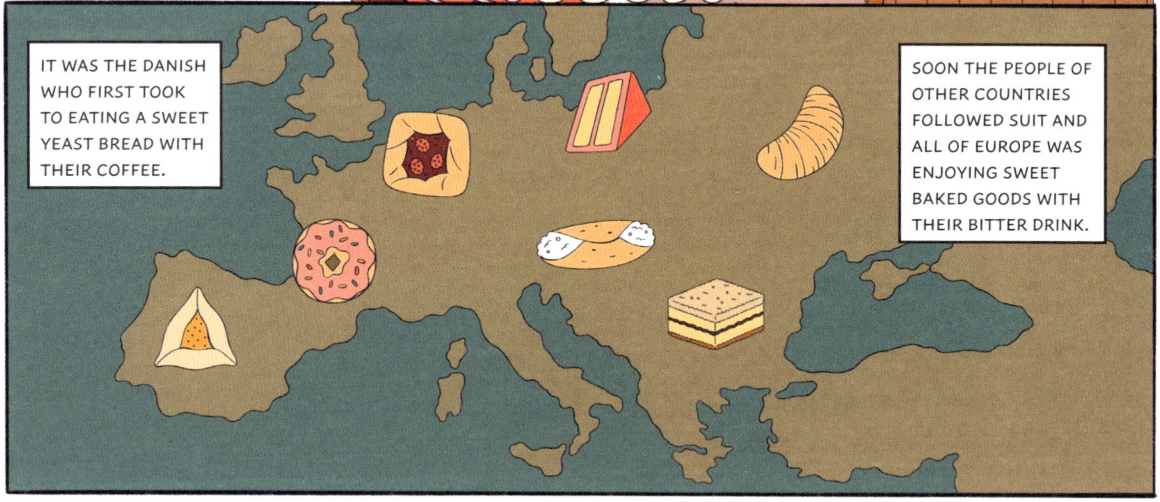
IT WAS THE DANISH WHO FIRST TOOK TO EATING A SWEET YEAST BREAD WITH THEIR COFFEE.
SOON THE PEOPLE OF OTHER COUNTRIES FOLLOWED SUIT AND ALL OF EUROPE WAS ENJOYING SWEET BAKED GOODS WITH THEIR BITTER DRINK.

THERE IS NO COFFEE IN COFFEE CAKE.

THE COFFEE CAKE WE KNOW IN THE UNITED STATES—AND THAT IS TYPICALLY FOUND IN JEWISH DELIS AND HOMES—IS A *SOUR CREAM* CAKE WITH A STREUSEL TOPPING (LIKE BABKA).

THE INVENTION OF THE BUNDT PAN IN THE 1950S GAVE IT ITS FAMILIAR SHAPE.

SOUR CREAM

THIS ROUND, TANGY DESSERT IS POPULAR ON SHABBAT AND FOR BREAKING THE FAST AFTER YOM KIPPUR AND TISHA B'AV.

SOMETIMES A MIXTURE OF WALNUTS, PECANS, OR CHOCOLATE IS ADDED WHEN THE BUNDT PAN IS HALF-FULL WITH THE SOUR CREAM BATTER.

AFTER THE REST OF THE BATTER IS POURED IN, IT IS TOPPED WITH THE STREUSEL, BAKED, AND OF COURSE SERVED WITH COFFEE.

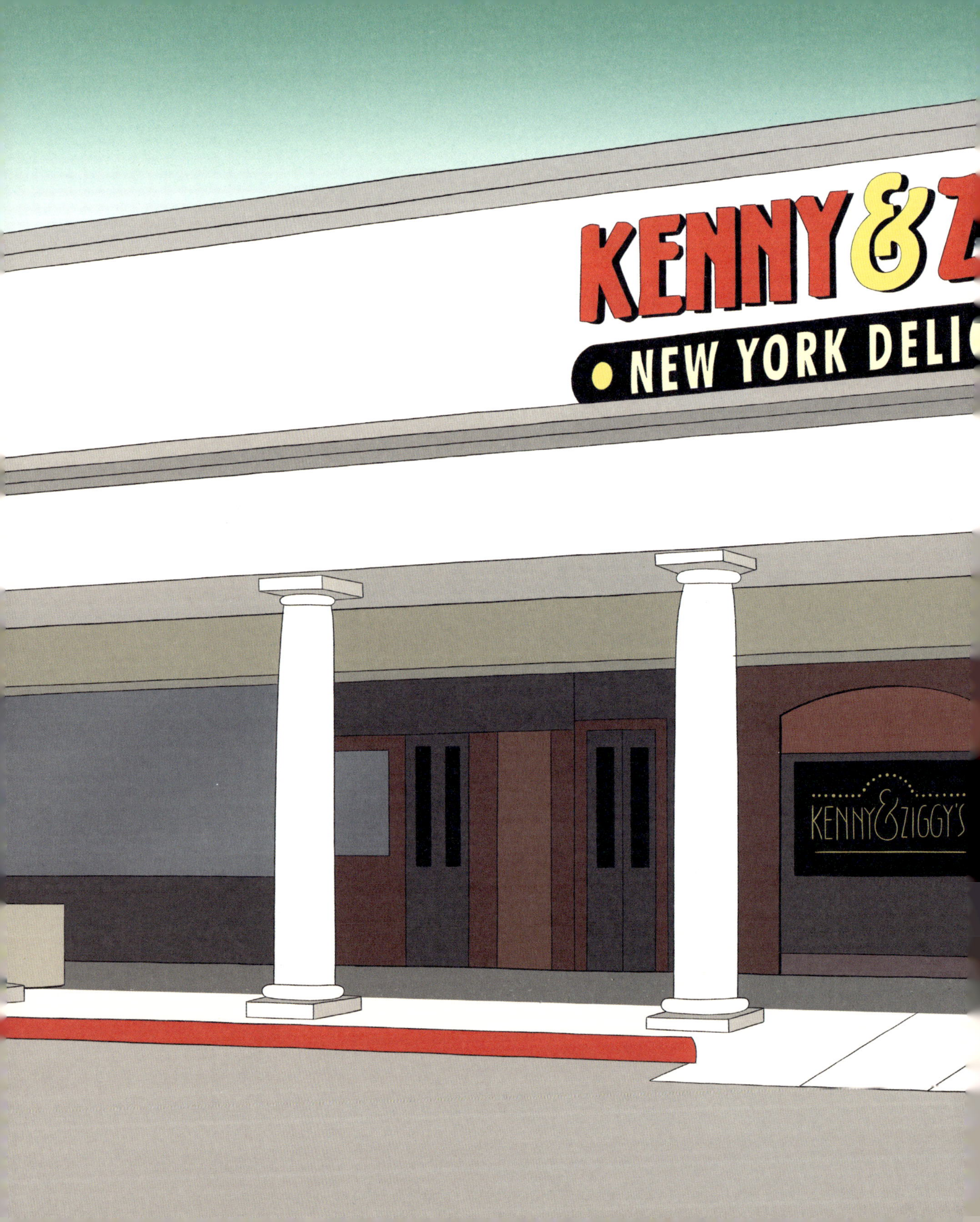
KENNY&
NEW YORK DELI
KENNY&ZIGGY'S

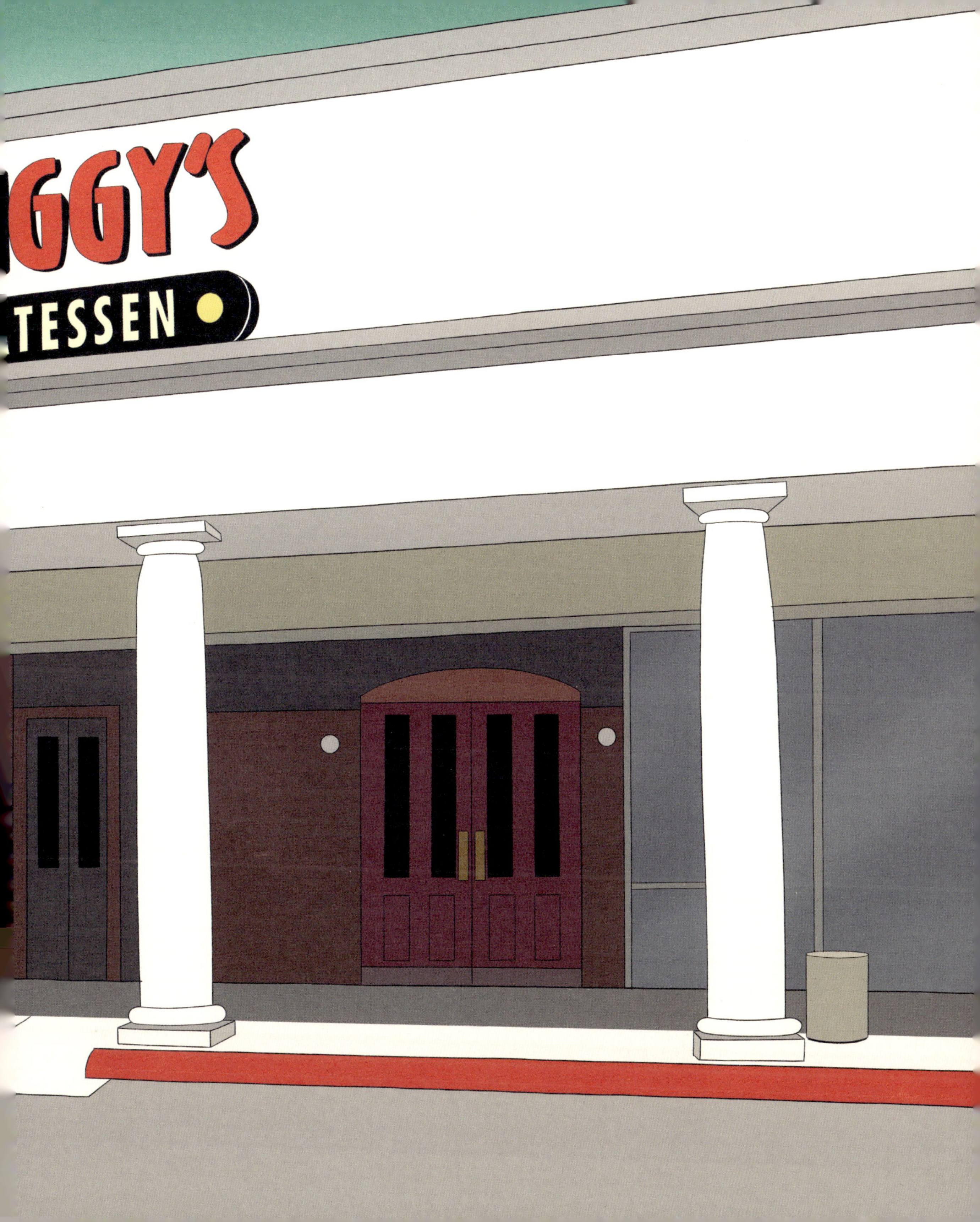
GGY'S
TESSEN

KENNY & ZIGGY'S NEW YORK DELICATESSEN RESTAURANT

1743 Post Oak Boulevard,
Houston, Texas

This Jewish delicatessen was established in 1999 in Houston, Texas, by Ziggy Gruber and Kenny Friedman. Ziggy's grandfather emigrated from Hungary at the turn of the century and settled on the Lower East Side. In 1927, he and his two brothers-in-law opened the Rialto Deli on Broadway, which stayed in the family through the generations. Ziggy spent his youth working in delis around New York until he went to culinary school in England. When he returned to the United States, he moved to Houston with Kenny Friedman and opened Kenny & Ziggy's, which, against all odds—it's in Texas!—would become one of the best Jewish delis in the country. In 2015, Ziggy and his deli became the subject of a documentary called *Deli Man*, which immortalized Kenny & Ziggy's as an essential destination for authentic Jewish food.

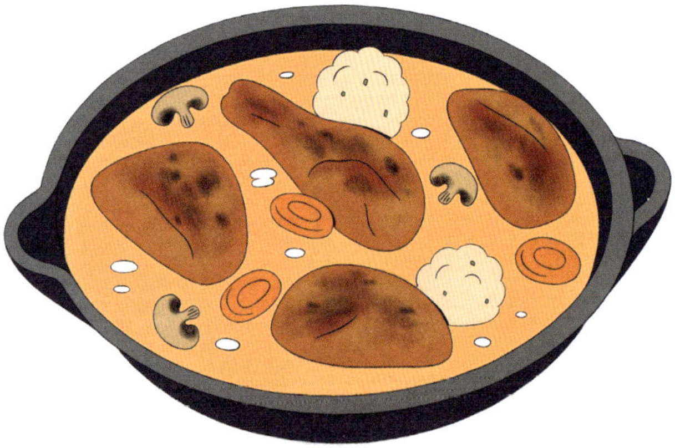

Interview with Ziggy Gruber, Owner of Kenny & Ziggy's New York Delicatessen Restaurant

What's the perfect order at Ziggy's, or what's *your* perfect order?

I like all kinds of things. Everybody today thinks corned beef and pastrami are really all of what the delicatessen is. I love pastrami like anybody else, but if it's a cold day, nothing beats a nice big plate of vegetable and potato soup, or you can have some kneidlach, some matzo ball soup. I love boiled beef flanken with some horseradish. I love goulash. I like stuffed cabbage. I mean, like, the old-school stuff.

Say someone comes in who's totally unfamiliar with Jewish food. What's the best way to introduce them?

The first thing they have to experience is what a real pastrami sandwich is—one that's been steamed for hours and hours and hours to break down all the tendons, dried for two days, and properly cut in an artisan way, because once they experience that, then they're gonna be open to eating the other stuff.

Matzo ball soup—I mean, who doesn't like chicken soup? It doesn't matter what culture you're in; everybody has some sort of chicken soup. But Jewish chicken soup, to have it with the matzo ball and a kreplach (dumpling), that's another thing that can get people really excited. Then if I try to get people to eat the Eastern European stuff, I like to start with a stuffed cabbage, 'cause our stuffed cabbage is made with beef and veal, and it's very light; it's delicious. But it's in a traditional Hungarian sweet-and-sour tomato-based sauce, and it's ground beef, so that's not so esoteric.

What's something that people tend not to order that you think is underrated and people should try?

I like chicken fricassee.

What's that?

Chicken that's been cut up and stewed for hours, with a lot of garlic, a lot of vegetables and tomatoes. But it also has gizzards and little meatballs. It's a delicious kind of mixture.

It sounds great.

To have that with a nice crusty bread to sop up all the gravy, it's very nice.

What's the difference between deli in the South and deli in New York?

I've operated on three coasts: here in Houston and in New York and in Los Angeles in the '90s. I cook and present my food the same way wherever I am.

Are the customers different in Texas, or are people the same everywhere when they come into a deli?

Customers are the same, but Houston is a very cosmopolitan city, so we have a lot of New Yorkers and people from Los Angeles and other parts. A lot of Canadians, too, because of the oil industry. People in Houston don't have much of a twang like some other parts of Texas. If you come into my store, you wouldn't think you're in Houston. You'd think you're walking in off Broadway [in New York City] because I built the store the same way. It's very rich with wood, and you see the salamis hanging up like crazy. We build beautiful stores.

Did the business change after the documentary (*Deli Man*, 2014, directed by Erik Greenberg Anjou) came out?

We were always a very, very busy operation, but it didn't hurt. It helped like anything else; it helped with our shipping. But what is very interesting, and sad at the same time, [is that] a lot of the delis that were iconic that were in that film, the majority of them are gone. It's heartbreaking.

Do you have hope that there's going to be generations of future delis taking their place?

The younger—I'll call them "heebsters"—they like to drink [laughs]. So the delicatessen... you'll see the way they build their stores; they're a lot different. I applaud it. The customer dictates what they're going to go to. People come to Kenny & Ziggy's from all over the country because we're kind of the "last of the Mohicans." With the atmosphere and everything else, it's a throwback. Look, will there be delicatessens? There's gonna be the odd deli still left. Is it gonna be like it was? Probably not. It's not gonna be the way it was when there were thousands of delis because

the first immigrants and first generation, this is all they ate. Now, young people, they eat everything. Everyone's a foodie! I always joke around. I say, "Most Jewish kids think sushi is a Jewish food."

It's different. Where a customer would probably eat this about five to six times a week, or even just a couple times a week, now you're looking at people eating different every day. To run a deli right, the labor cost is higher than a regular restaurant, and meat prices have compounded like you wouldn't believe. And people are just willing to spend so much. People don't realize most of the good Jewish delis are buying prime and choice meat. We are paying very high prices. But God forbid a sandwich is seventeen, eighteen bucks or more. They look at you like you need your head examined.

So maybe bringing in that bar business is the key to making sure that the margins are worth it for future delis.

They gotta make some shickered cocktails up there.

Well, it sounds like your deli is still going strong, all things considered.

Oh, listen, we have a cult following!

Drinks

DR. BROWN'S

I CAN'T RECOMMEND STRONGLY ENOUGH THAT EVERY ITEM IN THIS BOOK BE WASHED DOWN WITH A DR. BROWN'S SODA, THE JEWISH DELI'S MOST LOYAL COMPANION SINCE ITS INCEPTION IN 1869 BY THE SCHONEBERGER & NOBLE SOFT DRINK COMPANY IN MANHATTAN.

DR. BROWN'S
SINCE 1869
ORIGINAL
CREAM SODA

UP UNTIL THE EARLY 1980S, DR. BROWN'S KOSHER SODAS WERE EXCLUSIVELY DISTRIBUTED ALONG THE EAST COAST, STAKING THEIR SPOT EARLY ON IN THE REFRIGERATORS OF NEW YORK JEWISH DELIS.

D BERNHARD'S
SPECIALTIES

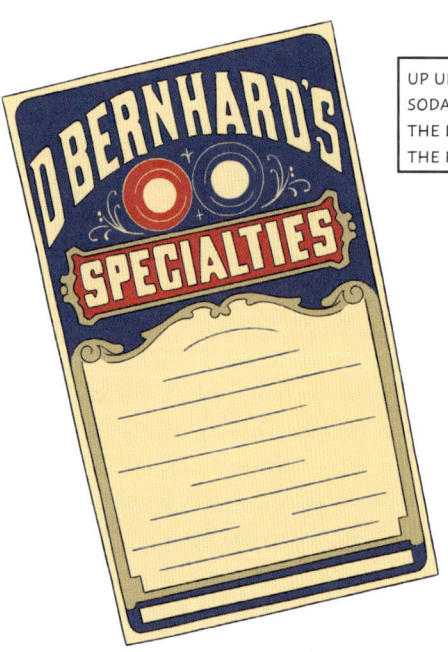

AN EARLY ADVERTISEMENT FOR DR. BROWN'S CELERY TONIC PROMOTED IT ALONGSIDE OTHER "MEDICINAL" DRINKS.

WHEN THE COMPANY WAS SOLD TO CANADA DRY, THE POPULAR FLAVORS WERE DISTRIBUTED TO GROCERY STORES ACROSS THE COUNTRY, AND THE BRAND WAS ESTABLISHED AS AN ICONIC SPECIALTY ITEM, ALTHOUGH 50% OF ALL SODAS ARE STILL SOLD WITHIN NEW YORK. EACH FLAVOR MAINTAINS ITS ORIGINAL RECIPE TO THIS DAY.

SINCE 1869
DR. BROWN'S
ORIGINAL
ORANGE SODA
NATURALLY FLAVORED

FLAVORS OF DR. BROWN'S

AN EARLY ADVERTISEMENT FOR DR. BROWN'S CELERY TONIC PROMOTED IT ALONGSIDE OTHER "MEDICINAL" DRINKS.

SINCE 1869
DR. BROWN'S
STATUE OF LIBERTY
THE ORIGINAL
CREAM SODA
FLAVOR FAVORITE FOR GENERATIONS

CREAM SODA

SINCE 1869
DIET
DR. BROWN'S
STATUE OF LIBERTY
THE ORIGINAL
CREAM SODA
FLAVOR FAVORITE FOR GENERATIONS

CREAM SODA

SINCE 1869
DR. BROWN'S
BROOKLYN BRIDGE 1883
NATURAL FLAVOR
CEL-RAY
CELERY SODA WITH OTHER NATURAL FLAVORS

CEL-RAY

SINCE 1869
DR. BROWN'S
CENTRAL PARK CAROUSEL
NATURAL FLAVOR
BLACK CHERRY
SODA WITH OTHER NATURAL FLAVORS

BLACK CHERRY

SINCE 1869
DIET
DR. BROWN'S
CENTRAL PARK CAROUSEL
NATURAL FLAVOR
BLACK CHERRY
SODA WITH OTHER NATURAL FLAVORS

BLACK CHERRY

SINCE 1869
DR. BROWN'S
ASTOR HOTEL NEW YORK
EXTRA DRY
GINGER ALE
WITH OTHER NATURAL FLAVORS

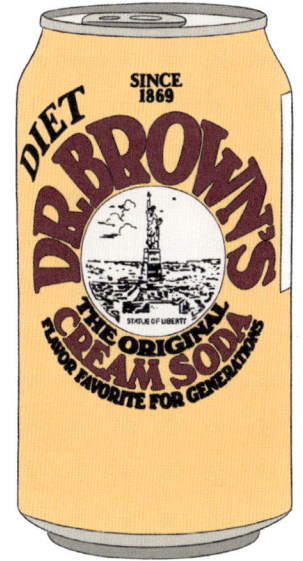

GINGER ALE

CEL-RAY

WITH A NICKNAME LIKE "JEWISH CHAMPAGNE," CEL-RAY NEEDS TO BE SINGLED OUT HERE.

FLAVORED WITH CELERY SEED, THE DRINK WAS ORIGINALLY CALLED CELERY TONIC AND WAS MEANT TO AID IN DIGESTION.

CEL-RAY
VITAMIN D
DR. BROWN'S
CEL-RAY
D
VITAMIN D
ADDED

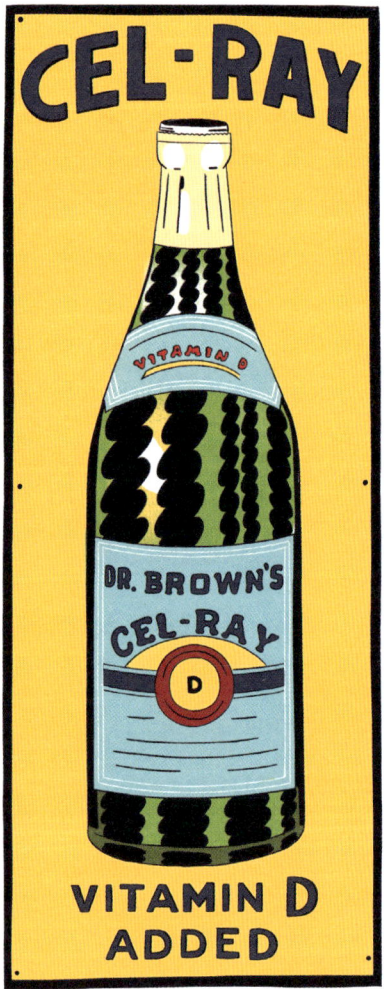

IT COVERED ALL THE BASES OF MARKETING SUCCESS: IT WAS ASSOCIATED WITH MEDICINAL SUPERFOODS AND HEALTHY BUZZWORDS, YET IT WAS SWEETENED WITH ENOUGH SUGAR TO MAKE IT COMMERCIALLY APPEALING.

SINCE 1889
DR. BROWN'S
NATURAL FLAVOR
CEL-RAY.
CELERY SODA WITH OTHER NATURAL FLAVORS
12 FL.OZS. (355 mL)

ALTHOUGH AN ACQUIRED TASTE, CEL-RAY MAINTAINS CULT STATUS IN THE JEWISH COMMUNITY, HARKENING BACK TO THE OLD-WORLD WAYS OF COOKING WITH FERMENTED ROOTS AND WORKING IN THE SUGAR INDUSTRY.

EGG CREAM

AN EGG CREAM IS A FOUNTAIN DRINK MADE WITH SELTZER, MILK, AND CHOCOLATE SYRUP—NO EGGS OR CREAM IN SIGHT.

A BROOKLYN ORIGINAL
SINCE 1900
Fox's
u-bet
NO HIGH FRUCTOSE CORN SYRUP
CHOCOLATE
FLAVORED SYRUP

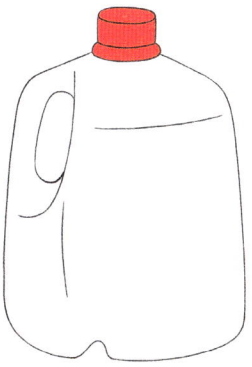

(IF YOU WANT TO GET TRULY AUTHENTIC, THE CHOCOLATE SYRUP HAS TO BE FOX'S U-BET CHOCOLATE SYRUP, MADE IN BROOKLYN SINCE THE BEGINNING OF THE TWENTIETH CENTURY.)

THERE ARE A COUPLE OF WORKING THEORIES ABOUT THE ORIGIN OF THE EGG CREAM. THE FIRST IS THAT IN THE LATE NINETEENTH CENTURY, A JEWISH TEENAGE THEATER ACTOR DISCOVERED A DRINK IN PARIS CALLED A CHOCOLAT ET CRÈME AND BROUGHT IT BACK TO THE LOWER EAST SIDE.

THE MORE POPULAR THEORY IS THAT IN THE BEGINNING OF THE TWENTIETH CENTURY, A CANDY SHOP OWNER NAMED LOUIS AUSTER INVENTED THE DRINK AND SOLD IT OUT OF THE AUSTER STORE ON SECOND AVENUE.

BECAUSE IT CAN'T REALLY BE BOTTLED OR CANNED, THE EGG CREAM HAS BECOME SOMEWHAT SCARCE. HOWEVER, ITS SIMPLE RECIPE AND CHEAP INGREDIENTS MAKE IT A SATISFYING ALTERNATIVE TO A MILKSHAKE.

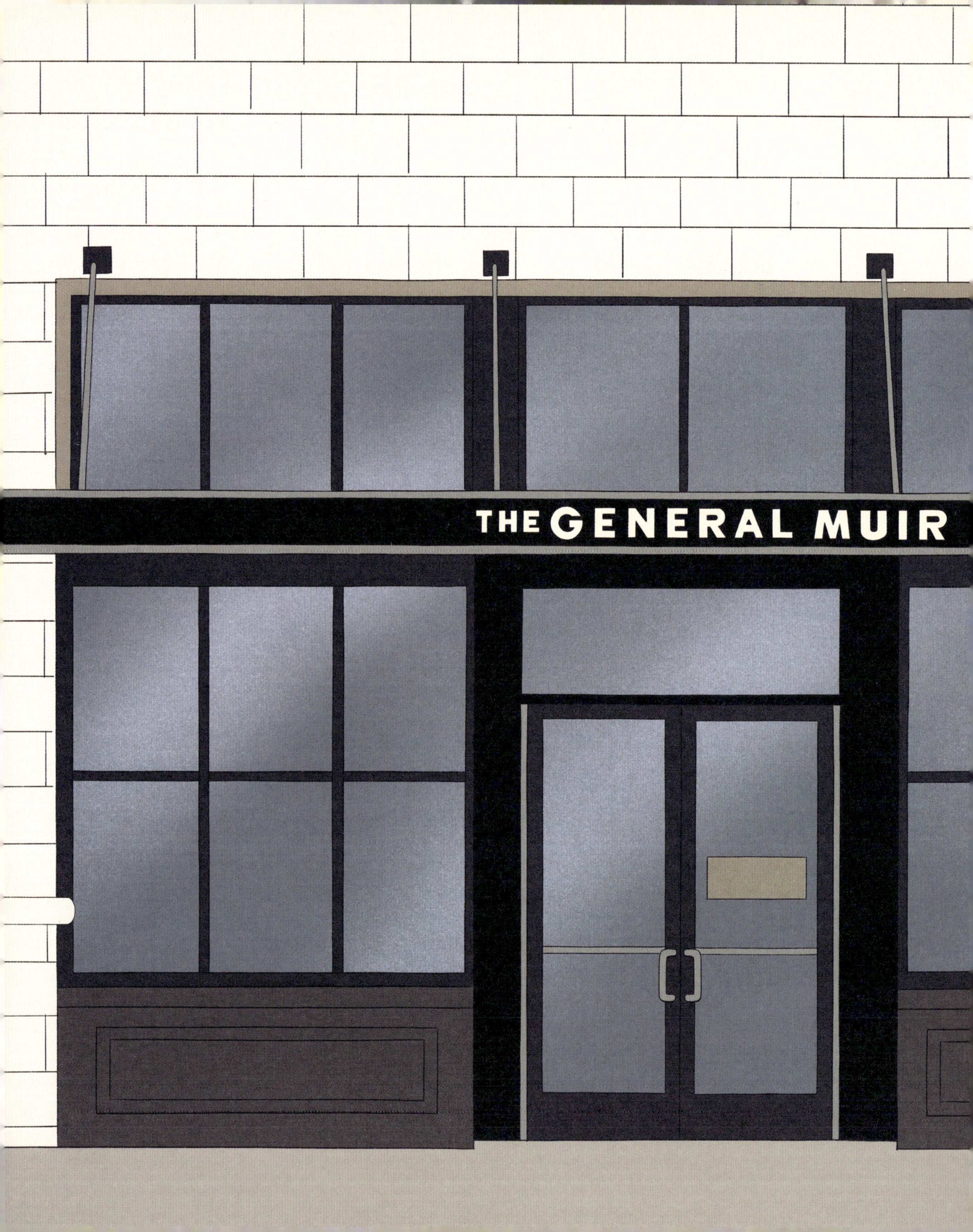
THE GENERAL MUIR

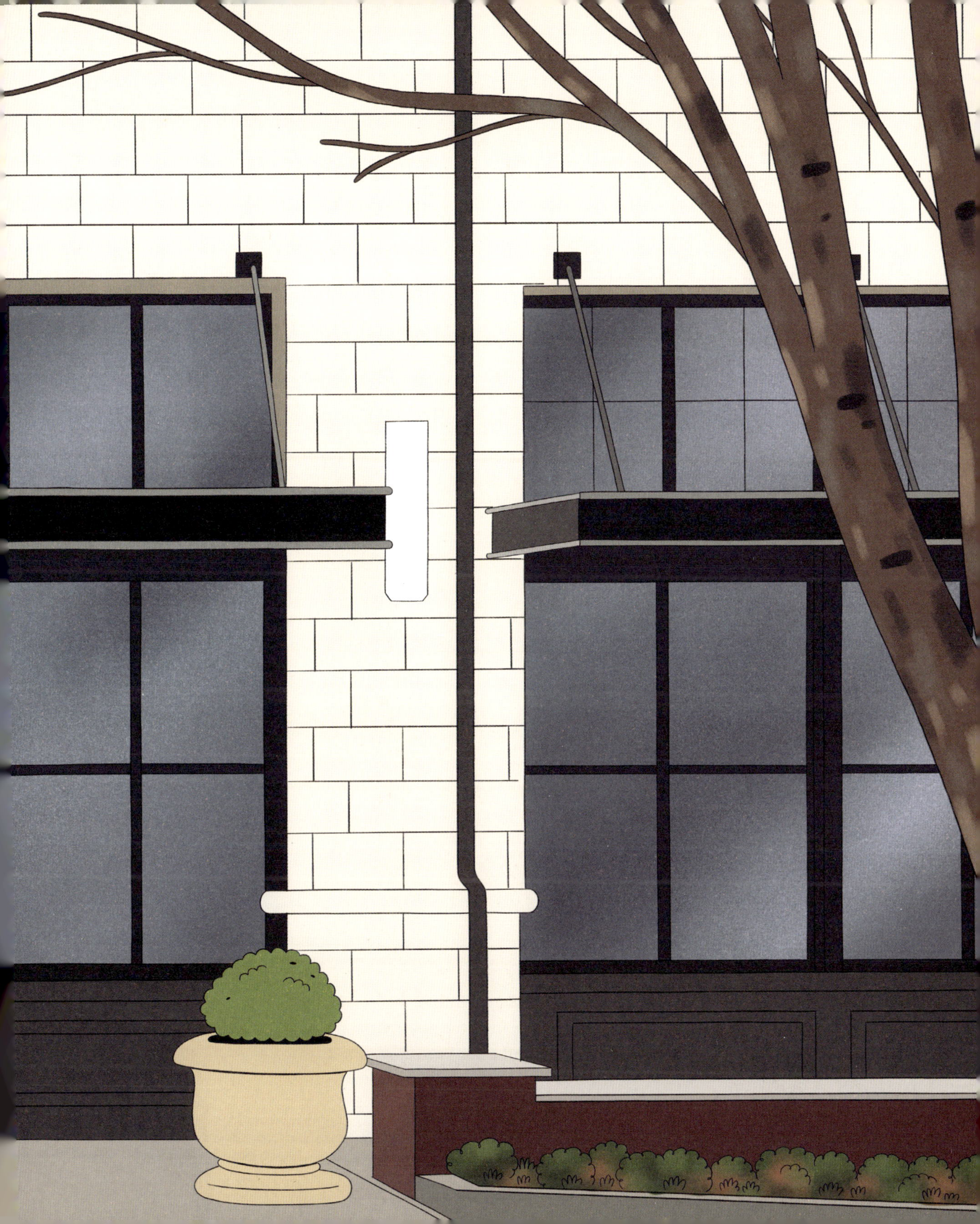

THE GENERAL MUIR

The General Muir has two locations in Georgia:

1540 Avenue Place, Suite B-230, Atlanta

6405 Blue Stone Road, Suite 240, Sandy Springs

Opened in 2013 at Emory Point in Atlanta, Georgia, the General Muir was founded by former lawyers and married couple Jennifer and Ben Johnson, along with Shelley Sweet and Todd Ginsberg. The General Muir takes its name from the refugee ship that carried co-owner Jennifer Johnson's grandparents to the United States. "The boat symbolized looking towards the future for them, and also remembering the past, and that's what we do when we open up a deli. We wanted to be a modern American restaurant that was a loving tribute to the Jewish deli in New York," says chef and co-owner Todd Ginsberg. After becoming a mainstay of the Atlanta food scene, the restaurant opened up a second location in Sandy Springs in early 2021.

Interview with Todd Ginsberg, Co-owner of the General Muir

Did you think it might be challenging to bring New York–style Jewish deli food to the South, or did you feel that there was already a market for it?
We're in the process of opening up a second General Muir right now, and we feel confident that there's a huge market for it. When we opened the first one, I don't think any of us felt as confident. We were going into one of the few Jewish neighborhoods in Georgia, but the majority of them are orthodox, and we weren't going to be kosher. So we weren't sure whose wheelhouse we would be in, but it just turned out that even the young kids just wanted to experience the delicatessen. We get a lot of Jews from New York coming to Emory.

Homesick New Yorkers?
Exactly.

When I talk to the old-school generation about the future of Jewish delis, they wonder how sustainable the business model is, but when I talk to the younger deli owners, I sense more optimism about what can be done with Jewish food.
Absolutely. It's completely sustainable if you treat it like a restaurant. If you look over the last twenty to fifty years at how restaurants fail, whether it's a deli or an Italian restaurant, there are similarities. You approach it from that angle, and then you're kind of working backward from there to develop what works.

I imagine you have to strike a particular balance between being respectful of tradition while trying to push Jewish food forward.
I wouldn't say that. Though the one thing that we are very traditional about are the holidays and those sorts of things. We don't really steer away from what a traditional pastrami or a corned beef brisket should taste like, because they are perfect as they are—why fix it? But we make them in-house, and we use quality beef.

I'm wondering what you might do traditionally versus non-traditionally. Is there a menu item that's important to do the way it's always been done? Or is there another item that's like, "This isn't your grandfather's _____"?
As the day unfolds from breakfast to lunch to dinner, we become less traditional, though even the breakfast items aren't very typical in a standard old-fashioned deli. We serve grits with roasted mushrooms, truffle sauce, and poached eggs, and rye toast sticks. We serve crispy pastrami instead of bacon—we don't do any pork products. But we kind of just went with our guts and with what tasted good, and what we ate as kids but want to taste better than when we were kids. We try to make the best Reuben. We try and make the best breakfast items. We definitely lean a little more Sephardic on the dinner menu.

Do the old-school customers come in and give you criticisms? Or are they excited?
No, they're excited. Though when we first opened up the

restaurant, people came in and they were like, "Well, this isn't a deli. There's none of this, there's none of that. . . ."

Older generations can be defensive.

Yeah, and they should be! They should be like, "Hey, why aren't you carrying the torch for us?" But at some point you have to say, it wasn't working then, it wasn't selling then, and it was more trouble than it was worth. It wasn't profitable. When we opened up the restaurant, we had to constantly consider what needed to be on the menu, and why, and what we want to do moving forward to take us to the next level. I think that's the idea of advancement: You have to adapt.

So you see the future of Jewish delis as adapting. That maybe the strictly traditional Jewish deli thrived in a time that doesn't exist anymore?

There was definitely a template that a lot of delis used from the '40s until the early '80s. And it ran its course. There are some restaurants that are still doing it. I think Kenny & Ziggy's is very traditional, and they're going to be fine. The ones that are great will stay around, and they can stay traditional.

Ziggy was telling me that he prides himself on having like four hundred things on the menu, but that the future of the deli is that it's going to need to be pared down to make it more sustainable.

One hundred percent. That's exactly right. We had to pare it down. The old delis felt like diners. The delis back when I was growing up in New Jersey had tuna melts, ham sandwiches, and ham and green pepper omelets. We wanted to do a fresh approach, and not be the restaurant where you come in and see five pages of menu.

That seems to be what's on trend for restaurants in general.

That's right. Menus in themselves have been paring down for the last twenty years.

The Future?

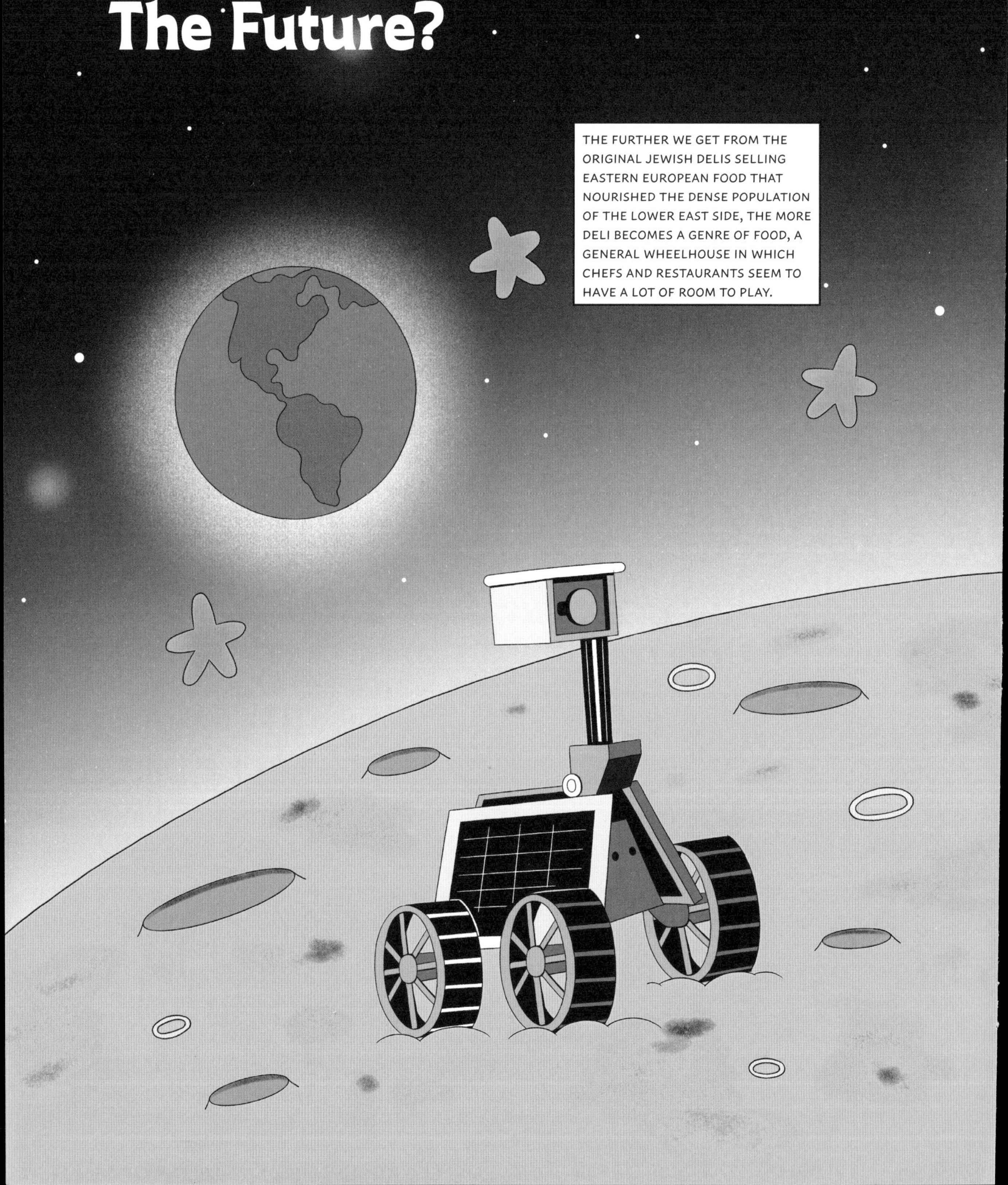
THE FURTHER WE GET FROM THE ORIGINAL JEWISH DELIS SELLING EASTERN EUROPEAN FOOD THAT NOURISHED THE DENSE POPULATION OF THE LOWER EAST SIDE, THE MORE DELI BECOMES A GENRE OF FOOD, A GENERAL WHEELHOUSE IN WHICH CHEFS AND RESTAURANTS SEEM TO HAVE A LOT OF ROOM TO PLAY.

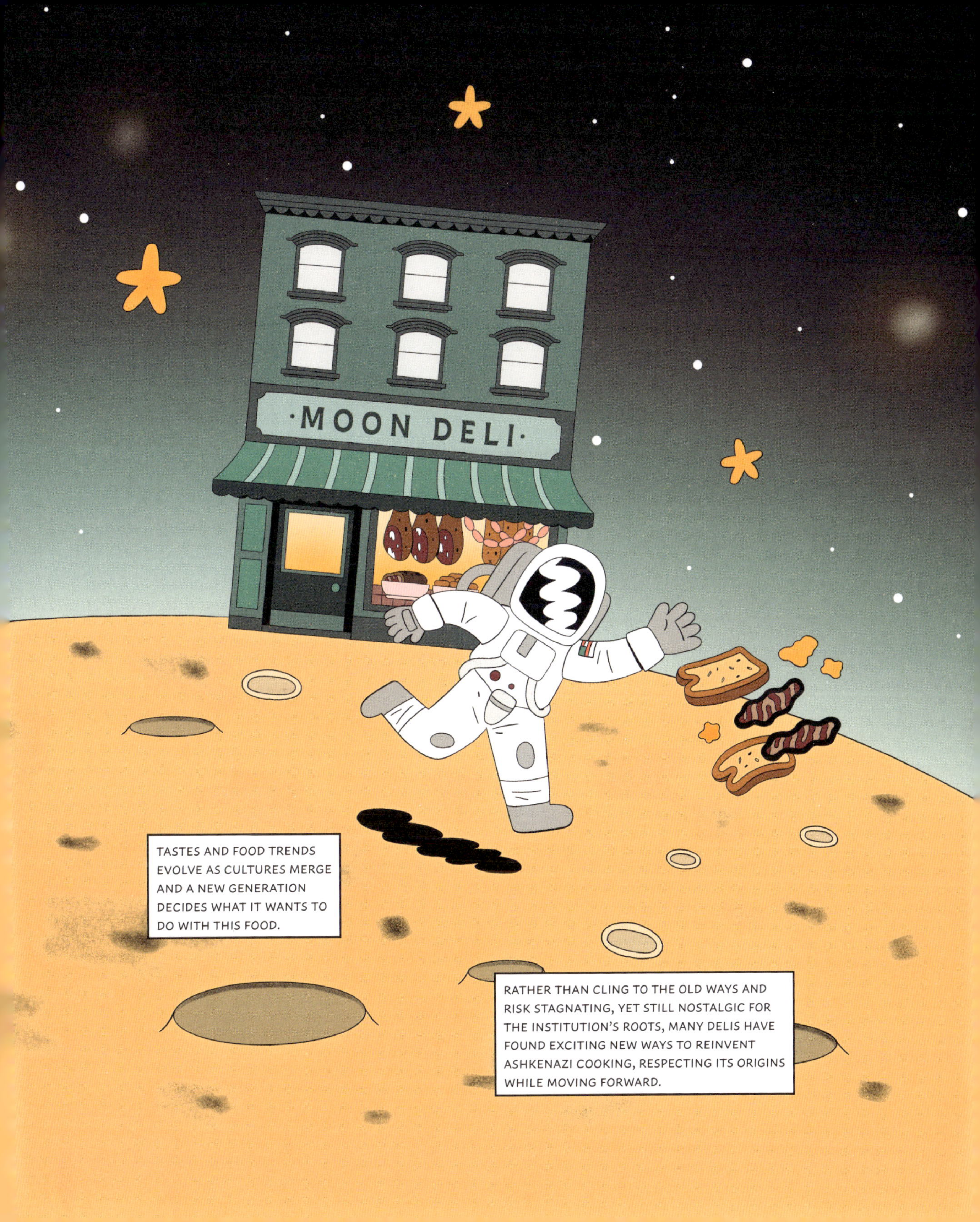
·MOON DELI·
TASTES AND FOOD TRENDS EVOLVE AS CULTURES MERGE AND A NEW GENERATION DECIDES WHAT IT WANTS TO DO WITH THIS FOOD.
RATHER THAN CLING TO THE OLD WAYS AND RISK STAGNATING, YET STILL NOSTALGIC FOR THE INSTITUTION'S ROOTS, MANY DELIS HAVE FOUND EXCITING NEW WAYS TO REINVENT ASHKENAZI COOKING, RESPECTING ITS ORIGINS WHILE MOVING FORWARD.

Fusion Foods

MATZO BALL RAMEN

SMOKED SALMON QUESADILLA

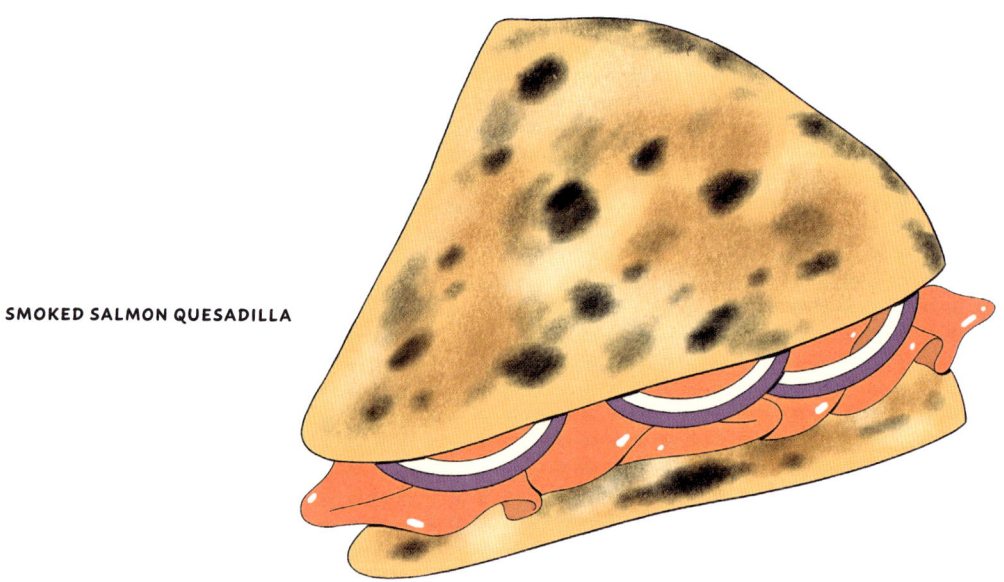

PASTRAMI AND KIMCHI SANDWICH

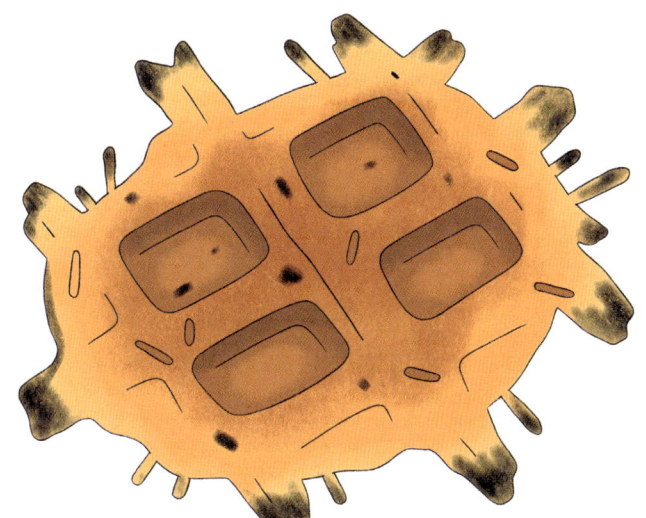

LATKE WAFFLES

ARTISANAL GEFILTE FISH

OTHER SANDWICHES

BROOKLYN TRANSPLANT

SABICH

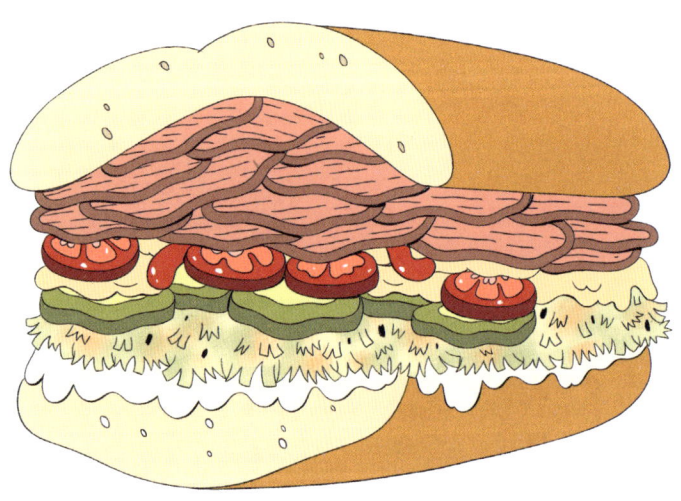

CARZLE
(AT THE DELI BOARD, SAN FRANCISCO)

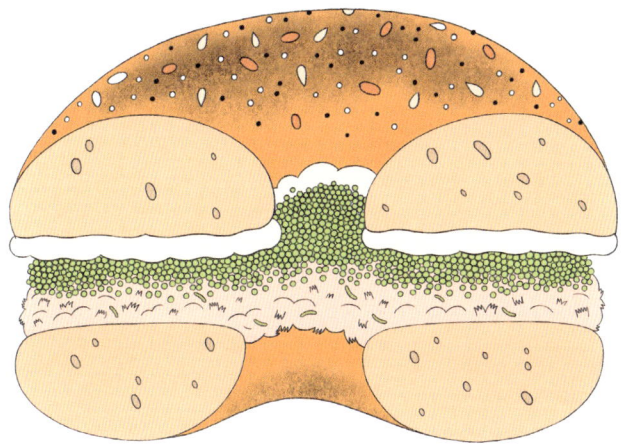

SUPER HEEBSTER
(AT RUSS & DAUGHTERS, MANHATTAN)

LATKE REUBEN

KNISH SANDWICH

CONTEMPORARY DELIS AROUND THE UNITED STATES

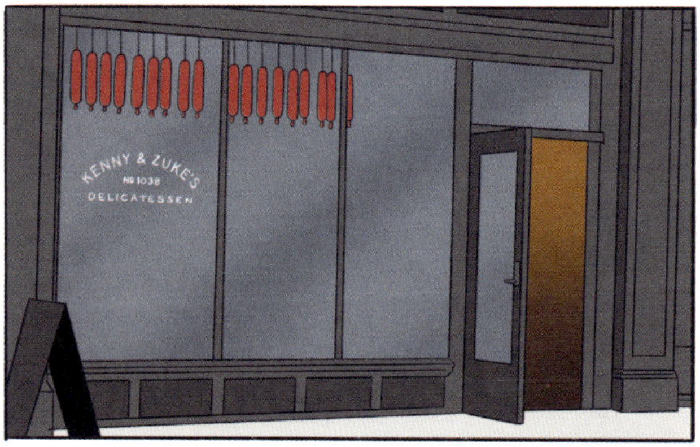
KENNY & ZUKE'S
No 1038
DELICATESSEN

KENNY & ZUKE'S

1038 SW Harvey Milk Avenue,
Portland, Oregon

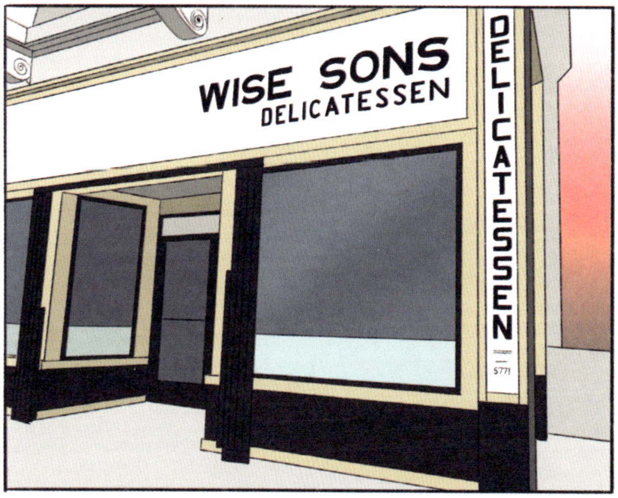
WISE SONS
DELICATESSEN
DELICATESSEN

WISE SONS JEWISH DELICATESSEN

3150 24th Street,
San Francisco, California

In addition to their flagship deli, they have several other locations in California and even one in Tokyo!

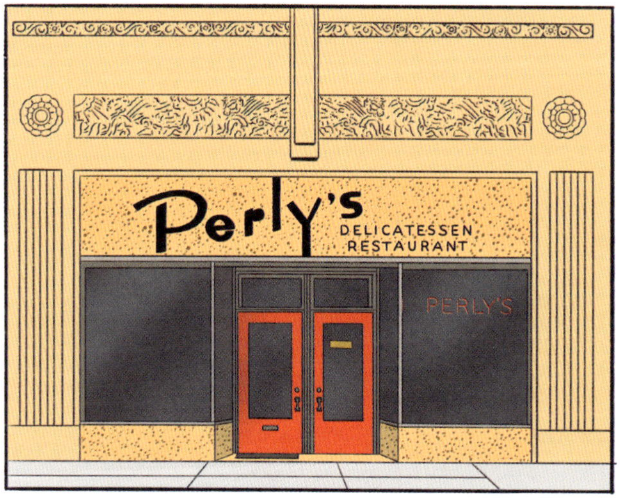
Perly's
DELICATESSEN
RESTAURANT
PERLY'S

PERLY'S DELICATESSEN RESTAURANT

111 E Grace Street,
Richmond, Virginia

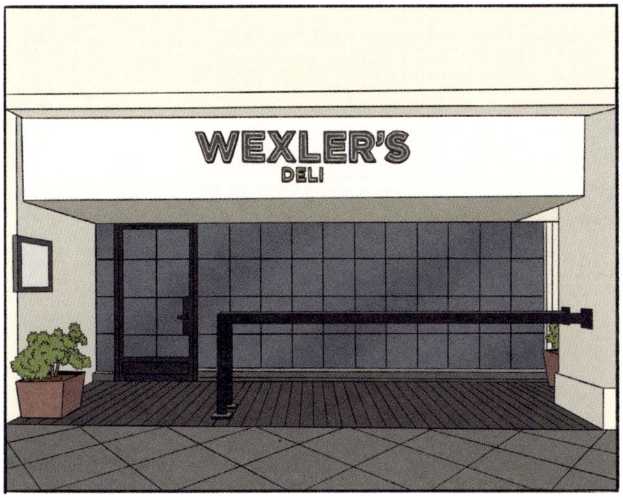
WEXLER'S
DELI

WEXLER'S DELI

616 Santa Monica Boulevard,
Santa Monica, California

and

317 South Broadway,
Los Angeles, California

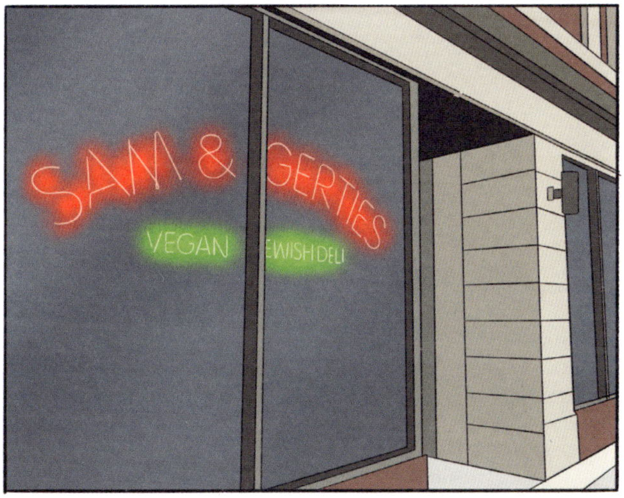
SAM & GERTIES
VEGAN
EWISH DELI

SAM & GERTIE'S VEGAN JEWISH DELI

1309 West Wilson Avenue,
Chicago, Illinois

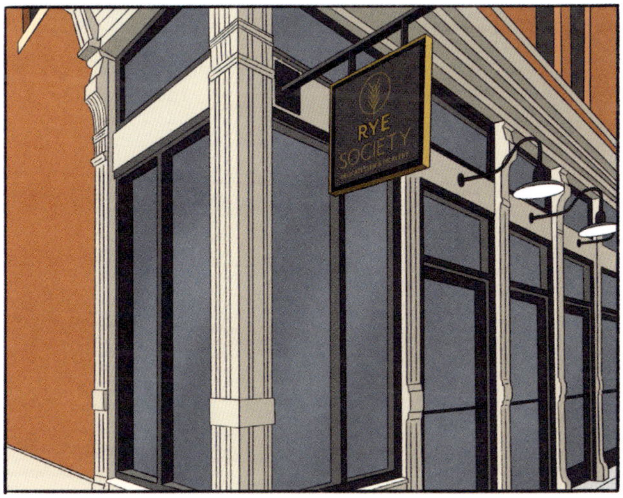
RYE
SOCIETY

RYE SOCIETY

3090 North Larimer Street,
Denver, Colorado

and

1401 Pearl Street,
Boulder, Colorado

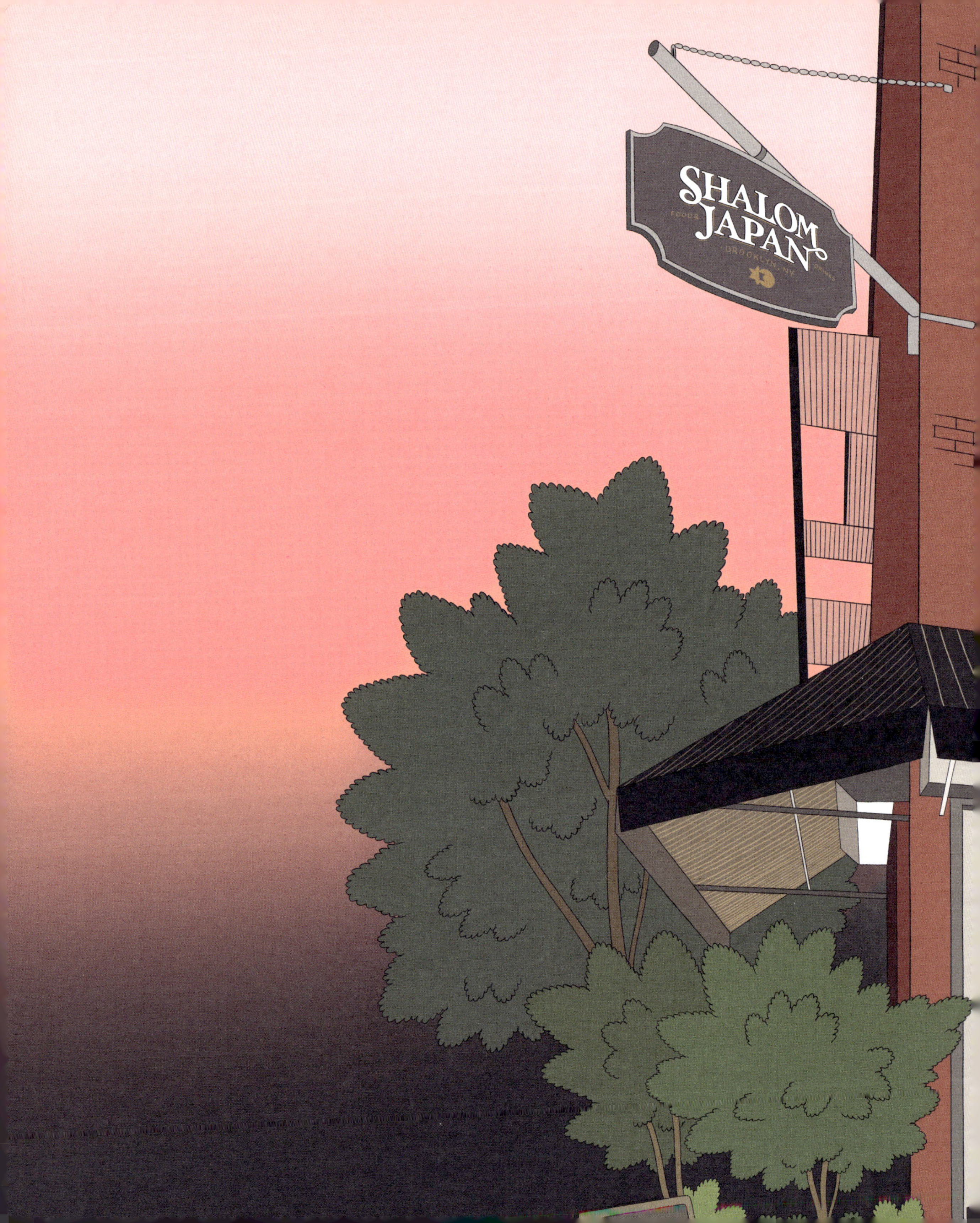
SHALOM JAPAN
FOOD &
BROOKLYN, NY
DRINKS

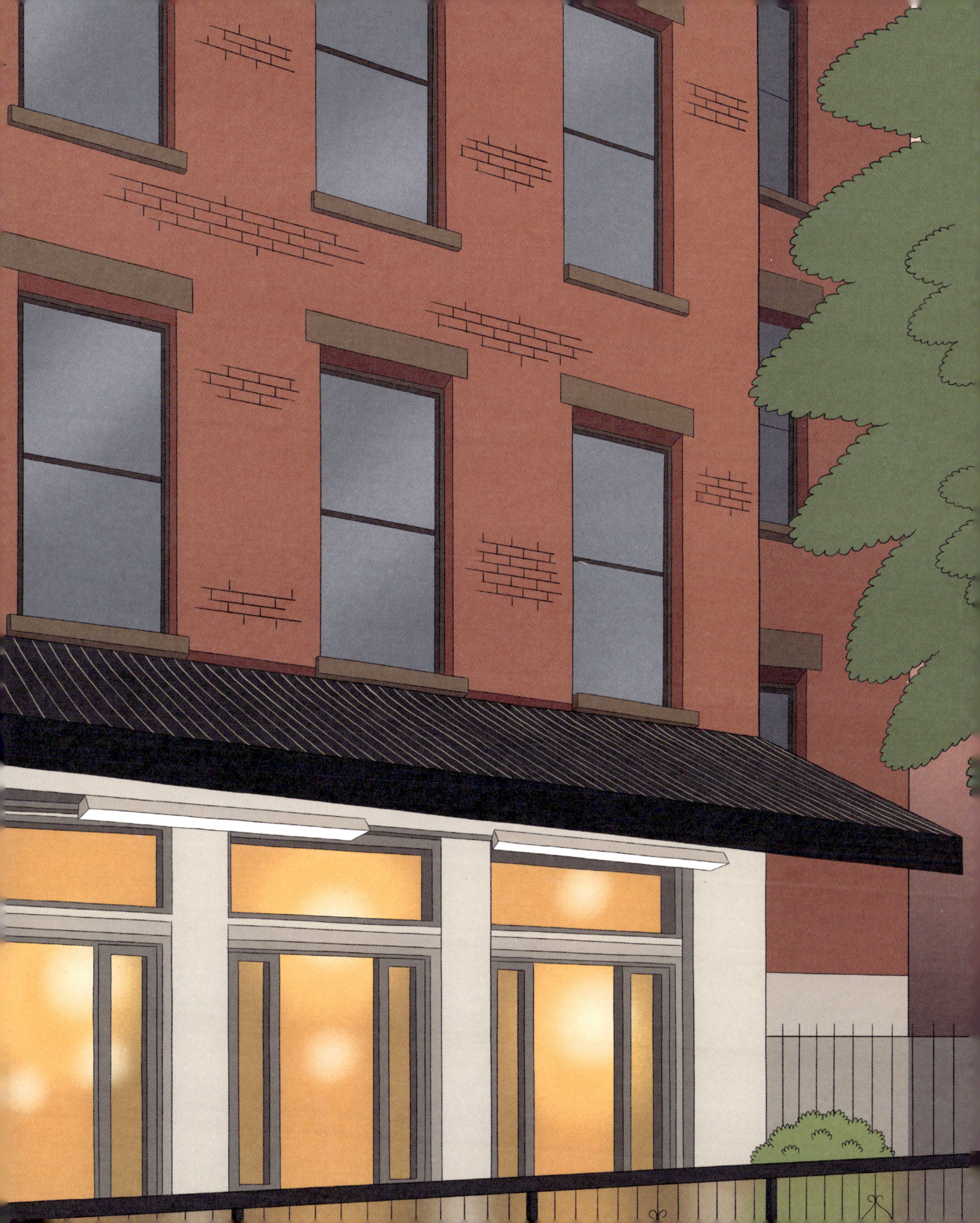

SHALOM JAPAN

310 South 4th Street,
Brooklyn, New York City

When chefs Aaron Israel and Sawa Okochi were dating, they came across a guidebook from 1983 that featured tours of Jewish neighborhoods in New York City, complete with recommendations that included a food-serving "kosher nightclub" called Shalom Japan. The name became a running joke in their relationship until years later when the now married couple were in between restaurant jobs and looking to start a new venture together. Based on foods shared throughout their life together, they opened up their own Shalom Japan in 2013 in Brooklyn (the original namesake had long since closed). Since then the restaurant has been pushing the boundaries of contemporary Jewish food, bringing in not only the flavors and traditions of the chefs' own cultures but of New York City as well.

Interview with Aaron Israel, Co-owner of Shalom Japan

How do the old-school Jewish customers react to your restaurant?

A lot of people come to the restaurant with a pretty open mind. It was a little bit of an uphill battle in the beginning because everyone thought this is just like some kooky fusion of Jewish and Japanese food. But we've been open now for seven years, and with the press we've gotten and everything, people understand that it's really more about our personal story.

Less a fusion of Jewish and Japanese food, and more about you and your wife meeting in the middle.

Some things on the menu are definitely pretty straightforward Jewish, some things are very traditionally Japanese, and a lot of things are from that story of family and coming together in life and through the restaurant.

I feel a sense of optimism from your generation about where the Jewish deli can go in the future.

Some people can approach Jewish food and think that the way they remember it is the way it is and will always be. But I think Jewish food is a really fluid thing. A [very traditional] Jewish deli is from a time that doesn't really exist anymore. That idea of a Jewish deli, from that first generation immigrating to America, it's faded because that's not where we are anymore. A lot of Jewish families are two, three, four, or more generations into living here. Restaurant work is hard. A lot of people think they want to do it and they start doing it and it's not so glorious.

And the odds are so stacked against you.

A lot of those people whose families had delis, they've maybe moved on to easier careers. I don't know if I want my kid to own a restaurant. That idea of a Jewish deli, I hate to say that I think it's a little antiquated, but I kind of do.

Jewish food is always evolving. Pastrami is a new thing; it was made here not that long ago. A lot of the food has roots wherever the people came from. They bring it and adapt it to the culture here. Like the knish. There was some other variation of it in Europe, and then it morphed into the knish we know when it hit New York as a ready-made prewrapped pastry lunch you could take on the go. A matzo ball is a version of a German bread dumpling but made with matzo. Gefilte fish is a Hungarian and

Romanian thing. Borscht is Russian and Polish. I have Polish friends who make great borscht.

So it's like, what's more Jewish than taking this food and adapting and fusing it? It's always been done that way.
People who didn't necessarily have a home base, who lived in various places and adapted to the local culture, brought in a lot of the local traditions and made it work with dietary laws—that's always been the history of Jewish food wherever Jewish people went.

At the restaurant, the way we look at it is this has really been happening with Jewish food all along, wherever Jewish people went. So what would happen if Jewish people set up a big community in Japan? And there *are* Jews in Japan! But what would that food be like? I think it might mean, for instance, instead of putting Manischewitz egg noodles in my matzo ball soup—hey, look at all these really cool noodles in Japan! Maybe I'll use ramen noodles

for it—that might work. Things like that might seem a little far-fetched to some people, but it's really just what's been happening all along.

Is that part of how you might describe the restaurant to someone? The hypothetical food of a Jewish community in Japan?
Yeah, but we look at it not as much of a macro thing as a micro thing. This is what *we* do, as a Jewish guy who met a Japanese woman, and this is the food that is meaningful to us.

It's personal.
The project is more personal, I would say. The strictly traditional Jewish deli—it's reasonable that they should keep going, and even that new ones should open up, but to not change or adapt is to ignore the entire history of Jewish food, which is about adaptation to new circumstances.

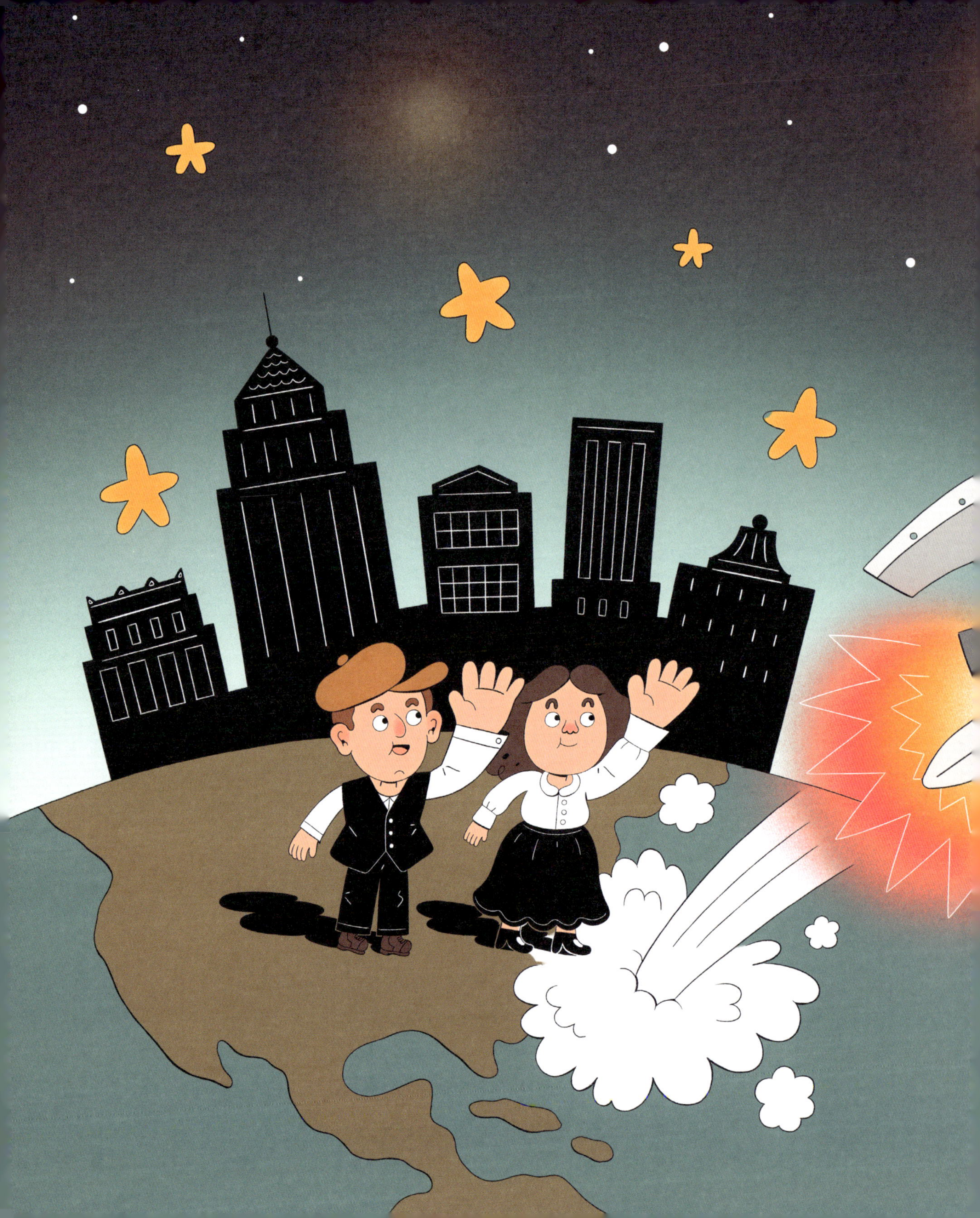

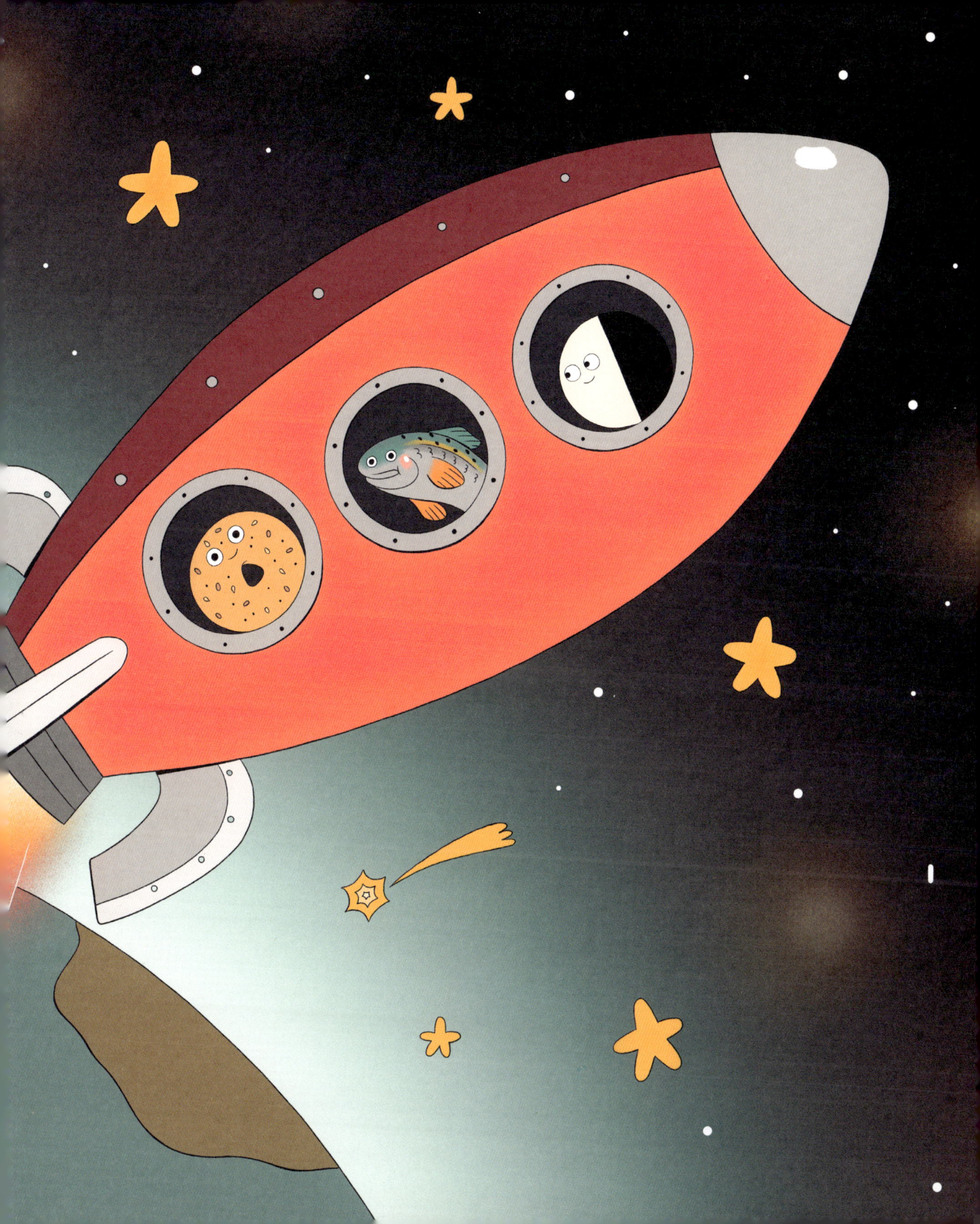

FURTHER READING
AND VIEWING

Books

The Bagel: The Surprising History of a Modest Bread by Maria Balinska (New Haven, CT: Yale University Press, 2008)

Encyclopedia of Jewish Food by Gil Marks (Hoboken, NJ: John Wiley & Sons, Inc., 2010)

Knish: In Search of the Jewish Soul Food by Laura Silver (Waltham, MA: Brandeis University Press, 2014)

97 Orchard: An Edible History of Five Immigrant Families in One New York Tenement by Jane Ziegelman (New York, NY: HarperCollins Publishers, 2010)

The 100 Most Jewish Foods: A Highly Debatable List by Alana Newhouse (New York, NY: Artisan Books, 2019)

Pastrami on Rye: An Overstuffed History of the Jewish Deli by Ted Merwin (New York, NY: NYU Press, 2015)

Russ & Daughters: Reflections and Recipes from the House That Herring Built by Mark Russ Federman (New York, NY: Schocken, 2013)

Save the Deli: In Search of Perfect Pastrami, Crusty Rye, and the Heart of Jewish Delicatessen by David Sax (Boston, MA: Mariner Books, 2009)

The 2nd Ave. Deli Cookbook: Recipes and Memories from Abe Lebewohl's Legendary Kitchen by Sharon Lebewohl and Rena Bulkin (New York, NY: Villard, 1999)

Video

The Deli Man, 2014, directed by Erik Greenberg Anjou

The Sturgeon Queens: The Story of Russ & Daughters, 2014, directed by Julie Cohen

ACKNOWLEDGMENTS

My wife, Nette Oot

My parents, Jane and Steve

Steve Mockus

Neil Egan

Juliette Capra

Melissa Clark

Danny Bernstein

Niki Russ Federman

Audrey Bachman

Lainie Schleien

Melanie Frost

Irwin Schlafman

Frank Silva

Dan Raskin

Josh Lebewohl

Ziggy Gruber

Aaron Israel

Todd Ginsberg

Ursula Siker

Mike Kassar

Evan Bloom

Leo Beckerman

Vinnie Neuberg

Ben Nadler is an illustrator, a designer, a writer, and a comics artist originally from Wisconsin. A graduate of the Rhode Island School of Design with a BFA in Illustration, he now lives, works, and enjoys the Jewish delis in New York City.